Physician Soldier

Number 166
Williams-Ford Texas A&M University Military History Series

Physician Soldier

*The South Pacific Letters
of Captain Fred Gabriel from
the 39th Station Hospital*

Edited by
Michael P. Gabriel

Texas A&M University Press
College Station

Library of Congress Cataloging-in-Publication Data

Names: Gabriel, Frederick R., 1914–1985, author. |
Gabriel, Michael P., 1962– editor.

Title: Physician soldier : the South Pacific letters of Captain Fred Gabriel
from the 39th Station Hospital / edited by Michael P. Gabriel.

Other titles: Williams-Ford Texas A&M University military history series ; no. 166.

Description: First edition. | College Station : Texas A&M University Press,
[2020] | Series: Williams-Ford Texas A&M University military history series ;
Number 166 | Includes bibliographical references and index.

Identifiers: LCCN 2020007521 | ISBN 9781623498948
(hardcover) | ISBN 9781623498955 (ebook)

Subjects: LCSH: Gabriel, Frederick R., 1914–1985—
Correspondence. | United States. Army. Medical Corps—Biography. |
United States. Army. Station Hospital, 39th. | Physicians—United States—
Correspondence. | World War, 1939–1945—Personal narratives,
American. | World War, 1939–1945—Campaigns—Pacific Area.
| World War, 1939–1945—Medical care—Pacific Area.

Classification: LCC D807.U6 G33 2020 | DDC 940.54/7573092 [B]—dc23
LC record available at https://lccn.loc.gov/2020007521

*All illustrations are from the author's personal
collections unlessotherwise credited.*

*This book is lovingly dedicated to the memory of
my dad and mom, Fred and Betty Gabriel.*

Contents

Acknowledgments

This book started out as a personal project to preserve and transcribe old family letters but quickly turned into something much bigger than I ever anticipated. Many people and institutions assisted me along the way, but any mistakes it contains are mine. First, I would like to thank the staffs of the National Personnel Records Center, the United States Army Heritage and Education Center, the United States National Archives and Records Administration, and the Pennsylvania State Library for helping me research their holdings and obtain copies of vital documents. Steve Appleby of the Eldred World War II Museum loaned me a copy of James Cawley's *Fr. Liebel's Letters*, which added context to many of my dad's remarks to his parents. The Eldred Museum is an undiscovered gem and has done much to commemorate not only local history but also World War II and all veterans. My thanks also go to the *Buffalo News* for granting me permission to republish Leo Hofschneider's letter and to the Kutztown University Research Committee for a grant in support of this project. I must acknowledge the editorial staff at Texas A&M University Press. Jay Dew initially expressed interest in this project and saw its value. Once the manuscript was accepted, Thom Lemmons and Patricia Clabaugh made the publishing process easy and clear, while Dawn Hall expertly copyedited my chapters. Similarly, my book greatly benefited from the comments of several manuscript reviewers who offered valuable insights into strengthening it.

Thanks also go to my friends and colleagues in the Department of History at Kutztown University of Pennsylvania for their help and support. I especially want to recognize Patti Derr, Mike Gambone, and Tricia Kelleher, who always made time to read drafts of the chapters. This book is stronger because of their good advice and suggestions. Anne Cardinal, the Department of History's secretary, helped with copying and always patiently listened to my stories about letters from the South Pacific. I also want to thank Susan Czerny, librarian at Rohrbach Library, and her student worker, Abby Scheuerman. Abby did an outstanding job of scanning and touching up the photographs found in this book. Bill Donner, in the anthropology department, offered me additional insights into the Solomon Islands and their inhabitants, based on his own experiences and extensive knowledge. My good friend Tom Tate, who possesses a great understanding of many historical topics, read an early draft of the manuscript.

One of the real pleasures in transcribing and editing my dad's World War II letters is that I have made new acquaintances, especially those who have a connection to the letters' contents. Among these are Jean Dearlove, Malcolm Parker's daughter, and Jim "Jamie" Cawley, an Eldred, Pennsylvania, native who compiled and published most of the Father Charles Liebel letters. My thanks go to Eddy Heyde's daughters—Holly Conley, Jude Russell, and Muriel Youmans—who generously allowed me to publish the photograph of our fathers on Saipan on V-J Day 1945. I had not seen this photo previously, but I am so glad that I finally did. Similarly, it has been wonderful getting to know better my numerous Gabriel, Farris, and Fagouri cousins—Vick's, Ester's, Lou's, and Joe's children. Being one of the younger members of this large extended family, I was not fortunate enough to grow up with them and did not know my grandparents, Louis and Dora. Two family reunions, several mass emails, and occasional phone calls helped me get to know them and identify many of the people and locations mentioned in the letters.

I also want to acknowledge my six brothers and sisters—Fred, Bernie, Nick, Mary, Gina, and Loree—for always supporting my love of history. This book is dedicated to our devoted parents,

Fred and Betty, and we were truly blessed to have them as role models. Lastly, my love and thanks go to my wife Sandy for her unlimited help and support in all my endeavors and to our daughter Katie. It is a great joy having her as part of our adventures.

Physician Soldier

Introduction and Travel Log

Over sixteen million American men and women served in the armed forces during World War II. From the conclusion of the war in 1945 until today, historians have examined nearly every facet of American participation. Much of this scholarship has centered on and continues to center on traditional military topics, such as battles, strategies, and key political and military leaders. The emphasis began to shift somewhat in the mid-1980s with the publication of Studs Terkel's Pulitzer Prize–winning book, *The Good War* (1984), a collection of interviews of "ordinary" soldiers and civilians who experienced the conflict. The fortieth and fiftieth anniversaries of Pearl Harbor, D-Day, and the end of the war further heightened interest, as did the realization that the World War II generation had begun to fade away. Tom Brokaw tapped into this trend and focused it with his best-selling *The Greatest Generation* (1998). Enthusiasm for the Greatest Generation continues today among scholars and the general public. Movies and television miniseries, such as *Saving Private Ryan*, *Band of Brothers*, and *Flags of Our Fathers*, attracted large audiences, and books and articles about World War II veterans continue to appear.

Despite this widespread interest in the Second World War, relatively little attention has focused on medical units. The United States Army published four institutional histories as part of its Green Book series, but these do not provide a feel for the individuals who served in this branch of the military. The same is true for Albert E. Cowdrey's *Fighting for Life: American Military Medicine in World War II*, a broad overview of both the European and Pacific Theaters.[1] A number of veterans wrote memoirs or published letters and diaries from their service in the medical corps, especially those who saw combat. For the European theater, these include Brendan Phibbs, *The Other Side of Time: A Combat Surgeon in World War II*, Allen N. Towne, *Doctor Danger Forward: A World War II Memoir of a Combat Medical Aidman, First Infantry Division*, Paul A. Kennedy, *Battlefield Surgeon: Life and Death on the Front Lines of World War II*, and Lawrence D. Collins, *The 56th Evacuation Hospital: Letters of a World War II Army Doctor*. Coverage of the Pacific is less extensive but includes James S. Vedder, *Combat Surgeon: Up Front with the 27th Marines*, an account from Iwo Jima, and Michael J. Lepore, *Life of the Clinician*.[2]

Other works have looked at the medical service from a social history perspective, as opposed to a military one. A particularly interesting work is *One Woman's War: Letters Home from the Women's Army Corps, 1944–1946*, Anne Bosanko Green's service at a number of hospitals in the United States. Somewhat similarly, Peter A. Witt's *Edith's War* examines the experience of a Red Cross worker in North Africa and Europe.[3]

Another veteran who left an extensive account of his service, somewhat similar to Green's and Witt's accounts, was my father, Dr. Frederick R. Gabriel, a physician in the 39th Station Hospital. In May 1944, five months after deploying to Guadalcanal, he wrote his parents: "I wish you would save all my letters. We are not supposed to keep diaries and by my letters I can keep a record of my overseas life. For that reason I will use a lot of dates and names." Fortunately, his parents had been keeping his letters long before this, and today over three hundred of these still survive. Gabriel also took a large number of photographs and collected others, totaling approximately five hundred. Many of these photos directly relate to his letters and in some cases offer additional insights. This adds a visual element to his story. Furthermore, he compiled a "travel log" with key dates in his military career from his induction in the army in July 1942 through June 1945. This timeline, which follows this introduction, helps make sense of the letters and photos, and it puts them into a larger context.

I first became aware of this collection of letters when I was a teenager, possibly when my dad brought them home after cleaning out my grandmother's house. He periodically spoke about his experiences in the war, but never in great depth, and I was only generally aware of where he served and what he did. After his death in 1985, I occasionally looked at the letters, and even contacted one of his friends from the 39th, Dr. Edward Heyde, but never did anything with them. About five years ago, however, I began to read the letters, which were not arranged in chronological order, and I noticed that some had begun to deteriorate. Therefore, I decided to scan and transcribe the letters to preserve them for the future. As I read more letters and placed them in order, I realized that they told a fascinating story that deserved a wider audience. The discovery of my father's photo albums from the war in January 2017 further convinced me of this.

The letters and photos begin in February 1942, when Gabriel was a resident at the Thomas Jefferson Medical College Hospital, and follow him and his unit's training at Camp Barkeley and Sheppard Field, Texas, and the Desert Training Center in Yuma, Arizona. The vast majority of the correspondences and pictures cover from January 1944 to December 1945, when he deployed to the South Pacific and was stationed on Guadalcanal, Angaur, and Saipan. Most of the three hundred plus letters are handwritten, and 222 of them are on V-mail.[4] Unfortunately, a number of gaps exist in the letters, especially in mid-1943 and fall 1944, but there is no indication that he did not write during this period. Either his parents did not keep these letters with the others, they were misplaced over the years, or perhaps they were lost in transit. Several of the letters are missing pages, but they are still included in the collection and marked "Incomplete." Furthermore, no letters exist after he returned to the United States in January 1946, even though he was not discharged until September. Gabriel may not have written as frequently, partly because he was hospitalized for much of this time, and/or his parents may have worried less with the war over and him back in the States.

Gabriel's correspondences and the accompanying photographs provide a gold mine of information on the war, despite the fact that the 39th Station Hospital saw only limited combat and was usually stationed in rear areas.[5] Furthermore, most of the letters were to his parents, whom he wanted to reassure, and they were monitored by censors to prevent the release of sensitive material. As such, these letters are different from the studies mentioned previously in that they provide a view of the war from a soldier serving in a supporting, rather than combat, role. The exact number of personnel who served in support services is difficult to determine and varied by theater and branch of service, but estimates range from 32 to 61 percent.[6] Therefore, Gabriel's experiences were not unique. Millions of others also served in similar capacities, but their stories are largely unknown because historians have mainly focused on the more dramatic combat aspects of the war. In this regard these letters offer the perspective of those who served behind the front lines, a more social history view of World War II.

The letters cover a wide range of topics, such as the varied responsibilities of medical officers, a Bob Hope USO show, the death of Franklin Delano Roosevelt, the end of the war in Europe, the atomic bomb, and growing frustration with the slow return of troops from the Pacific. Readers also gain insights into aboriginal populations in the Pacific and daily work and entertainment routines, especially movies and sports. In fact, Gabriel became an avid moviegoer during his tour of duty in the Pacific, and he mentions sixty-eight films by name. The letters also let readers see the war from the soldiers' viewpoint. As an example of his changing perspective, in late 1943 while still in the United States, Gabriel believed that the war would be over within a year. By summer 1945, after having been overseas for one and a half years, he predicted it would last another eighteen months. Gabriel frequently recorded the number of letters, newspapers, and packages that he received and how long they took to arrive. This shows the speed with which soldiers received mail and its importance to their morale.

The letters also offer insights into the home front, especially in rural north central Pennsylvania, as Gabriel responded to his parents' and friends' correspondences. He commented on bond drives, rationing, news from home, and a variety of domestic and international events, such as the San Francisco Conference. One reason that he was so well informed about events at home was because of Father Charles Liebel, a close family friend and the pastor of Saint Raphael Church in Eldred, Pennsylvania, Gabriel's hometown. In January 1943, Father Liebel began publishing a monthly newsletter and sent it to hundreds of area men and women serving in the military throughout the world. Copies of these remarkable newsletters, which local newspapers often reprinted, still exist and strongly complement many of the topics that Gabriel discussed.[7] Furthermore, Gabriel saved some of the postcards that Father Liebel sent the troops. Taken as a whole, Gabriel's letters and photos provide a day-to-day view of the Pacific war that has not been examined in any depth previously.

The vast majority of the letters are written to Fred's parents, Louis and Dora Gabriel. Louis immigrated to the United States from present-day Lebanon in 1903. After living on Long Island for several years, he moved first to Olean, New York, and then settled in nearby Eldred in 1910, where he married Dora Abdo Dan, who also arrived from Lebanon in 1903. A successful businessman and entrepreneur, Louis, along with Dora, operated a clothing store, and he also invested in real estate and oil leases. Fred, the couple's first son and third of five children, was born on July 9, 1914.

All of Fred's siblings and their families appear frequently in his letters. His eldest sister, Victoria, born in 1911, married George Fagouri, and they resided in Bolivar, New York, with their son Eddy and daughter Jackie. Born in 1912, Ester, Fred's second sister, lived in Eldred with her husband, Duffy Farris, and their sons, Paul, John, and Jimmy. Fred was especially close to his brother Louis. Despite a two-year difference in their ages, Fred and Lou were educated together from grammar to medical school. They graduated from Eldred High School in 1932, were proud members of the Class of 1936 at the University of Notre Dame, and then earned their medical degrees from Thomas Jefferson Medical College in Philadelphia four years later. Not surprisingly, Fred repeatedly mentions Lou, who served in the Fourteenth Armored Division, his wife, Martha Coleman, and their sons Tom and Don. Fred's youngest brother, Joseph, was born in 1924. He entered the US Army Air Corps in late 1942 and served at various locations in the United States. Others who frequently appear in the letters are Gabriel's many aunts, uncles, and cousins, who resided in Danbury, Connecticut; Bayonne, New Jersey; and elsewhere. He also repeatedly comments on friends from college and medical school, along with Father Liebel. One interesting aspect of the letters is that they note the many friends and acquaintances whom Gabriel ran into all across the Pacific. Such encounters must have given him a semblance of "home," as certainly similar meetings did for millions of other soldiers during the war. Such encounters also give some indication of just how many men and women served during the war.

Fred's letters to his parents tended to be different from those to his brothers, especially when he first entered the army and then deployed overseas. The letters to his parents are much more positive and reassuring, while those to Lou and Joe tend to provide a grittier view. The letters themselves logically divide into four sections: the United States, Guadalcanal, Angaur, and Saipan. While most of the letters were in his parents' possession, three came from his army personnel file and his hometown newspaper, the *Eldred Eagle*. I have corrected all spellings, except for Gabriel's ubiquitous use of "nite" and "tonite," and occasionally included punctuation marks to make the letters easier to read. I also removed multiple "continued" where Gabriel indicated he was switching to a new page. All the letters are addressed to Eldred unless otherwise noted, and the individuals mentioned are identified, whenever possible.

Graduation from the University of Notre Dame, June 1936. Gabriel's brother Joe (*on ground*), parents Louis and Dora; *left to right standing*, sister Victoria, brother Louis, Father Charles Liebel, cousin Sally Mansour, Gabriel, and sister Ester.

Travel Log

Table 1.

1.	July 24, 1942	Appointed 1st Lt. MC [Medical Corps], AUS [Army of the United States]
2.	July 29, 1942	Accepted appointment
3.	July 25, 1942	Ordered to MDRP [Medical Replacement Pool] Washing eff[ective] date duty Aug 8, 1942; date rank 8/8/42. Par 20, SO [Special Order] #198 WD [War Department] July 25, 1942
4.	Aug. 20, 1942	Ordered to 8 SC [Service Command], Camp Barkeley, Tex. Par 10, SO #224 WD
5.	Aug. 27, 1942	Left for Camp Barkeley, Texas
6.	Aug. 29, 1942	Arrived Camp Barkeley, Texas
7.	Statement of Commissioned Service	Requested: 9/16/42 Received: 10/8/42
8.	Sept. 5, 1942	Power of Attorney
9.	Oct. 8, 1942	Ordered to AMC [Army Medical College] for Tropical Medicine to arrive not later than 10/17/42 Par 1, SO 3 252 Hq, Cp Barkeley, Tex.
10.	Oct. 13, 1942	Left for Washington (order later amended to allow 2 days delay en route).
11.	Dec. 12, 1942	Completed Course Tr Med.

12.	Dec. 13, 1942	Leave of absence 7 days and 3 days travel time.
13.		Leave of Absence Requested 11/20/42 Granted 12/12/42 Effective 12/13/42
14.	Dec. 22, 1942	Returned to Barkeley, Texas
15.	March 1, 1943	Ordered to DTC [Desert Training Center], Yuma, Ariz, Par 18, SO #51 Hq Cp Barkeley, Tex. Left Cp Barkeley March 3, and arrived DTC Yuma, Ariz, March 5, 1943
16.	Feb. 3, 1943	will [Last Will and Testament] Typhoid—8/11, 8/18, 8/25/42, 10/8/43 Tetanus—8/11, 9/7, 9/28/42, 9/3/43 Smallpox—8/11/42 Immune; 10/8/43 Immune

**OFFICER'S IDENTIFICATION CARD 3 301767
(W.D., AGO FORM 65-1)**

17.	March 24, 1943	Ordered to Laguna, Ariz. To do physicals. Par. 1, SO #10, Hq. 39th D.T.C. Yuma, Ariz. Dated 3/24/43
18.	March 26, 1943	Par. 9. SO #65, Hq. D.T.C., Camp Young, Cal. Dated 3/16/43 Ordered to Chicago for 3 months course @ U. of Chicago (order received 3/26/43) Left for Chicago 3/27/43. To report there 3/27/43

19.	June 19, 1943	Completed 12-week course @ U. of Chicago @ noon Left Chicago 10:30 AM. June 20, 1943 Arrived Yuma 5:30 PM. June 22, 1943
20.	Sept. 10, 1943	Left DTC, Yuma, Ariz: for Sheppard Field, Witchita Falls, Texas (parap 22, SO. #192, CZ, DTC Banning, Cal. Aug. 30, 1943). Arrived: Sheppard Field: September 12, 1943.
21.	Sept. 20, 1943	Beginning 15-day leave (para # 13, SO #260, Hqrs. TS [Training Support?] and BTC [Basic Training Center] #3, AAF [Army Air Forces] Western TTC. [Technical Training Command], Sheppard Field Texas, 17 Sept. 1943.
22.	October 5	Returned from leave.
23.	October 16	Notified of captaincy; effective date of rank 10/5/43. (S.O # 278, Par. 16 War Dept. Wash. DC 5 Oct. 1943.
24.	Oct. 22, 1943	Nurses left us; October 26, 1943 new C.O.
25.	Dec. 27	Left Sheppard Field for Camp Stoneman, Cal. Arrived 31 December 1943 (PAR. 19, SO 355 Hq AAFTTC [Army Air Forces Technical Training Command], Sheppard Field, dated 21 Dec. 1943.
26.	Mon. Dec. 27, 1943	Left Sheppard Field, Texas.

	Fri. Dec. 31	Arrived Camp Stoneman, Cal.
	Mon. Jan. 10, 1944	Left Stoneman.
	Jan. 10, 1944	Boarded USS *West Point*.
	Tues. Jan. 11	1140 Lifted Anchor.
	Mon. Jan. 17	1300 Crossed Equator.
	Mon. Jan. 24	1200 noon Arrived Noumea, New Caledonia.
	Tuesday, the 25,	went ashore.
	Wed. Jan. 26	Left Noumea
	Fri. Jan. 28	Arrived Lunga Beach, Guadalcanal.
27.	Wed. Sept. 6, 1944	Boarded *Mormacport*; Sept. 7–to Tulagi
	Fri. Sept. 8, 1944	Went ashore @Banika, Russell Islands.
	Sat. [?] Oct. 13, 1944	Landed Angaur, Palau Islands–Yellow Beach.
	Sun. Oct. 21, 1944	39th began to function.
	Nov. 25, 1944	Lab. moved into Quonset. Dec. 1 – first blood chem.; "5 – first Kahn. [?]
	Mar. 9, 1945	Hospital moved into new area.
	Sun. May 20, 1945	Hospital ceased operating.

	Thursday, June 7, 1945	Left Angaur on *"Sabik"* (AKA-121)
	Tues. June 12, 1945	Landed Saipan.
	Sun. 17 June, 1945	I began to work @ 148 G.H. [General Hospital]

1

United States Introduction

Letters: March 5, 1942–January 8, 1944

After graduating from Jefferson in June 1940 with his medical degree, Gabriel obtained a general rotation internship at Saint Vincent Hospital in Erie, Pennsylvania, which ran until July 1, 1941. While there, he became friends with other young physicians who appear in his letters, such as Charlie Schaaf, "Jake" Brady, and Al Tocker. Completing his internship at Saint Vincent, Gabriel returned to Jefferson that August for a clinical pathology residency in the medical school's hospital. Gabriel wrote the first letter of this collection while there. He did not complete the residency at Jefferson, however. With the Japanese attack on Pearl Harbor on December 7, 1941, and the United States' entrance into the Second World War, Gabriel was appointed a first lieutenant in the Medical Corps on July 24, 1942, with his commission dated August 8.[1]

This was not Gabriel's first military experience. Both he and his brother Lou were members of the Reserve Officers' Training Corps during their four years at Jefferson. In summer 1938, they participated in a six-week advanced ROTC field camp at Carlisle Barracks, Pennsylvania. Ironically, in February 1940, Gabriel was denied an appointment as a first lieutenant in the Medical Corps Reserve, because at five foot three inches, he did not meet the minimum height requirement.[2] The advent of World War II changed this.

Now a member of the United States Army, Gabriel was initially ordered to the Medical Replacement Pool at Walter Reed Hospital in Washington, DC, and subsequently assigned to the 39th Station Hospital at Camp Barkeley, Texas, eleven miles southwest of Abilene. Activated on July 20, 1942, the 39th Station Hospital was a 250-bed facility "designed to function in the theatre of operations." The army operated a wide range of hospitals during the Second World War, ranging from small mobile units to evacuate battle casualties to major centers that could treat thousands of patients. Station hospitals provided general medical, dental, and surgical care for posts and bases that had a sufficient population to justify a hospital, but not a large one. Station hospitals usually had a bed capacity from twenty-five to nine hundred, and at times, they treated battle casualties, as did the 39th on Angaur.[3]

The 39th Station Hospital's initial cadre consisted of twenty-five enlisted men commanded by a second lieutenant, but its strength steadily grew as the unit underwent extensive personnel changes. During the course of the year, fifteen men transferred to other hospitals: five were assigned to officers' candidacy school, two entered the Air Corps, five became paratroopers, and three were discharged because of "essential civilian defence occupations." Still, by December, it consisted of 141 enlisted men and twenty officers.[4] The 39th faced difficult conditions for the first four or five months after its activation. "The living conditions at Camp Barkeley at this time [summer 1942] were a little rough due to the fact that the men were living in tents in an area formerly condemned for sanitary reasons." The area lacked adequate drainage, which resulted in thick, heavy mud after rain, and "a multitude of flies" inhabited the site. The soldiers' use of primitive pit latrines did not help this situation. Still, Gabriel realized that he was far more fortunate than many others. As he informed his parents in mid-September, "there is no use moaning over my present situation. In fact—it's a good one. I feel sorry for these other devils. I am lucky and I know it." The housing situation at Camp Barkeley gradually improved with the construction of hutments by October 1 and the installation of modern plumbing.[5]

Malcolm Parker photographs Gabriel near mess hall at Camp Barkeley, Texas, September 19, 1942. Note the mud surrounding the buildings.

Over the next several months, the 39th underwent intensive training. All personnel did basic drill, calisthenics, and received instruction in defense against both air raids and gas attacks. The unit even donned their gas masks on long marches when "passing a local hog farm." The enlisted men also received general instruction in medical records and administration, along with more specialized training for specific duties such as laboratory, surgical, and pharmacy technicians.

The officers, including Gabriel, the fourth one assigned to the 39th, endured the same conditions as the enlisted men. Gabriel arrived on August 29 and was followed two weeks later by Major Isaac F. Hudson, who assumed command of the unit. In addition to marches and physical exercises, the officers worked on map reading skills, "scouting and patrolling," water purification, and other aspects of command, such as military discipline and courtesies. The officers' average age was 32.4, making Gabriel one of the younger ones at 28, and they possessed professional experience ranging from one to fourteen years.[6]

A number of officers received advanced training in both military and medical areas. Gabriel took a three-and-a-half-

39th Station Hospital officers, Camp Barkeley, Texas, March 1943.

week course on chemical warfare in September, so he could train other members of the 39th. Soon afterward, on October 1, he was certified as a gas officer, after having completed a thirty-four-hour Defense against Chemical Attack training. One week later he received orders to proceed to the Army Medical School, in Washington, DC, for an eight-week course on tropical medicine, leaving Camp Barkeley on October 13. While in Washington, Gabriel took the opportunity to see the sites, including the National Zoological Park. He also requested and was granted a seven-day leave, with three days' travel time, effective December 13, the day after he completed the tropical medicine course. The leave gave Gabriel the opportunity to visit Eldred, but he did not spend the holidays there, as he returned to Texas on December 22.[7] The 39th continued its rigorous training, and in late January it received word that it would leave Camp Barkeley. In February, the unit's personnel repeatedly practiced pitching and striking their hospital tents. Additionally, they prepared for combat conditions by making a number of forced marches and receiving instruction on individual survival techniques.[8]

On March 3, 1943, the men boarded a train and headed west for the Desert Training Center (DTC) in Yuma, Arizona, and they arrived there two days later. Soon after this, the 39th received an influx of new personnel. In December 1942, thirty female nurses from Fort Devens, Massachusetts, were assigned to the unit, but they did not join the 39th until March 14 because of a lack of adequate housing. None of Gabriel's letters from the DTC survive, but his photos and later comments reveal that the nurses were integral parts of the unit. They received triangulation and other field training and presumably served in the wards and other areas of the hospital while stationed at the DTC.

The 39th remained at the DTC for twenty-seven weeks, "in conjunction with maneuvers and other troops undergoing desert training." This period allowed it to gain valuable practical experience functioning as a unit and a hospital. It spent the rest of March and the first week of April constructing hospital wards and setting up its medical equipment, employing the skills the unit had practiced so many times at Camp Barkeley. On April 8, the unit with its nurses was ready to operate as a hospital for the first time, and over the next three days, sixty patients were air-transported there from the 41st Station Hospital in Needles, California. During one four-week period, when other nearby medical units were split up for a large maneuver, the 39th

39th Station Hospital nurses receive triangulation training, Desert Training Center (DTC), Yuma, Arizona, June 1943.

expanded to five hundred beds to treat the influx of patients, many of whom were subsequently evacuated to other medical facilities. By July, an average of 206 patients occupied the hospital's beds each day. Overall, between April 8 and September 4, when the 39th ceased to operate, more than 2,400 patients were admitted to the hospital. Of these, twelve subsequently died, including four from heat exhaustion and sunstroke, which were the most common ailments. The unit's outpatient clinic also treated over 3,300 other patients, giving the 39th extensive practical experience in its primary function.[9]

The unit did not spend all its time treating patients while serving at the DTC. On July 21, personnel from both the 39th and the 37th station hospitals saw Lieutenant Edith Greenwood receive the Soldier's Medal for helping evacuate patients from a burning hospital near Yuma on September 16, 1942. Greenwood was the first woman to receive this honor, and *Collier's* magazine featured her on the cover of its April 15, 1944, edition. Gabriel knew Greenwood and commented on this to his family when she appeared in *Collier's*.[10] Gabriel's photos also show that there was time for recreational activities too. On August 22, the men and women of 39th enjoyed a day at a large swimming pool in Yuma, a welcome relief from the desert heat and sand. Such interactions continued while the 39th served in Arizona. Several months later, the officers and nurses enjoyed a grilled steak party. In October, one of Gabriel's friends, Malcolm M. Parker, married one of the nurses, Mary Metzger.

Gabriel did not serve at the DTC the entire time that the 39th was deployed there. On March 24, he received orders to go to Laguna, Arizona, to give physicals. Two days later he was sent to the University of Chicago for a three-month laboratory medicine course to receive additional training in bacteriology and parasitology.[11] Similar to when he was in Washington, DC, Gabriel used his free time to visit area attractions. On April 18, he returned to Notre Dame, visited with acquaintances, and saw the dramatic growth that the university had undergone because of naval officer training programs. Interestingly, on May 23, Gabriel witnessed a simulated air raid by two hundred "enemy" planes to assess Chicago's civil defense readiness. This offers insights into the American home front during the war.

Upon completion of his course, Gabriel returned to the 39th at the DTC on June 22 and continued to train and gain experience as a medical officer. Over the course of the next six weeks he held a variety of positions in the unit: he served briefly as dispensary officer and then was assigned his own ward, the Sixth, on July 18. On July 31, he and other members of the unit were "subjected to close overhead fire on [the] infiltration course," preparing them for overseas deployment and combat. Similarly, Gabriel built on earlier training and became recertified as the unit's gas officer after taking another three-day course on chemical warfare in early August. As a result of his performance, on September 1, Major Hudson recommended Gabriel for promotion to captain. Hudson wrote, "1st Lt Frederick R. Gabriel has clearly demonstrated his fitness for the responsibilities and duties of the position and grade for which recommended for over twelve months by serving as Medical Ward Officer . . . in an excellent manner."[12]

39th Station Hospital personnel on an infiltration course under live fire, DTC, June 1943.

When Gabriel received word of his promotion on October 16, the 39th was no longer at the DTC. Having completed their training in early September, the 39th prepared to leave Yuma, but officers from another hospital were assigned their barracks before the troop train arrived. This forced the 39th's officers to again live in tents for several days. The 39th finally left Yuma on September 10 and arrived at Sheppard Field, near Wichita Falls, Texas, two days later. The unit continued to train extensively in September and October, with road marches and overnight field exercises, including an extended eight-day maneuver near Vernon, Texas. This featured a mock strafing of the 39th's bivouac area by a fighter plane. The nurses participated in some of these exercises, suggesting that they would accompany the unit overseas, and by December 1, the 39th was prepared for deployment. Rumor had it that the 39th would serve in the Mediterranean or Italy, probably because of its extended desert training, but no one knew for sure.

The 39th also underwent a number of changes while stationed at Sheppard Field. On October 1, Lieutenant Colonel Jewell R. Wilson assumed command of the unit. Three weeks later, the female nurses transferred out, indicating that the 39th would deploy to an area that did not have adequate housing facilities for women. Instead, male medical and surgical technicians replaced them. During this period, Gabriel also received his second and last leave, this one of fifteen days, running from September 20 to October 5, during which time he visited his family in Eldred.

The 39th spent only three months at Sheppard Field before boarding a train and heading west to Camp Stoneman, a major debarkation center in Pittsburg, California, on December 27. The unit now numbered 174 enlisted men and 22 officers. The 39th spent New Year's Day at Camp Stoneman, and Gabriel had the opportunity to visit nearby San Francisco, but the unit's training period was rapidly coming to a close. The course of the war had changed in 1942 and 1943. Allied victories in North Africa, Sicily, and Russia marked "the end of the beginning" in the European theater. In the Pacific, Japanese expansion had

Gabriel on leave in Eldred, Pennsylvania, with parents and brother Joe, in front of the family store, September 26, 1943.

been halted at the Coral Sea, Midway, and India, and the Allies seized the initiative in New Guinea, the Solomon Islands, and the Gilberts. It was now time for the 39th Station Hospital to join other American forces overseas. Gabriel was aware of this situation, and his last several letters from this period repeatedly advised his parents not to worry if they did not hear from him for some time. He was obviously preparing them for his deployment overseas. Interestingly, the good news from Europe and the Pacific made him optimistic that the war was winding down. "Most experts think Germany will be out of the war by August or September at the latest. Japan will require several months more, but once everything is turned against her things will move along fast." Gabriel's views on this changed once he was overseas.

On January 10, the 39th Station Hospital left Camp Stoneman and boarded the USS *West Point* that evening for points unknown.[13]

[Jefferson Hospital Letterhead]

March 5, 1942.

Dear Folks:

   Two more days until the Black-and-Blue Ball.[14] I am getting
ready nicely—a haircut yesterday and a new bowtie today,
and now I am all set and eager. Brady[15] wrote me a couple
days ago, saying they planned to be here for the occasion.

   Work has been unusually heavy for the past two weeks.
Yesterday I was on call and didn't get to bed until 2:30 A.M.,
which made me somewhat tired today. I plan to get to bed
early tonite to even matters up somewhat. However, I can't
complain too much, because for the few weeks preceding this
present rush there wasn't too much night work.

   Louie hasn't written me since he went South. He probably
is much busier there than when he was at Ft. Myer.[16] I would
write to him if I were sure of his address. I do imagine that
a letter written to him at Fort Oglethorpe[17] would reach him
okay.

   Catherine wrote me this week. She says things are
proceeding pretty much as usual in Erie and that the hospital
has been usually rushed all winter long. In fact, they are
putting in another operating room.

   Dave Chase (the boy from Erie) phoned me the other evening.
He said his girl is coming down from Erie for the dance and
that he heard that [Alfred M.] Tocker,[18] with whom I interned,
is visiting in Erie. Presumably he came all the way from Texas
to see Joe's girl Lee. Better do something about that Joe.

   Margaret Curro was down this way Monday evening and
dropped around to see me. She wants to be remembered to Joe
and talked about what a nice time she and Taga [?] had the
evening we went out. Margaret says she is getting her vacation
sometime early in May, although she personally would prefer it
a little later in the summer.

   I am glad to know that you all are well (except Jackie and
Johnny) and that business is good. Incidentally, how are the

sick ones? I am completely over my cold now. There is a lot of it going around here now. I do hope that my recent episode will be my quota for the season.

Mary Ann called the other evening to see how I was doing and to learn what the news from home was. There wasn't much that wasn't in the "Eagle" that I had to tell her. Incidentally, I believe I read there that Timon Phelan[19] is in the Army now.

Well, as there isn't more news I'll close now with

Love,
Fred.

—————— ✦✦ ——————

Camp Barkeley,[20] Texas
Sept. 9, 1942

Dear Folks:

I received your letter of the 7th today, and I am glad to learn that Papa finally has gotten off on a trip. Here's hoping Mama will find time to do the same.

This has been another long, hot day, the kind that makes a person feel wilted when evening comes. Yesterday was pretty warm too, and in the afternoon we took our second ten-mile hike. They are in earnest about getting us in condition, it seems.

It was a surprise to learn that Louie has not yet left Benning,[21] though not the captaincy. He'll probably receive his transfer orders soon. They are rather slow about routine matters in the Army, I have learned. For instance, I will not receive my pay for August until the Hdqtr. here writes to Washington for some papers that should have been forwarded.

Of course I'll be very glad to help Joe go to school. If only I had known sooner I would not have signed up for the $18.75 bond each month and could have turned that amount over to him. I suppose I could stop buying them, but down here they are very insistent that everyone, especially officers, take out some. Even with it I think I can give him about the same *amount each payday without any trouble. And I suppose the simplest way to do it will be to send Papa $115 or $120.00 each month instead of a flat one hundred. I think I can do it because–at least at present—I am clearing $26.00 a month on room and subsistence allowance, which just covers my insurance and bond allotments ($6.90 plus $18.75). The balance of my base pay of $167.00 after the check to Papa is taken out will serve for my current operating expenses. I won't save anything but I didn't expect to anyway. And about this commuting business—it probably will be best for the first few months, but won't you run into trouble concerning tires and gas?*[22]

I am glad we are reconstructing so well after the flood,[23] *and that business is good. I certainly will be glad to see the stores again, but doubt if I will for a while yet.*

It must be the letter you received from me was the first one; I wrote again Sunday. There are some things in it I am particularly interested in, so please answer as soon as possible. Also, you needn't send them all airmail.

Joe is a bit confused about the typewriter. That instrument has been in the Bolivar store ever since it opened.

I do wish I'd get my travel and uniform allowance. Fall will soon be here and then we'll be required to wear expensive fall uniforms.

Well, I must close now.

> *Love,*
> *Fred.*

———— →← ————

> *Camp Barkeley, Tex.*
> *Sat. Sept. 19. 1942. P.M.*

Dear Folks:

This is a wet and windy Texas day. Rain prevents our usual Saturday afternoon jaunt into town, so I am spending this afternoon here in the Camp library, writing letters and looking up some material on the Big Dipper. We had a discussion about it last evening, and I want to see who is wrong.

*This noon I received your letter of the 16th and post-marked
3 PM. Your letter of the 14th was delivered to me a little less
than 72 hours after the post-mark. I have received the dough
twice and also the package of food. By now you must have
received my letter mentioning that I did receive that package.
The food had to be eaten that day because it attracts insects so.
Incidentally, did Ester receive the suitcase I returned?*

*So far I haven't received my pay for August. And the bond
won't begin to appear for 8 or 10 weeks I have been told.
Whenever you mention receiving a check, please mention the
amount so I'll know just which one you refer to.*

*In general, commuting to school doesn't work out too well,
though I don't imagine it will make any difference as far as
studies go in Joe's case.*

*I have written to and heard from Louie a couple times. He
seems to be much busier than I have been so far.*

*I plan to look up this party from Olean the first chance I get.
Both your letters are here before me now and I am trying to
clean up all questions you have.*

*This course I am taking in Chemical Warfare hasn't
changed my status with the 39th at all. Each unit sends a*

"Gas Mask Drill," Camp Barkeley, Texas, February 1943.

couple men to it so that they in turn can teach the fundamen-
tals to their fellow officers. It would be impossible for us all to
take it. The course is only a short one—about 3 ½ weeks. My
taking it won't send me anywhere necessarily, nor is it any
clue where the 39th might go. It is taught to all soldiers.

I am not working hard. In fact I sometimes wish I had more
to do, which I probably will get. When we have classes in the
evening, I spend the day reading and listening to the radio.
Last Saturday I was tired because the previous day we had
been in the field all day long, but I really wasn't very tired.

I am not sure when I did receive that package, but I believe
I wrote you that afternoon and mentioned the fact.

No, I have no idea where we will go, or even if we go. The
latest rumor—we call them outhouse rumors because most of
them originate there—has us going to a Station hospital in one
of the New England states or Middle Atlantic states. However, I
seriously question if we'll move before next spring. What I am
telling you is unofficial. I can get into trouble for writing things
like these.

Officers' tents, Camp Barkeley, Texas, fall 1942.

I have plenty of friends here all ready, but I'll look up this question of camel-riders first opportunity I have.[24]

The idea of living in Abilene has occurred to me and there are several reasons why I continue to live on the Post. In the first place—Abilene is a good 10 miles away and there is the question of time and transportation. Then, rooms there are extremely hard to get. Finally and the biggest reason—I like it here and I enjoy this. Living in a tent is a bit inconvenient but it is not hardship—at least it hasn't been so far. We have fun there and I might just as well get to know my fellow-officers as well as I can. Another thing—within the next two weeks hutments (ply-wood buildings, I think) are to be erected for us. Our enlisted men have already moved.

There is nothing I need, but if there is I will promptly let you know. There may be soon, too, as winter uniforms become official Oct. 15. And what I am doing then will determine what I wear.

I would like to be home now, naturally, but there is no use moaning over my present situation. In fact—it's a good one. I feel sorry for these other devils. I am lucky and I know it.

Well, that about covers everything.

I am sending this letter airmail because mail service is a little slow over weekends.

Love,
Fred.

———— ➔← ————

[From the Gabriel Personnel File, page 60]

Washington, DC
[Army Medical School]
Nov. 20. 1942.

Dear Major Hudson—

This week we began the second-half of our course, and I am happy to be able to report to you that things continue to move along satisfactorily here.

Our schedule is a heavy one, but the classes are well-arranged, and the instructors and lecturers for the most part

Gabriel (*on the right*) in a bacteriology lab at the University of Chicago, spring 1943.

are first-rate men in their fields. However, the subject matter is covered hurriedly, in a sense, because the course covers such a big field in a short time. It all makes for a full day of lectures and lab sessions, with plenty of outside reading for a chaser. Full days like these make the weeks go by quickly.

Seven from Barkeley are in this class, but some of them say they will not return to Texas and will rejoin their outfits elsewhere.

Before I rejoin the "39th" I would like to go home for a visit. Enclosed is a request for Leave of Absence. I trust you will see fit to act favorably upon it and that permission is granted.

> *Respectfully,*
> *Fred. R. Gabriel,*
> *1st. Lt. M.C.*

P.S. Thanks for the change in my orders; I finally am to get my paycheck, I hope.

[Camp Barkeley, Texas stationery; the letterhead consists of
a stagecoach and the bottom of the page contains the fort's
history.]

Chicago, Illinois
April 19, 1943.

Dear Folks—

After I got through phoning you this evening the operator
said I had another minute to go; so I don't know if I hung up
on someone or not.

Yesterday morning I went over to N.D. [Notre Dame]. The
campus was very pretty and I had a nice time there. I saw a
few priests I knew, but none of my classmates. In fact only one
of them is around, and I talked to him over the phone.

An odd thing happened to me there. I was looking over the
Navy's drill-house when I overheard a young man ask one of
the brothers if he knew Fred Gabriel, who graduated from N.D.
about 6 years ago. They turned around then, and there was
one of my fraternity brothers from Jeff. He had just finished his
second-year there and had come out this way for a few days
before going home. I don't know who was more surprised—he
or I. We had a nice talk about Jeff.

The Navy has taken over much of N.D. and will have more
of it next semester. They have quite a set-up there, including
two buildings they built. One is for classrooms and is behind
the Rockne Memorial; the other is the drill house and is located
in back of the gymnasium.[25]

Among those I saw at school was Brother Maurilius,[26] who
was in charge of Carroll Hall when we were freshmen. Carroll
is closed now, and he is working elsewhere. He seemed very
glad that I looked him up. I also looked over the Infirmary. The
nun in charge was very friendly and showed me all through
the building. She wants me to be sure to come back next time I
am there.

The weather changed a bit today and is raining. It was nice
enough yesterday—sunshine and quite comfortable without a
topcoat.

Speaking of clothes, Saturday afternoon I went downtown to a tailor and ordered a tropical worsted suit. It will be ready in about three weeks. I tried first to get one at the Post Exchange in the Stevens Hotel.[27] However, they had none that fit me and said they wouldn't, either.

The other evening I wrote to Louie. Tonite, besides this letter, I wrote to Joe and Uncle Mike.[28]

Ester wanted to know if we couldn't arrange for you to come out here and return with Louie. That would be nice, but I doubt if it could be arranged easily. Maybe I am wrong but I don't think we had better plan on it. We don't know—at least I don't—if and when he will get his leave. Nor do we know if he will come this way; I believe it is shorter not to.

Enclosed is a check—my pay for the first two weeks of being here. Not bad, is it? I don't know if you understand this, but these checks of a hundred dollars that go to you each month are for you, the same as before. Now, instead of my sending them, the government sends them. I had to make this allotment to a person, so I made it out to Mama.

Things are going along well here. My work keeps me busier than I'd like, but I guess I will survive all right. I am glad that things are well home, and with the girls.

Well it is late now so I'll say "goodnight"—Happy Easter.

Love,
Fred.

P.S. About Joe—I don't know, but I imagine they will keep him there until classes begin at the school where he is going. I don't know about Edmond either, but I heard he was working in an office.

F

[From the Gabriel Personnel File, pages 61–62]

Chicago, Illinois
Sunday: 23 May 1943.

Dear George[29]—

Yesterday the Rail Transportation Office at the Stevens refused to give me a TR [transportation request] covering Pullman for the return trip from Chicago to Yuma. They maintain it should have been granted along with that for the R.R. [railroad] ticket at the point of origin of my trip. I was unable to produce the TR for the R.R. ticket, as I never saw it.

At the time of my sudden departure from the 39th last March, the Personnel Officer informed me that he would send along some papers (I believe he said from the Transportation Office) for my signature. I never received those papers, and I believe they should be in my possession, at least a copy of them.

I would like to have this matter ironed out, and for your convenience I give the facts:—

I am entitled to R.R. transportation plus Pullman.

I was given a round-trip R.R. ticket.

Probably through my own error, I paid the Pullman fare from Yuma to Chicago. However, that part does not matter, as I will seek reimbursement when I return.

I have no copies of the TR involved (maybe I should not, but I was given the impression I should).

I never received some papers that I was told would be sent to me for signature. Please see what you can do about this affair.

Things are going along well here. It has been raining plenty of late, and we haven't seen many springy days. Today, in a mock raid to test Civilian Defense setups, Chicago is being bombed by 200 planes.[30]

News about the 39th has been rather scarce, and my latest was some time back. I trust all is fine with you-all.

Please give my regards to the boys (and the gals).

Sincerely,
F. Gabriel

1400 E. 53rd St.,
Chicago, Ill

[Camp Barkeley, Texas stationery; INCOMPLETE]

girl was keeping books.
  Well, I must close now.
                    Love,
                    Fred.

*P.S. Among our medical books near the radio is one I wish
you would send me. I believe it has a green color—Todd and
Stanford's "Laboratory Methods" or something like that.*[31] *Be
sure you sent it book-rates.*

——————— ➜ ⬅ ———————

[A.A.F [Army Air Force] Technical School, Chicago, Illinois,
stationery with a letterhead]

                    Sun. 12 Sept. 1943.
            [Sheppard Field,[32] *Wichita Falls, Texas]*
Dear Folks—
    Just a brief note to let you know we arrived here a few
minutes ago after a 2-day trip.
    This is a nice camp, and from what I have seen we will like
it here. It is an Air Force Camp.
    Seems to me a few from Eldred are here. Do you know
whom?
    On the train I tried to figure out my income-tax declaration.
However, I cannot do it as I don't know the income from the
houses.[33] And as regards, deductions—I am buying a bond a
month. However, Mama may have bought some more for me.
Can you file this form for me—my base pay is $166.67. Let me
know immediately, as the date [dead] line will soon be here. In
fact you probably won't receive this until the 15th.

39th Station
Hospital
wards, DTC,
July 1943.

9th Station
Hospital
personnel
enjoy a day
at the pool in
Yuma, August
1943.

Below is my correct address. Please notify the Eagle, etc. and tell Mrs. Russell[34] my address should include both serial number and organization.

I'll write you again tomorrow.

Love,
Fred.

Fred. R. Gabriel (0-485524)
1st. Lt. M.C.
39th Sta. Hosp.
Sheppard Field,
Wichita Falls, Texas.

Sheppard Field, Tex.
Wed. 15 Sept, 1943.

Dear Folks—

 This letter will be brief but it is good news. Although it isn't absolutely certain yet—beginning Monday the 20th I get 15-days leave. I expect to get home Wednesday morning on the train from Buffalo. I take the Missouri, Kansas and Texas [Railroad] to St. Louis, where I get the N.Y.C. [New York City] to Buffalo just in time to catch the Pennsy going south.

 At first I was not going to tell you, but surprise you with a phone call from Buffalo. Then I decided to write you now so you can tell Joe to come home the weekend of the 26th.

 I met Eddy Lambillotte[35] last nite.

 I am very excited about this trip and do hope I get final permission as well as the Pullman reservations. As soon as I heard today I went down to the depot and made arrangements. They are wiring ahead for them. Three of my best friends leave the same time for N.Y.C. We are trying to all travel as far as Buffalo together.

 I'll send you a telegram Monday noon regardless if my plans are changed or not. I may get there ahead of it but I'll wire you then anyway.

Fred.

———— ✈✈ ————

RESTRICTED

Special Orders)   *WAR DEPARTMENT*
No. 278)   *Washington, 5 Oct. 43*

EXTRACT

Par. 16 Announcement is made of the temp promotion of the following named officers to the grades indicated in their respective services AUS with rank fr date of this order:

1st Lt. to Captain

Frederick Raphael Gabriel   0485524   MC

By order of the Secretary of War:

G. C. MARSHALL,[36]
Chief of Staff.

Official:
    J. A. ULIO[37]
        Major General,
            The Adjutant General.

A TRUE COPY:

HERMAN BERKOWSKY[38]
1st Lt, Med Adm C

———— →← ————

[Sheppard Field, Wichita Falls, Texas, letterhead]

Wed. 11/3/43.

Dear Folks—
    Just a note to let you know that Louie and Martha and the baby are here. They arrived by bus yesterday afternoon and I spent the evening with them in the hotel.
    The baby is a darling. He was feeding when I first walked in, and he was afraid of me, but he got over it in a few minutes. Martha and Louie both look fine. They were surprised how tanned I am.
    There's no news, so I will close now.
                              Fred.

P.S. They are leaving tomorrow (Thursday); I believe Martha is going home Sunday.

Sheppard Field, Texas
Sun. Nov. 7, 1943

Dear Ester—

Tomorrow I am sending you a roll of #620 film. So far I have been unable to buy any in color, but will continue to look for it.

Well, finally saw Louie and family. They arrived Tuesday PM, Louie on a 3 day leave. Louie and Martha look fine and Tommy is a darling. Tommy was afraid of me at first but soon got over that. Martha and the baby leave for home today; Tommy probably wonders where his father is right now.

Today I received a Christmas card from Uncle Mike and this evening I am going to write to him. The last time I did so was while home. I also heard from Joe this week.

We are continuing with our training program here. Last week we completed an 8-day field trip and went out again to another place for 2 days. This Thursday we go out once more for a few days. Right now we are having quite a wind storm, which I trust will blow itself out before we get into the field.

Chaplain Service while on bivouac near Vernon, Texas, October 1943.

Strafing attack drill,
Vernon, Texas,
October 1943.

*Seven more weeks until Christmas–seven weeks to begin
and complete my shopping. Let me know if you have any
good suggestions for anyone. Don't forget, as I am way up the
proverbial tree.*

*Yesterday I bought myself a spare wristwatch for $21.27. It
is waterproof, shockproof, anti-magnetic, luminous face and
hands and a sweep-second hand. We were advised to have an
extra watch on hand and about 10 of us bought them at once.*

*No news forthcoming; things are more quiet now than they
were a couple weeks back.*

*Enclosed are a few snapshots which I wish you would give
Mama to hold for me.*

Well, I must close now. Tell the boys I said to be good.

Love,

Fred.

[Sheppard Field, Wichita Falls, Texas, letterhead]

Mon. Dec. 20, 1943.

Dear Folks—

Only four shopping days until Christmas doesn't worry me
because I have all that taken care of. Today I mailed out my
last package—a pair of leather-faced woolen gloves to Joe. He
may already have gloves but I couldn't think of what else he
would need, and besides it is so cold up where he is.[39]

The weather here continues to be coolish but nice. Today
was warm, and warm weather for a while seems to be due. I
remember how nice it was last year at this time. Seems much
longer than twelve months ago, however.

The mails must be swamped now. It takes your letters two
or three days longer than usual to be delivered to me. A day
of that may be lost here. I suppose my letters to you also are
on the way longer than usual. Don't get the idea that I am not
writing, because I am. When and if we ever leave here you
might not hear from me for a while, but that is because letters
are not to be mailed enroute. And if you ever don't get word
from me for quite a while, don't worry about that either. No
news is good news, and as I have so often told you, you will
hear quickly if there is bad news.

I have done quite well as regards Christmas cards this year,
having received some twenty of them. I have sent out about
that many, too. I have a few left over, which I will send you one
of these days, along with some clothes that are only in my way
here.

I am glad to know you are well and that business is good.
Don't overwork in the store during the holiday rush. I don't
know where you will find them but I hope you can find enough
help. How is Jimmy? From what Ester wrote in her last letter
he must have been pretty sick. I hope she calls the doctor next
time one of them are that ill.

Your package hasn't arrived yet, but I am sure it will in
a day or two. I have received packages from Ailene, Uncle
Louie[40] and Victoria.

*I have been writing a lot of letters lately. I wrote Louie
and Joe just the other day, and heard from Louie last Friday.
The last letter I had from Joe was about two weeks ago. The
December 10th "Eagle" arrived today. I read where Mrs.
O'Dell*[41] *got honorable mention San Francisco way. I have a
couple of good friends there. What is Mrs. O'Dell's address?
Maybe they live near each other.*

*Well, I must close now. I'll write you again before Christmas
but this probably will the only one you will receive by then,
so I'll now wish you all a Merry, Merry Christmas and Happy,
Peaceful New Year.*

Love,
Fred.

———————— ➔← ————————

[Sheppard Field, Wichita Falls, Texas, letterhead]

Christmas Day 1943.

Dear Folks—

*Believe it or not, but it snowed here last night. Not much
and it didn't last long, but it was snow. Yesterday afternoon
was wet; later it got colder and turned to hail and then snow.*

*I went to Midnight Mass here on the field. The altar was set
up in a hangar. About four thousand people were there and
seven or eight hundred of us received Communion. It was a
High Mass, of course, and the choir of enlisted men was very
good.*

*This noon we had a swell dinner. I believe it was even better
than at Thanksgiving, which is saying something. There was
plenty of everything, including the turkey, and all of it was
well cooked and served. I still am nibbling at the hard candy
and nuts each of us was given. A few days ago the mess hall
was decorated and a tree put up. Thursday nite there was a
little party for the enlisted men, to which we officers went for a
few minutes.*

*Yesterday I received a box of Syrian candy from Kalils.
When I gave some to one of our Jewish officers he said it*

was Jewish strudel. As yet I have not received your package, but I know the mail service is slow. Several of us have had packages in the mail for several days.

Joe wrote me the other day. He received my watch okay—I hope he managed to get home. Joe seemed to be doing all right in his work, too, from what he wrote.

I was going to phone home this morning but knew it would be useless to try to put through a call for that distance today of all times.

Christmas cards continue to dribble in. So far I have received twenty-nine, some from people I figured had forgotten me. One was from Fran, who wanted to know Joe's address. A real surprise was receiving a card from Shaffer. I had not heard from him in about two years. He is in a Chicago camp now.

A few days ago I sent home my last Christmas package, which were boxes of stationery for the girls. I trust they were received in time. Both of them let me know that the money for the children was received. I sent Martha a package, too, and yesterday received a card informing me that Louie and she had presented me with a year's subscription to Reader's Digest.

Thursday I expressed my gladstone[42] home, and in it I put a few things for which I have no immediate use. They were just getting in my way here.

All-in-all, this has been a good Christmas and I hope it was for you all too. Of course I wanted to be with you but that was utterly impossible. I would loved to have seen the children this morning. Boy—I really miss those devils. Well—maybe next year. Who knows?

I will close now.

> Love,
> Fred.

Carolers on Christmas Eve 1943, Sheppard Field, Texas (courtesy of Muriel Youmans).

[Sheppard Field, Wichita Falls, Texas, letterhead]

Friday 31 December 1943
[Camp Stoneman,[43] *California]*

Dear Folks—

By this time you probably have received my change-of-address card and know we have changed stations. We arrived here not long ago.

The trip out was long but we had fun. All the officers were together in one car. We passed the time reading, playing poker and in bull sessions. The meals were served to us and were good. Three or four times we got off the train near stations and walked around to get the kinks out of our legs. Twice I was able to buy newspapers. One was new, the other was 2 day old. Except for that I didn't know what was going on currently.

This is a big place where we are now. So far I have seen only a very small portion of it, but I think we will like it here, though we will be busy and have no idea how long we will be here. The weather isn't bad.

Several days ago I sent home some clothing. I trust you received them okay. More will follow in a few days.

I had a nice Christmas, though it was a wet day. It was raining like the devil when I went to midnight Mass but stopped by the time it was over. There was some snow on the ground Christmas Day, but not much and it did not last long. I trust you all had a nice Christmas and that Joe was able to get home.

I heard from Joe last week, though Lou has not written in over 2 weeks. That address you sent me arrived okay.

Our mail is censored—I think—so I have to be careful what I write. I heard in-coming mail might be also.

From what you write you must be having a real winter for yourselves. I haven't experienced any real cold weather in so long that I am curious how I would stand 20 below. I hope that real cold spell has passed.

While I write this I am listening to a newscast. The war news from all fronts is favorable. Looks like big things are shaping up all over, and in Europe at least, it is the beginning of the end. Most experts think Germany will be out of the war by August or September at the latest. Japan will require several months more, but once everything is turned against her things will move along fast.

Well, I must close now. I hope you all are feeling fine and please don't worry about me. I'll write you often as long as I can. Should you not hear from me for a while—don't worry about that either.

Love,
Fred.

P.S. I think these address changes were sent also to Fr. Liebel and the "Eagle"—not to anyone else, including Louie and Joe.

[Sheppard Field, Wichita Falls, Texas, letterhead]
My address at present is:

> Capt. Fred Gabriel 10-4855241
> 39th Sta. Hospital
> A.P.O # 9022, c/o PM
> San Francisco, Calif.
> Sunday 2 January 1944

Dear Folks—

This is a wet afternoon, good for staying in and writing letters. The tough part is that I have not much to write about, though. As I wrote you a couple days ago, we must be careful what we put into our letters. The mail of the enlisted men is censored; that of officers may be. We are supposed to censor our own mail, and our signature across the lower left corner of the envelope is a certification that the letter contains no military information.

We are on the West Coast; beyond that I cannot say anything. We have been here only a few days. We don't seem to be doing too much yet seem to have very little time to ourselves. How long we remain here I do not know. But remember—if you do not hear from me for a while do not worry.

This morning I expressed another package of clothing home. In it are my overcoat, 2 hats, summer uniform, and pinks.[44] *You might mention to Louie and Joe what the articles are. Joe won't be able to use officers clothing but Louie might want the overcoat.*

Mail from our last station has not yet caught up with us, so I have not heard from you in over a week. However, if should be coming along in a day or two.

Well, I must close now.

> Love,
> Fred.

[Sheppard Field, Wichita Falls, Texas, letterhead]

Wed. 5 January 1944.

Dear Folks—

Yesterday I received a letter from Ester. From it I know you have my new address. However, does that "24" after "San Francisco" belong there? Several others have by now heard from their homes and none seem to have it.

I saw Eddy Lambillotte a few times after he got back from furlough and he never said anything about cookies from Mrs. Hermann. However, I did not see him for several days prior to my leaving there and he may have received them then. Incidentally, that package you sent me has never shown up.

There isn't much I can tell you about what goes on here. I am kept busy and am feeling fine. Here's hoping you people all are as well as I am, and are not worrying about me.

Yesterday I wrote to both Lou and Joe. I haven't heard from either of them in a couple weeks. I told them that I had sent some clothes home and to help themselves to any of it they wanted. I am glad to learn that Joe did get home Christmas. New Year's Eve several of us went to a dance—stag. We met some old friends from Texas there, and we all had a good time. I have met some other friends here, too.

Well, I'll sign off now. I'll write 3 or 4 times a week while here.

Love,
Fred.

Sat., 8 January 1944.

Dear Folks—

This will be another brief letter, for really there isn't much to write about. We continue to be kept quite busy but not so much so that we cannot have some fun along with it.

The mail is beginning to come through quicker now, both the direct and that forwarded from Sheppard. Yesterday I received Christmas cards from two of my classmates at Chicago and a letter from Ester. I have not yet received the package you sent me, nor the cards. They should be in any day now, as others here are still receiving Christmas packages.

I would love to have seen the children when they awoke and saw their toys under the tree on Christmas morning. It must have been a sight. God willing—maybe I will be there when it happens next year. Things are really moving along aren't they? I don't believe Germany can last many months more.

Well, I'll close now. Remember what I said about worrying if you do not hear from me for a time.

Love,

Fred

➔ ←

2

Guadalcanal Introduction

Letters: January 19–September 4, 1944

When Gabriel and the rest of the 39th Station Hospital boarded the *West Point* on January 10, they became part of the nearly eight thousand soldiers that this former luxury liner was transporting to the South Pacific.[1] The ship's size did not mitigate the effects of rough weather, however, and not surprisingly, many men became ill, especially those who had never been at sea before, including Gabriel. Eddy Heyde, Gabriel's closest friend in the 39th recalled, "Seasick on the West Point for 3 whole days. Your father, [Malcolm M.] Parker and I (with 2 or 3 others) were in bunks in the bow of the ship and in the 1st 3 days of rather stormy weather that bow plunged up and down what <u>seemed</u> to be about 100 feet. We could only lie in our bunks all day, rising only to vomit or use the head. I remember your dad turned a ghastly shade of yellowish green (we were already taking Atabrine to prevent Malaria). Food never tasted better than on that first seasick free day."[2]

After overcoming the seasickness, Gabriel and others settled into an extended routine of finding ways to fill the days. Some of the activities included playing cards, such as bridge and scopa, an Italian game that many officers learned when they believed that they would deploy to Europe. They also spent time looking at the vast blue Pacific, which was so different from what they had ever seen. A week after departing, the *West Point* crossed

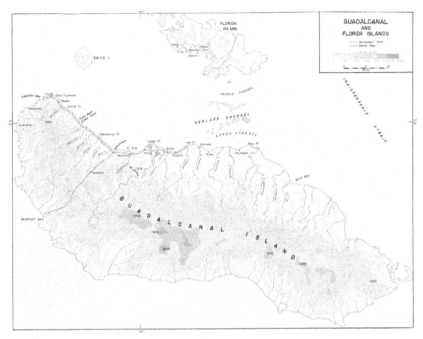

Guadalcanal and Florida Island. Map IV, from John Miller Jr., *United States Army in World War II>The War in the Pacific, Guadalcanal; The First Offensive*. Washington, DC>Historical Division, Department of the Army, 1949; reprint 1968.

the equator. The crew gave "Neptune" cards to any man who had never been in the Southern Hemisphere, but they omitted the usual initiation ceremony to mark this event.[3] On January 24, the ship arrived at Noumea, a major naval installation in New Caledonia, about eight hundred miles southeast of the Solomon Islands. Gabriel took this opportunity to briefly visit the island, the first of at least seven that he would set foot on over the next two years.

On January 28, the 39th disembarked from the *West Point* at Lunga Point, Guadalcanal, in the Solomon Islands, not far from the famous airstrip, Henderson Field.[4] Guadalcanal had been the scene of the first American offensive in the Pacific, and the Japanese had evacuated it in February 1943 after a bitter six-month campaign.[5] Once ashore, however, the 39th was not

Gabriel's Neptune card for crossing the equator, January 19, 1944.

activated. Instead, most of the enlisted men and officers served with other medical units on detached duty, while a small cohort maintained the unit's area and equipment. They also operated a dispensary for the 39th and other nearby units. Gabriel served with this small cohort, and his letters and photos offer insights into the day-to-day routine behind the front lines.

Many of Gabriel's letters, especially the early ones, repeatedly assured his parents that he was safe and well, and he even went so far as to write, "I am fine and having fun." The letters also describe some of his responsibilities. Gabriel served as the 39th's Sanitary and Malaria Control Officer, a critical role on the swampy, mosquito filled-island, and he succeeded in keeping the unit's area clean. During the eight months that the 39th spent on Guadalcanal, only one man contracted malaria.[6] Some of his other duties reveal how the military attempted to educate and engage the soldiers. Gabriel acted as the 39th's orientation officer, giving the enlisted men lectures on a variety of topics, and he served as the soldier voting officer, distributing absentee ballots for the November 1944 election. The army did not endorse any particular party or candidates but wanted to ensure that soldiers had the opportunity to fulfill their civic duty. He also continued to hone his medical training by attending a school on anesthesiology and meetings of the Guadalcanal Medical Society.

Despite these responsibilities, Gabriel complained of his prolonged "inactivity" and hoped to get back to treating patients and contributing to the war effort. In lieu of this, he and others in the 39th had plenty of time to follow the war closely over the radio, as they heard of Russian offensives, the Normandy invasion, and increasing American airstrikes on Japan. With the tide of battle beginning to shift against the Axis, he continued to optimistically predict that the war would end relatively soon. Members of the 39th also swam in the Pacific Ocean, collected seashells, and were mesmerized by the sunsets. Additionally, the unit organized volleyball and softball teams to keep morale up and give the men exercise. Gabriel headed two different softball teams while on the island, the "Atobrines" and a later one dubbed the "Eldred Eagles." Another activity that took up large amounts of time was going to the movies at one of the many outdoor theaters found on Guadalcanal. Gabriel provides his impressions of a wide range of motion pictures from future Academy Award winners, such as *Going My Way*, to *Tarzan's New York Adventure* and other less remembered classics. When not watching movies, members of the 39th saw United Service Organizations (USO) shows, some of which featured Ray Milland and other Hollywood stars, and Bob Hope and his troupe visited the island in August 1944. Gabriel was one of thousands of GIs who stood in line for hours ahead of time to see Hope perform.

Gabriel and a number of other officers also visited nearby Savo and Tulagi Islands. These excursions, along with their time on Guadalcanal, gave them the opportunity to meet some of the indigenous peoples who lived in the Solomon Islands. Gabriel comments on their appearance, negotiating skills for trade items, and their love of tobacco products. He also noted that some natives worked on coconut farms owned by white plant-ers. Similarly, he told his parents of the extensive farms that the army operated on Guadalcanal, a little-known topic. These farms helped supplement the 39th's rations, as food was another topic that frequently appears in Gabriel's letters. Despite serving in an exotic location with deep jungles, beautiful sunrises and sunsets, and a very different night sky, Gabriel commented that some of the landscape reminded him of home. He also observed that "life here isn't on a different plane, as I had imagined," be-cause the island was so "Americanized." "Things seem the same as they were in Washington, Texas or Arizona."

By September, however, the 39th's time on Guadalcanal was coming to a close. While General Douglas MacArthur's offensive through the Southwest Pacific approached the Philippines, Ad-miral Chester W. Nimitz's island-hopping campaign had secured the Solomon, Gilbert, and Marshall Islands, and parts of the Marianas. To support these operations, the 39th Station Hospi-tal left Guadalcanal for their first and only combat assignment.

[V-Mail]

Wed. 19 Jan. 1944
[U.S.S. West Point[7]]

Dear Folks—

I know this letter probably will not be very satisfactory but it [is] the best I can do at present. About all I am permitted to write is that I am at sea, and am well, happy and having fun. Concerning where and when we left, where we are going and when we expect to get there, I can say nothing. In fact, some of that information I do not know; even our C.O. [commanding officer] does not know yet where we are going.

This trip is a pleasant experience for me. The first couple days I was quite seasick, but since then everything has been fine.

I do not know where this will be mailed, and because I know how anxious you are for some word from me, I am now

USS *West Point.*

sending you two similar letters. This one by V-mail; the other by Air Mail.[8] This way I am doing what I can to have word reach you at the earliest possible moment. Just for the fun of it, let me know when you get each letter.

Well, I must close now. Please don't worry about me, for all goes well with me. And remember that it may be some time before you hear from me regularly or even again. However, I will write when I can. So love to you all.

Fred.

P.S. Finally received the Christmas package; also the playing cards; also Ester's money order and a package from Martha. Kiss the children "hello" from me.

[V-Mail]

SUNDAY, 23 JAN. 1944.

Dear Folks—

A few days ago I dropped into the ship's mailbag two similar letters (one airmail and the second V-mail). I did that because I want to get word to you as soon as possible, and I do not know which way is faster. Hence my using both ways. Let me know which letter (dated 19 January 1944) you get first.

Today I am writing only this V-mail letter. Not much has happened since last I wrote, so I will repeat myself somewhat. I am at sea and am well and happy (except for a little seasickness at first). Several things about this trip I do not know, but even if I did, I could write nothing about where and when we embarked, anything about the ship, where and when we expect to debark, etc. Maybe someday I will be able to, but not now. These letters I write are mailed here aboard ship but one of these days they should start Pennsylvania-ward.

I received all my Christmas packages, including one from Martha. Please thank everyone for me. And as I am not writing to many people, you will have to keep them informed of my address changes until I can do it. Remember it may be some time yet before you hear from me regularly, or even again. Don't forget to write often.

> *Love,*
> *Fred.*

———— ➔ ← ————

[V-Mail]

Wed. 26 January 1944

Dear Folks—

I plan to write several letters this evening and just finished one to Joe.

There still is not much to write. Or that I can write, for that matter. We are still at sea; now I have a very good hunch where we are going; I continue to have fun and get a big kick out of this voyage, though I must confess that I had a recurrence of my seasickness. I pass most of my waking hours reading, eating, gazing out over the waters and in that old Army game of "waiting in line." I have held Sick Call 3 times, too.

I was able to get ashore somewhere for a brief visit and bought a souvenir of the place and will send it to you soon.[9]

Incidentally, I sent home by Express a package of clothing from Texas on 12/23/43 and another from somewhere else a few days later. Be sure to let me know if you get them okay.

Love,

Fred.

This is the fourth letter I have sent you.
[on back is written "Received Feb. 12th]

[V-Mail]
To: PVT. JOE GABRIEL
A.A.F.T.T.C.[10]
HAMILTON COLLEGE
CLINTON, NEW YORK

Wed. 26 Jan. 1944

(1/31/43 [44]. Finally landed. S.W. Pacific island. Latest address: A.P.O. #709; c/o San Francisco, Cal.)

Dear Joe—

By the time you receive this you probably will have heard from home that I no longer am in the States. I have written them 3 letters since leaving and presume all or at least one of them will get there before this does to you.

Those letters were written at sea, as is this one. I can't say much—where, when, how long, etc. even if I did know. However I can say that I am well, having fun and a nice voyage. I was very sea sick at first but now am a regular old "salt."

It is hard to write a good letter; I kept wondering if what I want to say will be censored-out. I was able to get ashore somewhere for a brief visit. Sometime soon I am sending home a little souvenir of the place. If prices weren't so damn high there I would have gotten something for the children. But maybe it is just as well not to get into that practice, as I expect to see many interesting places before I get home again.

Well, Joe, I must close now. You had better reassure the folks about me or they will worry. Write when you can.

Love,
Fred.

I received your last letter.

———— ➔ ❮ ————

[V-Mail]
To: MAJ. LOUIS GABRIEL
Hq. C.C. "A", U.S. ARMY,
A.P.O. #446; c/o P.M.
NASHVILLE, TENN.

Wed. 26 Jan. 1944

(1/31/43 [44]. Finally landed. S.W. Pacific island. Latest address: A.P.O. #709; c/o San Francisco)

Dear Lou—

This letter is being written at sea and is not going to be a very newsy one. I am not permitted to say where and when we embarked, what our ship is, where we are going (I don't know that anyway) etc. I can write that, aside from a few days "mal de mer", I have and am having a very pleasant trip. I got ashore somewhere for a while and so, including Canada and Mexico, have set foot on four countries' soil so far in my time.

I wrote Joe this evening; also home. So far I have written them 4 times, but have no idea when they will receive them. These letters are posted and censored aboard ship. The first time I wrote them both V-mail and Air mail to make sure they would get word from me as soon as was possible.

I'll sign off now. Write when you can.

Love,
Fred.

[V-Mail]
*[CHANGE OF ADDRESS FORM WITH A HANDWRITTEN NOTE
BELOW]*

31 January 1944

Dear Folks—
*PLEASE ADDRESS ME AS SHOWN BELOW UNTIL OTHERWISE
ADVISED*

CAPTAIN   FREDERICK   R   GABRIEL   0-485524
(Grade)   (First Name) (Initial) (Last name) (Army serial number)

39th Station Hospital
(Company, battery, etc.) (Regiment, groups or other organization)

A.P.O. No. 709, c/o Postmaster, San Francisco, Calif.
*The above COMPLETE ADDRESS should be placed on ALL MAIL
sent to me*

MY CODE CABLE ADDRESS IS AMUTFI

Norml Signature Fred. R. Gabriel [signed]

SPACE BELOW FOR MESSAGE

31. Jan. 1944.
    *Am on an island somewhere in South Pacific area. Feeling
fine and having fun and worrying a bit about you worrying
about me. Have written you five times since leaving States and
sent you a radiogram[11] as soon as I could. Took a trip to San
Francisco before we left but could not contact O'Dells as they
had no phone.*
    *Received the Christmas package just before embarking; also
a letter from Ester. Will write you 3 or 4 times a week.*

Love,
Fred.

The above is my latest address.

[V-Mail]
[CHANGE OF ADDRESS FORM WITH A HANDWRITTEN NOTE
BELOW]

TUES. 1 FEB. 1944

Dear Father Liebel
PLEASE ADDRESS ME AS SHOWN BELOW UNTIL OTHERWISE
ADVISED

CAPTAIN   FREDERICK   R   GABRIEL   0-485524
(Grade)   (First Name) (Initial) (Last name) (Army serial number)

39th Station Hospital
(Company, battery, etc.) (Regiment, groups or other organization)

A.P.O. No. 709, c/o Postmaster, San Francisco, Calif.
The above COMPLETE ADDRESS should be placed on ALL
MAIL sent to me

MY CODE CABLE ADDRESS IS AMUTFI
Normal Signature Fred. R. Gabriel [signed]

SPACE BELOW FOR MESSAGE
This is an official change of address notification. Yes, I
finally dood it, and now am located on an island in the South
Pacific area. About the only things else I can write is that we
have not been here long and that the voyage out was pleasant
and interesting.

I wrote home a few times while aboard the ship but as yet
have had no word from them since leaving the States.

I'll sign off now, awaiting your next newsletter.
Sincerely,
Fred.

So. Pacific Area
Thurs. Feb. 3. 1944.

Dear Folks—

Mail finally has caught up with me and yesterday I received 5 letters, including 3 from you. Since I do not know yet how well my letters are getting through to you, I will repeat myself a bit here. Since leaving the States I have written you 6 times and sent you a radiogram. Three of the letters were written aboard ship.[12] I have received the Christmas package; also the 2 decks of cards; also Ester's money order; also a pkg of cookies from Martha. I have written to Louie and Joe since being here, and have sent change-of-addresses to you, Uncle Mike and Fr. Liebel. I'll leave it up to you to inform Mrs. Mae Russell. My other (older) address is okay but mail will get here sooner if the latest one (A.P.O. #709) is used.

I have sent you both V-mail and Air-mail; I don't know which is quicker though they want us to use V-mail if possible, I think because of the lesser weight. I believe letters to me will get here quickest if sent V-mail with an Air mail stamp. That way it will fly to the west coast, where it will be photoed and flown here. Another thing you might do—date your letters and answer any specific questions I might ask. Also acknowledge receipt of any packages, etc. from me. I sent home a package of clothing (via Railway Express) from Texas and another from California, and I may send home another. I will let you know if I do. I find I brought along too much clothing. Even though I sent most of my woolens home I doubt if I will have use for any of it. I told Lou he could have my pinks at home.

I can't tell you much about our trip, our ship or anything like that: Later on I may be able to. After leaving Sheppard Field we traveled 4 days to an area on the Pacific coast where we stayed for several days before embarking at still another place. During that several-day stay I got up to San Francisco once. While there I tried to phone the O'Dells but they apparently had no phone and I did not have time to look them up. I also phoned Dick Hoffman,[13] my Jeff roommate, who was at Mare Island Naval Hospital[14] but was informed that he had shipped out. Then I phoned one of my classmates at Chicago last summer. We arranged to meet somewhere downtown that evening but somehow missed each other. Funny thing—he was writing me a letter when I phoned him. I received it yesterday.

Well, I will close now. I am well and things go well here with me. I trust the same is with you, too. Don't worry about me and write often.

Love,
Fred.

My latest address:
A.P.O. #709
C/o San Francisco.
Rest the same

P.S. Enclose are some pictures taken in Texas. I never received the cookies from Selina, leaving too soon.

———— ➔ ← ————

South Pacific Area
Sun. Feb. 6. 1944.

Dear Folks—

This is a beautiful Sunday morning. I have just returned from Mass, where I received Communion, and from holding Sick Call. Sick Call doesn't amount to much these days. The usual cases seen being sunburn, athlete's foot and minor things like that.

Things continue to go well here. I am fine and having fun, so please do not worry about me. Our setup is not bad at all. We are living in tents but are enjoying it; the food is good;[15] we have set up a small PX, where toilet and laundry articles, tobacco, playing cards, etc. are readily obtained. Also they occasionally stock candies and cookies. The stock is rationed on the strength of the unit, but adequately. I believe the only time they sell out completely is when a shipment of beer or coke comes in, when everybody wants his own share.[16]

I still am not permitted to write very freely. The ship we traveled on was a good one, as you'll agree when I can name it. Meals were good. We were a bit crowded but no one minded. The weather for the most part was good. The ocean never was very rough; I guess the Pacific generally is not. The water was beautiful—sometimes green or a green-blue; usually it was an indigo blue, though at times it was lighter like a Prussian blue. Sometimes at sunset when there were small waves, the water just glistened gold in the sunlight. I did tell you I visited briefly somewhere on the way.

We aren't functioning as a unit yet. I spend my time writing letters or building little things around to make this place a little more livable. I am developing into quite a carpenter. Every day I do a little laundering, though drying the wash is a problem because of the frequent rains. Nearby is a nice sandy beach, where I swim daily in the ocean. There are plenty of palm and coconut trees around and all have eaten our fill of coconuts. Generally we are in bed by seven-thirty or eight, though last night I went to a movie. There are a couple nearby and the movies shown are recent. Yesterday I played volleyball, but usually it is too warm for that.

Every day I set my bedding, etc. out to sun. Somebody must stay around to watch for in five minutes a good downpour of rain will fall.[17]

I have seen many native men so far but only one woman. These natives are neither ferocious nor spectacular. The average adult male is five feet or under tall, and quite muscular. Many are red-haired, which looks funny, and they seem to go for pipes. None wear shoes; they wear only cloths, usually colored, around their waists.

Very nearby is a doctor from Olean, whose name is new to me.[18] *This morning I met a naval officer from Binghamton, who told me a doctor from Bradford*[19] *is on a nearby island.*

I have written quite a few letters lately and now am sitting back awaiting returns. A person really wants mail when overseas—no fooling.

Funny thing about being abroad—life here isn't on a different plane, as I had imagined, but maybe that is because this place is so Americanized. Things seem the same as they were in Washington, Texas or Arizona. And except for the realization that I am so damn far from home, I would think I never had left the States. Of course I reserve the right to change my mind if someone starts shooting at me.

Your letter of Jan. 21 just was delivered to me. That is good time—2 weeks. I have been using V-mail lately, which we are strongly urged to use. Incidentally, stationery is easy to get here.

Glad to know you received my clothes. Both packages? Yes, I got the relic.[20] Thanks. Haven't received the "Eagle" in a few weeks but papers come slower than letters. Received Fr. L. [Father Liebel] newsletter yesterday—he guessed close, didn't he? Must close now. Write often. I will write 3–4 times a week. Don't work too hard.

> *Love to all,*
> *Fred.*

————————— ➔ ← —————————

[V-Mail]

TUE. FEB. 8 1944.

Dear Folks—

This is Tuesday afternoon. I have just returned from school—an old story to me. It lasts only 3 days; I cannot tell you what we are studying.

Things continue to go well with me. I am fine, and eating like a horse. Daily swimming is my exercise. My weight is still about 142.#.

Last nite we had quite a rain—that is an old story, too, as this is the rainy season. Those 4-buckle rubber arctics[21] you sent me are a godsend. They are worth their weight in gold. Some units have boots issued to them, but I doubt that we will. I brought many things with me I could just as well have sent home but certainly not those arctics. I don't need anything. If I do I will let you know.

Will close now. Take care of yourselves and don't work too hard and do not worry about me. Still have received no mail from you with the #709 address but I am sure by this time you know it.

Love,
Fred.

———————— ✦ ————————

[V-Mail]

THUR. FEB. 10 1944.

Dear Folks—

This is a wet morning, so I am staying in and writing a few letters. I just finished washing some clothes. I rigged up a little fire place to boil the water. Drying them, as I wrote you, is quite often a problem because of the frequent rain. Clothes here soon begin to mold and smell sour so I sun them every chance I get.

There isn't much to write so my letters probably aren't very newsy to you.

One of the officers in my tent has a radio, which we turn on evenings. We get San Francisco and Radio Tokyo. This Jap broadcast is fun to listen to; their news reports sound like they are just eating the American forces. Then they play American music—to make us want to get home, I suppose. The announcer refers to us as the "orphans of the Pacific." [22] *Try to pick them up some time; we get it in the evening—I don't know when that would be in Pennsylvania.*

I'll sign off now. Had a letter from Joe yesterday, written Jan. 14.

Love,
Fred.

South Pacific Area
Sat. 12 Feb. 1944.

Dear Folks—

This has been a pretty swell day, though hot. It hasn't rained so far but the sky is clouding up fast now.

The mail man has been good to me these past 2 days—four letters: from Papa the 11th of Jan.; Martha the 10th; one from a nurse in Philly, and today one from Ester, written the 20th. I am glad to learn that all is well with you. I still am looking for one addressed #709. Vic wrote me the 15th.

We are not functioning yet; instead we are bivouacking here. Much of our time is spent fixing up around here and some nice work is being done by the men. We have to be rather imaginative as we haven't too much to work with. Yesterday, for instance, I made a pair of shorts by cutting the legs off a pair of suntans.[23] Not wanting to waste the pieces, I sewed together the cut ends of the legs, put a drawstring through the hemmed end and had myself a nice bag like a money-bag.

We haven't had so much rain these past few days and the sun really beams down, so much that a person can easily get a bad sunburn.

Yesterday I signed a pay-voucher for January and February. We get them together this time because we were sailing when the Jan. pay became due. Incidentally, we get 10% increase in base pay for overseas duty ($20.00 in my case); enlisted men get a 20% increase. I should be able to send money home occasionally because of the increase and because of no place to spend it here.

If my airmail envelopes look ragged it is because the heat has caused them to stick together and I have to pry them apart. Don't accuse anyone of tampering with them. I don't know if officers' mail is all censored yet or not. I believe that after they see we have learned what not to write they relax a bit. I wish I could tell you just where I am but I cannot. You can easily guess where, though.

In her letter Ester offered to send me a package. However, I am not asking for anything I absolutely do not need because I

*have enough on hand to start a store. Also shipping space on
ships is needed for necessities. Maybe, though, I'll be needing
something, in which case I will let you know.*

Well, I must close now, with

Love,
Fred.

P.S. Keep the letters coming.

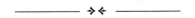

[From Eldred Eagle February 25, 1944, page 1]
"Communication"

Southwest Pacific
February 13, 1944

Dear Friend [Father Liebel]:

*The Newsletter was a very welcome piece of mail one day
this week. Much as I enjoyed it back in the States, it is doubly
welcome here. You called the shot when you said I am in the
SW Pacific. I am on a well-known island which of course I
cannot name.*

*This is the evening of a very beautiful Sunday, most of
which I idled except for going to Mass this morning. Now I am
catching up on my letter-writing ... life here isn't too bad—a
bit crude at present, but not too rough. We are bivouacking
until our unit begins to function. Thus we have spare time
which both officers and men spend largely in making our
set-up more comfortable. Considerable ingenuity is shown
in devising things. The weather presents considerable rain,
as this is the rainy season. When it gets warm, it really gets
warm, and changes for one condition to the other are frequent
and quick.*

*There are plenty of coconut palms on this island, as well
as plenty of jungle areas with multi-colored birds and flowers
and other forms of tropical animal and vegetable life. (Flash:
right now the President's address is coming in over the
radio).[24] However, in our immediate area things aren't too*

Soldier on beach near a sunken Japanese vessel, Kokumbona, Guadalcanal, 1944.

"jungly." This was the scene of severe and momentous fighting, and right now is tame compared to what it was a year ago, in all ways. ...

Speaking of our voyage out—it was pleasant and I enjoyed all of it except a bout of seasickness the first couple of days. We were on a good ship which of course cannot be named: made one stop on the way down.

One officer in the tent here has a radio but we don't play it much because it is a battery set. Evenings we tune in the army broadcasts from Frisco and LA on short wave. Last night it was particularly good and WEAL Baltimore came in strong on the longwave band.

News here is a bit scarce. Aside from radio newscasts from home and a daily mimeographed report, only the most important world news is put on this island. By the time newspapers and magazines reach here, the events are a week old. We have not received any so far, they will be welcome when they arrive. Our unit has subscribed to most of the popular periodicals and a few metropolitan newspapers.

The natives on this island—at least those I have seen— are a bit disappointing. Suppose I believe Hollywood too much. All those I have seen were men; the women stay close to their villages. They average about five feet in height, are well developed and wear only a skimpy bit of clothing if one could call it that. The men are dandy workers, smoke pipes almost constantly, and many are red-headed, believe it or not. Speaking of pipes, they are perhaps the most-desired things among the natives. These people speak pidgin-English, of course.

A M.C. [Medical Corps, Dr. Leonard] from Olean is with another unit nearby, and one at least from Bradford is with a naval hospital on a neighboring island. Our unit being new, is going through the souvenir-seeing stage of life abroad. There are plenty of Jap articles lying about, all evidence of the fighting. Right in our area are pill-boxes and fox-holes; and palms with their tops shot away are not a strange sight. To-day some of the officers "jeeped" to a native village to see "life in the raw." I missed out on that, being on duty. Am not too keen on random collecting of souvenirs because they will be too common at home after the war. However I have my eyes opened for something that may be particularly interesting.

Gosh, this is a long letter. Aren't you tired of reading? I am trying to determine how mail will reach me the quickest. Of course we are strongly urged to use V-mail and to advise our correspondents to do likewise. Personally I think that air-mailed V-mail would get here first, because it would be flown to the West Coast. I think that air-mail should reach the East quickly if it flies to the States which seemingly it does not always do. ...

Well, I'll close now. Give my kind regards to all the folks and friends, and keep the news coming.

Sincerely,

F---------------

Editor's Note: Portions of this letter that were personal have obviously been omitted.

[V-Mail]

WED. 16 FEB. 1944.
Somewhere in the So. Pacific

Dear Folks—

Your letters to me are coming through more regularly now, the last I received being written by Jeanette[25] Feb. 2 and reaching me yesterday (15th). I am glad to learn that you all are well and that you know I am well, too.

Things are going all right for us. We still are not busy but we keep busy just the same. For instance, for the past 3 days I have been supervising the building of a small recreation hall. We finished it this morning and it isn't half bad. Now we have a cool place to hang out in and a place to stay up evenings, for which we are happy.

Last night we had another ration of 2 bottles of beer.[26] I got my pair, as well as those of another officer who didn't care for his share. I drank some and am protecting the remaining bottles.

39th Station Hospital officers' rec hall, Guadalcanal 1944.

Yes, I received the relic okay. Ester wrote that a pkg. of clothes had arrived home, but failed to mention which.

I wrote Ester and Fr. Liebel this week; tonite I am going to write to Vic and Louie and Joe.

This afternoon is very hot; last night we had a severe rain. Well, I'll sign off now.

> Love,
> Fred.

P.S. If the Knieser's boys[27] *leave, who will run the store?*

―――――― ✦ ――――――

[INCOMPLETE]

P.S. got your new address from home. My latest is A.P.O. #709. 'Frisco

> Somewhere in So Pacific
> Thurs. 17 Feb. 1944.

Dear Lou—

By now you probably know, either directly or indirectly, that the above is my address. Things are going pretty well for us here, tho' yet we are only bivouacking and not functioning as a unit. Our area is pretty—in a grove of coconut palms. This was the actual scene (part of it, anyway) of very momentous fighting not too long ago. There are plenty of fox holes, old shells and other reminders about. Nearby on the ocean beach still are some of the landing-craft shot up in the invasion approach.

Naturally we see plenty of animals and vegetable plant life that is foreign to a Pennsylvanian like myself. Commonest are the coconuts—plenty on all the trees and easily obtainable. I have seen a few white birds that I think are parrots. Lizards are common, though the largest I have seen was about a foot long. He has been dubbed "Cecil" by us and has claimed our

39th Station Hospital soldiers on abandoned landing craft, Guadalcanal, 1944.

*tent as home. The other nite Cecil ate a box of cookies on me.
I have seen a few walking fish—perch, I was told. Then I
have seen plenty of insect-catching plants that fold up when
touched. I was told it grows in Texas but I never saw any of
it there. Not far from the unit areas are typical jungle—big,
shaggy trees, grass 8–10 feet high, vines like ropes and insects
by the millions.*

*The trip here was pleasant, though I was very seasick
twice and I mean sick. Also the vessel was crowded but no
one seemed to mind that much. Our ship was a good one—I
cannot name it, however. Only once was the sea choppy. Other
times only low waves were rolling and the water either indigo
or Prussian blue. Near some land it was green or green-blue.
I believe now am permitted to say we stopped at Noumea,
New Caledonia, en route here. I visited there briefly. The most
exciting things for me were the beer and hamburgers we
bought there.*

*Maybe I can give you some advice about certain overseas
conditions you'll want to know. I can't write them all at
once and will tell you more as I learn more. Like freshmen
in college or med. school we were subjected to considerable
misinformation. I'll try to give you straight dope, though*

remember I am speaking of this [box around word] place;
also—an outfit like yours probably will be in a more forward
position than we are.

  In the first place I brought along too damn much. I could
easily start a young store. For instance: woolens are absolutely
not needed here and what is more, they supposedly rot very
quickly in this climate. We have heavy and frequent rains
alternating rather suddenly with hot spells, though 4 days
without rain is unusual. We were told to send most woolens
home yet many of us brought along blouse, field and dress
O.D.'S.[28] I have a half-dozen cotton shirts and pants which
so far I haven't needed much though later on probably will.
Most of the time I run around with only shorts and T-shirts
(1/8 sleeve). Incidentally they are nice to have; replace your
underwear jerseys with them and use them for both purposes.
Good idea.

  Shortly before leaving I sent home for a pair of light weight
4-buckle rubber arctics. The Army ones are too heavy. Mine
have proved very, very useful. Engineers, etc., have rubber
boots issued to them but we don't rate them. Another useful
item but almost impossible to get even in the States is locker
sandals. Rubber are best. I never had any luck with wooden,
woolen or canvas ones. I think I will see if Papa can get me a
pair next time I write home.

  We weren't here a week before we set up our own little PX,
at which common "g i" needs like toilet and laundry soap,
other toilet articles, shaving things, playing cards, tobacco
(cigarettes 50¢ a carton), comb, cookies and hard candies
are obtainable. So don't be fooled on those things. I brought
along about 50+ razor blades (I have been collecting them for
the past 2 years) and about 30 bars of soap. Some things in
the PX are rationed on the strength of the unit but everyone
gets what he wants though maybe not just when he wants
it. For instance, already we have had a shipment (small) of
Ronson lighters,[29] excellent hunting knives, and I hear maybe
wrist-watches, too. So those overseas do pretty well. Common
clothing items are obtainable at the

[V-Mail]

SAT. 19 FEB. 1944
Somewhere in the So. Pacific

Dear Folks—

Today's mail brought me two letters: yours of Feb. 5th and the February newsletter. I was very happy to receive both.

You still use my old A.P.O. number, so I assume that by the 5th you had not yet received my radiogram or any letters written here. The ones you mention receiving were written aboard ship and probably mailed in New Caledonia. I now am permitted to say that we stopped there.

No, the apples and oranges in my Christmas box did not spoil. Lucky, wasn't it? I wrote Fr. Liebel a young book the other day; he'll probably pass it on to you.

About the box of candy you want to send me. I appreciate you wanting to do so but why send candy 8 thousand miles when I can buy it here? However, I wish you would send me 3 items (keep this letter for the postmaster):

1) 4 T-shirts (1/8 sleeve) size 34. Only 4.

2) 1 copy of Van Loon's "The Story of Mankind"[30] in the Pocket book (cheap, paper) edition. I don't want the good one.

3) Make up the balance of the allowable weight with unpopped popcorn, preferably in tin cans.

Should you be unable to get any of these items easily, just skip it as I don't [need] them very badly anyway. Must close now.

Love,
Fred.

[V-Mail]

MON. 21 FEB. 1944
Somewhere in So. Pacific

Dear Folks—

This is noon of a beautiful, lazy day. Not much doing for me, just cleaning up around, washing a few clothes, etc. Besides that I am doing a lot of letter-writing, even tho' there isn't much to write about. Saturday I wrote to Uncle George, Danbury and Bayonne.[31]

Yesterday was quite a big day. In the morning we had fried fresh eggs for breakfast. At noon we had a swell dinner of fried chicken and not the canned variety, either. In the afternoon I got your letter of Feb. 7th, using my new address and acknowledging my radiogram, so now that is over.

Last evening I went to a movie. There are several around and show fairly recent movies several nights a week. Earlier in the week I went to a U.S.O. show featuring some Hollywood stars—Ray Milland, Mary Elliott, Frances Faye and Rosita Moreno.[32] *Not bad, huh?*

In my last letter I asked you to send me 3 things. Now I will add a fourth. If any are available I would like a pair of rubber *locker sandals but I doubt if you can get any. If not, I have a pair which aren't too badly worn and which I can continue to use. Size 7 or 8. I have had no luck with wooden, canvas or felt sandals, so don't send any of these.*

Must close now.

Love,
Fred.

P.S. No newspapers have arrived yet.

[V-Mail]

THURS. 24 FEB. 1944
Somewhere in So. Pacific

Dear Folks—

This is Thursday evening. I have just put my two bottles
of beer on ice (which we were lucky enough to get) and am
writing this while waiting for it to cool. Another thing—tonite
we have electricity in our rec. halls. We really have fixed things
up here, if I do say so.

Today was hot and we have had no rain for three days. I
guess the worst of the rainy season is passing. The roads are
plenty dusty now.

There isn't much in the line of interest or news to write. I
still pass much of my time doing nothing in particular. I may
be assigned to a ward in a nearby hospital until we ourselves
begin to function. I play on the Officers' team in the 39th
volley ball tournament. We have lost both games so far but are
improving rapidly. We should do better from here on in. Boy!
this cold beer tastes swell! Today I received a card from Fr.
Liebel, using my #709 APO. I am trying to promote a trip to
this nearby island where a doctor from Bradford is located.[33]

I am writing you every other day. I figure my letters will
reach [you] about 2 weeks afterwards and by now should be
reaching you quite regularly. Your letters take 7–20 days. Fr.
L.'s card was written the 14th and came airmail. Tell him. Will
close now with

Love,
Fred.

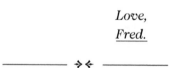

Somewhere in the So. Pacific
Sunday 27 Feb. 1944

Dear Folks—

This is Sunday evening, and it is stating it mildly to say
that I am tired. I just finished doing my washing and hanging
it on the line. The reason it wasn't done earlier is that I spent
the day visiting a native village. Instead of going to 11 o'clock

Mass, as I have been doing, I hitched down to another chapel about 5 miles away for 8 o'clock Mass and was back here ready to go by nine. I had good luck getting rides.

Another officer and myself and about fifteen enlisted men made the trip in 2 vehicles. After driving about 12 miles the road became impassible, so we got out and hoofed the last 3 miles to the village. The village itself was not spectacular, though its setting in real jungle was, consisting of about 20 small 1- and 2-room huts of thatched palm. The natives we saw were men and boys. The men seemed to be lazy and amused by us. The boys were the most interesting thing we saw—one fellow 11 years old, carrying a pipe and a cigar and smoking a cigarette, asked me for tobacco. I also saw another boy not over 3 years old puffing on a cigarette. As I told you before, tobacco and pipes are big items to these folks. We saw no women; I guess the chief locked them up when he saw us coming.

We went up there expecting to see something very worthwhile and to get good souvenirs. However, I personally was rather disappointed. The only things to barter for were grass-shirts, and they don't look like they would stand a trip to Pennsylvania. Next time I go to a village it will be to a bigger one.

We are fixed-up pretty nicely here now. Our two unit radios are in operation—one in the enlisted men's Rec. and the other in ours. They are darn good—right now we are listening to a recast from San Francisco coming in as strongly as Buffalo used to [at] home. All around the area we have planted palms, which improve the look considerably.

The mailman was good to me today—5 letters. And yesterday I had a very interesting V-mail from Louie. He typed it (which is very good on V-mail) and really got a lot on the page. It was written the 11th. Incidentally, both Airmail and V-mail have been reaching me in about 12 to 15 days. Louie gave me what low-down he could but said there really wasn't much to write about since I hear from you regularly.

(Flash—"Tokyo Ann" is now on the air. She speaks in

English to us "orphans of the Pacific." I heard she was the wife
of a traitor missionary. The famous Jap propaganda broadcast
"Zero Hour" comes on next.)[34]

By now my letters from here should be reaching you 3
or 4 times weekly. I think I sent only 1 letter after arriving
here before I sent the radiogram. No, I didn't say in it that I
had landed, though actually I had. There is something funny
about those messages. From some theaters "arrived safely"
is permitted. Here they are not. I doubt if even my APO was
on my wire. Also, we selected our sentences from a prepared
sheet. We couldn't mention arriving or destination at all, but
had to assume that our families would know that we must
have landed or otherwise we would not have sent anything.
Those messages never are sent from ships—I suppose we
maintained radio silence all the way—and usually not until
final destination is reached.

Today's letters were from Vic, Ester, Joe, Uncle Mike and
Mary Wrona. Mary still writes the best and nicest letters I
ever have received. I missed the boat very, very, badly there.
Uncle Mike sent only a note with a PX notification that he had
purchased and was sending me a Christmas gift—a billfold.
Poor Joe wrote that "Gerry" had married out on him too. I
assume she is that Syrian blond in Utica or is she Mrs. Pfeil's
niece?

Both the girls mentioned physical exams for married men,
the banquet in Olean, and both want to know if they can send
snapshots to me. Sure they can. Not by V-mail, of course.
Sending photos overseas is encouraged as a morale-builder, if I
remember correctly. And while I think of it—our incoming mail
is not censored. Write what you want. Vic also mentioned that
my cablegram left a bit to the imagination and that I probably
would like the "Eagle." I will get it when the papers get here.

If you haven't—how about buying me a bond during the
current drive?

I hope Louie and Joe got home at the same time okay and
that you all had a nice time.

Well, I'll close now and write you again in a couple days.

Love,

Fred.

P.S. Have been taking a few pictures but getting them developed is a problem.

P.S. I guess my letters reach you in about 2 weeks, too, don't they? The big difference between our mail and V-mail, I know now, is that V-mail must be shorter. However, typing and not-too-small writing permits plenty per page.

———————— ➔ ᐸ ————————

[V-Mail]
To: PVT. JOE GABRIEL (12100877)
A.A.F.T.T.C.—NORTH HALL
HAMILTON COLLEGE
CLINTON, NEW YORK.
MON. 28 FEB. 1944
South Pacific Area.

Dear Joe—

While waiting for a bottle of beer to cool (we got ice somehow, somewhere) I thought I would write you again. We get 2 bottle[s] 2 times a week.

I have received 9 letters in the last 2 days—6 from the family. Uncle Mike wrote me a note that he was sending me a Christmas present. You probably know most of the news from home.

In an old letter of yours you mention that the pictures you take are too small. Did you know my old camera—the one Paulie played with—recently was repaired? I doubt it is used much home. I have a camera with me and have taken a roll of pictures so far. Getting them developed here isn't easy.

Yesterday went to a native village. It was rather a disappointment to me—no native women, no good souvenirs, etc. However, it was exciting and coming back our vehicle got stuck in the middle of a river we were fording. One of the men also fell into some mud up to his neck. He says it was quicksand. I didn't see it but was told he was a goner until he grabbed a log. Some fun we got, huh?

Must close now. Write when you can and keep up the good work.

Love,
Fred.

P.S. I believe there is a Bolivar boy here.
AM LISTENING TO RADIO TOKYO NOW.

───────── ➔ ← ─────────

[INCOMPLETE]
[V-Mail]

SUN. [MON.] 28 FEB. 1944.

wrote that he had the car at school with him, had gone to the graduation dance and was soon to leave school.

Something in the "Eagle" reminded me to ask you—what ever became of the park? I remember we finished the tennis courts the day before the big flood.[35] What wasted labor that was!! And how is Park Ave.?

Early Mass today was at six. I planned to go but overslept. Instead I went @ eleven, which was a High Mass. And was it hot in the Chapel! Did I tell you that this nearby hospital now has a Catholic chaplain too? So the Catholics in the area have services more often.

Today I had a patient from Jamestown.[36] He knows some Olean people. I haven't seen Richardson or Eastman[37] in some time. And I never looked up Pfeiffer—I'll do it this week for sure.

Well—must close now.

Love,
Fred

[V-Mail]

WED. MAR. 1ST 1944.
Somewhere in So. Pacific.

(THE ELDRED NEWSPAPER HAS NOT YET BEGUN TO ARRIVE HERE)[38]

Dear Folks—

This is Wed. evening. We just finished playing volley-ball. The officers lost again but we have fun. I was going to type this but a machine was not available.

This morning I went to the dentist but he could find nothing to do on my teeth, which didn't anger me at all. This afternoon I had a chat with Sgt. Richardson [from] Bolivar. He also knew George has taken his physical. Later in the afternoon washed clothes. Today as somewhat rainy so they won't dry for a while. Usually it requires only several minutes. By using g-I laundry soap, plus plenty of elbow grease and a brush I can get my clothes to come out real white. Funny thing about my towels—when soapy water gets on them they look dirty even when they aren't. They are my only bother.

I have plenty of clothes with me. In fact much too much. Now I wished I had sent more of it home and used their weight for something like carpenter tools. I have plenty more use for them. Woolens are absolutely useless here, and I have considerable with me. The Sgt. told me not long ago he visited a former employee of Loops,[39] *now somewhere in the So. Pacific.*

The mailman continues to be good to me, and I am trying hard to keep him that way. I received a few old ones today— written early in January. They apparently came by boat. One was from Papa, written Jan. 3. I am glad that damn Bradford debt is cleared up. Also that day he forwarded me some income tax blanks. I am afraid you'll have to take care of it again for me. Ester can write a check. According to a slip with the blanks, in 1942 I filed a return of $49.52 and paid only half of it. I am in favor of paying this tax completely and promptly, and then receiving a rebate if any is due, than not pay it in the hope it will be waived because I am in the service, overseas or some other crap like that. So please pay any in arrears and what is due currently. Also, I believe my insurance premium is due soon; have Ester write a check for that too, not deducting the dividends.

Speaking of finances—yesterday I was paid for 2 months so you'll be getting a double allotment this time (3 hundred) and I find myself with plenty of cash on hand, for which I have no use. Sometime this week I will send you money orders for a hundred dollars or more, which I wish you would use to buy something for yourselves or for the house, but probably for yourselves.

I have thought of a good use for my extra twenty dollars per month for overseas duty (10% base pay). I suppose I should get another bond monthly with it but instead will give it to the girls to give Eddy and Paulie music lessons. Aside from bonds that will be the best use for it I can think of. The girls will not like the idea of taking the money and the boys won't like the idea of practicing but I think they'll see it my way. Besides, I'll get Louie and Joe and you to put pressure on them.

Not much in the line of news to write this trip. It isn't raining so much these days; we get good reception on the radio and really enjoy them; our newspapers and magazines came in today, probably on the same boat as the mail.

Before I forget, let me know—not you, Censor—if my V-mails are legible. If not I will make arrangements to use the typewriter.

Must close now and get caught up on the funny papers I have missed.

                                        Love,
                                        Fred.

[INCOMPLETE]
[V-Mail]

FRI. 3 MAR. 1944.
Somewhere in the Pacific.

Dear Folks—

Letter-writing again this evening after playing volley ball.
A couple days ago received the Dec. 17 and 24<u>th</u> issues of the
"Eagle." Today received the Feb. 18<u>th</u> issue you sent me air-
mail in an envelope the 21<u>st</u> (12 days travel time). Today's
mail also brought me yours and Ester's letters of the 21st of
Feb, plus a card from Father Liebel of the same date.

Louie wrote me recently; am glad he is going to Washington
and that Joe got home. Louie will probably ask for leave after
completion of his course. It is the same one I took a year ago
or a bit longer ago. Louie said he was writing Papa something
he found out about servicemen's income tax. I wrote you
about filing my returns. In addition to that you may want to
know I became Captain October 5th and I get a $25.00 bond
each month, plus the extra ones Mama buys me. Also I bought
$50.00 bonds for Notre Dame and a $25.00 fraternity one.

I think I will write you fewer airmails; by typing or using
2 V-mails I can write just as much. Incidentally, some here
today received Christmas packages of food—what messes they
were! I suggest you write me V-mail, too. I did get one from you
I believe (I get so many it is hard to remember from whom).
They will take 3 or 4 days longer but that won't matter much
as long as they arrive regularly. You can get my "Eagle" from
Mrs. Russell each week and send it to me in an envelope. You
need not air-mail it unless you want. That is a lot of postage.
Also, it weighs quite a bit and undoubtedly keeps some letters
from being taken aboard the airplane.

Somewhere in the So. Pacific
Wed. 8 March 1944.

Dear Folks—

Enclosed is the money-order for a hundred dollars, which I wish you would use to buy something for yourselves. Please let me know when you get it. Also enclosed is an income-tax bill of some sort. I wrote you that I want you to pay it for me, as well as my insurance.

This is early afternoon. I am going to 5:30-Mass. As far as I know, it is the only Lenten service nearby.

We have had quite a bit of rain lately, but the weather seems milder in general. Gosh! but I am tanned! Most of the time I don't wear a hell of a lot of clothes.

Building our Rec. hall was a good deal. Whereas we used to go to bed before 7, we now stay up late reading, writing, listening to the radio or playing 5¢ poker. I haven't been up after 11:30 since we left the States. However, I get up every morning about 6:30. The mornings here are nice, even when it is raining.

I believe I now can say that while we were aboard ship a rumor had it that it came over the radio from the enemy that they had sunk the very vessel we were traveling on.[40] We got a big kick out of that!!

Well, I'll close now. There really isn't much to write. I am receiving your mail okay and trust you are receiving mine.

Love,
Fred.

P.S. Am fine and still having fun.

———————— ➔ ← ————————

[V-Mail]

FRI. 9 MARCH 1944
South Pacific Area

Dear Folks—

This is a rainy afternoon, ideal for staying indoors and catching up on things that should have been done before.

*Today I received an airmail from you and a V-mail from Joe,
both dated the 23rd of Feb. So Louie and Joe did get home
together, or didn't Louie make it? What I have read about it is
confusing. I hope George gets his new store fixed up and the
stock moved before he has to go. I got the "Eagle" you mailed
in an envelope; I mentioned that before, I guess. A couple
days ago I sent you a money-order for a hundred dollars—for
yourselves, not me. What Sister Carmencita*[41] *told you means
nothing to me, surprising though that may seem. Incidentally,
when I write you I always have on hand your latest letters,
and usually mention their dates. Joe didn't have much to say.*

*Today also received a letter from Danbury. They have heard
from Vic recently, apparently, so they know the latest. She
(Edna)*[42] *said our cousin, Mary Dwailibe, had been there.*

*Things are the same here. I am feeling fine and looking okay,
too, I guess. At least no one complains about my looks. I am
very tanned now—I wish you could see me. Boy! how much I
mean that!*

Well, I'll close now,

> *Love,*
> *Fred.*

———— ➔❖ ————

[V-Mail]

> *SUN. 12 MARCH 1944*
> *South Pacific Area*

Dear Folks—

*This is a hot Sunday afternoon, and I am writing this
immediately after a big dinner. I try to rest or take it easy for a
half-hour after the noon meal. Funny thing about this weather—
it will rain like hell and in a couple hours be hot again.*

*One of the officers is here now, worried because he hasn't
heard from home in over a month. His family has the very bad
habit of not writing or withholding from him bad news. They
think they are doing him a favor that way. I hope you don't
have that foolish idea—if anything happens home I want to
know it straight and quickly.*

While I think of it—some say their V mails are being held up somewhere. Are [you] receiving mine okay? You can tell, because I write every second day. So far I have missed only once. They aren't long letters but they will let you know I am alive and kicking.

I never told you this, but at Sheppard Field our nurses were taken from us and were replaced with male nurses. I just heard they are in England with another unit. One disadvantage of female nurses here is that they interfere with our running around nude, etc.

Well, I must close now. Space is running out and there is very little to write.

Love,
Fred.

P.S. Birthday greetings to Papa, Jacqy, and P.J.

----------------- ➔ ← -----------------

[V-Mail]
To:
PVT. JOE GABRIEL (12100877)
T.D. A.A.F.T.T.C.—SOUTH DORM
HAMILTON COLLEGE
CLINTON, NEW YORK.

SUN. 12 MAR. 1944
South Pacific Area.

La Gab—

This is my siesta hour; I just finished writing home. Received your V-mail of the 23rd a couple days ago. So—I am not the only expert gunman in the family. I do believe, though, that I qualified with the more difficult weapon (Colt .45).

Funny story: when I visited their village a couple Sundays back, one of the natives (who spoke Pidgin English poorly) indicated to me he wanted his picture taken with a beautiful parrot on his shoulder. This I did, and indicated to him I would give him a copy of it if I ever came that way again.

He seemed very pleased and suddenly blurted out—"No
bullshit?"!

I met a fellow whose mother in Bolivar clerks for Vic and
George in the store. Also met another who until 10 years ago
lived in Rixford. He now lives near Ithaca, N.Y.

Went to 11:00 Mass this A.M. The Chaplain is a nice young
Irishman (Fr. Walsh) from up around Albany. A missionary
from a neighboring island gave the sermon.

Again not much to write. Am spending much of my time
making souvenirs for the family. Want a grass-skirt?

Must close now.

Love,
<u>Fred.</u>

P.S. Papa, P.J. and Jacqy. have birthdays this month.
WROTE THE GIRLS THAT I WOULD SPEND THE XTRA $20 A
MON. I AM MAKING FOR MUSIC LESSONS FOR EDDY AND P.J.

———————— →← ————————

[V-Mail]

TUE. 14 MARCH '44
South Pacific Area

Dear Folks—

This is about 9:00 PM. I have just returned from a movie,
which was pretty good. Also I saw it at an outside movie just
finished and located about a 2-minute walk from here. Pretty
soft, huh?

This morning the sun was very hot, though it rained hard
last night and again this P.M. This afternoon, too, I attended
an Island Medical Meeting,[43] *held at a hospital about 15 miles*
away. I have been there before and always enjoy the ride,
though the road is bumpy as the devil. These meetings are
pretty interesting.

There isn't much to write again. I played 3 games of volley-
ball tonite. I have become quite good at it. We have an outdoor
basketball court now. I shot baskets quite a bit and am pretty

Erecting water tank for the 39th Station Hospital shower. Note the basketball hoop, Guadalcanal 1944.

good at that too. I usually win when we keep score, though I am the only officer who plays.

Well, I have bragged enough for tonite, so I'll close.

Sincerely,

<u>*Fred.*</u>

P.S. I am waiting for 2 bottles of beer to cool.

———————— ➔ ← ————————

[V-Mail]

FRI. 17 MARCH 1944.

Dear Folks—
GOD BLESS YOU
at Easter
God bless you at Easter
And all the year through
And I shall be happy,

Just thinking of You—
Because, with His blessing
To hasten the Day,
Our Victory surely
Is well on the way!

                              Sincerely,
                              <u>Fred.</u>

[*The card has a Cross surrounded by flowers and US flags on it*].

───────── →← ─────────

[*V-Mail*]

                    SUN. 19 MARCH 1944
                    Somewhere in the Pacific.

Dear Folks—

   This is a very hot Sunday morning. I am writing this while
waiting to go to Mass. Yesterday I received letters from you
and from Joe. Also one from Fran. Selzer,[44] who is dietician
at an army hospital. A couple days ago your letter of the 28th
arrived. You mentioned you want to send me a radio. I have
changed my mind about needing one. We have three here,
to which everyone listens. So please do not attempt to send
it to me. Should I want one later, I will let you know. I am
surprised that George leaves so soon—I hope they get the store
moved by then.

   Thanks for sending the other things. It is okay to omit the
book.[45] I have found out that we will not need it, as there are
a couple volumes of it in our library. However, should you
buy it, just hold on to it. I may later ask for more things and
you can include it with them. I wrote you that it wouldn't be
necessary to send me the "Eagle" by first-class mail. However,
if you want to send it go ahead. I am rather anxious to receive
it more often than I have (3X so far).

   About the income tax—no, I paid <u>none</u> of it myself, leaving
it up to you. I recently returned to you a statement I received
concerning it. And even though need not pay it, don't I have to

file a return anyway?
See next page.

Fred.

Now, that part of the letter is over.

Last evening I saw a movie that was pretty good: "Ten Gentlemen from West Point." [46] I did write you that a movie has just been built only a block from here, and there are 3 others less than 10-minutes' walk away. This new one, too, runs every nite and in case of threatened rain we can get back in no time at all. The movies are out-door jobs but not bad.

Things continue pretty much the same for me. Not working officially yet, but trying to keep busy. Every day that it isn't raining I go swimming in the afternoon and play ball later. In the evening I go to a movie or stay in the REC. listening to the radio and reading, writing, playing—poker or reminiscing. Or plan about the future. Funny thing—over here we talk about the future and the past quite a bit. We may think about the present, especially the war and our being here, but seldom desires. Any talk about the present is about home, strikes, soldiers' voting, etc. We don't express opinions about military strategy and tactics quite as freely as we were prone to do back in the States. Now that we have a closer look at things we are content to let the professionals do the planning.

Space is running out again. Besides it is time to go to Church. So take care of yourselves.

Love,
Sincerely,
Fred.

P.S. I hope the girls aren't too upset about George, Duff leaving, and don't let on to them if they are. It will be tough enough on the fellows, leaving their families. How is Julia Knieser? [47]

[V-Mail—Typed]
To: PVT. JOE GABRIEL (12100877)
AAFTTC—TRAINING DETACHMENT
HAMILTON COLLEGE
CLINTON, NEW YORK.

SUNDAY 19 MARCH 1944
SOMEWHERE IN SOUTH PACIFIC.

DEAR JOE:

WHILE WAITING [for] EVENING CHOW I THOUGHT I WOULD
WRITE YOU. OUR MESS IN GENERAL IS GOOD. WE HAVE
DEHYDRATED POTATOES, CABBAGE, ETC. AND MOST OF THE
MEAT COMES FROM CANS. HOWEVER, OCCASIONALLY WE
GET FRESH MEAT, USUALLY GOAT THOUGH IT HAS BEEN PORK
TWICE AND BEEF ONCE. LAST SUNDAY WE HAD ICE CREAM,
WHICH ANOTHER OUTFIT KINDLY FROZE FOR US, WE HAVING
NO FACILITIES. WE HAVE HAD FRESH EGGS TWICE: MOST
GENERALLY THEY ARE "STRETCHED" OR POWDERED, AS THE
ARMY CALLS THEM. I DON'T GET UP FOR BREAKFAST IF I
KNOW WE WILL HAVE THEM.

THIS WEEK A MOVIE, LOCATED ONLY ABOUT A
THREE*MINUTE WALK AWAY, OPENED. BETTER STILL, IT
RUNS EVERY NITE AND AT A DESIGNATED TIME. MOST OF
THESE OUTDOOR JOBS BEGIN WHEN IT IS DARK ENOUGH.
THE FILMS SHOWN ARE NOT TOO OLD. LAST NITE I SAW
"TEN GENTLEMEN FROM WEST POINT." THE FILMS MAKE
THE CIRCUIT, SO I PLAN TO TAKE ALL MY BUSINESS TO ONE
PLACE, THEREBY SEEING ALL.

TONITE IS BEER NITE AGAIN (2 BOTTLES). USUALLY IT IS
MONDAYS AND THURSDAY. USUALLY, TOO, IT IS WARM. BUT
STILL IT IS BEER. WE GET A RATION OF COKES ONCE IN A
WHILE. OUR PX IS NOT BAD. IT STOCKS MOST THINGS WE
WANT AND SOME NOT OBTAINABLE TO CIVILIANS HOME. I
BUY QUITE A BIT CANDY, ETC. BUT OTHERWISE SPEND VERY
LITTLE MONEY. RECENTLY I SENT HOME A HUNDRED DOLLARS
AND TOLD THEM TO SPEND IT ON THEMSELVES. WITH MY
TWENTY DOLLARS A MONTH OVERSEAS BONUS I OFFERED

TO PAY FOR MUSIC LESSONS FOR EDDY AND PAULIE. SO FAR HAVE HAD NO WORD ABOUT MY OFFER, BUT DO HOPE IT IS ACCEPTED. MAYBE THEIR FATHERS WON'T LIKE THE IDEA. MAYBE I SHOULD HAVE WAITED UNTIL THEY LEFT.

BEING OVERSEAS CHANGES THINGS ALL RIGHT. IN THE PAST TEN DAYS I HAVE HAD FOUR LETTERS FROM DANBURY, ABOUT EQUAL TO THE NUMBER FROM THEM TO ME IN THE PAST TEN YEARS. DID MAMA TELL YOU ALL TO WRITE ME OFTENER? I HEAR FROM YOU ALL OFTENER. I DO APPRECIATE IT, TOO, AS MAIL CALL IS PERHAPS THE BIGGEST SINGLE ITEM HERE, AND THE FELLOW WHO IS LEFT OUT FEELS MIGHTY, MIGHTY LOW. I KNOW OFFICERS WHO ARE WRITING LONG*FORGETTEN FRIENDS IN ORDER TO BOLSTER THEIR CORRESPONDENTS.

I HEAR FROM HOME SEVERAL X A WEEK. HAVE RECEIVED THREE EAGLES SO FAR, BUT NONE RECENTLY. THEY WANT TO SEND IT FIRST*CLASS MAIL. COUSIN JOHNNIE MANSOUR [48] *HAS TAKEN HIS PHYSICAL; ABDO DAN HAS BEEN CALLED (I THINK); DUFFY PASSED TOO. ALSO HEARD FROM UNCLE MIKE AND FRAN SELZER. I THINK SHE HAS INTERESTS ELSEWHERE AND IS TRYING NONE*TOO*GRACEFULLY TO DROP ME FROM HER CORRESPONDING LIST, I BELIEVE. OH WELL.*

CAN'T OFFER UP ANY SUGGESTIONS ABOUT THE FUTURE, BUT MAYBE LOUIE CAN. KEEP UP YOUR GOOD WORK AND WRITE WHEN YOU CAN.

[this part handwritten]

> *Love,*
> *Fred*

P.S. ARE YOU SURE YOU ARE GETTING GOOD PRINTING WITH YOUR PICTURES? DO NOT BE MISLED IF THEY ARE GOOD PICTURES THEY DESERVE GOOD FINISHING.

[V-Mail—Typed]

Tues. 21 March 1944.
SOMEWHERE IN SOUTH PACIFIC.

DEAR FOLKS:

AFTER SKIPPING ME FOR A FEW DAYS LAST WEEK, THE MAILMAN HAS BEEN OKAY BY ME SO FAR THIS WEEK (10 LETTERS). SOME I AM RECEIVING NOW WERE MAILED LATE IN JANUARY AND APPARENTLY CAME OVER VIA BOAT. IN THE LATER ONES ARE A FEW THINGS I WANT TO ANSWER, SO HERE GOES. ... I AM GLAD THE FAMILY SUPPORTED THE LOAN DRIVE SO WELL. CAN YOU LET ME KNOW HOW MUCH OF MY MONEY YOU HAVE PUT INTO BONDS SO FAR THIS YEAR? I MERELY AM CURIOUS. I AM GLAD YOU ALL HAD SUCH A NICE VISIT WITH LOUIE AND HIS FAMILY, AND AM SORRY TO HEAR THAT FR. LEIBEL HAS BEEN ILL. I TRUST IT IS NOTHING SERIOUS. WHO ARE RUNNING THE NEW RESTAURANT? I BELIEVE ESTER MENTIONED IT ONCE BUT I HAVE FORGOTTEN. I AM GLAD ESTER FOUND A CAR, FOR THEY WILL NEED TO GET OUT ONCE IN A WHILE AFTER DUFFY LEAVES FOR THE NAVY. I HAVE BEEN WONDERING HOW MY EARLIER LETTERS GOT THROUGH TO YOU AND IN YOUR LETTER OF MARCH 1ST YOU LET ME KNOW BY SAYING YOU HAD NOT HEARD FROM ME IN TWO WEEKS. I KNEW THE FIRST MAILS WERE SLOW BUT DID NOT REALIZE IT LASTED THAT LONG. HOWEVER BY THIS TIME YOU MUST KNOW THAT SINCE WE LANDED HERE I HAVE WRITTEN YOU EVERY TWO DAYS. OVERSEAS MAIL OCCASIONALLY DOES GET TIED UP, SO DON'T BE ALARMED WHEN YOU DON'T HEAR FROM ME FOR A LITTLE WHILE. AS I SO OFTEN HAVE TOLD YOU, NO NEWS IS GOOD NEWS, AND IF EVER ANYTHING HAPPENS TO ME YOU'LL HEAR OF IT SOON ENOUGH. I DO HOPE LOUIS FINDS AN APARTMENT IN WASHINGTON. IN A LETTER WRITTEN BY YOU TWO DAYS LATER YOU SAY I NEVER MENTION HEARING FROM YOU. MAYBE I DID NOT USE THOSE WORDS BUT I USUALLY TRY TO ANSWER YOUR QUESTIONS AND COMMENTS ON THE THINGS YOU MENTION, OFTEN JUST TO REMIND YOU WHAT YOU WROTE OR TO LET YOU KNOW INDIRECTLY THAT I AM RECEIVING YOUR VERY WELCOME

*LETTERS. I BELIEVE I AM GETTING THEM ALL, TOO, FOR I
HEAR FROM ELDRED ABOUT FOUR TIMES A WEEK, INCLUDING
LETTERS FROM PAPA WRITTEN ON SUNDAYS. ALSO AT LEAST
ONCE A WEEK I HEAR FROM THE GIRLS AND LOUIE AND JOE.
THIS WILL SURPRISE YOU: IN THE PAST TWO WEEKS I HAVE
HAD FOUR LETTERS FROM DANBURY (AILEEN, EDNA, ESTHER
AND ABDO), AND AS I WROTE JOE, BEING OVERSEAS DOES
CHANGE THINGS, AS THAT IS ABOUT AS MANY LETTERS AS I
HAVE HAD FROM THEM IN THE PAST TEN YEARS. BOY! ISN'T
THIS A LONG PARAGRAPH?*

*THANKS FOR OFFERING ME JOE'S SHORTS BUT I DON'T
WANT THEM. I MADE MY OWN BECAUSE I WANTED TO GET
RID OF SOME OF MY CLOTHES. NOTHING GIVES ME MORE
PLEASURE RIGHT NOW THAN TO DISCARD THE WORN OUT
PAIR OF SOXS OR SHORTS. IT IS JUST LIKE FINISHING A
TOUGH EXAMINATION AND THEN TEARING UP THE NOTES
THAT I STUDIED FROM. WHEN YOU REALIZE THAT I MYSELF
MUST LUG AROUND MY PERSONAL BELONGINGS, YOU WILL
UNDERSTAND WHY I AM TIRED OF HAVING ENOUGH CLOTHES
ON HAND TO OUTFIT A WHOLE SQUAD. ALSO, I OFTEN WEAR
ONLY KHAKI UNDERSHORTS, WHICH ARE COOLER AND MUCH
EASIER TO WASH.*

*I GOT A BIG KICK OUT OF WHAT ESTER WROTE ABOUT
JOHNIE AT THAT BIRTHDAY PARTY. I, TOO, THINK PJ SHOULD
HAVE A TONSILLECTOMY. HE IS AT A GOOD AGE FOR IT.*

*THE DANBURY LETTERS SAID THEY ALL WERE GLAD I
ARRIVED SAFELY AND WAS WELL AND THAT THEY WOULD
WRITE ME AND WOULD LIKE TO HEAR FROM ME. I WILL TRY
AND ANSWER ALL THEIR LETTERS. ABDO WROTE THAT HE WAS
TO TAKE HIS PHYSICAL AND THAT JOHN MANSOUR ALREADY
HAD PASSED HIS. THEY WANT TO SEND ME SOMETHING.
THE ONLY THING IS AIRMAIL STATIONERY. THAT I NEED. SO I
TOLD THEM TO SEND ME SOME OF IT. I HAVE SOME ON HAND,
BUT IT IS NICE TO HAVE A LITTLE EXTRA AS IT CANNOT BE
PURCHASED HERE ON THE ISLAND. NEITHER CAN V*MAIL
SO FAR, FOR THAT MATTER, BUT I CAN ALWAYS GET SOME
FROM THE CHAPLAIN*[49] *OR THE RED CROSS. THE NEXT TIME I*

REQUESTED A PACKAGE FROM YOU I WAS GOING TO ASK FOR LIGHT*WEIGHT AIRMAIL PAPER AND ENVELOPES, BUT NOW WILL NOT NEED TO.

LAST NITE I SAW ANOTHER MOVIE AT THIS NEW PLACE JUST NEXT TO US. IT WAS A SCREWY PICTURE AND NOT WORTH WALKING EVEN THAT FAR TO SEE. AND WHILE I THINK OF IT … I HAVE MEANT TO TELL YOU NOT TO MISS SEEING "A JOURNEY FOR MARGARET" [50] *AND BE SURE TO TAKE MAMA. IT IS ABOUT THE DARLINGEST FOUR OR FIVE YEAR OLD GIRL.*

THIS IS AFTERNOON AND IT IS RAINING. LUCKILY I WENT SWIMMING THIS MORNING. THE WATER IS A LITTLE QUIETER THEN THAN LATER, BUT FOR SOME REASON OR OTHER, SEEMED MUCH, MUCH SALTIER. IT REALLY BURNED MY EYES. BOY! ONE DAY WE HAD LOTS OF FUN IN THE WATER. THE WAVES WOULD COME IN ABOUT TEN FEET HIGH AND JUST PICK UP EVERYONE AND CARRY THEM IN. THAT REALLY WAS FUN. THAT WAS THE ROUGHEST WATER I HAVE SEEN, ANYWHERE.

WE GET BEER AGAIN TONITE. THIS WEEK WE ARE GETTING IT FOUR TIMES INSTEAD OF THE USUAL TWO TIMES. WE WILL HAVE ICE AGAIN, TOO. TODAY FOR DINNER WE HAD STEAK, THE SECOND TIME SINCE WE HAVE BEEN HERE. WE ARE GETTING FRESH MEATS AND VEGETABLES OFTENER OF LATE. AT FIRST WE HAD ONLY CANNED MEATS AND DEHYDRATED VEGETABLES. EVER SEE DEHYDRATED CABBAGE AND POTATOES? THEY AREN'T TOO BAD.

THIS WEEK I HAVE HAD LETTERS FROM TWO OLD FLAMES. FRAN SELZER, WHO IS IN ALABAMA, AND FROM LORRAINE SADD. [51] *LORRAINE SAYS OUR RESPECTIVE FAMILIES HAVE NOT BEEN KEEPING IN TOUCH WITH EACH OTHER LATELY, AND THAT EVELYN'S* [52] *HUSBAND HAS GONE INTO THE ARMY AND THAT EVELYN IS BACK HOME FOR THE DURATION.*

THIS HAS BEEN A LONG LETTER, SO I WILL CLOSE NOW.

> *Love,*
> *Fred [handwritten]*

P.S. HOW DO [YOU] LIKE THE TYPING WITH CAPITALS?

[V-Mail—Typed]

Thurs. 23 March 1944.
SOMEWHERE IN SOUTH PACIFIC.

DEAR FOLKS ...

LAST NIGHT I WROTE TO LOUIE AND JOE, AND THIS MORNING WILL WRITE TO YOU AND THE GIRLS. I TRUST THIS LETTER FINDS YOU ALL DOING WELL; I AM. I STILL HEAR FROM YOU ALL OFTEN, AND HOPE YOU KEEP IT UP.

YESTERDAY WE RECEIVED OUR FOURTH BATCH OF PAPERS AND MAGAZINES. INCLUDED WERE THE EAGLES OF JAN. 14, 21, AND 28. FOR A WHILE WE WILL WANT FOR PAPERS AND MAGAZINES TO READ, THEN FOR A WHILE WE WILL BE SNOWED UNDER WITH THEM. SPEAKING OF SNOW, THE 21ST WE HERE WENT INTO FALL, WHEREAS YOU WENT INTO SPRING.

I HEARD WE CAN NOW TELL THE NAME OF OUR SHIP. IF NOT THE CENSOR WILL BLACK IT OUT AND THIS NEXT SENTENCE WILL BE MISSING TO YOU. IT WAS THE SS WEST POINT. BEFORE IT WAS TAKEN OVER BY THE GOVT. IT WAS THE SS AMERICA, THE LARGEST PASSENGER SHIP EVER BUILT IN THE COUNTRY. I READ SOMETHING IN NEWSWEEK ABOUT IT SEVERAL MONTHS AGO. I BELIEVE THIS VESSEL NEVER SAW CIVILIAN USE, BEING FINISHED ABOUT THE TIME WE ENTERED THE WAR. LET ME KNOW IF THIS PARAGRAPH IS CENSORED OUT. IF IT IS, I WILL NOT TRY AGAIN. I HELP CENSOR OUR MENS MAIL NOW, AND HAVE A NEW SLANT ON CENSORSHIP. SOME OF THESE BOYS THINK THEY ARE CLEVER, THE COMMONEST TRICK BEING REFERENCES TO BOOKS OR MAGAZINE ARTICLES ABOUT THIS ISLAND. HOWEVER, I HAVE ACCESS TO THE SAME ONES THEY HAVE AND ALWAYS LOOK UP THESE REFERENCES. OTHER THAN THAT, I DO NOT BELIEVE THEY WOULD DELIBERATELY TRY TO REVEAL ANYTHING THEY SHOULD NOT. BUT OCCASIONALLY SOME ONE WILL INADVERTENTLY MENTION THINGS THEY SHOULD NOT, AS NAMES OF UNITS, DISTANCES, MILITARY OR ISLAND INSTALLATIONS. PICTURE* TAKING RECENTLY WAS BANNED HERE EXCEPT BY OFFICIAL PHOTOGRAPHERS. WHEN WE COULD TAKE THEM WE WERE NOT TO TAKE ANY MILITARY

INSTALLATIONS WHATSOEVER AND GRAVEYARDS COULD NOT BE SHOWN WITH MORE THAN TWO GRAVES. WHY AM I WRITING ABOUT THEM? I ENJOYED READING IN THE EAGLE ABOUT THE SUMMARY OF THE YEAR'S EVENTS. SEEMS LIKE ALL MARRIED WOMEN HAD A CHILD AND MOST PEOPLE HAD THEIR APPENDICES (PLURAL FOR APPENDIX) REMOVED. A DOCTOR PRACTICING HOME LAST YEAR REALLY WOULD HAVE BEEN BUST.

OCCASIONALLY I THINK ABOUT WHAT I WANT TO DO AFTER THE WAR. THE WAY I FEEL NOW I AM GOING TO TAKE THINGS QUITE EASY. WHEN I SEE THESE OLDER DOCTORS AND WHAT THEY HAVE LEFT AFTER WORKING NITE AND DAY I KNOW IT DOES NOT PAY. THEY COME INTO THE ARMY AS CAPTAINS WITH NOT AS MUCH YEARLY PAY AS THEY MADE IN TWO MONTHS OF PRACTICE. AND ALL THE WHILE SOME S.O.B. OR SLACKER IS STAYING HOME AND STEALING THEIR PATIENTS. I HAVE HEARD THAT STORY FROM SO MANY OF THEM. I STILL DON'T KNOW WHAT I WOULD LIKE TO GO INTO. RIGHT NOW SURGERY OR EAR, EYE, NOSE AND THROAT LOOK GOOD TO ME. STILL AFTER I GET OUT OF THE ARMY I WILL NEED ONLY ABOUT ONE YEAR MORE OF WORK TO BE ELIGIBLE FOR CERTIFICATION AS A PATHOLOGIST, AND THAT IS NOTHING TO SNEEZE AT. PATHOLOGY IS A HELL OF A GOOD GROUNDWORK FOR ANY FIELD OF MEDICINE. ANOTHER THING I THINK I WOULD LIKE IS GROUP*PRACTICE OR CLINIC WORK, WHICH IS THE COMING THING ANYWAY IF THESE DAMN POLITICIANS DON'T TAKE OVER MEDICINE, AS THEY ARE TRYING LIKE HELL TO DO. INCIDENTALLY, I WANT YOU TO OPPOSE ALL YOU CAN THIS RUBBISH OF SOCIALIZED OR STATE MEDICINE. HEALTH INSURANCE IS A GOOD THING BUT IT IS AN ENTIRELY DIFFERENT THING, THOUGH THESE New page [handwritten]
(I WRITE CONTINUATION BECAUSE INDIVIDUAL COMPONENTS OF A MULTIPLE V MAIL CANNOT BE NUMBERED, THOUGH DIFFERENT PAGES OF OTHER LETTERS IN THE SAME ENVELOP CAN BE NUMBERED)
DAMN ADVOCATES OF IT TRY TO CONFUSE THE ISSUE AND

GET SUPPORT BY SAYING THEY ARE THE SAME WHICH THEY MOST CERTAINLY ARE NOT. IF THESE POLITICIANS WANT TO DO SOMETHING FOR THEIR COUNTRY, AS THEY MAINTAIN THEY DO, THEY OUGHT TO COMMIT MASS HARI*KARI. AS I SEE THEIR IDEA OF SOCIALIZED MEDICINE, I WANT NO PART OF IT. BUT TO GET BACK TO MYSELF: I WILL SUGGEST TO LOUIE THE PLAN OF PRACTICING TOGETHER, POSSIBLY WITH A COUPLE OTHERS. MAYBE JOE WILL DECIDE IN FAVOR OF STUDYING MEDICINE, TOO. OR SOME OF THE NEPHEWS. I HAVE INQUIRED LOTS ABOUT THIS PLAN. MOST WHO HAVE EXPERIENCE WITH IT SAY IT IS EASY, BUT ALMOST ALL AGREE IT A MISTAKE FOR A FEW TO BUILD A HOSPITAL OR BUILD*OVER ONE.

WE HAD A PRETTY GOOD RAIN LAST NIGHT, WITH MORE WIND THAN I HAVE SEEN SINCE LEAVING THE STATES. WE SHOULD BE HAVING LESS AND LESS RAIN FOR A WHILE NOW.

I HAVE GONE TO THE MOVIES FOUR NIGHTS STRAIGHT NOW. A COUPLE TIMES IT WAS CRAZY, BUT AFTER ALL A CRAZY SHOW IS BETTER THAN NONE. THIS NEW MOVIE PLAYS EVERY NITE, SO I PROBABLY WILL BE A REAL MOVIE FAN AS TIME GOES ON.

THE MAILMAN CONTINUES TO BE GOOD TO ME. BESIDES THE FAMILY, I RECENTLY HAVE HEARD FROM UNCLE MIKE, LORRAINE SADD AND VICTORIA'S FRIEND, MRS. MILLER. LORRAINE SAID THEY HADN'T BEEN HEARING FROM US AS OFTEN AS THEY WOULD LIKE. ALSO, EVELYN'S HUSBAND IS IN THE ARMY AND EVELYN IS BACK HOME UNTIL HE RETURNS. SAY, HAVEN'T I WRITTEN THIS TO YOU BEFORE? OR MAYBE TO THE GIRLS. TODAY I HAD A V FROM LOUIE. THIS ONE WAS SENT THE SAME DAY AS THE AIRMAILED V MAIL, WHICH I RECEIVED OVER A WEEK AGO. HE SENT THEM THAT WAY TO SEE HOW THEY COMPARED IN DELIVERY TIME. THIS IS NOT A TRUE COMPARISON, THOUGH, AS MAIL ARRIVAL HERE HAS BEEN A BIT IRREGULAR OF LATE.

I AM GLAD ESTER BOUGHT THAT CAR. IF SHE IS GOING TO LOOK AFTER THOSE THREE CHILDREN AND HER STORE AFTER DUFFY GOES INTO THE NAVY, SHE WILL NEED SOME

RELAXATION ALL RIGHT. THAT OR A SIEGE IN A SANATORIUM.
YESTERDAY I WENT TO MIDWEEK MASS AND NOVENA
SERVICE AGAIN. GOSH! LENT IS THREE*FOURTH OVER
ALREADY. GUESS I WILL HAVE TO GET READY FOR THE EASTER
PARADE. FOR IT MUST NOT BE NEGLECTED, EVEN OVER HERE.
WE GET BEER AGAIN TONITE. I HAVE SAVED MY RATIONS
FOR THE PAST THREE TIMES, AND NOW HAVE ON HAND
SIX BOTTLES. NOW I PROBABLY WILL HAVE TO STAY AWAKE
NIGHTS GUARDING IT. ALSO, I KEEP IN MY "REFRIGERATOR"
A FEW CANS OF FRUIT JUICE AND A COUPLE OF PEANUTS.
I USED TO BUY COOKIES IN TWO*BOX AMOUNTS, BUT NO
MORE. WHILE I WAS EATING ONE, THE ANTS WERE EATING
THE OTHER. BOY! THEY MUST SMELL FOOD AND HOW THEY
CLIMB UP EVERYTHING FOR IT! A BOX OF FOOD OPENED HERE
MUST BE EATEN EMPTY AT ONE SITTING FOR THERE IS NO
SECOND ONE.
MUST CLOSE NOW.

Love,
Fred. [handwritten]

CAN YOU READ THIS EASIER THAN HANDWRITING?
[handwritten].

———————— ➤ ← ————————

[V-Mail]

TUES. 28 MAR. 1944
South Pacific Theatre.

Dear Folks—

   Am writing this while awaiting to go to the movie. I have
been going almost nightly. Some of the pictures are good, some
poor—but all are entertainment of a sort.
   Recently had a letter from Andy Lasichak,[53] *our classmate*
who told you to have me write him, and an Easter card from
Aileen. Saturday received the "Eagle" of Mar. 10th.
   Today was rather a routine day. This morning I helped
censor mail, washed some clothes and did some work I will
keep a secret from you for a while. This afternoon I attended

a meeting of the Island Medical Society and afterward went swimming and played horseshoes. This evening we played three furious games of volleyball.

I am glad you all are well and things go well with you. They are with me, too. Am now listening to a re-cast of Bob Hope. Radio reception of late has been swell. Glad you are having no trouble with my income tax; I have more money and bonds than I thought.

Well, space is running out, so I'll close now.

Love,
Fred.

P.S. No packages received yet.

———————— ➔ ⬅ ————————

[V-Mail]

THURS. 30 MAR. 1944.

Dear Folks—

Well, tomorrow is payday again. Hasn't this last month gone by quickly? I haven't heard if you received the $100.00 money order yet, or if the girls will let me pay for music lessons for the boys.

Today, while down the road (I always start to say "down town," but there is nothing here even resembling a settlement of any kind), I stopped in to see Sgt. Richardson. He was not in, though this boy from Barden Brook is located just a short ways from our area.[54] A short time ago, while hitch-hiking, I was picked up by a fellow from Bradford.

I have contacted a fellow who will develop pictures for a fairly fair price. Therefore, I may be sending you some from time to time. Strictly speaking, picture-taking is forbidden except by official photographers. However, I am going to take some of ourselves, our area, etc. These are non-military subjects, and I doubt I will get in trouble over them.

Of late I have been a steady movie-goer, and am going again this evening. This movie is quite popular and a person must get there early to get a seat. It is an outdoor movie, with bench seating but they are not uncomfortable.

Our magazines and papers are beginning to arrive more regularly and often. You can send me the "Eagle" airmail if you wish—it really is nice to get it quickly—but I don't mind if it comes slower. It still is news to me.

Fred.

-Next page.

So Paulie is five years old? How time flies! I looked up my birthday lists a couple weeks ago and knew he had a birthday coming up. I will send him a present pretty soon. Gosh how I would like to see those kids!!

I had a letter from Charlie Schaaf a few days ago.[55] *He is in England with a general hospital, and located not far from the unit with our old nurses! I told him to look them up if he had a chance.*

This is beer nite again and luckily we have ice. I am now on my second bottle and can feel the effects. Beer has quite a bang here, maybe because our blood is concentrated by excessive sweating.

I sent [the] Lambillottes a letter the other day. They must feel terrible about Nunny.[56] *I am afraid plenty of homes will get death notices before this is over.*

The radio is coming in good now. Reception has been very good lately.

Well, I must close now.

Love,
Fred.

——————— ✦ ———————

[INCOMPLETE]
[V-Mail]

SUN. 2 APRIL 1944

Just returned from Mass and found some mail—yours and Ester's letters of the 20th and the "Alumnus" and 2/25 "Eagle" together.[57] *Thanks for sending them. I saw my letter;*[58] *also that a Notre Dame Club met at APO # 708. I know where it is; maybe someday I might get to one of these overseas meetings.*

Hear you have a V-mail reading glass. How is it? Can you read me alright? I try to write large. Yours are very plain and easy to read. Glad you received the money order okay. Remember that is for yourselves or the house—not me. It is about time you started looking out for yourselves and not us children.

I do hear often from Louie and Joe; also the girls.

You say the weather home is cold. I could go for some cooler days and enjoy them plenty.

Not long ago we had an air-raid alarm. I should not admit this, I suppose, but secretly I was glad. I want to be bombed once and see some actual fighting before I go home. Of course, I don't hanker to be in any sea battles.

Well, space is running out, so I'll close now. Am feeling fine and am tan as a native.

Love,
Fred.

P.S. Have not looked up Eastman yet but will do so soon. May send you some pictures soon, too.
Nothing came of the air-raid alarm, being only an alarm.

———— ➔ ← ————

[INCOMPLETE]
To: PVT. JOE GABRIEL
A.A.F.T.T.C.
HAMILTON COLLEGE
CLINTON, NEW YORK.

THUR. 6 APR. 1944
South Pacific Area

La Gab—

This is now Good Friday. I began this [letter] last evening but was dragged off to a good movie: "Eyes in the Night" with

Ed. Arnold—a propaganda picture but enjoyable.[59] *Since this movie opened in our backyard (3 minute walk from here) I have gone almost nitely. This week saw "Air Force" and "Mrs. Miniver" the pictures.*[60]

Had [a; letter partly missing] letter from Louie yesterday. He writes all goes well and that a Jeff classmate of mine is here on the Island.[61] *I must contact him. Today I walked over to the outfit of the Eastman boy from Barden Brook. He was out and I left no message.*

A hospital nearby has SCAT (Service Command Air Transport) Nurses now, which means we no longer run around here nude. It rained a few minutes today. Funny thing—it seems that every time I put my bedding out to air the rain comes.

Have finished making souvenirs for Mama and the girls and now am making some for Pop and you boys. For the ladies I made beautiful necklace-bracelet sets of matched snail shells. I made all different styles and they are nice. Some shells I got from natives; others I got from the water near a coral reef. Incidentally, about the reef is beautiful coral and gorgeous yellow, green and blue fish. Also saw there blue starfish (I never believed there were such things really before) and a young octopus. Near the reef are sharks, I am told. Anyway—these shells are the exoskeleton of snails. They are put underground so the sun will not bleach them and ants can eat away the flesh.

———— ➜ ⬅ ————

[V-Mail - Typed]

EASTER SUNDAY 9 APR. 1944.
SOUTH PACIFIC THEATRE

DEAR FOLKS ...

THIS REALLY WILL BE MORE OF A NOTE THAN ANYTHING ELSE. HOWEVER, IT IS MY DAY TO WRITE YOU AND I WANT TO SEND SOMETHING.

THIS MORNING THERE WAS A HIGH MASS AT 10:30 INSTEAD OF THE USUAL LOW MASS AT 11:00. THERE MUST HAVE BEEN

Memorial Chapel and military cemetery. The island chaplain
designed this chapel, and native laborers constructed it,
Guadalcanal 1944.

*THREE HUNDRED FELLOWS CROWDED INTO THAT ONE
ROOM AND OVER HALF OF US RECEIVED COMMUNION. THIS
ISLAND HAS A CENTRAL MEMORIAL CHAPEL,*[62] *WHERE ABOUT
FIVE HUNDRED ORDINARILY ATTEND MASS ON SUNDAY. THE
CHAPLAIN SAYS THAT THIS MORNING THERE WERE AT LEAST
TWO THOUSAND THERE. IMAGINE THAT.*

*I HAD A PLEASANT SURPRISE AT MASS THIS MORNING. I
WAS WALKING UP THE AISLE TO GO TO CONFESSION WHEN
I SPIED ONE OF MY JEFFERSON CLASSMATES. HE WAS A
VERY GOOD FRIEND OF MINE. IN FACT, WE WERE PARTNERS
IN LABORATORY, HIS NAME IS LEWIS FRANK,*[63] *AN ITALIAN
BOY. AS WE WERE PAIRED OFF ALPHABETICALLY, HE AND I
WORKED TOGETHER. IT REALLY WAS A SURPRISE SEEING HIM
THERE. HE IS NOW ATTACHED TO THIS HOSPITAL LOCATED
ONLY A FIVE MINUTE WALK AWAY. I JUST NOW RETURNED
FROM VISITING HIM. WE TALKED OVER SCHOOL DAYS AND
BROUGHT EACH OTHER UP TO DATE ON CLASS NEWS. FRANK
HAS BEEN OVERSEAS SOME TWENTY-MONTHS, AND REALLY
IS ANXIOUS TO GET BACK TO THE STATES. HE HAS BEEN
STATIONED IN NEW ZEALAND AND NEW CALEDONIA, AMONG
OTHER PLACES.*

WHEN I LEFT HIS TENT, HE GAVE ME A FIFTH OF WHISKEY. I HAVE TO BE CAREFUL WITH IT, AS A FELLOW MIGHT GET HIT OVER THE HEAD FOR LESS LIQUOR THAN THAT.

LAST NITE SAW A "JOURNEY FOR MARGARET"; PLAN TO GO TO THE MOVIE AGAIN TONITE IF IT DOESN'T RAIN, WHICH IT PROBABLY WILL.

TODAY RECEIVED A LETTER FROM PAPA. YES, I CAN READ YOUR V-MAILS WITHOUT ANY TROUBLE. I HOPE YOU CAN READ MINE AS EASILY.

MUST CLOSE NOW.

Love,
YOUR SON,
Fred.

———————— ➔ ← ————————

[Airmail Stationery]

Wed. April 12. 1944.
So. Pacific

Dear Folks—

This is the evening of a beautiful day. I again am writing you while waiting to go to the movie. I just came in from gazing at the sunset. Gosh—it is beautiful. The western sky is filled with fluffy white clouds and flaming pink sunrays; in the east are lacy clouds that range in color from grey to purple, with pale blue sky showing through the patches. It really is something to see. The stars here at nite are not as large or as bright as they seem to be in either Texas or Arizona, but just the same the sky at nite is beautiful and lonesome, and the air is warm and about the only sound heard are crickets chirping. Listening to them reminds me of that pond back of the house in the flats. Remember when we were kids we would go out on the back porch to watch the crows meeting in those 2 big trees in the field and later on at dusk how the crickets would begin to sound off? I would like to be listening to them now. That is what I thought about last nite. I couldn't go to sleep so I went outside the tent and stayed awhile; the moon was so bright I believe I could have read by it.

Today I sent Louie an airmail and enclosed in it a wrist-watch strap made of aluminum from a foreign plane.

Tomorrow I will answer Joe's last letter of two days ago and enclose one for him. Sometime this week I hope to get off to you and the children a box of souvenirs. It will be some weeks en route, as it will go out via boat.

Today I received your letter of Mar. 28, with the enclosed stick of gum and N.D. [Notre Dame] K. [Knights] of Columbus[64] *card. I don't know why you think I am not getting all your mail. I hear from you about 3 times a week, and at least once from the girls, Papa, Lou and Joe. I usually mention how much mail I get, but I cannot itemize them. Some mail is delayed a few days but it does get to me. Thanks for offering me a pen but I can get a fairly good one in our PX.*

A few days ago I got your Mar. 23rd letter with the clipping about Herb Geuder.[65] *Lorraine did not say anything in her letter about her grandmother's death. Easter Sunday I received Pop's V. of the 26th. And that afternoon I mailed one to you.*

No change in my routine here. However, we can't stay here forever not functioning and it will suit me swell when we do begin to operate. Right now I am listening to the radio. I believe that I now can say that a broadcasting station recently began to operate here on the island.

Last week I tried to look up both Richardson and Eastman— but no soap; neither were in.

I think I will go to bed early tonite. I played three games of volleyball this evening, and am tired. This evening, too, we had steak again, which is twice now within the past week. Another thing I like is the fact that we occasionally get pineapple pie, which is one pie I do eat. We get good pastries.

Well, I must close now.

Love,
Fred.

P.S. This week received the "Eagle" of 2/11 and 3/3.

[V-Mail]

FRI. 14 APR. 1944.
South Pacific.

Dear Folks—

   Just returned from seeing a punk movie and about Texas,
of all places! Today received your letter of 3/30; the Airmailed
"Eagle" of 3/31; Pop's V-mail of 4/2, plus a letter from Joe. So
you see I do all right. Sorry to hear about poor old "Butch"
Russell. Lately have had letters from 2 of my fellow-interns,
both now in England—Charley Schaaf of Erie and Al Tocker.
Also heard from an Erie girl, who is now a navy nurse in
Australia.

   How is everything and everyone at home? I hope Ester
and the boys are not feeling too bad about Duff leaving. I am
fine and doing the same. Yesterday sent both Lou and Joe
wristwatch straps of aluminum in airmail letters. Early next
week will send you a box of souvenirs, but it must go by boat
and will be a long time en route. No packages from you yet,
and should I need anything I will let you know. Will write you
a longer letter next time.

Love,
Fred.

P.S. Who writes the airmails? Our chaplain religiously reads
my "Eagles." Heard from Vic today, too.

—————— ➔ ⬅ ——————

[Airmail Stationery—Typed]

SOUTH PACIFIC
WED. 19 Apr. 1944.

DEAR FOLKS ...

   I AM WRITING THIS DURING MY SIESTA HOUR (12:30–1:00). I
DID NOT WRITE YESTERDAY AS I WANTED TO ENCLOSE THESE
PICTURES AND THEY WERE NOT READY THEN.

   I ALSO SENT OTHER PICTURES TO LOU, WHICH HE WILL
SEND ON TO YOU. THEY ARE ABOUT THE SAME AS THESE, AND

*I SENT THEM TO HIM DIRECTLY INSTEAD OF THEM BEING SENT
BACK AND FORTH BETWEEN YOU. YOU WILL SEE THAT THERE
ARE TWO KINDS OF PICTURES; I TOOK THE SMALL ONES AND
YOU CAN SEE WHAT A POOR FINISHING JOB WAS DONE. I HAVE
NO WAY OF GETTING ANYTHING BETTER. THE LARGE, CLEAR
PICTURES I GOT FROM AN OFFICER AT A NEARBY HOSPITAL
"WHO HAS CONNECTIONS." ANYWAY, THESE PICTURES WILL
GIVE YOU A BETTER IDEA OF OUR ENVIRONMENT THAN I AM
ABLE TO DO WITH MERE WORDS. PLEASE SAVE THEM FOR ME.
I HAVE A FEW OTHERS, AND WILL NOT SEND THEM, AS I THINK
THEY WOULD NOT GET BY THE CENSOR. I AM KEEPING ALL MY
OWN NEGATIVES AND MAYBE SOMETIME WILL GET A GOOD
PRINTING JOB DONE ON THEM.*

*SGT. RICHARDSON OF BOLIVAR WAS HERE TO SEE ME THIS
MORNING. I SHOWED HIM AROUND THE AREA, MY PICTURES
AND WE HAD A NICE VISIT. HE COMES OUT THIS WAY OFTEN,
SO I WILL BE SEEING HIM. WHEN I GET A CHANCE I AM GOING
DOWN TO HIS PLACE TO SEE THE PICTURES HE HAS. BEING
IN A PHOTO OUTFIT HE HAS SOME DANDIES AND GOOD
FACILITIES.*

*TODAY RECEIVED THE AIRMAILED "EAGLE" OF THE
SEVENTH OF THIS MONTH, THE LAST "NEWSLETTER" AND
A LETTER FROM VIC. FUNNY THING ... ALL TOOK EXACTLY
THIRTEEN DAYS TO GET HERE. YESTERDAY HEARD FROM
BOTH LOU AND JOE. THEY ARE DOING WELL, AS YOU KNOW.
HAVEN'T HEARD FROM ESTER IN A COUPLE WEEKS, BUT KNOW
SHE IS PRETTY BUSY. I ASKED FOR DUFF'S ADDRESS WHEN I
LAST WROTE HER. I KNOW HE IS AT SAMPSON.[66]*

*NO PACKAGES FROM YOU YET, BUT WILL BE GETTING IT ONE
OF THESE DAYS. HERE IS SOMETHING YOU CAN GET ME FOR
MY BIRTHDAY: I WOULD LIKE A RUBBER STAMP TO MAKE USE
OF V*MAIL EASIER. I WANT ONE FOR THE UPPER RIGHT HAND
CORNER (SENDER'S ADDRESS, ETC.). I GET SO DAMN TIRED OF
FILLING THAT IN. PLEASE HAVE THE STAMP MADE TO FIT IT
WELL AND EXACTLY LIKE THE SAMPLE I AM ENCLOSING. THE
APO NUMBER WILL BE A BLANK, AS IT MIGHT CHANGE. I ASKED*

THE CO [commanding officer] JOKINGLY IF THE RANK SHOULD
BE LEFT BLANK, TOO, BUT HE ONLY LAUGHED AND SAID
NOTHING.

REMEMBER THE "DEAR FELLERS" LETTERS OUR INTERN
GROUP AT ERIE HAD TO KEEP IN TOUCH WITH EACH OTHER?
WELL IT STOPPED WHEN SCHAAF WENT TO ENGLAND AND I
CAME HERE. ANYWAY, WE ARE TRYING TO REVIVE IT AGAIN. I
WILL LET YOU KNOW HOW WE ARE DOING WITH IT.

I JUST SENT YOU VIA BOAT A PACKAGE. IT WAS TOO BIG
TO SEND OTHERWISE AND YOU WILL GET IT AROUND JULY
FIRST. IN IT IS A GRASS SKIRT FOR WHOMEVER WANTS IT, A
BRASS ASHTRAY FOR POP AND SIX NECKLACES (I KNOW IT IS
BAD POLICY TO WRITE ON THE BACKS OF PAGES BECAUSE
IF THE CENSOR CUTS OUT SOMETHING, HE CUTS OUT
BOTH SIDES BUT THIS LETTER WILL BE HEAVY ENOUGH
WITH THE ENCLOSURES AND I WANT TO LIGHTEN IT). AND
BRACELET MATCHED SETS OF SNAIL SHELLS. THEY ARE
SIX OF THEM AND IN FOUR STYLES, INCLUDING ONE FOR
JACY. INCIDENTALLY, THIS IS THAT SECRET THAT I WROTE
YOU ABOUT. MAMA, YOU TAKE YOUR PICK OF THE SETS AND
PASS THE OTHERS ON TO THE GIRLS, MARTHA AND LIZ.[67]
SHE WILL BE DOING MORE THAN EVER NOW FOR ESTER,
SO I AM INCLUDING ONE FOR HER. THESE SHELLS ARE THE
SKELETONS OF ONCE*LIVING SNAILS. SOME I GOT MYSELF
IN THE OCEAN; OTHERS I BOUGHT FROM NATIVES, THOUGH
I MADE ALL THE SETS MYSELF. I WAS OFFERED FIFTEEN
DOLLARS PER SET BUT DO NOT NEED MONEY THAT BAD AS
YET. ANYWAY, THESE SNAILS ARE KILLED THEN BURIED UNDER
GROUND TO PROTECT THEM FROM THE SUN WHILE ANTS
EAT AWAY THE FLESHY PORTION. THEY CAN BE CLEANED BY
WASHING WITH WARM WATER AND SOAP. HOT WATER WILL
BLEACH THE SHELL AWAY. THE CLASPS ON THE SETS ARE
CHEAP, AS ARE THE CHAINS (DOGTAG CHAINS), BUT THEY
ARE ALL I HAD AVAILABLE. THESE CHAINS MAY RUST OR
LEAVE A SKIN MARK BUT MAYBE NOT. I MADE ONE SET WITH
A CRUCIFIX PENDANT WHICH IS PRETTY. HOWEVER, THE WAY

THE SHELLS ARE PUT TOGETHER MAKES THEM TEND TO ROLL
OVER. OTHERWISE IT IS PRETTY. TELL MOM TO TRY THEM
ALL ON AND TAKE HER PICK FIRST AND YOU SEND ONE TO
MARTHA. WELL, ENOUGH ABOUT THEM. I HOPE YOU RECEIVE
THEM OKAY AND LIKE THEM. LATER ON I AM SENDING THE
CHILDREN LARGER SNAIL SHELLS AND BASKETS MADE OF
COCONUTS. SAY NOTHING TO THEM ABOUT IT, OR THEY WILL
GET VERY IMPATIENT WAITING FOR THEM.

THINGS ABOUT STATUS QUO HERE. THE WEATHER
CONTINUES A BIT DRIER, A BIT HOTTER AND BEAUTIFUL DAYS
AND SUNSETS AND SKIES AT NITE. I WISH I COULD GET A
COLOR PICTURE OF A SUNSET. THEY REALLY ARE BEAUTIFUL.

WELL, I MUST CLOSE NOW. I SAW A GOOD MOVIE LAST NITE
"INTERMEZZO." ANOTHER SWELL RECENT ONE IS DUE SOON:
"SONG OF BERNADETTE."[68] WE ARE BUILDING A SOFTBALL
FIELD IN OUR AREA AND I AM HELPING WITH THAT, SO I WILL
BE PLAYING A LITTLE BALL.

Love,

[this portion handwritten] <u>Fred.</u>

P.S. Enclosing also a booklet I bought in Noumea, New
Caledonia.

—————— ➔ ⬅ ——————

[Airmail Stationery]

South Pacific
Sat. 22 Apr. 1944

Dear Folks—

In spite of rain last night and for a couple hours today, this
has been a hot day. Rain will come down heavy and then a
half-hour later the sun will be hot again and the ground dry. It
is surprising how quickly the earth soaks up the water.

Today I received the package containing the popcorn, T.
shirts, shorts and the book "Into the Valley."[69] Thanks. I was
unable to read the postmark date on it so do not know how
long it was on the way. Three other officers got packages today,
too, all apparently coming on the same boat. Yesterday I got

Pop's V. of Easter Sunday—yes I am able to read them easily.
Also heard from Jake Brady, now somewhere in the Central
Pacific where he saw action early in February.

Last night the earth shook for a couple minutes and we were
quite excited to think we had experienced a 'quake. Today we
heard differently—it was a naval action.[70]

Right now I am listening to the news of the war. It sounds
very good, doesn't it? I wish things really would open up soon
and this thing get over with. Still, time really is moving along.
We have been on this island twelve weeks already.

Last night I wrote a few people including Fr. Liebel. In the
past few days I have written all my fellow-interns. One—from
Dunkirk[71]*—I have not heard of in 2 years so I wrote his family*
for his address. I wouldn't be too surprised if he were in this
theater. Say, quite a few from around home are down this
way, aren't they? While I think of it, please send me Timon's
address. I haven't written him in a long time now and do want
to keep in touch with him. I see where Regina is to be a WAVE.
I think more women ought to go into the services—they are
doing a good job. Incidentally, a few Red Cross girls arrived
here this week.[72]

Sometime next week I am going to visit a neighboring
island. The natives there supposedly are very interesting. I also
want to go to the other island where I believe those doctors
from Bradford are.

I haven't so much spare time now, for "in addition to my
other duties," I now am our Sanitary Officer. It isn't hard and
fits in well with some of my other duties.

I still have a little more work on the rest of the souvenirs. In
that package I did send you, I forgot the ashtray. I will put it in
the other. I hope you like the sets; also the pictures I mailed a
few days back. This week I finished another roll, so may have
more for you soon.

I already have asked you to send me one thing (rubber
stamp); in my next letter I will request a couple more, all of
which can be sent together.

It is nice that Duff likes Sampson. Has George had definite word when he'll leave? I doubt that fellows coming in this late will get overseas. Our part of the states has plenty overseas now, all right.

The other day that boy from Bolivar visited me.[73] *He has some swell pictures, he says, and I want to go down [to] see them. I looked up Eastman once but he was not in, so I'll try again.*

"The Song of Bernadette" played nearby last nite but I did not see it, though I expect to soon. From what I have read, it is some picture. Our chaplain saw it and he is the only one who did not like it. He thought it extremely boring.

Now that their dad is away, I suppose you see more of Paulie and Johnnie than ever, if that is possible. Gosh! I would like to see them.

Well, must close now.

> *Love,*
> *Fred.*

———— ➜ ← ————

[V-Mail]

> *FRI. 28 APR. 1944.*
> *South Pacific Area.*

Dear Folks—

This is noon of a beautiful day—the sun is hot, there is a cool breeze coming in from the ocean and the sky is filled with lazy white clouds, all fluffed-up. I have just finished chow and am writing this while resting for a half-hour or so—my siesta.

Yesterday received Mom's letters of April 4, 11 and 13. Thanks for the clipping about Hofschneider—wasn't it swell? In his last letter Louie wrote he had just received an announcement of Hofscheider's wedding, probably from his wife in Indianapolis. I wrote her for Leo's address. I think I will send the clipping to the N.D. "Alumnus."[74]

Today am writing Joe and Lou (c/o you as you wrote he'd be coming home on leave) about a possible lead for Joe—Medical

Administrative Corps Officer's Candidate School @ Camp
Barkeley, Texas. He has only a month to go, so had better make
inquiries fast.

Will close now. Tomorrow will write you a long airmail
again.

Love,
Fred.

———————— ➔ ← ————————

[V-Mail]
To: PVT. JOE GABRIEL
HAMILTON COLLEGE,
CLINTON NEW YORK
A.A.F.T.T.D.

FRI. 28 APR. 1944.
South Pacific.

La Gab–

Just a note to advise you to investigate the feasibility of
Medical Administrative Corps O.C.S. (Camp Barkeley, Texas).
I hear it is worth looking into. Also hear Lou is coming home
on leave after Washington; ask him about it, huh?

Mama sent me a newspaper clipping of a letter written to
his mother by Leo. Hofschneider of Rochester, N.Y., our N.D.
classmate. It is well worth reading.

All well here. Status quo.

Say, Joe. Occasionally get me a roll of #616 and/or #120
film. If I buy this camera I wrote you about, I'll need the latter
(#120).

Love,
Fred.

[V-Mail]

WED. 3 MAY 1944
South Pacific Area.

Dear Folks:

This will be a short letter. Tomorrow I will write you a longer one, telling about the trip I took today to a nearby island. We just got back—it is about 8 o'clock now—and we got up before 6 to catch the boat.

It is raining again this evening, though we had a swell day for our trip. Four of us officers made up the party. Sunday another and myself plan an excursion to another place we have been wanting to visit.

Well, until tomorrow—

Love,
Fred.

———————— →← ————————

[Airmail letterhead]

South Pacific
Thurs. 4 May 1944.

Dear Folks—

Last nite after returning from visiting a nearby island[75] I was tired and wrote you only a V-mail. This morning I will tell you about our little excursion. Eight of us went over but only 4 were from our Unit. Three of us went as guests of the fourth, who supposedly was to do some inspecting over there. I suppose a bit of that was done along with our sight-seeing. We left here about 8 o'clock in the morning in our own boat. Having it gave us more freedom than if we went over in the regular boat. We got there about 11 o'clock. The trip over was swell. Except for a couple minutes rain at first—just enough to make us take our things inside—the weather was warm and sunny, and fortunately for me, the water was smooth. They kept kidding me about how seasick I would get, but I fooled them about that. You know this island we are on isn't too small and most of it I have never seen. This boat trip gave me a chance to go by most of one end of it and what I saw was pretty. It is much more hilly than I realized—some peaks being over 6,000 feet—and low hanging clouds cover most of the hilltops. Between the ranges of hills are areas that are not now jungly, and from where we traveled by they looked just like that farmland around Bolivar and Richburg.[76]

The island we visited is much smaller than this one and as we approached it, we could see all of it in one look. It reminded me of a green center-piece in the middle of a big blue rug. The vegetation along the shore was dense but not overgrown with tall brush and vines as it is in some places I have seen, and it came right down to the water, with almost no sandy beaches in between. When we were close enough, we could plainly see 3 small native villages of thatched huts set in clearings in the palm groves, and just before we landed, a native in a native canoe came out to escort us in. No sooner had we gotten on land than the C.O. of the outfit we were to inspect drove up in a jeep and took our group to his area. The others followed in another vehicle.

Native fishing village, Solomon Islands 1944.

*We planned to stay there only four hours and in order not
to waste time went to the largest village for a "look-see" while
awaiting lunch at the Army mess. Our "inspector" had been
there only a week before and knew the village chief, so the first
thing we did was look him up. That is the way things are done
and it is best not to barter in the village, take pictures, etc.
without his permission.*

*We found Chief Billy very pleasant, very cooperative and
anxiously awaiting some rice he had been promised on the last
trip in exchange for a couple bunches of bananas and a few
shells of snails. I don't know how old the Chief is, but he looked
and talked more like an old Southern Negro than like the
natives on this island. His wife carried a 15-month old baby in
her arms—I suppose "on her hip" is more correct—that was*

Gabriel and Chief Billy with his family, Savo Island, May 3, 1944

very sweet and smiled all over the place when talked to. The Chief's 16- and 18-year-old daughters had just come in from the bush, where they were planting a garden, and the Chief, his family and the other natives all were anxious to have their pictures taken. I took a dozen or so on the trip and do hope they come out well. If so—they will be coming your way before too long.

Rice, sugar, and calico are big barter items with these natives. They seem to have plenty of tobacco and would not swap for that; they had bananas, war clubs, fresh eggs (I saw plenty of chickens) and tomatoes that grow no bigger than English walnuts, to exchange. Our group got all these things for a little rice, sugar, and an old mattress cover. Besides that, we got them to pose for a lot of pictures.

I could talk easily with the natives and rather acted as interpreter for our party. It is hard to out-bargain those devils—they know what they wanted and would give very little in return for it. In all other respects, though, they were okay. They like Americans.

We returned to the Army area for a good lunch, which was welcome as we were plenty hungry by that time.

After lunch we drove about 5 miles through a palm plantation to the other big point of interest on the island. That was a river bed in a narrow canyon. Dense vegetation grew over the walls of the canyon and atop its ridges. Trees there on the ridge grew very tall—I believe it was a good 300 yards from their tops down the sides of the canyon to the river bed. Near the head of the river bed was a smaller canyon heading off to the right. Through it flowed a small stream. Its walls, too, were steep. They were almost hot to the touch and stream and sulfur fumes issued from them.[77]

On this trip I saw for the first time some wild orchids. They grow on a vine that lives parasitically on big trees. I saw also some giant tree-ferns or fern-trees. They grew up to about 60 feet high and the branches resembled plant ferns only were much, much longer, averaging between 8 to 10 feet in length.

That island bears an active volcano, we were told, though we did not get to see it or the smoke from its crater.

When we got back to the landing at 2:30, our vessel wasn't there so we went swimming while awaiting it. In about 30 minutes it showed up and we left.

The return trip was as pleasant as that out, though it was much cooler and ahead of us we could see the mist of a rain. Several times we saw small schools of horse mackerel, about 3 feet long and probably weighing 12 to 15 pounds each, jump about 10 feet out of the water. I was told they act like that when chased by sharks and/or barracuda.

We got back to the beach here about 6:15; just too late for late chow. And were we disappointed because we so hungry! You see, the return trip took longer because we zig-zagged a bit to escape squalls.

Anyway, we got back safely to our area about 7.

We had a darn good day, we all agreed. By "we" I mean the four from our outfit: Capt. [Emanuel] Feit, Lts. [Herman] Berkowsky and [Clifford] Worsley, and myself.

Sunday Capt. [Wesley R.] Burt, one of our dental officers, and I plan on visiting still another nearby island. The C.O. has given us permission to make the trip and said he might go along with us if it does not rain. Rain or shine, Burt and I are going and I know we will have a good time.

Gee whiz! I didn't realize I was describing this in such detail. I am glad I have, though, as it was a very pleasant trip and I wanted you to "get the feel" of the things we saw.

Yesterday's mail I picked up today, as the Post Office tent was closed by the time I got back here. There were a couple letters from you, which I will answer tomorrow.

Until then.

> *Love,*
> *Fred.*

[V-Mail]

FRI. 5 MAY 1944.
South Pacific Area.

Dear Folks—

Yesterday received your airmails of 4/17 and 4/18 and today
Papa's V of the 24th. Glad to know all goes well with you all.
I get the "Eagle" quite regularly as well as letters from the
boys. About Bob Johnston—I often wondered what became
of him. Thanks for the "Lake Shore Visitor."[78] You need <u>not</u>
send it regularly, as I don't know many of those written about;
however, I would like clippings about acquaintances. I have
quite a bank account, huh? I ought to make a good catch for
some girl. If safety deposit boxes are available in Eldred bank,
please get me one, and we all can use it.

Yesterday looked up Eastman. He is a very pleasant fellow
and we had a nice visit together. I don't remember any of his
family but he knew me. We live only 10 minutes' walk away
from each other. We will look up this Sgt. Pfieffer and have a
get together.

About this gardening—let me caution you about over-
exerting yourself, especially in the hot sun and just after meals.
Go easy on that stuff.

Whose lumber yard is where we planted sweet peas?

Am glad Duff likes Sampson and writes often. I can imagine
how much the boys miss him. I sent Joe a tip—don't know how
good it is. Must be—gave you the idea I was lonesome over
here—you mentioned it twice. I am not, though. I am enjoying
it here as much as a person can. Thanks for the gum. We do
get it once in a while, but it is one thing always acceptable, so
send me a little whenever you want to.

Please send me some garden seeds:—

one package each of cucumber, tomato, watermelon,
cantaloupe, and celery seeds.

2 packages each of green onion, red radish, lettuce,
parsley and peas.

some peppermint seed (nanna)

any of these that are impractical or not readily available just skip.

one package each of 3 different flowers.

Must close now.

Love,
Fred.

Heard from Joe and Uncle Mike today.

———— ➔ ← ————

[V-Mail]

MON. 8 MAY 1944.
South Pacific Area.

Dear Folks—

Just received letters from you, Vic and Lou. Glad all is well and Lou got home. I envy him. Hope something good opens for Joe—Lou seemed to think it would. Glad you got the pictures OK and will get me the rubber stamp. About asking for packages—wait until you get the letter I sent last week. You probably know why I do not request more of them—they take 8 to 10 weeks to get here; I have enough clothes; food would spoil and other things I need I can get here. So you see there really is no need asking for things I cannot use. All I want, besides a few special items I have asked for, is regular mail from you. That will satisfy me fine.

A couple days ago I requested some seeds; to it please add only a handful of unroasted peanuts with shells. I will plant them too.

I wrote you a long account of the trip I made Wed. May 3 to a nearby island. Tomorrow I will write you about a trip made yesterday (Sunday) to still another island [Tulagi]. The doctor from Bradford[79] *I wanted to call on was not there, but by using his name we (Capts. Burt and [Edward C.] Heyde and Lt. [John] Long, a navy man and myself) were invited to a swell steak dinner at the Navy hospital there. Yesterday in our area a fellow killed a crocodile 13 feet long and weighing over 1000 lbs. And I used to fool around near where it was killed!!*

I wish you would save all my letters. We are not supposed to keep diaries and by my letters I can keep a record of my overseas life. For that reason I will use a lot of dates and names.

Must close now. Don't worry about me—I am just fine and dandy.

Love,
Fred.

CAN YOU READ THIS OKAY?

"Crocodile (13' 3"; 1,000 pounds) killed with one shot through the eye by PFC Jesse Pirtle in the lagoon in our area. Killed the day previously. 39th Station Hospital," Guadalcanal May 7, 1944.

[V-Mail]

SAT. 13 MAY 1944.
South Pacific.

Dear Folks—

This is a drizzly Saturday afternoon. I am using it to catch up on my correspondence. That plus reading. We got in another batch of magazines and papers today.

I have not received any mail these past 2 days. Hope I hit tomorrow. Of course I know you are writing and deliveries have been mixed up of late.

It has rained almost every evening this week. Last night I went to the movie regardless. Saw Bonnie Baker in "Spotlight Scandals"[80]—a different picture, I must say.

Things still the same here, but it can't last forever. Am getting a bit fed-up with inactivity, as are we all. We want to do something to help end this business.

Heard from Louie and Joe lately.

Will close now and write again tomorrow.

Love,
Fred.

───────── ✦ ✦ ─────────

[V-Mail]
Mother's Day

Somewhere in the Pacific
Sunday 14 May 1944.

Dear Mom—

Just a brief Mother's Day greeting that must travel half way around the world to reach you. It will be late on arrival, but none the less sincere. I just wanted to tell you that if I had to choose one day that I could be home, I would select this day for it. But alas—I had no opportunity to choose, so I am over here, dreaming that I am home.

By the grace of God, I will be there a year from now.

Sincerely,
Your son,
Fred.

[V-Mail]

MON. 15 MAY 1944.
South Pacific Area.

Dear Folks—

This is my favorite writing time—in the lull between
athletics and the movie. At this time all of us usually gather
here in our "Wreck Hall," reading, writing, or on Mondays
and Wednesday, waiting for the beer to cool. These past 2 days
have been unusually hot, so cold beer is really welcome tonite.

Yesterday and today—I received your letters of 4/20 and 5/4.
I will answer them now.

Who is this Mrs. Rogers helping you with the housecleaning?
Housecleaning is a perennial gag in the funnies, but there is
something nice about not being around while it is in process,
just the same. So you ordered my stamp through the bank?
It ought to be a good one then. You need not worry about the
pliers not being what I ordered. I can use any kind of pliers
okay. I am surprised that Duffy finished his boot training so
soon—how time does fly! And while I think of it—thanks for
the 2 sticks of gum. I can use them.

Yesterday the new chaplain (Catholic) at the nearby hospital
starting having 2 Masses on Sunday—7 and 11. I went to the
early one; 11 is a little too late. The chaplain's name is Fr. Kuhn.

Well, my softball team, the ATOBRINES, finally won a game.
We beat Supply 9–5 yesterday afternoon. These games are a lot
of fun, reminding me of the games that used to be played in the
flats back of the Electric Co. I have not played in a couple days
as I hurt my leg a little. It is nothing serious and I am going to
play in tomorrow's game.

This morning's sunrise and the sunset this evening really
were gorgeous. It is hard to imagine how many colors are there
at once. I do wish my camera was good enough to take color
pictures.

Well, I will close now.

Love,
Fred.

P.S. Received an "Eagle" today.

[V-Mail]

THUR. 18 MAY 1944.
South Pacific.

Dear Father Liebel—

I suppose if pleasure at receiving the "newsletter" was the criterion, I should write you much more often than I do. But truthfully—there is darn little to write about from my sideline seat. We have been here some 4 months—bivouacking!! So you see, our activities are a routine. The advent of nurses and R.C. [Red Cross] girls[81] here hasn't lightened up the social sky. It is purposely made difficult to meet them; a barb wire fence is around their barracks, and no fooling, either. Fortunately we still have nitely movies, often in the rain.

I heard about Lou, Joe, and Duffy being home. George not called yet, etc. I am kept well up on the goings-on home.

Recently looked up James Eastman; I hear there is a Pfeiffer here too. A Jeff classmate of mine[82] is at a hospital a block away, the same one where Dr. Leonard, Olean, is stationed.

Well, until the next time then.—

Sincerely,
Fred.

P.S. Received the May issue.

——————— ➔ ← ———————

[V-Mail]
To: PVT. JOE GABRIEL
AAFTTC
HAMILTON COLLEGE
CLINTON, NEW YORK

FRI. 19 MAY 1944.
Somewhere in So. Pacific.

Dear Joe—

There is almost nothing new to write about from here. After some 14 weeks of it, we still are bivouacking, with no immediate prospect of change. How about you—know where

*you are going? Should you go to Sheppard Field I will fix
you up with one of the cutest and sweetest girls you'll ever
meet. Her name is Lorraine, too; she works in the PX there—a
beautiful Texas gal.*

*I am now able to get around without hobbling; a week ago
I developed a charley horse in each thigh while playing ball. A
surprising number of our men have gotten on the sick book via
softball—but it's a good game, regardless.*

*In recent letters, I have read about Lou, Duff and yourself
getting home. How I would like to. We are starting to say:
"Golden Gate in '48".*

*One of our Chinamen, in his broken English, refers to a good
fellow as the "cream of the crotch!" The others Chinaman's
name is HIM JEW.*

*Haven't had a letter from Uncle Mike in some time, though
he did pass on to me a letter he received from Lorraine.*

Must close now.

Love,
Fred.

*P.S. DID YOU GO TO THE BALL?
AM SENDING A FEW PICTURES HOME OCCASIONALLY.
I GOT LOTS OF GOOD FROM EASTMAN'S "HOW TO MAKE
GOOD PICTURES."*[83] *GET IT.*

➔ ←

[V-Mail]

MON. 22 MAY 1944.
South Pacific.

Dear Folks—

*As I write this here in the "Wreck Hall," it is literally raining
cats and dogs outside. And is the wind blowing! So much
so that almost a half of the room on that side is wet. Did you
notice in the picture of this building that it is opened but
screened on all sides? Thus rain easily comes in.*

Today has been a rather usual day. I worked a bit this

morning. This afternoon we officers had a "scrub" game of softball and had a lot of fun at it. Later, in a regular intra-company game the Ward Boys beat Supply 11–7. The game was very funny. One of the officers playing for Supply— [George B.] Hughes, who incidentally put on captain's bars today,—hit a home run with the bases loaded. The best part of it was that he has not played ball in years. Was he cheered!

Today our PX got in a pretty good supply of canned and bar candy, cookies and cigars. These items are not always on hand, though fruit juices, etc. are.

Yesterday was a nice day. I went to 7:00 o'clock Mass and then fooled around the rest of the morning. In the PM there were 2 ball games. In one of them my "Atobrines" lost to the "Male Nurses" (we call them Male WACS [Women Army Corps]) 10–7. Do you wonder how my team was named? ATOBRINE is a drug we take to suppress symptoms of malaria, and I am our Malaria Control Officer.

For dinner yesterday we had an unusual fruit salad of native bananas, pineapple and papaya. Papaya and avocado are 2 fruits (I guess they are) I have met since going to California and then coming here.

Last night we saw a childish but rather entertaining movie: "Tarzan's New York Adventures."[84]

Today's mail included letters from Ester, Vic, Charley Schaaf (in England) and one from Geo. Rubenstein, my fellow intern from Dunkirk. He is nearby—APO #708.[85] I wish we could get together over here somehow. Maybe we can, who knows?

This is a long letter, but since I found out you cannot easily read typed V's I have decided not use it.

Vic writes she is putting in considerable time at the store and that Jacy has taken to walking off. Reminds me of how Joe used to do that. Ester wrote about the boys being home and about Johnnie's birthday party. I can't keep track of birthdays anymore, since I lost my list. Guess I will get up a new one.

Enclosed a few pictures in my last letter, as I will do occasionally. You'll get a good idea of this place from them.

I wrote Gino[86] a letter but it was returned because of

insufficient address. Can you send me it complete? Please save
them all for me.

    Well, will close for now. Am feeling fine, so do not worry
about me.

Love,
Fred.

P.S. THE GIRLS' LETTERS AND SCHAAF'S ARRIVED IN 11 DAYS.
A FRIEND IS BUYING ME SOME CAMERA THINGS IN PHILLY AND
WILL SEND YOU THE BILL.[87]

———————— ➔ ⟵ ————————

[INCOMPLETE]
[V-Mail]

WED. 24 MAY 1944.
So. Pacific.

    on whom we operated twice so it couldn't stink-up the
place. Since being here, the boys have acquired a beautiful, pet
parrot; at one time they had live star fish and a baby shark;
four wild baby pigs run around our area. Today I saw the
latest—7 baby chicks! Where they were picked up, I cannot
guess. Maybe they are wild.

    Hope you do not worry where Joe is next stationed. There
really is no need to, you know. Should he go to Sheppard I will
fix him up with a sweet and beautiful Texas gal, just right for
him.

    Right now am listening to the radio war news. It is very
favorable in all theatres, don't you think? I do hope things
open up some and hurry along this damn mess.

    Did I ever tell you I wrote Wynette?[88] *I did and heard from*
her not long ago.

    Well, time to close.

Love,
Fred.

P.S. Please send me a list of birthdays of you, us children, and
the children.

[INCOMPLETE]
[V-Mail]

> *SUN. 28 MAY 1944.*
> *South Pacific.*

Dear Folks—

The movies we have been seeing lately have been punk. I just returned from one, and it was an all-time low. It was a cowboy picture full of impossible happenings. I don't mind cowboy pictures once in a while, but this one was really something.

Yesterday and today were unusually hot and beautiful days. I worked a bit yesterday morning, holding Sick Call as a relief, the regular man being away, and afterwards inspecting the area. I watched a ball game in the afternoon and then went swimming. Last nite saw "Ladies' Day."[89] The sunset last evening was gorgeous. The whole sky was striped pink and right in the middle of it was the brightest quarter-moon.

We finally figured out what produced a shadow in the western sky along towards evening. It is produced by an island several miles away.[90]

Today I received a letter from Joe and the "Eagle" of the 19th. I wish someone would tell Mrs. Russell that officers get "leave"—not furloughs and that enlisted men get "furloughs"—not leave. There is a distinct difference. Joe

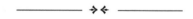

[V-Mail]

> *WED. 31 MAY 1944.*
> *South Pacific.*

Dear Folks—

Wrote you last evening but here goes again, anyway. Does anyone home get more mail than you?

Dinner this noon was pleasant because our new mess hall is completed, and today for the first time we ate sitting down. It is not elaborate but good enough. Instead of living

*in unscreened ward tents, we officers are to get screened
pyramidal tents, holding 3 or 4 men each.*

*Monday evening Capt. Burt and I went down to Service
Command to visit Capts. Feit, Heyde and [Malcolm M.] Parker.
We had dinner there, after which they took us over to the
Officer Club to drink beer and play poker. We had lots of fun.*

*Yesterday afternoon the undefeated team in our intra-
company was defeated by the Male Nurses, much to most
everyone's joy. Some spirit in that game.*

*April 15th "Colliers" cover is a nurse I knew in the desert.
Read the story of her getting the Soldier's Medal; it is mixed up
a bit, but essentially correct.*[91]

Saw "Cowboy in Manhattan"[92] *last nite.*

Love,
Fred.

—————— →← ——————

[V-Mail]
To: PVT. JOE GABRIEL
C/o MR. LOUIS GABRIEL

WED. 31 MAY 1944.
South Pacific.

Dear Joe—

*Was glad to receive your letter of the 15th; have since heard
you are en route to Florida. Good luck, and don't let your new
post and/or new work throw you. Just do your work as best
you can reasonably, don't worry, have a good time and let
things go at that.*

*Both O. and E. M. [officers and enlisted men] of our outfit
have a new fad, sling shots! Bats and parakeets inhabit these
coconut palms and they knock them down that way. They are
so high up they are stunned by the stones. Several have been
hit. The pets who have or have had since being here include:
puppies, 8 chicks, cats, baby shark, starfish, octopus, 3
parakeets, a bat! I told you about the skunk we had in Texas*[93]
and the crocodile killed here. Some outfit.

Glad you went to the Ball. Tell me about your date.

I didn't know being a track man was part of your physical. You should see me run bases—my legs still are sore. Would like to see your Yearbook, which I will do one of these months. I'll see what I can do about those two watch bands; it will be a couple weeks anyway, as I have no light-weight aluminum on hand. Tomorrow am sending home a pkg. containing seashells, brass ashtray made of a 37 mm shell[94] and a good Jap canteen lid and with writing on it.

At first thought I would not care for souvenirs, but now am changing my mind somewhat. Am also trying to collect a pictorial record of my army life. Say—did I ever tell you about my "Travelogue"—a record with dates, special order numbers, etc., of all my Army schools, moves, etc.[95] I suggest you keep one.

Did you see the April 15 "Colliers"? The cover picture is a nurse I knew in the desert. Read the story about her getting the Soldiers' Medal. It is a bit mixed up, but mostly true.

Most of the shows I have been seeing lately have been none too good. Last nite it was rather good! "Cowboy in Manhattan." The world premiere of a movie showing Bing Crosby as a priest[96] showed here last month but I did not get to see it.

I have been made our Orientation Officer[97]—current events, etc.—and now will have something else on my hands.

Well, must close now. Write.

Fred.

--------------------- ➔ ← ---------------------

[V-Mail]

WED. 31 MAY 1944.
South Pacific.

Dear Father Liebel—

Thank you for the postal cards that I receive occasionally. Am awaiting next "newsletter."

No need to change the scenery for the next act of our little play here, for from all we don't hear, things will be the same for

*a while yet. It is a bit monotonous, this easy life of inactivity, but
I can't say I envy those who went the other way an awful lot.*

*I haven't seen Pfeiffer at all yet or Eastman in some time.
Had a letter from Timon the other day. Among my last news
from home is Joe on way to Florida, Duffy to Maryland, George
not called yet, and Pop Victory-gardening actively.*

*Am sending home a few pictures occasionally that you
might like to see. Oh yes—you might make it known that
gnashing of teeth will be spared if stamps and stationery sent
overseas (in bulk) are separated by wax paper; also—more
and more airmail to us comes via boat apparently (3–4 weeks
en route).*

*Yesterday was just another day here. This letter is barren
but it is a greeting.*

Sincerely,

Fred

——————— →← ———————

[V-Mail]

THURS. 1 JUNE 1944.

South Pacific.

Dear Folks—

*Tomorrow promises to be an unusual day for us—2 fresh
eggs a piece for breakfast and fried fresh chicken for dinner!
The chicken dinner sort of celebrates our new (screened-in)
mess tents.*

*Yesterday, I went to 6 P.M. Mass and then to confession for
First Friday tomorrow. After Mass we saw a good movie: "This
Land is Mine."[98] However, it was a war propaganda picture,
and we are getting a little tired of them. Tonite "The Great
Impersonation"[99] is playing. I have seen the movie schedule
for the next two weeks; several good and rather recent ones
are listed.*

*I am being sent to school again. It is a one-week course in
Anesthesia, given at a hospital about 12 miles away. It consists
of clinics from 8 to 11. Today was the first day. Another of our
officers, now on Detached Service, also attends.[100] I meet him*

half-way, ride the rest with him, and on the way back stop at his place for lunch.

Wrote Fr. Liebel and Joe yesterday.

Love,

<u>Fred.</u>

———————— ✈ ✉ ————————

[V-Mail]

THURS. 1 JUNE 1944.

FROM THE ARCTIC

TO THE TROPICS
WHEREVER I MAY
ROAM
I SEND THIS CARD TO TELL YOU
I'M THINKING OF YOU BACK HOME!
HAPPY FATHER'S DAY

Fred.

[The letter contains a cartoon of a dog wearing a uniform while skiing, sitting under a palm tree, and standing on a beach with a rifle.]

———————— ✈ ✉ ————————

South Pacific

Sunday 4 June 1944.

Dear Folks—

 This has been a long day, beginning at 6 this morning, when I got up for Mass at 6:15. Now it is late evening, and we just came from the movie. We saw "The Spoilers," with Marlene Dietrich, Randolph Scott and John Wayne.[101]

 Our team played two games today. We beat Supply this morning and lost to Ward Boys this afternoon. A third game was played but I didn't get into it—it was for men over 34 years old—I told them to ask me again in 1949.

 Yesterday morning I got back early from this series of Clinics on Anesthesia I am attending. The officer giving them

*became ill, so there wasn't much doing. I got back here about
10 A.M., just in time for mail call, at which I received your
letters of the 23rd and 26th and one from Vic (23rd also).
Thanks for the gum and the blotter. Now to answer you.*

*I am glad to know you received my package. I presumed
you refer to the bracelet sets—you didn't say. How do you like
them? I hope they were alright. As yet I have not received the
slipper package; it will be along soon, so please do not forward
me the duplicate pair. I made myself a good pair of locker-
sandals by cutting the toes and sides out of an old pair of
shoes.*

*That was awfully nice that Uncle Lou and Albert visited
you.*[102] *It has been a long time since we have seen them. It was
in 1939 for me, I do believe. Remember when Hitler went into
Poland early in September that year we listened to the war
news at Uncle Louie's house? Mama, Louie, Joe and I made
that trip. Or maybe Joe wasn't along; I am not sure now.*

*So Joe is in Florida, doing practical work? I would be just
as well satisfied if he didn't get any more army college work.
He must have worked like a devil on that stuff, and too much
is too much. The seeds have not arrived yet and I will put them
in a tin can when they do. We have plenty of cans—the candy
comes in them. That is the only way to keep ants away from
food here. So much mail comes this way that it is doubtful if a
package would come by plane. Eight ounces is the largest we
can send airmail, and even then it is only a chance it will go
that way, regardless of postage.*

*I knew Uncle Mike was coming back to the States for
reassignment, but did not think it would be so soon.—I really
would like to be there when he comes to Eldred. He will have
plenty of stories to tell, that boy will, or I miss my guess.*

*On our radio and a daily news sheet that is put out here on
the island we get all the important news from all over the world.*

*Today I received letters from Louie and from [the] Schaafs in
Erie. One of their girls answered the letter I sent them when I
heard about Eddy's death. Lou sent a very nice and newsy letter,
as he usually does. He doesn't write very long ones, but he gets*

in all the details and writes about exactly the things I want to know. He told me about the last few weeks at school, his leave, about home and you-all, and last but not least—Tommy. He said something nice about the other six children but added that sweet as they were, Tommy was best.

Did he tell you about visiting my former landlady in Washington? I must write her—he said she was so glad he called on her. Poor Mrs. Metcalf—she was very good to me. I often wondered what became of her. Say, what is this business of Joe and an engagement ring? I knew he met some nice gals in Utica, but did not think anything serious had developed.

Yesterday I did something very unusual for me—I took a nap in the afternoon. I slept about 3 hours, maybe because it was raining. The rain began at noon and kept up rather heavily for over 15 hours. It kept us all in last nite, me playing 2 games I have learned recently—gin rummy and cribbage. Both are fun. Can you play them? If not, I will teach you someday.

I have plenty of plans for the future. One is to get you and Pop away from the store occasionally and show you a good time.

Well, it is late now, so I will bring this little "visit" to a close and say goodnight.

> *Love,*
> *Fred.*

P.S. Received Pop's V of the 23 and the last Eagle Friday.

> *F.*

———— ✈ ————

[V-Mail]

> TUES. 6 June 1944.
> South Pacific.

Dear Folks—

Right now I am happily listening to radio comments on the taking of Rome.[103] *The news these days really is good, don't you think?*

*In the past 3 days we have had no Anesthesia clinics, but
anyways at 8 o'clock Capt. Heyde and I arrive there, visit a
few minutes, and then come home. He usually brings me all the
way back. The drive to this hospital is very pretty, especially
where it skirts the sea, and I enjoy riding along with the top of
the jeep down.*

*Today had a letter from Bayonne, everything is okay with
them. Yesterday had letters from Danbury and from Fr. Liebel.
Both enclosed several swell pictures. The ones Esther sent were
of her family and Joe (Gabriel) was in some of them. He looks
big in that overcoat. Fr. L's pictures were of Eldred's Main
Street and made me more than a little homesick.*

Last evening saw "Always in My Heart."[104] *In it was a
harmonica-playing comic who looked a lot like me. Boy! Did
we 39'ers laugh! Everybody was staring at us and wanted to
know what was so funny.*

Love,
Fred.

P.S. Heard from Louie Sunday. Is Uncle Mike home?

————— ➔ ← —————

[V-Mail]

THUR. 8 June 1944.
South Pacific.

Dear Folks—

*This is a beautiful moonlit night. I have just returned to the
area from the Service Command. Major [George D.] Vermilya,
Lt. Berkowsky, and I spent the evening with Capts. Feit,
Parker and Heyde there. We had a swell steak-and-French fries
supper, after which we went over to the Officer Club for a few
hours.*

*I didn't go to "school" this morning. Instead I spent the
whole morning fixing up our magazines, arranging them so
they didn't look like a strong wind had blown them around.*

Last evening we saw a very good movie—"Princess

O'Rourke." It was quite funny. Olivia de Havilland and Robert
Cummings played in it.[105] Before going to the movie I went to
Wed. P.M. Mass.

We are fixing-up our area quite a bit. I'll tell you about it in
my next letter.

Love,
<u>Fred.</u>

—————— ➔❧ ——————

South Pacific
Sat. 10 June 1944.

Dear Folks—

Well, what do you think of the invasion?[106] We get hourly
radio news reports, so we probably are following it as closely
as you are. We first heard that the actual invasion had
started while at the movie Tuesday evening, when a special
announcement was made.

We really ate well today—fresh eggs for breakfast and steak
this noon. We are to get ice cream once a week and some
kind of deal has been cooked up where we get mustard, chili
sauce, etc. once in a while. The building of our new mess tents
was really something, and having tables and tableware has
perked-up things around here. We eat more slowly and sit
around a while after meals now. Before we wolfed-down the
food and beat it.

James Eastman stopped around to see me this morning.
He was here earlier in the week but I was away at the time.
I showed him some of my pictures and he told me I might get
film developed at their place. I do so hope so, as many of them
aren't good at all because of poor work.

Yesterday I received the June newsletter and also heard
from Joe. I believe I did write you that both Fr. Liebel and
Esther Dan[107] recently sent me some swell snapshots; Esther
sent group and family pictures and Joe was in some of them.
Fr. Liebel's pictures were of Main Street, and one was taken of
the whole town from Oak Hill Cemetery. I showed them to the

officers and many were surprised that Pennsylvania had hills that were covered with forests and not coal mines.

I am giving Joe a watch band for his birthday. A fellow is making it for me, as it is too elaborate for my talents. I will send it to Louie, so he can see it, and he will send it on to Joe. I expect to have it in the mail in a day or so, so he should get it by the 24th.

How did Uncle Mike look to you? Joe wrote that he was the same "old Uncle Mike," and that he has done quite a bit of traveling. Here's hoping he gets a nice assignment and one not far away from Olean. I'll probably be hearing from him soon and will be anxious to learn where he is going.

So far I have received only one package from you, but please do not repeat on any of those I haven't gotten yet and do not send me anything I do not ask for. Today we moved into our new tents and it is surprising how much useless and excess things I have accumulated. These tents, by the way, are pretty snozzy. Four officers to each one, and each of us has a separate closet. They are screened tents, with wooden floors and electricity.

Enclosed are a few more pictures that I wish you would save for me. And while I think of it—Esther Dan wants a picture of me. Would you please have Ester locate the negatives and have printed for Esther D. 1) the picture of Louie and I at Sheppard, 2) the picture of Joe and I taken home last October and 3) the one of Mom, Pop, Joe and I? Maybe there are extra ones of them home but I doubt it. Let me know in your next letter if these negatives can be found.

You mention sending me the packages first-class mail. I think that if you ask Glenn he will tell you that all packages coming this way travel by boat, and the only place where they might go faster by first-class mail is in getting to the West Coast.

I wrote Fr. Liebel the other day and will again do so in a week or two. Then I will thank him for the rosary and prayer book, but you save them for me at home.

Today I got last week's "Eagle" (June 2). I also received the one with the article about Joe, plus the clipping of the same thing. Yes, I received the clipping of the Schaaf boy and I do believe I am receiving all your letters. From the things you write and the questions you ask, I sometimes wonder if you receive the letters I send you—I still am writing at least every second day—and if you do get them, if you read them. I specially try to answer your questions and you ask me the same thing over three or four times. Are you receiving about 4 letters from me each week?

This week I went to Mass twice—Wednesday, as usual, and Thursday, the feast of Corpus Christi. Mrs. Schaffner of Bolivar told Vic that a Fr. Gabriel of Bonaventure is here @ #709.[108] *I will look him up.*

Well, it is late now, so I'll close.

> *Love,*
> *Fred.*

P.S. Happy Father's Day and many more of them, Pop

———————— ➤ ◄ ————————

[V-Mail]

> *Sunday 11 June 1944.*
> *South Pacific.*

Dear Folks—

Note that I am using the rubber stamp [an arrow points to the "from" address "FREDERICK R. GABRIEL, Capt. MC. Aus. 0-485524]. Thanks.

This morning I went to 11 Mass, after straightening up and settling our new quarters. We used it for the first time yesterday. Major Vermilya, Capt. Burt, Lt. Berkowsky, and myself are together; Maj. [Glen E.] Snyder, Capts. [Donald W.] Johnson and Hughes and Lt. [Albert S.] Elliott are in the second, while Capt. Birdsall and Lts. [Abraham A.] Weisberg and Worsley are in the third. There are only 12 of us living

*here now; the 12th—Lt. Col. [Jewell R.] Wilson, the C.O.—lives
alone in his tent. The other nine of our officers are away on
Detached Service.*

Last night we saw a funny show, "The Devil With Hitler."[109]
Tonite we saw "Rhythm of the Islands";[110] *it made us hoot
when they showed it as a tropical paradise with beautiful
women, etc.*

*This morning I sent you an airmail with a few more
snapshots. I also sent some to Joe. This afternoon I finished
packing a box of souvenirs to send you.*[111] *Expect it in 6 or 7
weeks. In it are 1) a brass ash-tray for Papa, made from a big-
gun shell. It can be cleaned well with vinegar and salt. 2) Two
tin cans of various seashells, one for Ester's children and one
for Vic's. 3) 6 large shells (lemon sized) keep what you want
for yourself and give one to the girls and Louie. 4) a couple
pieces of coral—good for putting in fish bowls 5) a large,
irregular multiple seashell, good for a paper weight. Please
give it to Father Liebel for me.*

*Also included are a woolen shirt, pants, and field jacket; I
have no use for them here. Maybe this fall you can give them to
Louie or Joe.*

*I forgot—also in the package is a Jap canteen, with cover—
for me!!!*

*Should you or anyone else want any shells, coral, etc. just
let me know. It strikes me funny—you know how I dislike
knick-knacks around the house and here I am sending you a
bunch of them. Still, these are good souvenirs and reminders of
this place (as though I will ever forget it).*

Well, must close now.

*Love,
Fred.*

[V-Mail]

> TUE. 13 June 1944.
> South Pacific.

Dear Folks—

I just returned from the movie. It was good—Jack Benny in "Meanest Man in the World."[112]

Right now three of us at this table are here writing letters and discussing what a change has been made here. We sit here, without any shirts, listening to our radio and saying this is <u>almost</u> like home.

Today a new thing I have charge of—Orientation—held its first session. It was pretty good and the men showed quite a bit of interest.

Yesterday afternoon another officer and myself visited a local (Island) art show. It really was surprising how much and how good work has been turned out. It included all kinds of drawings and paintings, souvenir-making and some native work, like weaving. Yesterday the "Atobrines" beat the league-leading Administration.

Today I had letters from Duffy and from Lorraine. Also saw James Eastman again.

Well, must close now.

> *Love,*
> <u>*Fred.*</u>

P.S. Tomorrow am sending Joe his birthday present, a really nice watch band that I had made for him.

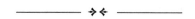

> South Pacific
> Thurs. 15 June 1944

Dear Folks—

I'll begin this letter now but doubt that I will finish it before I leave for the movie. We are going early as there is to be a U.S.O. Stage show in conjunction with it, and the place will be packed. I don't know how many go there each nite, even for the poorest shows, but I estimate at least 15 hundred. Which reminds me—last evening there was a "Community Sing" short. The songs were popular college ones. There was scarcely any singing until they played the N.D. "Victory March." Then you should have heard that crowd sound off. It seems as most everyone there knew the music and the words.

The feature last evening was a Sherlock Holmes show— entertaining but otherwise none too good.

This afternoon I accompanied some of the men on a trip for gravel. We went down towards the west end of the island about twenty miles, much farther than I had been before. Gosh! but it was a beautiful drive. Much of the way the road skirted the sea, and as we drove along we could see the curving beachline just ahead of us. The water close to the shore was green, while out a ways it was a Prussian blue. The air was clear and nearby islands to our north and west were plainly visible. The inland side of the road bordered low, heavily wooded hills that reminded me very much of those up around Coudersport and Gaines.[113]

Well, I am off to the movie now.

Well, I am back again. There was no USO show, but we did see a good and very funny movie—Don Ameche in "Girl Trouble."[114]

Your letter of June 6 arrived today. I am glad you heard from Joe after he arrived in Tampa.[115] He is pretty good about writing, so I'll be hearing from him soon.

I can't imagine where that large confirmation class of 110 all came from. Are they all from Eldred, Sartwell and Duke Center?[116] I probably will read the list of names in the next "Eagle." For the past few weeks I have been getting the copy you airmail me just 7 or 8 days after you get it, which is very good time.

Thanks for taking care of my insurance for me. I heard from Duffy yesterday. He wrote me from Bainbridge.[117] He didn't write much about what he is doing, probably because he hadn't been there long. I wrote him just a couple days ago.

Say, what is this surprise package you sent me? You said

*Joe bought one and you got one for me, too, but you didn't
mention what it was. I am anxious to find what the thing
is. Incidentally—lately my pajamas have begun to give out,
so would you please send me 2 pairs in addition to the one I
now have on the way? Also—if you can get any without too
much trouble, I'd like 2 wrist watch snap pins. I don't know
if that is the correct name for them, so here's a picture of what
I am referring to.—it is the thing that holds the strap to the
watch. Some have springs on both ends; some only on 1 end. I
will take either kind. If you can't find any, that is all right, as
straight pins do just as well. [There's a drawing of a watch,
pins, and strap].*

*I had planned to send you a few more pictures, but now
think I will postpone it until next time.*

It is late, so I'll close with

Love,
<u>Fred.</u>

P.S. Here are 3 photographs after all.

---------- →← ----------

[V-Mail]

FRI. 16 June 1944.
South Pacific.

Dear Folks—

*I have just returned from the movie. It was a cowboy
picture again, about the fifth in the last eight evenings. Today I
saw the movie schedule for the second half of the month; some
good ones are listed. Which reminds me—do you people ever
go see them?*

*All day long we have been talking about this morning's
radio report that Japan was bombed. I listened to several of
the hourly newscasts, hoping the targets bombed would be
identified. However, all that was said was "the heart of Japan."
Gosh! I hope it was Tokyo.*[118]

Today I received Papa's long letter of May 28th. I have

*received later letters from you, by the way. In it was something
that makes me believe this surprise package you were sending
me (before I requested it) is the identification bracelet. Is that
right? Also received the "ALUMNUS" today.*

*So far have not received any but that first package from
you, nor the saw blades Mama put in an envelope. I should be
getting some of these things in a week or two—you said one
was mailed May 9th.*

Must close now.

Love,
Fred.

───────── ➔ ← ─────────

[V-Mail]

Sunday 18 June 1944
South Pacific.

Dear Folks—

*Thanks for the package, which I received today, containing
the pliers, chisel, saw blades, book, etc. Everything was just
what I wanted, so thanks again. Yesterday I received the single
saw-blade. Both packages probably came on the same boat. I
suppose the book*[119] *was the one Louie said he wanted me to
read; I have started it, and find it very good.*

*I just returned from the movie. It wasn't so good—a Frank
Buck jungle affair.*[120] *The one last evening wasn't so hot either,
but it was a double feature. Right now there are a couple
U.S.O. shows here on the Island which I hear are good. I'll take
them in when they come this way.*

*Your letter of the 9th came yesterday, too. See—I used
the stamp on this one. Let me know how it photographs.
Incidentally, that stamp-pad is a good one. I'll have to hide it
or the office men might "borrow it."*

*I haven't yet heard from Joe since he went to Florida, but
probably will soon. Louie has written only once since he went
back, so I'll be hearing from him also.*

*We officers have a ping pong table in our REC and I have
been playing a lot, though that does not detract from our usual*

softball. My team won another game today. The company is
organizing a hardball team, so that is one more recreation we
will have.

Today at noon we had something for the first time—soup.
We also had fresh chicken (second time) and a good salad
of native bananas, pineapple and papaya, a fruit that is
something like a melon (cantaloupe). Our meals are very
good, I think, though of course we get some things I don't like
(remember me, Mom?). We feel better, too, since we have our
new mess tents. Friday, the officers' shower was finished; in
it also are a wash-basin with faucets and running water. All
the comforts of home we have now, but they don't begin to
compare to the real thing.

Must close now.

Love,
<u>Fred.</u>

P.S. We get steak a couple times a week now.

———————— ➔ ← ————————

South Pacific
Thurs. 22 June 1944

Dear Folks—

This has been another beautiful day—long and quiet and
lazy. Right now it is evening and a nice cool breeze is blowing
in from the sea. That happens almost daily making for good
sleeping. I sleep like a child, straight through until morning. Of
course, if I drink a beer late, I often have to get up during the
night once or twice.

I had a nice mail call today. There were 9 pieces including
your letter of the 13th and the airmailed napkin. Thanks for it,
but there was no great need to get it here in such a hurry. None
of the others have them yet, but several have sent home for
them. I also received an "Eagle" and the "Lake Shore Visitor."
Both come quite regularly now.

Vic mentioned in her last letter that Mama was considering going to Danbury with Uncle Mike. I hope she did, as it would be a nice trip for her and a bit of change of surroundings for a couple weeks. Apparently Uncle Mike didn't go to Charleston. Lorraine wrote that he might do that. Of course he could stop there on the way to N. Carolina—they must be somewhere near each other. Say—I wonder if Louie and Uncle [Mike] can get together now that both are in the South.

So Ester did visit Duffy in Philly? That is good. She'll probably tell me about her trip when she next writes. I won't mind taking a trip there. I plan to, too, but guess I will put it off for a few months. There probably are plenty of cities elsewhere I'll see before I visit an American one again. Still, the way the war is progressing for the Allies maybe I'll be home much sooner than any of us expected a few months ago. The Americans seem to be doing okay by themselves on all fronts. Gosh! I hope the Jap fleet does come out and fight. There is no doubt in my mind that the Americans will defeat them decisively, after which we'll be in the Philippines by early fall. Those are my guesses, anyway. Now if only the Russians would make war on Japan the "Rising Sun" would be set in a big hurry. I imagine the Nips will fold rather quickly once real bombing of their cities gets under way.

Well enough of grand strategy. I had better leave that to the generals and admirals. They don't try to tell us how a hospital should be run and I shouldn't tell them how the campaign should be fought.

Apparently I forgot to let you know that I bought a new army watch not long ago, so you need not have Uncle Mike buy one for me. I now have 2, and both keep good time. Really I have 3, as Joe still has my gold doctor watch. He asked me for it while I was at Sheppard. He can hold it for me until I get home. Yesterday I worked on another plain aluminum watch band for him. When it is finished and sent to him that will make three, including the fancy one now en route to him for a birthday present. I hope he likes it and can use it. The measurements were taken from the watch I wear.

Yes I received the "Eagle" telling of Joe's graduation as well
as a single clipping of the same thing. I'll have something in
there about me soon. Our Public Relations officer is getting
interviews from each of us—both officers and men—to send to
our home newspapers. It is a routine and almost stereotyped
thing, so do not attach too much importance to it.

There is an awful lot of building going on in the area these
days. I don't know where all the lumber is coming from, but
all of the "tent" offices and several of the men's tents are being
replaced by screened-in hutments. These hutments are worlds
better than tents and I wish all the men could get them. If we
are here much longer, maybe they will. We think the officers'
three hutments are swank compared to the big ward tents we
lived in. They are much improvement in all respects. Now, for
example, we try to keep our shoes shined, which we thought
was useless when we were living on the ground.

Speaking of living on the ground reminds me that that was
what Mama always said she wanted, which in turns reminds
me of something else. You know that double lot on the corner of
Elm and Main streets, where Albrights used to live? I believe
Mrs. Whittemore now owns it, at least that half bordering on
Elm. I wish you would ask her if she would consider selling it,
and for how much. I think that is a nice location. Also—ask
the present owners of that old Ed Smith place the same thing.
While you are at it, tell Mr. Marsh I wouldn't mind having an
option on that large lot between the furniture store and Mrs.
Mitchell's. I guess this real estate thing runs in the family.

We got a new medical officer yesterday—a Captain [Stephen
H.] Harris from Rhode Island. About all I know of him so far is
that he has three days less Army service than I have (twenty-
two months) and hasn't been abroad very many weeks.

Most of us run the radio on the hour to get the hourly
newscasts. We have heard some welcome news that way
this month. One is coming over the air now (6 P.M.) but it is
essentially the same news we have been hearing all afternoon.

Today was the first time I have been swimming in quite
some time. I rather got out of the habit when I hurt my

legs ("charley-horses") a few weeks back. None of us go as regularly as we used to. I guess the novelty of the thing is wearing off. From now on, though, I am going to make an effort to go every day.

We are building a new incinerator and today I went down to a Navy salvage yard for some scrap iron. Which reminds me, on a card today from Fr. Liebel he mentioned that Bouser Morris[121] and a couple others from home are nearby. I believe I know where. What is the A.P.O. number? Also—I lost Gino's address. Please send it to me.

Well, I must close now. I trust this finds you all as well as it leaves me.

Love,
Fred.

P.S. The two pictures of the 3 boys were swell. The devils look very lovable. I'd like pictures of them on the new swings.

Enclosed are a few more snapshots. I am also sending some interesting ones to the children—both sets of them.

Don't forget what I asked you.

F.

-------------------- ➔ ← --------------------

[V-Mail]

FRI. 23 JUNE 1944.
South Pacific Theatre.

Dear Father Liebel—

During the past few days the mailman has brought me your letter and the postcard for Eastman and myself, which will be passed over tomorrow. Thanks for them.

Sorry I can't write you "newsier" letters but really I cannot. Things are the same old thing for us, day after day. I'll bet that if we did get a call to set up our hospital, none of us could believe it. But in spite of the mild monotony of this lazy life I continue to enjoy being here. I am happy and as contented as can be expected; in fact, probably more so. I get along okay and am feeling in the veritable "pink." We could do with a bit *of social life but that seems to be beyond our reach. Maybe that stage will be reached with the "civilization" of this island. Officers now are required to wear Class A uniforms;*[122] *no more running around native-fashion.*

We get hourly news reports via the radio, and really have heard some heartening ones this month. The way the war is progressing for the Allies now, maybe we will be home sooner than most of us dared expected a few months ago.

I'll bet our winter weather (2 days old now) is hotter than your summer. It is on the torrid side but not as muggy as I anticipated. Most of our days are beautiful—long and lifeless and quiet; evenings of late have been coolish and ideal for sleeping. Sunrise, sunsets and the nite skies are really something here. They make an individual feel alone and so insignificant. The Southern Cross and Milky Way are easily seen. Day break and darkness break quickly here and rain squalls come up suddenly. These latter often catch me off balance with practically everything I own, out sunning.

There is nothing in my frequent news from home that you do not know. Hear from Joe occasionally but from Louie only once since he returned. I get the "Eagle" and "Lake Shore Visitor" in good time; pass the latter along to some of the Catholic lads.

Say—should you desire it, if you'll send me the width of the strap-end of your wristwatch and the circumference of your wrist I'll make you an aluminum watch band, like I sent my brothers.

I have an idea where Bouser Morris, etc. are.

Well, must sign off now. Until the next time then—

> *Sincerely,*
> *Fred.*

[V-Mail]

> FRI. 23 June 1944
> South Pacific.

Dear Folks—

Instead of going to the movie tonite and seeing "Tarzan,"[123] I am staying in and writing letters. I just finished one to Fr. Liebel and a birthday greeting from me to Joe. I heard from him today; apparently MacDill is a nice place and Joe likes it there.

This has been another hot and beautiful day. I was caught off balance, though, this afternoon when it suddenly began to rain and I had practically everything I own out to sun. Thus it goes!

Pop wanted to know if your airmail makes good time. Yes, it does generally (8 to 12 days), though today's letter from him was dated the 4<u>th</u>. Apparently at times there is so much mail that some comes by boat. Service to you is a bit faster, I believe.

About Uncle Mike being only a corporal: sometimes the Table of Organization (how many of each rating allowed) of a unit may be filled. Then there will be no promotion without vacancies occurring.

> Love,
> <u>Fred.</u>

P.S. Asked Ester for a list of birthdays but she must have forgotten. Will you remind her?

[V-Mail]

> SAT. 24 JUNE 1944
> South Pacific.

Dear Folks—

This won't be very newsy, but I do want to answer 3 of your letters now lying before me, 2 of which came today.

I am awfully glad I am not around during Spring housecleaning. That is one time I'd gladly leave home. Aren't you a bit late in finishing it this year?

The airmailed napkin arrived a few days ago and already is in use; air mail is faster than first class mail, which crosses the ocean on boat. Yes, Fr. Leibel sent me that set of pictures of Eldred; in fact he sent me 2 sets and also a set for Eastman, which I delivered today to him as he came to see me again. Which Tuohy girl was asking about me? I read in the "Eagle" that their aunt (I think) was in Eldred.

The address of my Washington landlady is MRS. ELIZABETH METCALF; 405 ASPEN STREET N.W.

Yes, it is funny I never got the package with the slippers. I got the one with the popcorn, underwear, etc. that you sent about the same time. I will get it, though.

I think it is wise to have P.J's tonsils removed. The last time I saw them, they were much enlarged. Who is going to do the operation? Wintermantle?[124]

No, I haven't received the seeds. I thought I did tell you that before a couple times. The tools arrived about a week ago and have seen considerable service already. They were just what I wanted. The "Eagle" of last Friday came today—very good time.

Here are 2 things I wish you would send me; in a few days I'll request a couple more, (after I am sure what I want).

a folding carpenter ruler—about 72 inches long and not too good, as I'll probably break it.

three bars of shaving soap, either Palmolive or Colgate. Our PX has none and I don't like tube shaving soap.

Well, must sign off now.

Love,
Fred.

P.S. Joe can vote as of today, can't he? Remember how close he came to being named "Sterling"? Paulie will get a kick out of that story!

F.

South Pacific
Mon. 26 June 1944
Dear Folks—
   This is only a note, just an accompaniment for the enclosed
pictures (12).
   Please save them along with the others for me.
   I'll write you later this evening.

Love,
<u>*Fred.*</u>

————— ➤← —————

South Pacific
Mon. 26 June 1944

Dear Folks—
   This is the usual time for movies, but Capt. Burt and
I decided to stay in and write letters instead of going. We
thought it wouldn't be good ("Sing a Jingle")[125] *but the others*
just returned from there and said it was very entertaining.
Besides that there were 2 good shorts, one about beautiful gals
in swim suits. Gals, beautiful or otherwise, go over big here at
this stage of the game.
   Lt. Berkowsky, the junior man in our hutment, is also here
at the table writing a letter to his wife. He said he just wrote
something about me, so I am going to write about him. He
is a very nice fellow and we have lots of fun. His wife had a
daughter a couple of months ago, their first child, and he has
never seen her. About 4 times a week he reports to me the
baby's latest weight. We always kid Hy, as we call him, about
being henpecked. He is, too, though he swears up and down
that he wears the pants in his family, and the he gets in the last
words "Yes Dear."
   Right now the 10 PM news report from San Francisco
is coming over the radio. It is encouraging news but the
same darn thing we have heard every hour all afternoon—
Cherbourg is just about taken, the Americans on Saipan are
advancing, the Russians are going to town again, etc.[126] *I*

don't know how the war, either front, can last another eighteen months. The Allies certainly are forging ahead everywhere, and what is more important, are destroying the enemies' power to make war. The Axis is back on its heels and must know they cannot hold out much longer. They'll start feeling around for a negotiated peace in a short while.

Well, for all practical purposes, we now have been here five months, and have six months overseas service under our belts. Gosh! how that time has gone by. In a sense it seems like years since we arrived here and at the same time it seems only a few weeks. I guess that is because the days are long, yet time just flies. Anyway, this easy life is getting us impatient to set up our hospital, which must take place sometime. We can't stay here for-ever. Besides, the area is pretty well fixed up now, and it is our experience that when that has been accomplished, we are moved out and someone else moves in to benefit by our labor. Well, time alone will tell if our luck, or whatever it is, still holds out. We all are hoping so.

Yesterday I heard from Louie, the first time since he returned to Campbell. He has been busy, he wrote, and also that they have a nice large house and he wants you to visit him. Why don't you? The change will do you good. Kentucky should be a good place to relax—they have a nice climate. Tommy is walking now, and Louie is anxious to get a picture of him tottering along. I finished another roll of film myself today. We have found out that it doesn't pay to keep film in the camera too long—the heat and moisture make the emulsion run.

Enclosed is a note requesting some things, some for the second time. You can present the note to the Post Office.

Must sign off now.

Love,
Fred.

P.S. In another envelop am sending home some snapshots.

South Pacific
Mon. 26 June 1944

Dear Folks—
Please send me the following:—
- *one carpenter's folding ruler—72 inches*
- *three bars (round) of shaving soap*
- *one "male" electric plug [includes a sketch]*
- *one "female" electric socket [includes a sketch]*
- *one ball-hammer—small size; if you cannot get it easily,
  skip it as I don't need it very badly [includes sketch].*

Sincerely,
Fred

Sketch of electric plugs and hammer from June 26, 1944 letter,
Guadalcanal.

[V-Mail]

> *Tues. 27 JUNE 1944*
> *South Pacific.*

Dear Folks—

Today heard from Esther Dan, who says Uncle Mike and Celia [Cecelia] Moses are to be married. Any truth to that? Lots of soldiers who have been overseas a while make up their minds then about marriage. Also had Pop's letter of the 18th; glad to know Joe will phone you regularly. Yesterday had a letter from Joe, written while waiting for his phone call to get through to you. He likes it there, and has taken a couple trips to nearby cities. He also mentioned a little more about his Syrian girlfriend in Utica, the one to whom he wanted to give a ring.

Yesterday we held the regular monthly exam of the men; this afternoon another unit for whom we hold sick call. Later this afternoon we had another Orientation session, one of the majors discussing insurances, pensions, etc. for the servicemen.

We just returned from the movie, a film about the British Coastal Command.[127] It showed how its planes protect convoys from German submarines.

This week I am sending you some more pictures, both new and old. They spoil fast in this climate, and if I keep them here, they won't last much longer. I'll take them down to the Island censor for his okay and then send them via boat. I am keeping here a representative but small groups of pictures of the family and Eldred. By the way, are you getting ready those pictures for Esther Dan?

The 10 P.M. news is coming over now, and it continues to be good, with the Axis being pushed back and bombed heavily everywhere. I don't see how they can hold out much longer. Apparently the poor Finns feel they have had about enough.[128]

We are starting a new softball league, in which I have a team that somebody dubbed the "ELDRED EAGLES." Can you beat that? The first I knew of the name was when I read it on the bulletin board. That's just like the people home calling

*Irene and Bill Scott "Citty" and "Skid-di." Do they really call
them that? Say—do you suppose I should send Mrs. Russell
a picture of the team to put in the paper? Maybe I could even
promote uniforms from her. Wouldn't that be something?*

*Before I forget—my bonds will come to you a bit irregularly
for a month or two; today I doubled the allotment to $37.50
I hope you record all bonds that I buy, so I can have the
information for my income-tax returns. Did you rent a safety-
deposit box at the bank for me?*

Well, must close now.

Love,

Fred.

———————— ⇥⇤ ————————

[V-Mail]

THUR. 29 JUNE 1944

South Pacific.

Dear Folks—

*For some reason I am pretty tired tonite. Maybe it is because
I played ping pong for an hour this morning and softball this
afternoon. Anyway, after I finish this I am going to bed. It
is cool again this evening, so I shall sleep well. I usually do
anyway.*

*We—"The Eldred Eagles"—lost the game, incidentally, to the
"Texas Longhorns." Tomorrow we play the "Chow Hounds."
There are four teams and all have similarly descriptive
names.*[129]

*Right now we are having another of those periods of
irregular mail service. I have not heard from you for 3 days
but I am not worrying, as I know tomorrow is the next day
I will get a batch of letters—hope so, anyways. Some of the
others have had no mail in about a week, and a couple are
feeling pretty blue about it. Funny how the moods of the men
changes when mail gets slack.*

*Today, I had my teeth cleaned. An enlisted man did it, so
I don't know if I have any cavities as he might not say so.
However, I have no reason to think I need to have dental*

attention. I guess nobody likes that, do they? While I think of it, how are Mama's teeth? I hope she has no more trouble with them.

This morning I mailed the coconuts to Aileen's children. I thought it would be nice since she has been so good about writing to me. In a couple days I will get one off to Tommy. Esther Dan wanted some pictures of me and now I have a couple for her. Plenty of fellows are sending pictures home— we see them by the dozens every day while censoring mail.

Who would think that tomorrow is the last of the month? Gosh! when we first got here I never dreamed we would see July here, and here it is and here we are! Well, we can't stay here forever. Tomorrow is pay day, too. I draw about 45 in cash each month, of which I spend less than half. That is why I increased my bond allocation to a 50 dollar bond monthly. One of these days I am going to send another 25 dollar one to Notre Dame.

The boys just came back from the movie. I didn't go as I saw it at Sheppard. We saw a different, but only fair, movie last nite: "The Strange Death of Adolph Hitler," the story of a double of Hitler's who was killed by his own wife because she thought he had taken her children from her; she didn't know it was her husband she shot.[130] The double looked really like old Shicklegruber.

I just went over to the Chaplain's tent for more V-mail (that's) why I don't ask you for it—he supplies everyone). There is a bright half-moon, yet the sky is clouded now and few stars can be seen. I went outside about 2 this morning, and the sky was so beautiful and star-studded that I stood there for a few minutes with my mouth open.

The newscaster just mentioned the nomination of Dewey and Bricker by the Republicans.[131] The election this November is going to be interesting and probably close. Were Dewey a bit older and this not a war-time election I think he would be elected easily. Ever since my intern days, when I first noted it, I have been literally amazed at how strongly opposed most medical men are to Roosevelt. You probably know we here will vote by overseas ballot.

We still heckle Berkowsky about being henpecked and have nicknamed him "Subservient." Every nite while writing letters we take him for a ride. He takes it well and usually gets back at us when we play cards, at which he often wins. Lately we have been playing a lot of "Scopa"[132] an Italian game we learned at Barkeley when we thought we were going the other way. We were told that was how the natives there determined how and who would buy the drinks. We figured we would go prepared to drink like old-timers.

Charley Schaaf hasn't written me in several weeks, but I imagine those in England are pretty busy these days. Still, according to announced figures, the Invasion casualties were not nearly as great as was expected, at least by me. That certainly is a happy failure of expectations, though, isn't it? I was thinking the other day that several Duke Center men in the Air Corps have been reported missing in action.[133] I hope no more from home are reported as such.

We have several maps around, on which we follow the progress of the war. That is part of my duties as our Orientation Officer. The map of the Pacific is hard to follow unless it is a large one because there are so darned many islands to watch.

Well, must close now, hoping the mailman has something for me tomorrow.

Love,
Fred.

——————— ⇥⇤ ———————

[V-Mail]

FRI. 30 JUNE 1944.
South Pacific.

Dear Ester—

We just returned from Wallace Beery in "Salute to the Marines."[134] It wasn't so good, even in Technicolor.[135] We have been subjected to some rather poor pictures these past couple of weeks. Now to see what July brings us. Isn't it hard to believe that July is here? It doesn't seem over a few weeks ago that we landed here—yet we have 6 months overseas duty to our credit—it begins with the overseas trip.

The mailman hasn't been so good to me—5 days now without a letter. And I am not the only one. Practically the whole unit has had a let-down. I continue to write plenty, though, and this afternoon wrote to Duffy.

This afternoon my "Eldred Eagles" won a game 9–7. Yesterday we took a ride [were defeated] badly: 16 to 0. I guess maybe that is why I played so hard today, scoring 3 runs. Funny thing—the volleyball court has been deserted since the ball field was finished and volleyball was played as much then as the other is now.

I am waiting to learn when P. J. will have his tonsils removed. I'll bet he'll put on weight then. How tall is he now? In these recent snapshots he seemed taller than when I last saw him, last October. Johnny looks bigger, too, but with the same look in his eyes. And Jimmy—the only way I remembered him was as he was sitting in his crib, with his feet hanging down between the rails and trying to peek through. Gosh! how I'd like to be with them now, even if only for a few minutes. But things like that must wait for a while yet. Maybe another 18 months or so. Well, if they go by at the same speed as the last few have, even that won't seem long.

James Easton was here to see me, I was told, but I was not around. He is a very nice fellow. Incidentally—I have no direct way of looking up Monroe's son-in-law but will continue to ask around. What kind of an outfit is he with? That address I received wasn't too revealing.

We recently have received some good books for our library. Right now I am reading "God is My Co-Pilot,"[136] which is pretty interesting. I just finished Walter Lippman's "U.S. Foreign Policy,"[137] not a storybook but really good. Louie sent it to me and he also liked it very well.

Esther Dan wrote me that Uncle Mike and Cecelia Moses were planning on being married soon, which was news to me. Well, I am glad for them if it is true and I hope it is.

Another officer and myself bought a new G.E. [General Electric] electric iron for ten dollars. Now I'll wear pressed clothes for a change.

Must close now.

Love,
Fred.

───────── ➔ ← ─────────

[V-Mail]

FRI. 30 JUNE 1944.
South Pacific.

Dear Folks—

That 4-page v mail I wrote you last nite exhausted my supply of news and just about my writing arm too, though today I did write to Ester and Duffy.

This morning was paid—$44.10. Did I ever tell you that over half the money the outfit actually receives each month is sent home? That is pretty good, isn't it? In fact I believe it is closer to 70% than 50%.

The "Eldred Eagles" redeemed themselves this afternoon and beat the "Chow Hounds" 9–7. I scored 3 of our runs.

This evening we saw "Salute to the Marines." It wasn't too good. These past 2 weeks we haven't been having such good ones anyway.

James Eastman was here today but I was away at the time. Tomorrow begins another month.

Love,
Fred

[V-Mail]

SAT. 1 JULY 1944
South Pacific

Dear Folks—

Again it is the same time, same place and same thing: just back from the movie, writing in our hutment and kidding the married ones about being henpecked. Tonite there is one variation, however. I didn't go to the movie, having seen it before, and besides, I am O.D. (office of the day) today, which means I should stick around.

Today's mail brought me no letters but I did get the package containing one pair of pajamas, popcorn, peanuts and seeds. The p.js will be put to immediate use (just as soon as this is finished), as the others have seen their best days. You know— we have had only 2 popcorn "parties," the last one a couple month ago. I guess we have lost our appetite for it; at least that appetite is dulled. It is the same way with other things we haven't too handy—probably a protective mechanism on the part of Mother Nature.

Come to think of it, both yesterday and today I did receive "Lake Shore Visitors." I pass them on to some of the other Catholic boys after finishing with them.

Well, as I have nothing to write about (anyway) I'll close now.

Love,
<u>Fred.</u>

———————— ➔ ◆ ————————

South Pacific
Mon. 3. July 1944

Dear Folks—

The mailman has finally remembered how to spell my name and yesterday and today I received letters from you, Joe and Charley Schaaf in England.

Charley says they are pretty busy with invasion wounded and that he couldn't say too much for them or do too much for them. Joe seems to be having fun at Tampa. He, too, mentioned about Uncle Mike getting married but said it wasn't definite as yet. I should be hearing from Uncle soon, and no doubt I'll get the lowdown then.

Who writes those letters to me? Some of them are rather puzzling and quite often they leave me up in the air. For example, they'll tell me the last part about something and forget I don't know what it is they are talking about. Doesn't she read the letter before they are sealed in the envelope?

From your letter of June 23, I assume I have asked you to send me one or 2 spring-guards for wrist-watches; I don't recall having asked for them, but you wrote you were trying to get me some "watch-bracelet pins." In case we are not talking about the same thing, here is what I want: it is the thing that holds the wrist-watch strap to the watch. [Hand-drawn picture of a watch showing the part] Please send me one or 2 of them, with the spring on 1 or both ends.

Also—if you can easily find one, please send me a cheap pocket watch, not over three dollars. I have 2 good wristwatches, so really don't need it, but thought a cheap pocket watch wouldn't be a bad thing to have. Remember the $1.50 watches I used to have? That is the kind I want.

So you didn't like the movie "Lost Angel"?[138] I thought it was good and the little girl was very sweet. I don't believe "The Sullivans"[139] has come to this island yet; I understand it was very good. The movie where Bing Crosby plays the part of a priest is still around and most everyone who sees it has liked it very much. This past week I missed 3 movies because I had seen them not so long ago. The schedule for this month has some good ones listed.

I am sorry Tommy Slavin[140] and I didn't meet. If he was only 30 miles away, I think I know where he was. At a fork in the road near our area is a "39th Station Hospital" sign. It is only about 75 yards away. That may be the one Tommy saw. Jimmy Eastman was here today. The last time he was here we had our picture taken together. I gave him a print of it today. One of these days I am going down to his place and see his pictures.

That certainly must have been a pleasant surprise—Dr. Dineen calling on you. Was he going to Sayre to seek a hospital appointment? Probably he was. The last I heard he was resident in Medicine at St. Francis in Pittsburgh.[141] *I have written to him a couple of times since being in the Army but never have had any answer from him, so I won't bother again.*

Both yesterday and today have been very hot. Fortunately there is a good breeze blowing now. At 6:30 Mass yesterday I saw 4 nuns and 2 priests. I have heard conflicting stories concerning them, so will say no more until I get the correct dope.

Yesterday the "Oklahoma Oakie" beat us in soft ball. I played the whole game but didn't do so hot. But I can't be flashy all the time, can I?

Enclosed are a few pictures. Tomorrow or Wednesday I will send you several more by boat as there are too many to go airmail.

Well, I'll sign off for now.

Love,
<u>*Fred*</u>

————— ➜ ⇠ —————

[Written on same page at bottom of letter]

2 July 1944.

Dear Folks—
Please send me the following:
- *one or 2 wrist watch spring-guards. 5/8 inch long.*
- *A cheap pocket watch.*
- *2 triangular files, about 6 inches long and about ¼ inch wide on a side.*

Sincerely,
<u>*Fred*</u>

[V-Mail]

TUES. 4 JULY 1944.
South Pacific Theatre

Dear Folks—

The mailman is my pal again (5 letters today). Included was yours of June 20th. Yesterday I had one from Ester and also the 2 packages of seeds. Thanks for them. I have material enough for a real vegetable garden now, huh? Incidentally, we get them fresh here occasionally.

Last evening three of us attended a party at the Service Command. We had a nice time—cocktails, buffet supper. Afterwards there was a dance but we could not even get near one of the girls. Instead we played poker and listened to the band, which was not bad.

Holidays over here do not mean much. Yet even without looking at the calendar I would have known that this was the Fourth. There is something about them that sets them apart. As I wrote Vic—they are a little hotter, longer and lazier than other days and people have the feeling of quietness and do-nothing. I guess it is about the same all over, but especially in smaller towns, from what I gathered from our discussions of the subject today.

There was a big baseball game here on the island this afternoon, to which I listened on the radio. I didn't go because after those couple of drinks last night I didn't feel much like sitting out in the hot sun for a couple hours or so.

Did I tell you James Eastman was here yesterday? I gave him a copy of a picture of us together. My copy I sent you in my last letter. I now have this package of pictures I wrote you about all ready and will get them in the mail tomorrow.

The sky suddenly clouded up this evening and I think we are due for a good rain. There hasn't been much of it these last 3 weeks and things are quite dry. The rain will be welcomed by some.

In Pop's letter of the 25th he mentioned Duff's one-day visit. Sounds like he had a 36-hour pass. Ester wrote that he likes it at Bainbridge but that he is naturally greyer about the temples.

Well, this rain is beginning to fall. Sounds like it will be on the heavy side.

Must close now. Take care of yourselves.

Love,

Fred.

P.S. Thanks for the birthday cards, which I received yesterday.

South Pacific
Sat. 8 July 1944.

Dear Folks—

Although it is a few hours early, the boys just finished singing "Happy Birthday" to me when they saw me reading the cards I got from you. Now they are kidding me about being old and bald and tell me I should have been married a long [time] ago, as by the time I'll get home I will be too old and rundown to have children. Things really would be bad, wouldn't they, if what they say were true. Gosh, I wouldn't want that to happen home, let alone over here.

Being O.D. I couldn't go to the movie this evening. Instead I stayed home and caught up on all my back correspondence. That wasn't hard to do as I haven't received much mail these past 3 weeks, though during the early part of this week I did get 3 or 4 a day. Thursday, Friday and today I didn't fare so well. Air mail apparently is coming through slowly these days, slower than V-mail. I still use the V's mainly but when I have enclosures or know it will be a long letter I use airmail.

Since Wednesday afternoon it has been raining several hours a day and has been a bit cool. Today, however, was warmer, with no rain and lots of sun. It dried up the puddles that sprung up around here of late and enough so that there could be a ball game this afternoon. We have a game tomorrow morning; our game Friday was rained out.

We have some good books now and today I finished one I thought was swell, except a bit sad and pathetic: "Reunion on Strawberry Hill."[142] *It was the story of a family of children—especially career-seeking daughters—who wanted to put their elderly parents in an institution instead of letting them finish out their lives on the old homestead. Most of it centers around the reunion at the homestead on the parents 48th wedding anniversary. The book left me a little depressed though with some definite ideas.*

I know you two will never face the situation of the parents in that book and that you will never have to worry about anything as long as we children are alive. Except possibly us, huh?

Yesterday morning I went down to the Service Club and saw the Island Orientation Officer—you know I am our Orientation Officer. He was an interesting fellow but quite a talker and I didn't get a chance to say much in the hour-and-a-quarter we talked. He seemed pleased at the way I was handling things and asked for suggestions on several matters. We discussed government-controlled Medicine a lot. He, like me, feels it is a bad thing but probably in the offing. Although he is about 36 and a professional music teacher he still plans on studying to be a doctor.

Besides reading these new books, lately we in this hutment have taken to playing bridge. We have fun but only one of us—the Major—knows a hell of a lot about it. I imagine we will catch on after a little time at it. We have started a ping-pong tournament among the officers, too. Last night I drew up the schedule for it.

Every Saturday morning, both as Sanitary and Malaria Control Officer, I inspect the area. I rate the tents on neatness, cleanliness, etc. and then type the results and put them on the bulletin board. There really is a hell of a lot of attention paid to housekeeping now that I have started to do so.

This morning I sent a coconut to Tommy. Wednesday I purchased a $25.00 bond for Notre Dame. You probably are

*in the midst of the 3rd bond drive now. We have no regular
drives, like you do, but the whole Army tries to have 100%
bond-buying among the members of the command.*

　　Well, I am fresh out of news, so I'll close.

With Love,

<u>*Fred.*</u>

───────── ➔ ← ─────────

South Pacific

Mon. 10 July 1944

Dear Folks—

　　*It is now 9 P.M. and I need not tell you where I have been.
Tonite it was "Gangway for Tomorrow"*[143] *and only a fair
picture. It was the story of 5 people who drove to work in a
war plant together telling the stories of their lives. Of course
there was a moral to it, and it might briefly be stated: "Back
the Attack!"*

　　*This has been an unusually hot day though last nite was
cool (68°). We all remarked about it and blamed our getting
up late for breakfast on that. It is nice sleeping these cool
nites. I haven't done much this whole day long. This morning
I finished reading another book; this afternoon I spent 2 hours
watching a fellow cut a piece of sheet iron with an acetylene
flame. The roof of our new incinerator cracked yesterday
and as Sanitary Officer I had to see that it was put back into
working order in a hurry, which necessitated the iron sheet,
cut to measurement. There was no ballgame this evening,
which is an unusual occurrence around here. We had a good
game yesterday morning, though we did lose by one run after 2
extra innings.*

　　*Except for being my birthday, yesterday was the usual
Sunday. And being July 9th didn't change it much, either. After
going to 6:30 Mass we had the ballgame, which lasted until
11:30 (it began at 9:30, in case you were wondering). We were
going somewhere—just anywhere away from the area—after
dinner but because it looked like rain, we stayed in and read
and played ping pong instead.*

*Today I received 2 letters from you, plus the airmail
envelopes and an "Eagle." Thanks for the envelopes; this
letter will go into one of them. Eating too much starches and
sugar should be avoided by Pop, but taking plenty of fresh
vegetables is a good thing. We are getting them more regularly
all the time. Some are imported and the rest is raised here in
the Island on regular Army farms. Did you know the Army
has units that do farm work just like there are units that drill
wells?*[144] *Which reminds me that this movie and story idea of
always being about someone in the Air Corps irks me. It gives
the impression that only the Air Corps is doing anything to
win the war. Most of them in that branch of the service talk as
though they thought so, too. Anyway, the poor infantryman is
beginning to get some recognition. A bill recently was before
Congress to increase their pay.*[145] *They deserve it, there is no
doubt about it. They are the boys who really win the victories.*

*Well, the war continues to move along fast and favorably for
our side, doesn't it? We listen to all the newscasts and follow
the battle lines on maps. It is a very interesting thing to do.
The Russian front is the one that moves the fastest. They really
are moving and can't be more than 500 miles from Berlin.*[146]
*Maybe they will get there before the Americans and British do
via the western front. Just so somebody does and before many
more months. That will suit me fine.*

*I had a letter from Vic yesterday. In it Eddy enclosed a
note asking me to write him another V-mail. I did once and I
guess he was pretty proud about the matter. What I will do is
occasionally send each of the children V-mail with drawings
on them. I can't draw myself but don't think I will have much
trouble in finding someone who can. Drawings will go through
the mail all right but I wonder how they will photograph. I
know the best way to find out, which I shall do.*

*You mentioned Louie sending on to Joe that gift watch band.
Now I know it got there, something I had wondered about. Joe
will probably mention it in his next letter. I hope he tells me
more about his work. He has not said very much about it.*

Both the girls mentioned taking the children swimming,

which is a darn good thing. So Barden Brook is still the swimming hole. Where do they go now—up to Crowley's? I remember we used to go there as well as to Heaths, by the railroad trestle. I haven't been swimming much myself these past few days, but plan to go more often while I have the chance.

A directive recently came out that only official photographers were to use cameras here, which means no more picture-taking for me. Therefore you need not try too hard to get film for me. The size is #116, though, in case you do get some. Why don't you have some snapshots taken of yourselves to send me? I really would like some. The latest I have of you were taken home last September.

This has turned out to be a rather long letter, hasn't it? I'll close now.

Love,
Fred

---------- ➔ ⬅ ----------

[V-Mail]

TUES. 11 JULY 1944
South Pacific

Dear Folks—

Today's mail brought me letters from Fr. Liebel, Aileen, Duffy and the "Newsletter." The three of them report everything okay, and the "Newsletter" brought me up to date of the local items. This has been a coolish day and late this afternoon it rained. Again I pretty much loafed away the whole day though I did one good thing this morning. I spent an hour—and half writing a letter to Eddy and Jacqy, and had to postpone the one to P.J. and Jay until tomorrow. Two in one day would be too much. Writing good letters to children is not easy.

The other day I heard from Brady. He was on a troop transport, bound for a battle with the Japs. I think I know where. His wife now is in Olean and deals with Uncle George's store. Ask him about her; maybe you will bump into Mrs. Brady there some time.

Tonite's movie was "Sahara."[147] *I had seen it before but enjoyed it just the same.*

I'll close now.

Love,

Fred

P.S. I will send Johnny in Danbury something. The watch band pins probably will be in soon. I'll let you know when.

———————— →← ————————

[INCOMPLETE]

South Pacific Theatre

Wed. 12 July 1944.

Dear Uncle Paul and Uncle Jay[148]*—*

I am sending you a few pictures of here, from which I hope you will get some ideas of this place. Too bad you aren't here so you could see for yourselves. There are lots of things to see here that you do not have [at] home. Take these coconut trees for example. On this island they are as common as apple trees are back in Eldred. Besides being used as a healthy drink by the natives, the milk of the coconut is used to make face soap. The trees are raised on farms, which are owned by British or Americans, but the work is done by the natives.

A coconut tree is a pretty sight. They grow to be two or three times as high as your house; their trunks are about as big around as an electric-line pole and often just as straight. In fact, they are used for poles. These trees have leaves and branches only at the top, the rest of the trunk being bare. The branches come off the tree top like the spokes of an umbrella— they are on all sides and hang down. Underneath and in between the branches is where the coconuts grow. The tree raises coconuts all year around, but the coconuts all are not the same size at once. Some will be young and small; others will be old and like the one I sent you; and the rest will be in between in size.

Native members
of a labor
battalion.
The man on
the right is
wearing typical
native dress.
Pipe smoking
was common,
Guadalcanal
1944.

When a coconut gets to be a big size it becomes ripe and falls to the ground. Sometimes a strong wind will shake them down even before they are ripe. We have to be careful when we walk under these trees that a coconut does not fall and hit us on the head. That would be a good trick to play on the Japs but don't want it to happen to us, I tell you.

———————— →← ————————

[V-Mail]

> THURS. 13 JULY 1944
> South Pacific

Dear Folks—

We really are getting rain these days. It rained all last night and off and—on all day long. The sky will suddenly cloud up, the wind begins to blow and then a heavy rain will fall furiously for a few minutes. It will stop just as sudden and the sun comes out again.

I had a letter today from Joe, in which he acknowledged receiving my birthday present. He is going to send me a picture of his "Edna." Louie wrote me yesterday. You probably already know what he said, so I'll not repeat.

I received the 4 wristwatch pens. Thanks for them. You sent

2 of each side, all of which I can use. Two of them are being
used already; the other 2 will do for spares. You know, I don't
remember asking for them only that once, about 2 weeks ago.
I probably did before that, too, as I thought of it several times
but never while I was writing to you.

Today was strictly routine, nothing different happening; in
fact nothing at all happened.

Well, until the next time.

Love,
<u>Fred</u>

———————— ➔ ← ————————

[V-Mail]

SUN. 16 JULY 1944
South Pacific

Dear Folks—

Friday morning I finally got to use my fishing tackle. Major
Vermilya, myself, and Mangion[149]—one of our men—went
fishing. The place was nearby and near the mouth of a river
and right around there the scenery was beautiful. For a change
we weren't looking at these eternal palms and tall grass. I and
the Major didn't catch any but Mangion did.

This Mangion is some fellow—I believe I told you about him
before. He is Maltese, his people now live in Tunisia and he
speaks Syrian. He springs it on me every once in a while. He
has worked all over the world for Henry Ford and lived in the
Syrian district of Detroit. He is about 36 years old and speaks
English with an accent. The British want him to join their
Intelligence Service.

Saturday morning we held our usual inspection of the area.
I am our inspecting officer because of my sanitary duties. The
men have taken much better care of their tents since we began
these weekly inspections. Some of them are as clean and neat
as the work of the proverbial Dutch housecleaner.

In the afternoon we had a ball game. I didn't want to play
but as the "Eagles" were short of men, I did. Had a lot of fun
too, though I missed supper.

This morning I went to 6:30 Mass. Eleven o'clock is a bit too late for me. Besides, it usually is uncomfortably hot by then. After Mass and breakfast, I cleaned out my foot locker and then went swimming. The water was quite rough and I didn't stay very long.

We have coined a new phrase around here: "wising off." It means about the same as "popping off" or just plain getting smart. I guess it began during the card game here in the hutment. Practically every noon and in the evening while waiting for movie-time, four of us play cards. Usually it is an Italian game—"Scopa." After the movie we have what I am doing right now: letter-writing. Burt, Berkowsky, and I are at it now. Major Vermilya usually writes his letters in the morning after censoring. I am too tired of reading letters then to begin writing them.

Today I watched the 39th baseball team play a game with a C.B. [Construction Battalion] outfit. The game almost was rained out but the sun shone again and the game went on. The C.B.'s won 5–4, though it was anybody's game until the end.

The movie this evening was "Boston Blackie goes to Hollywood."[150]

Love,
Fred

P.S. Received the second napkin via airmail Friday. Thanks.

———————— ➔← ————————

[V-Mail]

TUES. 18 JULY 1944.
South Pacific.

Dear Folks:—

It is later than I thought so I will postpone until tomorrow the long letter I had planned to write. A couple different things have happened this week, so for a change I can write about something besides softball and movies.

So—now I'll answer the last 2 letters from you.

Thanks for sending that money to Dave Chase in Philly for me. I just had a letter from him, saying he had sent me the package.[151] *The cost was lower than I expected.*

That was nice of Dermott Tuohy[152] *to look up Joe and to take him out. I hadn't even thought of Derm. in a long, long time, though I recall he was in Washington while I was there. He was then on his way South and stopped off to see his aunt.*

Let me know what Mrs. Whittemore's mother says about that corner property. I have an idea what Mr. Marsh will say.[153] *About the safety deposit box—I guess we'll have to keep our bonds in the safe in the store.*

By the time I get out of the Army, I'll have my name on lots of bonds, won't I? You know I now get a $50.00 every month, taken out of my check.

Glad to know you heard from Uncle Mike. He'll probably be writing me one of these days. I hope so anyway.

Must close now.

Love,
Fred.

———— ➔ ← ————

South Pacific
Thurs. 20 July 1944

Dear Folks—

Although this is only midmorning, the sun already is very hot. Yesterday afternoon and evening it rained steadily and last night was a bit coldish, which gives you some idea how changeable the weather is here. This is the winter season and supposedly is rather rainless but that certainly hasn't been the case these past four weeks.

Today is the second anniversary of the activation of our unit. To celebrate the occasion there is to be a little party this evening, at which beer and refreshments will be served. I don't know if the celebration includes more than that or not, but doubt it. The unit came into being at Cp. Barkeley, Texas, and the cadre that formed it came from Cp. Bowie. [154] *Not many of that original few are with us now. In fact, we have had since then quite a turnover of both officers and men. Too, we have had several leave us since being here, all for medical reasons. Most of them are back in the States now and probably should not have been sent overseas in the first place. One bad thing about losing men is that we never know how well the replacement will fit in. So far all of them have gotten along swell. This is a good outfit and everywhere we have been men have tried to transfer to us.*

Nineteen more days and I will have been 2 years in the Army. That time has gone by quickly, especially the last twelve months. We were back in Yuma when I passed my one-year mark. I'd like to know how many more marks I'll see roll around before I get into civilians clothes again.

Monday morning at the hospital across the way was a parade and concert by the Royal New Zealand Air Force Band. [155] *They were pretty good, though I believe I have seen better. Anyway, it was interesting to see how they marched and went through formations. They do it a bit differently than American bands. At the concert they played several popular American pieces.*

That afternoon I went swimming and later played softball. In the evening I took in the movie—per usual. We'd be rather lost here without our ball games and movies. Sunday afternoon I sat in a rain to watch a game. From a spectator at the game—a C.B.—I learned definitely where Bouser Morris's outfit is. It is where I thought.

Tuesday and Wednesday morning from 8 until 11 I attended meetings of the island orientation officers. Some good men talked to us and we got some ideas about running our own orientation programs. One very interesting talk on the development of the Japanese Empire was given by a Hawaiian who had made quite a study of that subject. Tuesday evening was our weekly Orientation hour. I gave a review of that book Louie sent me on the Foreign Policy of the U.S. It is some book.

Original cadre of the 39th Station Hospital celebrate the unit's second anniversary. Jesse Pirtle, who shot the crocodile, is seated second from the left, July 20, 1944, Guadalcanal.

Last nite we stayed in because of the rain and we had an interesting evening on U.S. geography. We tried to see if we could name the 48 states and their capitols. That is much harder to do than a person would think at first. Most of us could name about 45 states easily but the last 2 or 3 gave us trouble. This morning one officer won a ten-dollar bet by writing the names of all the states in less than 10 minutes. He just finished in time.

Yesterday I sent you a package containing some woolen clothes and my bible. I am not using them and am tired of lugging them around. Tomorrow or the next day I will send you—not airmail—another package of pictures and negatives. I will not be sending you any more pictures, or very few at most, for a while as we now are forbidden to use cameras unless we are official Army photographers, which I am not.

A newscast just came over the radio. The war news all is heartening. We especially like the news that the chiefs of the Jap. army and navy have been replaced.[156] *That must mean that Hirohito*[157] *is plenty worried, if it doesn't indicate much more than that, which I do hope it does.*

Mail service is a bit slow again and during the past 3 days I had only one letter (yesterday from Joe, a V-mail). V-mail comes through pretty well during these slack periods. How about my mail to you—does it run low for a few days and then catch up in batches? I still write at least 4 times a week, and if it is V-, usually use more than one page. If I get a multiple V-, they seldom come the same day. Do you receive them that way, too? I figure you must have at least one piece of mail from me practically every day.

Speaking of packages—I believe I have received everything you have sent me except that package in March containing the slippers, and of course the ones you have only recently sent me. The last thing I received was the package of envelopes; before that it was an airmailed napkin.

Wasn't it too bad about the circus fire in Connecticut and the big ammunition explosion in San Francisco?[158]

I have received the last "Eagle" and "Newsletter."

Am enclosing snapshots—of our hospital in the D.T.C.; the occupants of the 3 officers' hutments (2 of ours); one of myself gazing at a bit of sculpturing.

Some of the others may want prints from my negatives that I have sent home; if so, I'll let you know which ones and you can have them printed and forward to me.

Must close now.

> *Love,*
> *Fred.*

P.S. If you have one or can get one readily, please send me a book with the Arabic alphabet

[V-Mail]

SAT. 22 JULY 1944.
South Pacific.

Dear Folks—

This morning Maj. Vermilya and I went fishing. It looked like a good time for it, but when we got to the mouth of the river we found the water very muddy. It must have rained back up in the mountains, but it didn't rain here. Anyway, after fishing for over an hour without a single bite we came home. The rest of the morning was spent in the weekly inspection of the area.

I am back in the souvenir-making business again. This time it is a P-38. P.J. will tell you what kind of airplane it is. I worked all afternoon on it and have finished about half. If I had all the material on hand I believe I could complete it in another afternoon.

This evening was our perennial ballgame. It was a good game, too. You should see the interest shown in them—just like the World Series back home. Tonite we saw a good movie: Claudette Colbert and Fred MacMurray in "No Time for Love."[159] *Those we have seen this week have been pretty good.*

The mailman ignored me today again. Whenever there is anxiety in the Pacific our mail service drops off.[160] *In a day or two I'll probably hit the jackpot.*

Must close now. Will write again tomorrow.

Love,
Fred.

———— ➜ ← ————

[V-Mail]

SUN. 23 JULY 1944.
South Pacific.

Dear Folks—

Being Officer of the Day and not allowed to leave the area, I missed the movie this evening. I console myself with the fact that it is raining. Too bad, too, as there was something special. It is this New Zealand band I saw earlier in the week.[161] *Besides their music-playing, they parade and do comedy dances.*

This afternoon was fairly cool but this morning really was hot. We had a game at 9:30. One of the boys who was playing without a hat and who hadn't eaten breakfast passed out from the heat. He came around okay but I imagine he won't be very frisky for a day or two. He is the second one of our men to do that since being here. The other time was at Mass the first Sunday here.

The mailman was good today. Besides 2 letters from you and 1 from Lou, he brought me my name-bracelet. Thank you very much. It is just what I wanted and makes a good birthday gift. Several of the officers have admired it.

The "Eldred Eagles" aren't doing so well these days so maybe I had better wait until we get a reputation before I send a picture of the team to Mrs. Russell. Really, though, some of our losses were very close games, which we should have won.

In a recent letter Esther Dan said you had sent them our pictures. Schaffner is lucky to be home on leave, though I guess he has done his share. I never met him here; in fact I haven't seen Richardson in quite a while now.

I heard Gino has moved from where he was but I'll write him anyway. It was Eastman who told me.

Eldred really must have gone in big for this last bond drive to sell that much. It hardly seems possible that such a small town could do so well.[162] *How much of that amount was purchased by the Gabriels?*

Who is helping in the store while Jeanette in on her vacation? I noticed a new handwriting in one of your letters— at least I think it was a different one. How is business these days and do you still have trouble in getting stock? I read recently where more and more goods are being released for civilians and that some war factories are getting ready to make their old products again.[163] *That is encouraging and*

*so does the war news continue to be: I follow the battle lines
on maps each day and they do change a lot, especially on the
Russian front.*

    Well, must close now.

Love,
Fred.

———————— ➔ ◆ ————————

[V-Mail]

TUES. 25 JULY 1944.
Somewhere in Guadalcanal.

Dear Folks—

    *As you can see, I now can reveal my location as
Guadalcanal. Yesterday we heard we could name it.*

    This will be a short letter as I want to go to bed early.

    *Am glad you received the box okay. It was on the road quite
a while. You'll be receiving another wooden box and a couple
small cardboard ones too. I told you I got that name bracelet
you sent me. Mail call continues to be a bit lean though I got
a letter yesterday and again today. Am surprised Fr. Liebel
took that money, thinking it came from me. While in Chicago
I sent him ten dollars, which he returned as he didn't want
contributions from servicemen. I am planning on sending him
a souvenir, too.*

    *For once I'll be glad to see payday (5 days away). Buying a
bond and paying 10 dollars towards a radio this month has
me down to my last dollar. Usually I have plenty on hand. That
one dollar will hold me for 5 days.*

    *Yesterday I wrote to Louie and Joe. Tomorrow I will write to
the girls. Am glad everything goes well with you all; the same
holds true for me also.*

    Send me Uncle Mike's address if you have it.

Love,
Fred

[V-Mail]

THURS. 27 JULY 1944
Somewhere in Guadalcanal

Dear Folks—

This has been a pleasant day and the first in some time
without rain. It was not too hot, either. After censoring this
morning, I studied for a couple hours and before I realized it
was time for lunch. This afternoon I watched a hardball game
between the 39th and the outfit to which Eastman belongs. I
didn't see him there. Our team wasn't its usual good self and it
lost 5–1. After supper there was a game here, and the "Eagles"
beat the "Texas Longhorns."

I didn't receive any letters today, but did get that pair of
pajamas from you. Thanks. I am pretty well stocked in them
now. Pajamas are the only thing I use in the line of clothing
that I cannot buy here. If I had known that would be the case I
would have gone aboard the boat with much less luggage than
I did. In my last letter to Louie I told him what I had learned
about preparing for overseas. Usually the people who give
advice about that officially haven't been overseas themselves
and really don't help a lot. Advice from someone who has gone
through it is the thing.

The other day I was appointed our Soldier Voting Officer[164]
and tomorrow am going to a meeting concerning it. The details
probably will be explained to us. The Army really is leaning
over backwards to provide soldiers with an opportunity
to vote and it has set up quite a machinery to care for it.
However, the Army doesn't permit any political activity, etc. by
or to the soldiers.

In a recent "Lake Shore Visitor," I read a silly, illogical and
misleading article on Federal medicine written by a professor
at Villa Maria College.[165] I felt like writing him and telling
him how wrong he was, but I wasn't sure enough of my facts.
Besides, he probably wouldn't be a good thing to do. There is a
sequel article in another issue I received just today. I haven't
read it yet but am interested to see what more he has to say on

the matter. You probably know how I feel about this subject.

Our PX is now taking orders for Christmas presents. I looked through the catalogue. Much of it was toys, candy, magazine subscriptions, and smokers' supplies. I don't think I'll deal through them, so I can postpone my shopping a while. Yet it is something to think about, especially since time moves along so swiftly for us.

Well, must close now. Everything is okay here, and I trust they are with you too.

Love,
Fred.

———— ➜❦ ————

[V-Mail]

FRI. 28 JULY 1944
Somewhere on Guadalcanal

Dear Folks—

We just got back from the movie and in the nick of time. It has started to rain and we left here unprepared for it. I never did like to wear a raincoat. I believe I'd rather get drenched than wear one. They get me as wet as the rain itself would.

This morning the C.O. and I attended a meeting of Soldier Voting officers. They did explain the details and recent changes in regulation concerning it. We in the Army have one advantage over you—we can vote and yet are not subjected to a lot of political talk and propaganda.

This afternoon I went to another ballgame, but I didn't have such a good time. The playing by our team was sloppy, the sun broiling and the thing dragged on and on. We got back here an hour later for supper.

Today received no mail from you but did hear from Duffy and Andy Lasichak. Duff's letter was some 6 weeks getting here, so it really wasn't newsy in the true meaning of the word. Andy said the government had recently surveyed his hospital (he was rejected for service) to see how many residencies they would have available for returning service men. I think

*I'll start thinking about the matter and line up a few good
residencies. Must also now write a couple more letters.*

Love,

Fred.

––––––––––– ➔ ← –––––––––––

[V-Mail]

SUN. 30 JULY 1944

Guadalcanal

Dear Folks—

   *Guess what 2 things I did today! Now I am forgetting one,
since this is Sunday. I went to Mass, watched a ballgame and
just returned from the movie. It was pretty poor ("Doughboys
in Ireland")*[166] *but the game was swell. It was between a
Hawaiian outfit and another team that is perhaps one of the
best in the So. Pacific. The Hawaiians won 3–2. There was a
big crowd there. Everything was just like a game [at] home
except that all the spectators were male and no one was selling
peanuts.*

   *This afternoon our team (39th) had a game. One of our
sergeants was hit with a ball sustaining a possible skull
fracture. I took him to the hospital for x-ray and observation.
He was feeling pretty good when I left him.*

   *Yesterday I heard from Uncle Mike, whose letter was written
about 5 weeks ago. He was awaiting reassignment. I heard
from Joe, too. Today I received a letter from Ester and the
"Alumnus" from you. That particular issue seems to be this
year's yearbook. There was no class news in it, did you notice?*

   *There is a beautiful full moon tonite. It lights up the whole
landscape and there are only a few clouds to shut off the light.*

   *This was another short letter. I am tired and want to get
some sleep.*

Love,

Fred

[V-Mail]

MON. 31 JULY 1944
Somewhere on Guadalcanal

Dear Folks—

Well the mail finally came through today. I received about a dozen letters and papers as well as the package from you containing the shaving soap, electrical plugs and 2 hammers. It made good time. Thanks for it. The hammers aren't just what I wanted but I can use them. I gave the small one away, as I have one like it.

Am glad the package with the shells, etc. got there okay. That was nice the family supported the bond drive so well. I just learned that the interest on those bonds is taxable. Did you know that?

As I told you, if you have trouble finding any of these things I ask for—just skip them. The same applies to the pocket watch. I really don't need it, nor most of the items I requested.

Have written several letters tonite, including Fr. Liebel, who sent me some pictures, and Uncle Mike. Heard from Lorraine today, and from a friend in England, so there are 2 more to answer.

This Gabreski[167] from Oil City who shot down 28 planes is a brother (I believe) of our fraternity brother at Jeff; also N.D. Must close now.

Love,
Fred

———— ➔ ← ————

[V-Mail]

TUES. 1 AUG. 1944
Somewhere in Guadalcanal

Dear Folks—

Was going to write you an airmail on the stationery I received from Vic today but knew I didn't have enough to say to make it worthwhile.

Things same here. I continue to be in excellent health and spirits and manage to keep busy in spite of the fact that I have

*plenty of time on my hands. James Eastman was here today,
the first in a couple of weeks. He wanted the negative of he and
I together, saying his folks saw the picture and liked it. He has
a lot of pictures himself and one of these days I am going to his
place to see them.*

*We had a good orientation hour this afternoon. An outside
speaker discussed "The Rise of the Japanese Empire." It was
very interesting and instructive. This morning we were paid.
I drew a few cents under twenty-five dollars, which is $18.75
less than usual (on account of the extra bond allotment).*

*The weather today was pleasant, much cooler than it has
been of late. It hasn't been raining so much lately, either,
though we will get showers that are heavy but last only a few
minutes.*

Must close now.

Love,
Fred

———————— ➤ ← ————————

Somewhere on Guadalcanal
Thurs. 3 August 1944.

Dear Folks—

*This is another beautiful night. There is a bright full moon
that lights up the earth and the sky but dulls out the stars.
Clouds aren't heavy or plentiful but when one floats across the
moon the stars seem brighter. The skies here really are pretty
on a star-lighted night. Being south of the equator we can see
many stars and constellations that are not visible to you.*

*The movie this evening was pretty good but I am tired of
shows that are filled with music—especially girl singers—and
are about war. I read somewhere that musicals are the most
popular with servicemen but I doubt very much that the same
can be said about war movies.*

*I don't write you airmail very much, do I? This is the
first in some time. I am using the stationery I received from
Vic. Whenever anyone writes that they want to send me
something—what do I want—I usually ask for airmail paper*

and envelopes. Now I have enough on hand to last me months and months. And many of the envelopes are not so good because the heat sealed them.

Air mail continues to be a bit slower than V-mail in reaching us. Incidentally, you might use it more often in writing me, especially for shorter letters.

I had a letter from Lorraine today. She and 3 others just visited in Cincinnati, though it wasn't her regular vacation. She said she hadn't yet decided where to spend it. I don't know if I was supposed to read between the lines on that or not. Lorraine wrote that Uncle Mike is at Camp Van Dorn, Miss.[168]

These past couple days have been quite busy in conjunction with my duties as our Soldier Voting Officer. I am passing out cards that the individual soldiers send back home as an application for a State Absentee ballot. Some of the men seem very desirous to vote; others just aren't interested. The Army is strictly impartial and says no soldier can be compelled to vote.

No, I won't be ashamed to ask you for anything I need, but you are beginning again to put in things I don't ask for. My stock of clothing is getting top heavy once more. Tomorrow I'll go through it again and give away some of my excesses like undershirts and shorts. If that pocket watch you have home— that used one—runs, it will do nicely. I really don't need it as I have two good wristwatches but sometimes I don't feel like wearing them, as when I am working or on a trip into the hills.

Tomorrow I am sending a gift to Fr. Liebel. It wasn't what he wrote he wanted but I think he'll like it. No doubt you will get to see it, maybe soon or maybe not for a month or so. It all depends on whether it goes via airmail or by boat. Sometimes packages go out by boat regardless if the postage [is] paid on them.

A couple of articles, or items, I should say, on the front page of the recent "Eagle" were so well written and free of typographical and other errors, that they stood out. I wondered who wrote them. Has something new been added to the paper's staff? And just for the devil of it—ask Mrs. Russell sometime

*who sponsors those articles that recently have appeared and
which always end up with how precious is good eyesight.*

*Isn't this breakfast birthday party a new-fangled idea?
I don't recall having heard of them before. Yet Mom seems
to have gone to a few these past several weeks. We have
good breakfasts here, though only once a week do we get my
favorite—plain but fresh toast. Then let me put on all the
butter I want. We get French toast and pancakes each three
times weekly. Speaking of butter—we have fresh butter most
all the time now.*

*Tuesday's Orientation lecture was very good. A guest
speaker discussed the "Rise of the Japanese Empire." It was
quite timely and especially well received by us, being in this
theatre.*

*Since being in the Army I have had plenty of experience as
a speaker. I have talked to the men about chemical warfare,
venereal disease and sex, tropical medicine, sanitation, and
a few other things. I wonder sometime if they don't get tired
listening to me sound off.*

Well, I'll close now.

Love,
<u>Fred</u>

——————— ➔ ← ———————

[V-Mail]

FRI. 4 AUG. 1944
Somewhere in Guadalcanal

Dear Folks—

Saw "Moontide"[169] *tonite. It was pretty good. Next Tuesday
we have a treat—Bob Hope*[170] *and troupe in person! Not bad,
huh?*

*Had another good mail today, including your letter of July
26th and the package of paint brushes. Thank you.*

*To answer your questions. I have received 2 pairs of
pajamas and 4 napkins (maybe only 3. I am not sure now).
Anyway packages are coming through in good time.*

Today finally finished handing out the ballot cards. Was that a chore! Not so hard, but monotonous. I had to explain the thing to most of them individually so you see why I am happy it is over.

This P.M. sent fifty dollars ($50.00) to the Jeff Alumni Assn. It can be deducted from my income tax files—remember that when they are figured out for next quarter.

Must close now.

Love,
Fred

———— ➔ ⬅ ————

[V-Mail]

SAT. 5 AUG. 1944
Somewhere in Guadalcanal

Dear Folks—

This has been a strictly routine day all the way through. Up at 6:30, breakfast at 6:45 and censoring of mail for about an hour. After that the C.O. and I inspected the area, which finished up about 11 o'clock. From there until lunch at 11:45 I played ping pong.

I read until about 2, when Burt and I went swimming. The water was rough and dirty so we didn't stay long. Coming back here I cleaned up my area of the hutment and then went to the "early show" at 3:45. I did that so I could see the ball game this evening. After the game I went to Confession and read until we went to the movie about 7. It was very good. Ginger Rogers in "Roxie Hart."[171] I had seen it before but think I enjoyed it more this time.

This is another beautiful evening. A cool breeze is blowing in from the sea, just north of us. The moonlight is bright enough to read by. It was the same early this morning. I got up about 3:30 and the sky was so pretty I stayed up a few minutes to look at it.

Burt, Berkowsky and I are here, writing letters and listening to the radio next door. We do this every evening. Coming back

*from the movie we stop at the "Wreck Hall" for a cold bottle
of beer or a can of fruit juice. Then we come back and write
letters. We still kid Berkowsky about being hen-pecked. He got
sore this evening when someone showed him a cartoon of a
wife leading her husband around on a string and told him it
was he and his wife. He didn't like that.*

*Mail was lean again today. I didn't get any myself but still
have a few to answer that I received earlier this week. I got
another letter and the "Newsletter" from Fr. Liebel. Also one
from Vic and from a nurse in Philly. According to the radio,
there is quite a serious transportation strike there.[172] Hearing
that make the fellows here swear plenty. They'd just love to
have those strikers stationed here for a few weeks and then
they would think twice before leaving their jobs, no matter
what the reason. I myself believe that policy would work well.*

*I am glad I sent that canteen home. An order came out today
prohibiting sending back of any more Jap souvenirs of any
kind.*

*Well, will sign off now. Am fine and happy and trust you are
too.*

Love,

Fred

———————— ➔ ← ————————

[V-Mail]

SUN. 6 AUG. 1944

Somewhere in Guadalcanal

Dear Folks—

*Am O.D. again today, and am staying in this rainy evening
and writing letters. Have written 7 so far. Writing them is one
way to get them in return.*

*Not much to write about again. This has been a regular
ordinary Sunday, lazy and all that. Fortunately it was cool.
Did take a trip down to Service Command this afternoon to see
Capts. Heyde and Parker about their soldier ballots. They were
the last 2 I had to see in the whole outfit. Thank golly that job is
over. I was getting fed up with it.*

*Did a little housecleaning again today, cleaning out my
footlocker and bedroll. Am getting it in pretty good shape now.
Very little junk.*

*It has just started to pour again and I have to go out in the
rain to make rounds.*

Must close now.

Love,
Fred

─────────── ➤ ➤ ───────────

[V-Mail]

WED. 9 AUG. 1944
Somewhere in Guadalcanal

Dear Folks—

*What do you think—the package containing the slippers
and book arrived yesterday. The candy was in good condition,
though some had melted on the shorts, and the slippers are
just right. Thanks for them. I believe the package was lost
because the A.P.D. number was smeared, like it had gotten
wet. It finally reached me via the Army Postal Directory
Service.*

*Last nite I was too tired to write you. I sat for five hours
straight at the show. Boy! was there a mob there to see Bob
Hope! I estimated the crowd at 8,000. It started at 7:30 but
some were there already at 1:30 just to make sure of a seat. By
3:00 the regular benches were filled. Those coming after that
brought their own benches, chairs, boxes, etc. We went over at
4:30, just right after supper. Fortunately, I had a swell seat. No
one could sit or stand in front of me and I could see everything
fine. Besides Bob Hope, there were Frances Langford, Patty
Thomas, Jerry Colonna, Tony Romano (guitarist) and Barney
Dean.[173] Frances Langford sang and Patty Thomas, the other
woman, was the dancer. The show, which lasted about an
hour, was good and I enjoyed it very much. However, I doubt
that I would again wait 3 hours to see it—not in less than a
couple years, at least. Still, I am glad I saw it this time and
would have felt that I missed something if I hadn't. Bob Hope*

is a good comedian. Some of the jokes he told were dirtier than most of us expected.

Today was a fine day again, though the sun was a bit on the too-hot side. This morning I read for a couple hours. This afternoon I played ping pong for a while and then went down to the library at the Service Club. T/4 [Technician Fourth Grade] [Charles W.] Strippy [Jr.], who helps me with Orientation, and Cpl. [Lorenz W.] Winterland went along. We were looking for material for the next week's lecture, which will be on the Electoral College, election of President and other federal office-holders. I thought this subject will be appropriate in view of the coming election. No electioneering understand; the Army absolutely prohibits that.

We saw a good softball game this afternoon. The 39th All-Stars, selected from the 4 teams in our league played the regular 39th team. The All-Stars lost 8–6, though I think they outplayed the other team. 3 or 4 "Eagles," incidentally, play with the All-Stars. These 2 teams are playing a 3-game series, so it is anyone's win yet.

I did something just now that most people never do— reached up and plucked a banana from a stalk. We have it hanging here in the hutment. A couple weeks ago when we bought it from the natives, the fruit was stony hard. They now have ripened almost to the point of being rotten.

Mail service is mixed up again for airmail, though V's get through in good time. The last I received, from Pop and from Danbury, came through in 9 days. Esther [Dan] wrote that Abdo had left that day for the Navy, and that her parents were a bit upset about it. In his letter of the 30th Pop mentioned how much in bonds the family had just purchased; also, that you had sent me the brushes and the watch. The brushes arrived about a week ago. You need not have gotten me a good watch. I wanted only a cheap pocket-watch like you used to get us when we were young. So far I have had good fortune with my wristwatches, though I am very careful of them. Most of our officers who bought these government wristwatches have had trouble with them, mostly due to moisture. In the Desert it was the sand that messed them up. You see, we have had both extremes.

I sent Fr. Liebel his present, a tortoise shell cross inlaid with mother-of-pearl, a few days ago. It isn't big but is very pretty. I hope he likes it. He won't get it for a while as it was too big a package to go airmail. It is about 2 inches high.

It rained most last night, yet by about mid-morning the sun had dried up the ground pretty well. The sun here really comes out strong after a rain.

Lately I have heard from Lorraine, Louie, Joe and Andy Lasichak.

Well, this letter is long enough for one sitting, so I'll close now.

Love,
<u>Fred</u>

———— ✈ ————

Guadalcanal
Fri. 11 Aug. 1944.

Dear Folks—

Remember this stationery?[174] It is some I found today during one of my frequent housecleaning jobs on my foot locker. I have carried it around long enough, I believe, and now will use it up. I have lots of things—stationery, clothes— that I am doing the same with. I am trying to use them up or wear them out and thus get them out of my way.

This has been a comfortable week as regards the weather— not too hot and not much rain. Nights are cool. These past 2 I found that sleeping <u>under</u> my mattress cover was not quite warm enough, so now I sleep in it. That way I am nice and warm.

I didn't go to the movie this evening as I had seen this particular film twice before. Instead Capt. Johnson and I popped some popcorn and drank cold beer. Gosh! it was good. We had a little fresh butter to go with the corn. Johnson likes popcorn as much as I do and we two ate enough for 6 *people. Over in the enlisted men's dayroom we could see 4 of the fellows who hadn't gone to the movie either, so we popped another washbasin-ful and I took it over to them. Boy! How these poor devils went for it.*

Today I got in a few hours reading. I did another thing that made me feel good. I played ping pong with 2 of the best and beat them both. One of them—Maj. Snyder—I especially like to take over. We often play a series of games and he usually wins by one game. Yesterday and today, though, I beat him quite handily, winning 5 games out 6 today.

This evening there was another softball game between the regular 39th team and the 39th All-Stars. This game was different, though, because the Regulars pitcher, an excellent one, pitched for the All-Stars. That was done so the teams would be more evenly matched. They were pretty equal at that, the score being 3–3.

I went swimming this afternoon at the beach of the hospital nearby. While there I saw my Jeff classmate[175] as well as Dr. Leonard of Olean. He is a captain M.C. and knows Uncle George.

The eleven PM war news is just coming over the radio now. It certainly is good, especially about the bombing of the Jap mainland and about the Allied progress in Brittany.[176] The way things are going against them from the east and from the west and from the south and from the air, I don't see how the Germans can hold out much longer. It must be obvious to them too that defeat is coming their way before long.

In his last letter Louie mentioned that he was not being moved, after all. Which is good news or not, as one chooses to look at it. I know he would like to be stationed nearer you. Still it is questionable if he actually could get up to Eldred any oftener. On the other hand, you people could see him by getting on the noon train. You'd be in Harrisburg late the same afternoon.

Incidentally, how did you and the girls get up to Buffalo— train or car? I believe that was the first any of you had been there in several months. Pop and I drove up when I was home last. It was late September or early October. I do not recall which now.

Tomorrow I am O.D. again. Each of us who take turns at it gets it once a week. Of course we have more officers than 7 but only lieutenants and captains are it; those on Detached Service are excused. Being O.D. isn't bad. We are required not to leave the area, to inspect it 3 times (once between midnight and 6 in the morning). I usually make that round about 2 A.M. The funny thing is that I awaken about that time all by myself. I just concentrate on the matter for a couple of minutes before going to bed. I was going to say "before I go to sleep" but I don't think I am awake that long. Usually I am asleep within a minute or 2 after my head hits the pillow. These other fellows can't figure it out.

Yesterday afternoon I and two of the enlisted men (Strippy and Winterland) went down to the Service Club library to browse around and to look up a couple books we were interested in. There is a nice setup there and a nice collection of books.

I have a couple of pictures to send you. They'll be in this letter or in the next airmail.

Will close now.

Love,
<u>Fred.</u>

———————— ✦ ✦ ————————

[V-Mail]

Mon. 14 AUG. 1944
Somewhere in Guadalcanal

Dear Folks—

The lights were off last nite when we got back from the movie. Thus no letter to you. The movie was pretty good, but one I had seen before. Tonite we saw an excellent one "Holy Matrimony," with Gracie Fields and Monty Woolley.[177] The movies these past 2 weeks have been pretty good.

I put in a rather full morning. There were 4 matters I had to attend to "downtown" so after finishing censoring the mail I got a jeep and started out. The places I went were rather far apart but the people I wanted to see were in and things went along smoothly. Still it was lunch time when we got back. This afternoon I read for about 3 hours, played ping pong a while and then showered and got ready for supper. Our meals lately, by the way, have been very good. After supper the Colonel, Burt, Berkowsky, and I played "Scopa" (that Italian card game) until movie time. We play it almost every evening and most morns.

A few minutes ago I had some of Lt. Weisburg's birthday cake. I washed it down with a can of cold tomato juice, my pre-bedtime drink.

Wednesday morning I went to 6:30 Mass as usual. About 9 I went swimming with Wes Burt. The water is very calm in the mornings and it was ideal swimming. The water cool and the air warm. I had lots of fun floating. I can't swim very well but I can float very well.

Yesterday afternoon I read a while and then took a nap. Being O.D. Saturday, I had to make rounds during the nite, which I did at 1:30. Of course that left me a bit tired and sleepy the next day. We get so much shut-eye here that I wonder how we'll act when we get home. The same thing about movies; after seeing them 7 nights a week here, when we get back we'll either be so sick of them, we will never care if we don't see another, or the habit will keep us going.

I have done pretty well about packages lately. Yesterday I received 2 from you (1 was a pair of pajamas; the other contained the steel tape and the measuring stick) and one from Dave Chase, who sent that camera stuff. Today I had a package from Wynette. Our chaplain, who lives in California, told me [that] film and popcorn were quite easy to get there, so I wrote her for some of each. That was about 3 months ago. Unfortunately, they weren't easy at all to find but she sent me 2 films and 2 popcorns. I don't know when we'll be permitted

to use our cameras again, but when we are I'll have about
a dozen rolls of film. James Eastman stopped by Sunday
morning.

Love,
Fred

———— ➔ ← ————

[V-Mail]

WED. 16 AUG. 1944
Somewhere in Guadalcanal

Dear Folks—
This has been a moist, windy afternoon. I believe a rain is
coming up. At least dark clouds are forming to the east and the
wind seems wet. We could use a good rain. There hasn't been
any for several days and the roads are dusty. A little fell early
this morning, but only for a few minutes.
I didn't do so much today. Worked around and then read a
while this morning. After dinner I wrote a couple letters and
read until about three. I had planned to go swimming then but
instead stayed here and played ping pong. I have been doing
that considerably as late. We have a table in our "Wreck" Hall,
as have the enlisted men in theirs.
The outfit hasn't been playing much softball this past week-
and-half (as you probably noticed from my letters). I don't
know why. Perhaps because of a let-down following the high
interest in the championship series a couple weeks ago.
Yesterday was a beautiful day. Even early in the morning
the sun was hot and the air warm. I went swimming about
10, but didn't stay long as the water was rough. Besides I was
the only one around. I don't like to go swimming alone. In the
afternoon the Island Medical Society had a meeting at this
hospital nearby (we are not permitted to mention the names
or number of units here). The meeting was interesting, being a
case history with autopsy reports of one puzzling case they had
there recently. I figure out the diagnosis pretty closely. Gosh! I
am getting rusty medically. Before I even can go into practice

I'll have to go into a hospital for a year or 2. I already have my eye on a couple good residencies. Wish I knew what field I want to go into. That way I could make some really definite plans. No specialty particularly attracts me, while several seem very good. Maybe when I get my hands into real Medicine again a bright light will strike me. One thing I am rather sure of—I don't want to be a lab man or a pathologist. Internal Medicine would be good, as would Surgery or Ear, Eye, Nose and Throat.

I have on hand your letters of Aug. 1 and 4, which I will answer now. I didn't say I was interested in Marsh's building—only the big lot between the store and Mitchell's. I think that would be a nice site for a home. Our store must be much improved by the new lights. I am not kidding, when I say I'd like to see them and soon. Joe writes me occasionally but Louie not so often. So Joe is being moved. I'll be interested to learn where. Wherever it is—I know he will like it and do well and be able to take care of himself, so don't worry about him. If you do worry don't let him know about it. Louie must be kept pretty busy these days.

Just returned from 5:30 Mass, which I usually hear on Wednesday evening.

This evening after the movie I will write Louie and Joe. Also Uncle Mike since you sent me his new address.

Today received the "Eagle" from you, and some more pictures from Fr. Liebel, who also sent me that list of all those from the borough and township in the Service. Really are a flock of us, huh. Incidentally, last week I sent you a picture of the 39th ball team (not my "Eagles"). I prefer that neither Fr. Liebel nor Mrs. Russell make copies of that picture. Someday I may take a picture of the "Eagles" for them—but later.

I notice Papa only takes fifty dollars of my allotment check each month. I thought he wanted a hundred. Tell him to go ahead and take that much if he needs it. And while I think of it, please let me know when the fifty-dollar bonds start coming to you in place of the twenty-five.

*It is nice that papa gets out to the leases often and that he
takes the boys with him. Do you get out Ma? You should while
summer is here. Before you realize it, it will be winter again
and you know what that means. I'd like to bury my face in
snow right now.*

*So Mary Chrisman passed away. I hadn't thought of her in a
long time. I wonder to whom she left her money and property.
Wouldn't it be nice if she left it for a community hospital or
library of something like that.*

Must close now.

Love,
Fred

———————— ➔ ← ————————

[V-Mail]

THURS. 16 [17] AUG. 1944
Somewhere in Guadalcanal

Dear Folks—

*As far as weather goes this has been a comfortable day. As
far as having accomplished much during it, this has not been
very successful. The most good I did was read for 2 or 3 hours.
Lately we have received several good books which interest me.
I am reading a few medical journals too.*

*Tonite we saw a cowboy movie, the first in sometime. For
a while we had them frequently, at least it seemed that way.
Tonite's wasn't too bad.*

*Your letter of July 28th came today. I thought I did mention
receiving the identification bracelet, which got here about 3
weeks ago. I read in the "Eagle" about Herb Geuder again.* [178]
*I do hope he gets home. After being over here that long he
deserves a long furlough. I hear from Joe often and Louie
occasionally. About me wanting you to send me some shorts—
no, no, no!! Please send me nothing I do not specifically ask
for.*

Well, I must close now.

Love,
Fred.

[V-Mail]

FRI. 18 AUG. 1944
Guadalcanal.

Dear Folks—

After a night and morning of heavy rain and drizzle this has turned out a very beautiful evening—the kind that makes a person want to sit on the porch or putter in the garden after supper. I am spending it listening to the radio. Again it is my turn at O.D. so no movie for me tonight. And as long as I have to stay in I will get an early start on my evening's letter-writing.

The mail man was friendly to me today. I got five: from Mom, Pop, Joe and Mrs. Metcalf. Also Duffy. Not bad, huh? Your letter, Mom, again makes me think you are not getting my mail or you are not reading it. Here's why I think so. You ask why I don't write airmail; and you offer to send me another hammer and some stationery. Please don't even think of sending me anything—even a straight pin—unless I specifically ask for it. I know if you get the idea I need something, sure as shooting you will be sending it to me, whether I need it or not. And while I think of it—please do not you send me anything for Christmas and do not let anyone else do so. I have enough stuff here to go into competition with the government in several departments. I do not like to write things like that but if I do not get rid of my reserve stocks somehow, one of these days I will use them for a big bonfire.

About those football tickets from N.D., send them to Joe if he wants them. Otherwise, destroy them. Thanks for the newspaper clipping. I put it on the bulletin board where several had read it. The writer, incidentally, wasn't 100% correct.

For reasons I will explain at a later date, I never planted my garden. That is why I never mentioned it. However, we planted some flowers around our hut that are doing beautifully. This is good growing country, no fooling.

At the Orientation hour Tuesday, we heard a nice discussion on the Philippines by a Filipino chaplain from Chicago. He

hasn't been in this country so very long, and so knew what he
was talking about.

Well, must sign off now.

Love,
<u>Fred</u>

──────── ➔ ← ────────

[V-Mail]

SUN. 3 SEPT. 1944
Guadalcanal.

Dear Folks—

This letter may be a mixed up [one] as a poker game here
in the hutment is distracting me. They wanted me to sit in but
I played cribbage for a couple hours this evening and want to
write a few letters now.

I straightened up my footlocker this morning again. Every
time I do that I arrange it better. Besides doing that I went
down to Service Command with one of the men to buy some
things he couldn't buy here. This afternoon I watched a ball
game here in the area and napped a while. The movie for this
evening did not sound good so I stayed away. Those who went
enjoyed it and said I missed a good one.

Yesterday I went down to Jim Eastman's place to visit him.
He has a lot of interesting pictures and from them I found out
who his family are. I thought his sister was the only one I knew
but I did recognize his mother too. I don't recall having seen
his father before.

Last evening I accompanied Capt. Heyde to a Navy unit to
visit a friend of his. We had supper there and then went down
to the beach to watch the sun set. It was a beautiful sight and
[for] once after all the movies show one thing of the tropical
islands correctly. As I wrote you before, the weather is getting
to be like what it was when we first arrived on this island.
After the sun went down we went over to their officer's club
for a while. It is pretty nice and was fixed up in nautical style.
Afterwards we played cards and listened to the radio until
about 10:30, when Lt. Long,[179] Heyde's friend, drove us home.

We are getting plenty of rain these days. My officer's raincoat leaks a bit now, but I got a new one this morning and in a funny way. Capt. Feit gave me a raincoat he found last nite. It is a new one and fits me even better than my own. So now I am ready for wet weather with the best of them.

Things are the same here. I am feeling just fine and hope this finds you all the same.

Love,
Fred.

———————— ➔ ← ————————

Guadalcanal
Sunday 3 Sept. 1944.

Dear Folks—

Just wrote you a V-mail. Now this airmail to enclose a few snapshots and cards I do not want to have around here anymore. One is my cabin assignment card on the "West Point." Another is my "Neptune Card," a card which all travelers get when they cross the equator for the first time. Ordinarily some little ceremony accompanies that event (crossing the equator) but such revelry is out for the duration. Two others are a postal card and a picture of Eastman and myself. The rest are pictures of a nurse friend and of Ester's three. I just received them several days ago. I am keeping the best one with me. Doesn't P.J. look sad in these pictures? Apparently he wasn't feeling well when these were taken.

Well, I must close now.

Love,
Fred.

[V-Mail—Not Shrunk]

MON. 4 SEPT. 1944
Somewhere in Guadalcanal

Dear Folks—

This has been a pleasant day, nice and cool. The sky was cloudy most of the time and thus the sun didn't get too hot. I have been busy all day long (for a change) and am pretty tired now. However, I wanted to write tonite, for tomorrow I may not be able to.[180]

Today I received letters from you, Ester and Duffy. It is nice that Louie and Joe were home together, even if for only a few hours. So Mama and Joe journeyed to Utica? I hope Mama enjoyed the trip; I know Joe did, and suspected he would be traveling up that way if he got home. Say, Duffy wrote something about Louie being a proud father again. Louie wrote they were expecting in December. Who is wrong here? Is it I?

Yesterday I sent you two letters, a V. and an air-mail containing a few pictures, negatives and cards. Please save them all for me.

Well, I'll close for this time and write again when I can.

Love,
Fred.

P.S. HEARD TODAY THAT ONE OF OUR OLD NURSES, NOW IN ENGLAND, WAS PRETTY BADLY INJURED IN AN AUTO ACCIDENT.

→ ←

3

Angaur Introduction

Letters: September 1944–June 5, 1945

The 39th Station Hospital left Guadalcanal on September 6 aboard the USS *Mormacport*. The unit spent the next thirty-eight days on the vessel, except for brief stops at Tulagi and then Banika in the Russell Islands, where Gabriel made a short visit. During this extended voyage, the *Mormacport* sailed through what Eddy Heyde described as "a first class hurricane." [1] Gabriel presumably wrote the opening letter of this section before the storm, because he makes no reference to it.

The 39th's destination was Angaur, the southernmost island in the Palaus, located at the far western end of the Caroline group, about six hundred miles east of Mindanao. Military planners believed that bases in the Palaus could offer valuable support for US forces advancing toward the Philippines, but others unsuccessfully argued that the islands should be bypassed. On September 17, 1944, elements of the US Army's 81st Division landed on Angaur, "a rough coral rock" two and a half miles long and less than a mile wide, shaped like a pork chop. The Japanese mined phosphate on the island, which contained two artificial lakes and a salt swamp. A garish maze of coral outcroppings and caves covered Angaur, and they provided the Japanese innumerable defensive positions, as did a mix of coconut, coniferous, and broadleaf trees, one of which caused a painful rash similar to poison oak. Although overshadowed by the US Marines' bloody fight

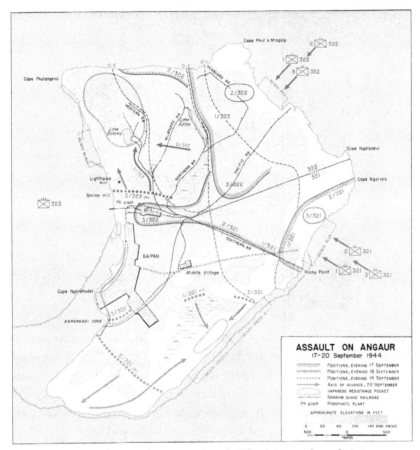

Angaur. Map VII, from Robert Ross Smith, *The Approach to the Philippines*. Washington, DC>Center of Military History United States Army, 1996.

on Peleliu, which lay ten miles north, Angaur was one of only two sites in the Pacific islands campaign where the Japanese inflicted more casualties than they sustained. The other was Iwo Jima. In all, the Americans suffered 2,558 casualties securing the island, which quickly housed four squadrons of B-24s.[2]

Gabriel and the rest of the 39th Station Hospital landed on Angaur at Yellow Beach near Saipan Town on October 13. As they went ashore, the men watched American warships pound Japanese positions on the northwest side of the island. The unit then spent the next eight days waiting for their equipment to be un-

Uroshi "Poison Tar" tree, which caused a painful rash, April 1945, Angaur.

loaded and set up. Finally, on October 21, the 39th became operational when it took over the treatment of the 17th Field Hospital's 373 patients, exchanging tents with that outfit so it could deploy to a new area. Fighting continued on Angaur through October 23, and members of the 39th occasionally heard bullets whistle past their area during their first few days on the island.[3]

The 39th faced harsh conditions during its first months on Angaur, where temperatures ranged from 75 to 94 degrees with high humidity. Most of the unit's facilities and living areas were under tents, which quickly deteriorated, and the men erected "crude improvised screening for the kitchen and operating room." Inadequate latrines and the heavy casualties from the extended combat resulted in swarms of flies inhabiting the island. The widespread use of DDT and other insecticides eventually brought this situation under control, but the difficult conditions remained. A diarrhea epidemic, which lasted through November, debilitated hundreds of soldiers, and it was followed by an extended outbreak of hepatitis. If this was not enough, a powerful typhoon swept through the Palaus from November 6 to 10, heavily damaging the unit's area. The 39th initially lacked adequate bathing facilities for patients, and those who were ambulatory were sent back to their home units for this. By the end of 1944, the 39th had treated nearly two thousand patients, including 144 battle casualties, one of whom died. Other patients included forty-five of the approximately 190 natives on Angaur, and twenty-five Japanese prisoners of war. The unit also operated an outpatient clinic that treated another 2,600 patients during this time. Eddy Heyde recalled this difficult period by writing, "I was anesthetist and psychiatrist. I used to interview my patients by Coleman Lamp at night sometimes. The horrendous stories some of those fellows told!"

The 39th's situation gradually improved. By December, its operating room, X-ray facility, laboratory, and other departments had been relocated into Quonset huts. In March 1945, the unit moved to a new area with a hospital constructed of prefabricated buildings. A truck also regularly delivered water, which allowed for the construction of a shower for patients. The material conditions for the soldiers of the 39th, both officers and enlisted men, also began to improve. The Red Cross maintained a recreation room for both patients and members of the 39th, and the hospital area contained an outdoor movie theater. Unit personnel were also "able to shower for about an hour daily when water is made available to them from the tank on the water truck." Gabriel and the others also welcomed the arrival of refrigerated "fresh food" ships because it meant better meals. As it had on Guadalcanal, the unit again established athletic teams to help maintain the soldiers' morale. Mail call also had a large

39th Station Hospital during the typhoon of November 6–10, 1944, Angaur. Note the two soldiers outside on the right side of the photo.

39th Station Hospital dental clinic after the typhoon, November 7, 1944, Angaur.

impact on morale. Gabriel continued to keep a running account of how many missives he received each day, commenting, "Mailless days do something to a person."[4]

Large gaps exist in Gabriel's letters during the first several months on Angaur. Although his photos captured the island's blasted landscape and the effects of combat, the letters that do survive reveal little of the hardship that he and the other members of the 39th experienced during this period. Whether this was because of censorship, his not wanting to concern his parents, lack of time, or a combination of all three, one gets little sense of the actual conditions, aside from him being extremely busy. He informed his parents that he and his tent mates each did the work of at least two men. His responsibilities included running the 39th's laboratory; supervising his own ward, number 13; and periodically serving as officer of the day. Gabriel welcomed the opportunity to treat patients again, especially after his long period of inactivity on Guadalcanal, and he occasionally commented on them. He noted a patient born with only one kidney, another who suffered from a liver abscess, along with others who had diabetes, tuberculosis, and communicable diseases. Gabriel also took several photos of his ward and patients, including two Angaur natives. In addition to these duties, Gabriel served as the Insect Control Officer, and he conducted a two-day school on this important topic for others stationed on Angaur.

Gabriel also filled his letters with comments on day-to-day life and larger events, such as the death of President Franklin Roosevelt and the end of the war in Europe. Although heartened by the progress in the Pacific, as late as June 1945, Gabriel believed that the war would last much longer. "We here get a laugh from how optimistic you folks home and in Europe are about an early defeat of Japan. Most of us in the Pacific think we know better. ... I believe you will find that another 18 months will be required before the Japs see the light of day." Perhaps the bloody fighting on Angaur and other islands made him less sanguine than he had been on Guadalcanal. Still, this did not prevent him from contemplating his eventual discharge from the army, and he comments on the military's new point system for demobilization announced in May 1945.

Following the securing of the island, the 39th was temporarily assigned to Angaur's permanent garrison, which at times numbered over ten thousand. On April 24, 1945, the unit received orders assigning it to the 10th Army and instructing it to prepare for deployment to a "Forward Area" in early June. On May 20, the unit hospital ceased to function, in preparation for this move. Since January 1, 1,457 patients had been admitted, and the 39th's outpatient clinic saw an additional 8,788, most of whom were members of the US Navy, Marines, Coast Guard, Merchant Marines, and natives who had remained on the island. The unit's annual report summarized its time on Angaur: "The 39th Station Hospital had a very capable staff and rendered excellent medical and surgical service to members of all services based on the island." Further proof of the unit's service came when two of its officers, Major George D. Vermilya and Captain Kersey C. Riter, later received bronze stars for their efforts in maintaining medical services during the first two months on Angaur.[5]

On June 7, 152 enlisted men and eighteen officers of the 39th Station Hospital boarded the USS *Sabik* (AK-121) for their next, and last, assignment. Rather than deploying to a forward area, however, the unit disembarked five days later at Pier Able 6 on Saipan in the Mariana Islands.[6]

[V-Mail]

Somewhere at Sea.

Dear Folks—

As you can see, we are now en route somewhere. Where and when we will get there—I cannot say; in fact I do not know.

We are having a pleasant trip and so far I have not been sick. Here's hoping I stay this way. This ship is not as large as the other I was on but we are more comfortably situated.[7] We mess three times daily and meals are excellent.

I live in a deckhouse with over a dozen other officers, 5 from our unit. The rest all belong to one outfit and are a nice group. They are the biggest men, though, reminding me of a N.D. [Notre Dame] football squad.

When this will be mailed is problematical, as is how often you will hear from me. In any extent, please do not worry about me. I am fine, having fun and tired of doing nothing.

Love,
Fred.

———————— ➔ ← ————————

[INCOMPLETE]

[no date][8]

-2-

will keep me busy for weeks catching up. Too bad I can't do some of that now while I have so much spare time on my hands. I have plenty of spare time, no fooling, and spend several hours a day doing "brink duty,"[9] besides which I get about 10 hours of sleep each nite. I am glad to get in this rest now because maybe later when we get ashore I won't have time for it.

I have learned to play cribbage and play several series of games daily. That game is a sort of fad with the 39th right now. That and bridge, which I am learning now. There are several good bridge players in the outfit and one of them gives 3 of us beginners a 2-hour lesson every afternoon. I am catching on pretty well and should be able to give Joe a run for his money some day. He wrote me he was learning the game too.

By now P.J. must be a regular schoolboy. I wish I could have seen him getting ready to go for the first time. It is a big event for him, and for Ester, too. I remember my first day of school——over 24 years ago. That is a quarter of a century, a whole generation ago. Time really moves along, and more so for me all the time.

Reading continues to occupy my attention for 3 or 4 hours a day. Besides medical journals, I have read a few books from the ship's library. One story I read—for the second time, incidentally—made me feel so sad I didn't finish it. We have that book home—"A Lantern in Her Hand."[10] Funny how it struck me that way. Maybe I am homesick, because it is the story of a family.

I am writing this in the officers' mess, or "ward," as it is referred to here. We have been aboard so long now that we talk like sailors, or Navy men any way.

We say "deck" instead of floor, "forward," "aft," "portside," "starboard," etc.

I have become acquainted with several marines on this voyage, the first I have known very well. The enlisted men as a rule are very young and quite cocky; their officers are about the age of other officers and they, too, have an opinion of themselves that isn't entirely justified. Still when pinned down they will admit the Army and Navy are helping out somewhat to win this war.

Someone just told me that mail is going out tomorrow. If that is true you may get this letter in a week or 10 days.

I'll close now. Don't worry about me.

> *Love,*
> *Fred.*

Pacific Area
Mon. 23 October 1944

Dear Folks—

Missed writing you yesterday. Things continue to keep us rushing around here but we are coming along fine. The people from whom we took over left yesterday and the going is smoother because of it. [11] *They just congested the mess halls, etc. and delayed our moving over into this area.*

The lab is doing better than I expected at this early date. We haven't all the equipment set up; in fact, our present quarters are not big enough for all of it. My medical ward is full and humming. None of the patients are very ill but they require plenty of attention anyways once they get into a bed. However, I have good ward boys and we have things systematized the way we want them, which always helps out plenty.

Today a new medical ward was opened and it was "given" to me, though actually it will be run by another officer who is on Detached Service with us. The type of patients who will go to the new ward are like those who are sent to mine—general medicine.

Inside view of Gabriel's ward 13. Two of his ward men are located in the right center. Patients are seen on the left and right, two of whom are natives reclining.

Having patients is really fun. I enjoy caring for them. Then, too, it is nice to be working again. Loafing is all right if it is taken for short intervals frequently, but 8 months of doing nothing is something else.

I am Medical Officer of the Day today and am now on duty at the Dispensary. The night force[12] *is here now, too, and are making so much noise that I can hardly concentrate on this letter. I now know what the patients mean when they say they cannot sleep at night because of the noise from here.*

Today I had a letter from Uncle Mike, my only mail in 3 days. Mail service is a bit irregular again, as it has been every time there is a campaign on in this area, as you may have noticed. I haven't heard what this evening's radio news is, but the last I heard the Philippine push was ahead of schedule. I knew it was coming up but had heard it was scheduled for a month later than its actual date; I heard November 20th, whereas October 20th was that "D" Day.[13]

Well, I'll close now.

Love,
Fred.

➔ ⬅

Somewhere in the Pacific
Fri. Nov. 3, 1944

Dear Folks—

I feel that I can do better than a V-mail tonite, so here goes this. Besides, I have a bit more time.

I set some kind of a record today. This morning was the third in a row that I went to Mass and received Communion. It was All Saints' Day, then All Souls' Day and today was a First Friday. We go to Mass in a Red Cross building, which is just across the road from the hospital. I have met 2 priests there. One is a blond-haired German Army chaplain; the other is a red-headed Irish Marine. So you see we do have variety.

This has been another pleasant day—not too hot. In fact, a slight breeze has been blowing most of the afternoon and evening. It is blowing into the tent quite noticeably now, and is

"Backyard" of the 39th Station Hospital officers' area, near their original hospital site. Note one of Angaur's lakes in the background, January 1945.

very welcome as it will be good for sleeping. I sleep well on my steel bed and mattress. Not only that but I use a sheet under me.

Only 3 or 4 times since leaving the States have I needed a blanket for cover at night. Usually a mattress cover does me nicely, even when others use 2 blankets. Funny thing but lots of bed covers usually keep me awake. Some nights I cover myself with only a bath towel or the tops of my pajamas and it is sufficient.

I just stopped to watch a 10-inch land crab lumber through the tent. He certainly made a lot of noise, even in the dirt. The way they drag their feet makes one think they are a much larger animal. They are pretty good size at that and not very pleasant to look at, either.

At mail call today I hit a small jackpot—a card from Fr. Liebel, 2 V-mails from Joe and one from a friend in Erie. He is interning at St. Vincent's now and wrote me about the hospital and my friends there. Joe wrote about the hurricane[14] he checked not long ago. I had not read much about it but I gather it was really something. Fr. Liebel sent a picture-postcard of Rock City.[15]

Joe mentioned sending me a book. I am anxious to see what it is. I am anxious, too, to see what you-all are sending me for Christmas. Just like a child, the thought of Christmas packages intrigues me. I'll probably open them right in the post-office tent and not even wait to get back here. I have heard several others say that they too were anxiously awaiting their Christmas packages. I guess—and hope—I never get too old to enjoy getting them.

I am pretty tired this evening. I have been all day long. I was up rather late last night and was called at five this morning to see a patient. It is odd but being up early in the morning like that, even for only a few minutes, affects me more than staying up until then does. I guess I am one of those people who do their soundest sleeping late rather than early.

Well, Heyde is brushing his teeth and fixing his mosquito netting over his bed, so I think I will too.

Love,

Fred.

P.S. Has anyone else mentioned to you the book I did—the one I read on the ship "A SYRIAN YANKEE"?[16]

"Capt. Manny Feit attracts attention of guard while I hustle picture of Jap P.O.W.'s washing their mess gear." November 1945, Angaur.

Wednesday, 6 December 1944

Dear Folks—

This has been one of the coolest days we have had in several weeks. In fact I had to put on a T-shirt under my outer one in order to be warm. To you, this probably would be very warm, but to us it is quite a change from the usual hot day. During the past few days we have quite a bit of rain and overcast skies. Come to think of it, we haven't had a real sunny day this week.

Well, the lab is growing all the time; as was expected of us when we moved into our new quarters. While we were located in the tent we had facilities and room only for routine urine tests and blood counts. But since then we have expanded. Last Tuesday we began doing blood chemistries, yesterday we ran the first blood tests for syphilis and by the end of the week we expect to do bacteriology. Not bad, huh? Now we have a real lab. But there is one fly in the vinegar, or is it ointment—the boys in the lab are overworked as it is, and with all this extra stuff, it will be that much worse. I am trying to get another man or two assigned to us but no luck so far.

Yesterday was a rat-race for me. My ward was torn down to make room for progress and in short notice I had to inventory everything and turn it back in to the Medical Supply Officer. Boy—was he made unhappy by that! "Unhappy" is our word for angry or sore. Incidentally it is my roommate—Lt. Berkowsky. Berkowsky and Captain Heyde, the other tent mate, and I console ourselves with the thought that we are the 3 busiest men in the unit. And that isn't exaggerating much. Each of us is doing enough work for 2 men. Heyde is our anesthetist, psychiatrist, Sanitary Officer and has 3 wards. Berkowsky is in charge of Unit Supply, Medical Supply, Transportation, Utilities and Pharmacy. I have my lab and the ward and am Insect Control Officer.

No mail again today which makes 3 in a row now. However, on the 3rd I received 4 letters—you, Ester, Charley Schaaf in Paris and a fellow in Philly.

Gabriel, Herman
Berkowsky, and
Eddy Heyde,
January 1945,
Angaur.

39th Station Hospital on Angaur, Palau Islands, January 1945. Gabriel's ward, number 13, is on the left end of the tents, and the headquarters are on the right.

Your letter of November 16th I'll answer it now. I do write to
Danbury every time they write me. Only last week I wrote to
Aileen. Thanks, but you need not send me any chewing gum.
Our PX has it occasionally, as does the Red Cross. Incidentally,
the Red Cross takes pretty good care of the hospital and its
patients. No, the shaving brush hasn't arrived yet. I don't know
for sure where Louie is, either, but I think he is in France or
Holland. [17] *About the flashlight, I just drew one from Supply*
last week.

   Well, I'll close now.

   In a few days I'll request a few items from you.

                              Love,
                              Fred.

────────── ➔ ← ──────────

                              Sunday, 10 Dec. 1944.
Dear Folks—

   Well, the mail did come in today and I got 10 letters and
2 "Eagles," all of which made me very happy. Even 1 letter
would have made me feel good after a whole week of hearing
"nothing for you today, Captain." Among the letters were 4
from you (Nov. 9 and 21 airmail; Nov. 23 and 26, v mail). I'll
try to answer them all here at once.

   I am glad to learn from the earliest of these 4 letters that you
are hearing from me regularly (I believe in subsequent letters
I learned that didn't last very long) and that all the packages I
sent you arrived okay. I was wondering about that very thing
just this morning. Donny Frisbee's [18] *address makes it seem*
unlikely that we'll get together—at least not unless one of us
does a lot of moving. In another letter I did explain to you why
you need not send me a flashlight—I already have two.

   I am sorry I haven't mentioned it before, but the "Eagle"
you airmail me arrive regularly and in good time. Back on
the "Canal" I was getting them in 7–10 days. Both those that
arrived today were airmail; one was just 1 month old (Nov.
10) and the other was a week younger. After mail gets coming

through a little better, I don't doubt but what I'll hear of the local goings-on almost as someone outside the county does.

I certainly was sorry to hear about James Moses' accident, and am awfully anxious to hear how he is making out. Jim is a very nice fellow, and I do trust he comes along fine.

So Joe Bush is going to open a dry-cleaning plant in Eldred? Well, I don't think the borough alone will support them, but I do believe that a good plant, doing good work and giving good service will draw a paying volume of business from the borough and the territory surrounding. The problem of gasoline and deliveries might give them a little trouble right now. I haven't seen Joe in a long time, and I don't recall just when now. I believe it was shortly before I came into the Army. And I haven't seen his brother—Lulu, I believe—since he married and that was years and years ago. At least, so it seems.

What you said about women carpenters and how they probably will polish every nail they drive amused me—And it reminds me of a remark someone made this week. We were uncrating the incubator out in front of the lab here and what a job that was! The crate and its nails must have weighed over 200 pounds. Some of the boards had at least 1 nail every 2 inches. One fellow watching us sweat it out said, "I'll bet some of the damned women defense workers put that thing together. Who else would waste all those nails?"

It was nice that Papa could stop off at Sayre and see Martha and Tommy. From all I hear, Tommy must be a big boy now. The last pictures I saw of him showed that he has grown a lot.

Another of the letters of today was from Joe. I don't recall very much what he said, except that all was well with him. I was so excited about all my mail that I read them all hurriedly and poorly. I guess the whole hospital was excited after mail call. Getting or not getting mail makes a big difference to a fellow over here.

Gee, this is a long letter, isn't it? I meant to tell you about a little trip I took today, too, but will hold that off for tomorrow or the next day. Things are slowing down a bit now and I will have a little more time to write you.

Love,

Fred.

P.S. Also heard from Vic and Fr. Liebel; also got the "Newsletter." He has me wrong about this Philippine fracas.

———————— ✦✦ ————————

[V-Mail]

Sunday, 17 December 1944

Dear Folks—

    This has been a beautiful day—but so hot that it could not be enjoyed much. There weren't many clouds in the sky, nor much breeze and so you can see why the sun seemed to be bearing down directly upon us. This would have been a good day for doing nothing. However, being my day as O.D. I couldn't get away that easily.

    I saw a good movie last night. Teresa Wright and Gary Cooper in "Casanova Brown." [19] It was quite good. I don't know if it is a new picture or not, but I never heard of it before.

39th Station Hospital movie area, January 1945, Angaur.

*That was the second movie I saw this week. Earlier Berkowsky
and I went to a nearby Marine outfit to see "Doughgirls."[20] I
believe I wrote you about it, what a crazy picture it was. We
have movies right here in the Hospital area two or three times
a week. However, they are held outdoors (so are all the others,
for that matter) and the sound effects are not so good. As I
look back on it, the movie we attended every nite back on the
"Canal" was a good one: it was a 35-mm machine (double).
The acoustics weren't bad and it was only a stone's throw from
our area. Come to think of it. Guadalcanal in many ways was
not such a bad place after all.*

Love,
Fred.

————— ➔ ◄ —————

[V-Mail]

Tues. 19 Dec. 1944

Dear Folks—
   *Well, I have been quite a playboy today. This afternoon I ate
early chow and went to a softball game. And after that I went
to a movie.*

A sand-bagged ward tent, 39th Station Hospital, January 1945, Angaur.

A league has been started here and the 39th has a team in it. So far (3 games) we are undefeated. Their playing again will help me two-fold 1) amusement 2) give me something to write about. The game today was good, incidentally, but was played on a rough field.

The movie wasn't so good but it was funny in spots. And there was a couple of shorts and a "community sing" thrown in; so I got my money's worth.

No mail today, but otherwise this hasn't been such a bad day. I was quite busy in the ward, having a full house now. I like to keep at least one bed open for emergencies, etc. but even that is occupied.

The sun wasn't so hot and the weather was quite comfortable this afternoon.

Well, until tomorrow.

> *Love,*
> *Fred.*

———————— →← ————————

[V-Mail]

Christmas Day 1944

Dear Folks—

Well, thus passed my 3rd Christmas in the Army, and I cannot say it was an unpleasant one. On the other hand, I rather enjoyed it, though I have been very busy from 7 this morning until now: 11 PM. The day was warm and sunny and things went off smoothly, including a good mail call. The only disappointing thing has been that I didn't write you a nice long letter, as I had planned. But just the same—my thoughts were with you all the day long. I kept thinking how lucky we children were to have such good parents and how big a time you always made Christmas for us. I believe that is one big reason why Christmas will always be my favorite season. And if I ever marry—I probably should say "when" instead—and have children, I am going to make it a big event for them, too, like you did for us.

We didn't have fresh turkey for dinner—ours came out of a can, but it was good anyway. And we had most of the things— including the spirit—that made a real American holiday.

Love,
Fred.

———— ➔ ← ————

[V-Mail]

1 January 1945.

Dear Folks—

This New Year's Day really has been a scorcher. Being O.D. yesterday, I had this afternoon off. Spent it—part of it, anyway—writing letters and cleaning up the tent. The rest of it I spent riding around the Island. About 3 o'clock I met the Chaplain, who has a jeep. I asked him if he was going anywhere. He said that he wasn't, but that he would take me for a ride if I wanted. And so it began.

No mail today, but hear there will be some for us tomorrow. Do hope I get some of it.

Had an easy morning, taking off at 11 to go to Mass. Until tomorrow.

Love,
Fred.

HOW IS MY INCOME TAX DOING?

———— ➔ ← ————

[V-Mail]

Tues. 23 Jan. 1945

Dear Folks—

I began this on a typewriter but I will finish it by hand.

This has been another swell day—the work was light, the weather fine and everything went smoothly. The only fly in the ointment is that our food is a bit on the weak side. Even that will be remedied, as I hear another "fresh food" ship is being unloaded now.

Your letter of the 13th was one of 3 I got today. So Uncle Mike and Celia [Cecelia] finally did it—well more power to them. I am anxious to read all about the wedding. That is too bad about Joe Kunkel and good news about Dar Feheley.[21] Too bad, too, about Frohnapple's toilet; I trust Harry fixed it okay.

Well, until tomorrow.

Love,
Fred

———————— ✦ ————————

[V-Mail]

WED. 24 JAN. 1945
Somewhere in the Palaus.

Dear Folks—

I sat through a few minutes rain this evening to see the end of the movie (Judy Garland and Mickey Rooney in "Strike Up the Band").[22] It was pretty good, and one of the best we have seen here in some time.

Say, how are Aunt Maggie, Uncle George, Peggy, etc.? You haven't mentioned them in some time. I trust they all are well. How is Tommy making out with the draft? I presume Johnny is still in the army band.

Today was another light day. It is fun not having much to do but sometimes I find myself wondering how to spend the time. Of course I don't have to think very hard to recall something that should be taken care of.

I am feeling fine and hope this finds you all the same. Be sure you take care of yourselves.

Isn't the war news good to listen to these days?

Love,
Fred.

[V-Mail]

THUR. 25 JAN. 1945
Somewhere in the Palaus.

Dear Folks—

Haven't much to write about this time, so I feel justified in using this V-mail.

We were somewhat busier today but still were not rushed. I was called out of the movie this evening (I am O.D.) but it was a third-rater, so I don't mind.

Our meals jumped today—steak, fresh potatoes and butter. What a treat! I ate enough for 2 people. I guess we all overdid it a bit, but it was a swell dinner.

No mail again today: better luck tomorrow. I suppose I should not expect mail every day. We did have a lot of it for those 3 or 4 days and even at that I believe some of the officers still expected more Christmas packages.

Well, must close now.

Love,
Fred.

———— ➤ ← ————

[V-Mail]

FRI. 26 Jan. 1945
Somewhere in the Palaus.

Dear Folks—

No mail from you in 3 days now, so tomorrow should be a different story. I hope so anyway. Mailless days do something to a person. I try not to let it bother me much because I know you write often and besides you have plenty of other things to do.

This has been another "ordinary" day. There was a heavy rain for a while this morning but afterwards the sun came out hot and heavy. Work is still on the light side but I am not complaining about it at all.

*I listened to the 6 o'clock news this evening and things
really are going our way in the Philippines aren't they? I didn't
hear about the goings-on in Europe but I heard the Russians
are less than 150 miles from Berlin.*[23] *At that rate, Germany
can't stay in the war much longer.*

*I had 2 letters today—from Jim Eastman and my classmate
Andy Lasichak.*

Love,
Fred.

———————— →← ————————

[V-Mail]

Fri. Jan. 26. 1945
Somewhere in the Palaus.

Dear Folks—

*When you make up my next package please include a couple
of cellophane covers for pictures, passports, cards, etc. that
are carried in wallets. Darn if I can think of the name of them
now, but you'll know what they are. I'd prefer the folding type,
and there is no hurry for them.*

*We must carry our identification card on us and I notice the
cellophane envelope or jacket, or whatever it is, I enclose it in
is wearing out. Here's how the thing I want looks unfolded.
[drawing of a trifold]*

Love,
Fred.

[INCOMPLETE]
[V-Mail]

MON. 29 JAN. 1945.
Somewhere in the Palaus.

Dear Folks—

In case my letter of yesterday worried you—I am fine
today. It must have been a hangover, alright, although several
in the outfit are complaining of slight reaction from that
immunization shot of a few days ago.

A "fresh-food" ship came here recently and our meals are
much better. Sunday morning we had fried eggs and real "live"
oranges. Yesterday noon we had a turkey dinner good enough
to make me think I was home. This morning we again had
fried eggs and fresh apples, so you see we are doing okay.

Today received 2 packages from you. One was the Kleenex;
the other contained the fruit cake and nuts. Thanks for
everything. A whole load of packages came in, which must
about finish off our Christmas mail.

Our PX recently received a good stock of fruit juices,
pretzels, potato chips, candy, cookies, stationery, cigars, etc.,
so there isn't much chance of our going hungry, is there?

———————— ➤ ❮ ————————

[V-Mail]

THURS. 1 FEB. 1945.
Somewhere in the Palaus.

Dear Folks—

I just returned from the movie, and feel a bit disappointed.
It was not nearly as good as I had heard it was. Or maybe I
had expected too much. The ballgame I saw this afternoon was
a let-down too, as the Hospital team lost its first game (in 12
games). At that, they are leading the league.

Took a few minutes off today and went down and looked
over the new hospital area. It will be real pretty when all
fixed-up, and will be as big as this present one is crowded. It

will be in a grove of coconut palms. Incidentally, I am taking a few pictures of the lab, the wards, etc. and will pass them on to you as soon as possible.

Today had a letter from Brady. He is up around [censored] somewhere (I think) and has figured out correctly my location. His wife and daughter are in Olean.

No mail from you today, but yesterday there were two letters (19th and 17th), so you see how good the mail service is. Did I tell you I just had a letter from Louie, a V-mail, that got to me in only 21 days? He mentioned hearing from you people regularly.

The war news certainly is good. By the way they are going, both Germany and Japan must see that very evident handwriting on the wall. I hope it sells the date to surrender and that it is very, very soon.

Love,
<u>Fred.</u>

P.S. THE BEDROOM SLIPPERS YOU SENT WILL DO NICELY.

———————— →← ————————

[V-Mail]

FRI. 2 FEB. 1945.
Somewhere in the Palaus.

Dear Folks—

Received 3 airmails this morning—the "Eagle," a letter from Vic, and a letter from you in which was enclosed the card of thumbtacks. Thanks a lot. Vic's letter was a long one and she told me all about Uncle Mike's wedding, something I had been wanting to know. Apparently the wedding was pretty and the breakfast afterwards was very nice too. Wouldn't I really have liked to have been there? Oh boy!

This afternoon rode around the island with the island surgeon, collecting samples from all the water points so we could analyze them in the lab. This island has changed a lot

Terrain near one of the beaches on Angaur. Note the blasted trees and rugged terrain, December 1944.

since we have been here. Grass and vegetation are beginning to grow back improving the looks a lot and covering-up a lot of the battle scars.

Well, until tomorrow.

Love,
Fred.

P.S. DOES THIS PEN WRITE TOO FINE FOR V-MAIL?

———— ➔ ← ————

[V-Mail]

Somewhere in the Palaus.
2 February 1945. Friday

VALENTINE
GREETINGS
Fred.
[Huge hand-drawn heart with arrow through it].

[V-Mail]

WED. 7 FEB. 1945.

Somewhere in the Palaus.

Dear Folks—

Just returned from the movie. It played the Notre Dame "VICTORY MARCH" quite a bit; otherwise it wasn't so good. [24]

This has been a pretty fair day, cooler than yesterday by a lot. We held Ward Rounds this morning, and had turkey for supper. Today we had some-thing new—Coca Cola. Each man was allowed to buy 12. I don't care much for it—especially when it is warm—so I gave mine to my patients. My ward is less than half-full now, which isn't good in lots of ways. I am afraid they might close it down, which I wouldn't like. I do not want to get away from caring for patients if I can help it.

No mail from you today, but did receive one from Danbury. All is well there, though they are worried because they think Albert has been sent abroad.

Until tomorrow, then.

Love,

Fred.

——————— ➔ ← ———————

V-Mail]

8 FEB. 1945.

Somewhere in the Palaus.

Dear Folks—

I know I should write you air mail more often but it is much easier for me to use this form. And I know that as long as you hear from me you don't care what it is.

Just returned from the movie. It was a ghost story but different. It was impossible, of course, yet was done so nicely that it did not insult the intelligence of the people who saw it, like so many movies do.

Today received a package from you containing the 2 calendars. They are nice and will come in handy. Thanks. Also had a letter from you, which reminds me—you occasionally write something that makes me believe you mix me up with someone else or that I ask you for things and then forget about it. For instance, you say you will send me ink as soon as you get the rubber bands. I don't recall asking for rubber bands or are they something you will use to wrap the ink in? No kidding. I have so darn much stuff that I haven't room for even an extra pair of socks.

I was just thinking that all the days seem alike here and holidays and anniversaries pass unnoticed more often than they are remembered. I don't know how many birthdays I have slipped up on. Can't do much about them, anyway, as long as I am marooned here.

Just heard tonight that 2 of our officers are being sent back because they have ulcers of the stomach.[25] I really hate to see them go, as both were real swell fellows and nice to work with.

Am anxious to get Uncle Mike's new address so I can write them. Heard he was going to Texas; also heard to Louisiana. Anyway, it will be a warm climate.

Business here in the Lab is picking up; that on the ward is still slow.

Love,
Fred.

———————— ➜ ⬅ ————————

[V-Mail]

MON. 12 FEB. 1945.
Somewhere in the Palaus.

Dear Folks—

Christmas packages still are coming in, and yesterday I got 2. One was from you. The other was from Vic. In your package was popcorn, candy, olive-oil, the book. Thanks very much for everything. I know what trouble you put yourselves to, getting ready and sending packages to me.

This is Lincoln's birthday, but it was not celebrated very much here. Naturally, it would not be. One day here is pretty much like any other.

Supper tonite was good—roast pork, apple sauce, swell gravy and spinach. Of course I don't eat spinach. Our meals have been exceptionally good this week.

This evening we officers played another soft-ball game. We lost, but we had fun. The weather was ideal for playing, too, which helped a lot.

Today received some pictures of snow scenes back home from Fr. Liebel, which even in pictures made me shiver a bit. Also received Pop's typewritten letter of Jan. 21st, in which was the inventory figures. You two (Mom must have had her share of the credit) certainly have done wonderfully well. I hope I do half that good.

I can imagine that it is difficult to get away for a short vacation. Why not do it the way I saw Germans do it in a movie—look at pictures of where you would like to be and imagine you are there, having fun. Or else, close the store a little early and read some good magazines and books during the evening.

Want to write Joe yet tonite, so will close now with

Love,
Fred.

———————— ➔ ← ————————

[V-Mail]

WED. 14 FEB. 1945.
Somewhere in the Palaus.

Dear Folks—

I believe I am correct in believing this is Ash Wednesday as well as St. Valentine's Day. I got up too late this morning to go to early Mass and could not go later as I was O.D. and am not supposed to leave the area. Besides that, I was busy much of the day.

Hard to believe, isn't it, that another Lent has started? Wonder where I will be a year from now and what changes will have occurred. Sincerely hope the beginning of Lent finds me home and the war over. The way the news sounded tonite

the end must be somewhere in sight for both Germany and
Japan. Hope their eye-sight is good.
   On mail call today—none from you.

Love,
Fred.

——————— ➤ ← ———————

[V-Mail]

THURS. 15 FEB. '45
Somewhere in the Palau

Dear Folks—

   Today received letters from you and from Joe. Both were
dated January 28. They were the first mail for me in 3 days,
incidentally. Glad to know all is well with you and that the
weather is a little less cold. Also am glad to learn that my
bonds and allotment checks are reaching you regularly. Am
glad Pop has decided to spend no more money on real estate.
Hope he sticks to that decision. It is nice to know that you had
word from Louie. My last letter was some time ago.

   Joe mentioned that he has a furlough coming up in a few
weeks. Good for him—he has been working hard and hasn't
been home in quite a spell now. He said his present status
there is confused. I feel he would be wise just to sit back and
let things happen as they will.

I weighed today—138# stripped, my usual weight.
Until tomorrow.

Love,
Fred.

——————— ➤ ← ———————

Somewhere in the Palaus.
Tues. 20 February 1945.

Dear Folks—

   I ate so much for supper tonite that I believe I could fall
asleep right here at my desk. It was a swell meal—fresh fish
(haddock), fresh potatoes, fresh butter, vinegar beets, fresh

celery, coleslaw, apple pie and cheese. That "fresh-food" ship
I wrote you about did get here, you see. Can you blame me for
stuffing myself when a meal like that comes along? We did
pretty well yesterday, too—fresh eggs for breakfast and fresh
turkey for supper. We get so damn much canned foods that I
get a big kick out of the word "fresh."

Remember me writing that my ward had several empty
beds? Well, I was the O.D. yesterday and I fixed that up a bit.
I admitted 4 medical patients and I sent them all to myself.
When we were busy 4 patients coming in at once was nothing
on the ward, but taking care of them today was more work
than I have done along that line in a week and it did tire
me plenty. Gave me that big appetite also. Doing 4 complete
histories and physical examinations is no easy job.

Which reminds me–you never said anything about my
mentioning a man from Smethport,[26] who was a patient here. I
just heard yesterday that he was in Hawaii in a hospital.

In his last letter, Joe described a funny haircut he had
just gotten. The barber who did it must be a brother of our
barber because he has some poor workmanship of his [own]
running around our area. He cut my hair last week but before
he started I told him I was in no hurry and hoped he wasn't
either. He knew what I meant, all right, and gave me a good
cut, which is something many of his customers cannot say.

I am a little stiff and sore in the back and legs from
yesterday's game. It takes something like that to make me
realize how run down we are physically, so to speak. Back
on the Canal we played volleyball and softball quite a bit and
kept in trim. We hope to devote more time to athletics when
we get to our new area. Incidentally, I hear we are to start
moving shortly after the first. Moving the ward won't be too
bad but moving the lab equipment is going to take a lot of time.
I imagine the trucks we have will be plenty busy for a time.

Mail call is a bit slim again; and today was the 3rd. straight
one for me with nothing handed my way at the post-office.
Hope I get a big handful tomorrow. Funny how mail and

the thought of it influences our lives here. Mail call is about
10 o'clock, which breaks up the morning nicely, both the
expectation beforehand and then the reading of it afterwards.
Mornings here go by very fast and I believe it is for that reason
alone. But, boy, how the whole day drags when there is no
mail! But I should not complain. I believe I receive as much
mail as any of the officers.

Louie hasn't written me in 3 weeks now but I realize he has
not too much time to devote to it. Probably writing to Martha
regularly is about all he has time for. Joe writes about twice
every three weeks.

A couple of days ago I enclosed several snapshots in my
letter. Here are 3 more. I trust they give you some idea of life
here and that you can see for yourselves that things are not too
rough.

Love,
Fred.

P.S. Did you or did you not receive a money order for one
hundred dollars from me about the middle of last August? I am
still saving the stub and want to get rid of it.

You never mentioned receiving a pair of wooden elephants I
sent you from Guadalcanal, either. [27]

F.

———— ➔ ⬅ ————

[V-Mail]

WED. 21 FEB. 1945
Somewhere in the Palaus.

Dear Folks—

Had a swell mail call today—7 letters including 3 from you,
one from Vic and the "Newsletter." Your letters were of the 4th,
5th, and 7th, and they made good time getting here, besides
bringing me up to date on the latest Eldred goings-on. In the
other 2 pieces of mail I received were the "Eagle" and a snow-
scene picture from Fr. Liebel.

Winter scene near Eldred from Fr. Charles Liebel.
Note the war bonds sign.

Thanks again for offering to send me some things, but really
there is nothing special I need right now. My needs are simple
and few, and aside from a little food now and then, I am pretty
well taken care of. Our meals are better of late and besides,
food doesn't keep well out here. That is why I asked for tinned
foods. In the next package you might send me a jar of mustard
and some sandwich cheese or sandwich spread. But please
don't send them too often or too much. HAD A LETTER FROM
LOUIE TODAY. WRITTEN THE 24TH.

I didn't know until recently that Peggy's husband was in the
service and I wondered how Tommy was making it with the
Draft board. And while I think of it—I had never written them
because I never have received a letter from them. I realize they
are busy but I also know they see you often enough to know
how I am doing.

Thanks for the calendar from Fr. Chemaly.[28] I will keep it
right on my desk. Incidentally, I will try to get you a picture
of me at the desk. The store calendars you sent me arrived

several days ago. They are pretty (I cut off the advertising part) and I have them both in use in the lab.

About the READERS' DIGEST—Martha and Lou gave me a subscription for Christmas. We are swamped with magazines here and I seldom read them anymore, at least not like I used to.

That is surprising news about Joe going to school in N.J. I will be anxious to hear more about it.

Until tomorrow, then.

Love,
Fred.

——————— ➔ ← ———————

[V-Mail]

FRI. 23 FEB. 1945
Somewhere in the Palaus.

Dear Folks—

Just returned from a vaudeville show put on by soldiers, and it was very good. The orchestra was exceptionally good and so were the singers. And they had some real funny gags.

This has been a rather busy day for me. My ward is filling up again and I have a few interesting cases. While I was away this evening a boy with tuberculosis was admitted. I haven't taken care of one of those in a long time. I also am caring for diabetes, another thing I haven't had in months and months.

The mailman was pretty good to me yesterday but today not so much so. However, I did receive a pretty valentine from my Uncles Paulie, Johnny and Jimmy of whom I am very proud. I sent them valentines, too. I do hope they received them.

I have a few more pictures to send home, so probably will be doing that shortly.

Love,
Fred.

Somewhere in the Palaus
Sat. 24 Feb. 1945.

Dear Folks—

This has been a windy, windy day—not hard, but steady all day long. And with it comes the dust. You know this "rock," commonly referred to as an island, is all coral. Hence dust and dirt are its middle name, and they really have been blown around today. The wards, the different departments and clinics, etc. are hard to keep clean because of the dust.

Enclosed are a few more snapshots. I'll send you them from time to time. Which reminds me—pictures of this island will be mailed you from Rochester, N.Y. in a few weeks. I ordered some from a stranger who lives in Olean, no less. I was telling him where to send them and he looked up so surprised when I said Eldred, and said "don't tell me you are from Eldred, Penna!" He lives on First Street and knows Uncle George. These pictures from him are various scenes about this island. Don't get the idea that all the rough and rocky stuff shown in the result of fighting, as it is not. Much of the place is naturally that way.

Today had a V-mail from Martha, thanking me for the gift I sent Tommy at Christmas. She seemed quite pleased with it and also mentioned how nicely Donnie was getting along. That was the first I had heard from her in some time. Say, what did I send Tommy?

Thanks for the cellophane jacket, which Pop enclosed in a letter of the 11th. Paulie looks sweet even from the back in that picture, doesn't he? I'll never forget that weekend in Chicago.

I know where this Dorrion[29] *boy is located and will look him up if I get a chance (which isn't likely)—it isn't far away by air. Is his mother a Rew girl?*[30]

Thanks for the things you are sending for my desk. I had a stapling machine, but it got rusty.

So Abdo is in England? I rather expected he would be there one of these days. I am anxious to learn more about this school

Four soldiers explore the caves and coral formations on
Angaur, January 1945.

Joe is going to. I'll no doubt be hearing from him one of these days. He writes quite often.

I have shown Fr. Liebel's snow scene to several people and invariably they ask what that white stuff is. When I tell them they say "Snow? What's snow?"

Well, I will close now.

Love,
Fred.

──────── ➜ ← ────────

[V-Mail]

WED. 28 FEB. 1945
Somewhere in the Palaus.

Dear Folks—

Here is the last of the month already. Time is passing unbelievably fast, a thing that is rather frightening to think about.

Just returned from the movie: "KEYS of THE KINGDOM."[31] *It was good but heavy, if you know what I mean. It was about a Catholic missionary.*

Those 2 of our officers were evacuated today. They both rather hated to leave, and we all hated for them to leave. Anyway, they'll be back in the States. I believe, though, that I would rather stay here a while longer than go back because of [an] ulcer.

This was to be my afternoon off, but I was busy anyway with monthly inventory, reports, etc.

Well, tomorrow is another day and another month. No mail now for 3 days.

Love,
Fred.

Somewhere in the Palaus.
Thurs. 1 March 1945.

Dear Folks—

*Just returned from the movie a few minutes ago. It was
pretty punk but fortunately did not last long. I couldn't have
sat through another reel. The movies here, incidentally, take
me back to my childhood, as the audience sits in darkness
while reels are switched by hand like they were way back
when Frank Slavin ran the Eldred show.*

*This has been a rather busy day for me. I worked but a short
time in the ward this evening and then put in the rest of the
time in the lab. This afternoon I was running the Receiving
Office as well as holding Medical Clinic. Being busy does make
time go very quickly.*

*The wind has blown more-or-less continuously all day
long though not very hard. But last nite—for a few minutes
I expected the tent to be blown away. As it was, it just about
toppled over and was it dusty in there. My mattress cover was
just plastered.*

*Today was the 4th straight mailless day. One of these
mornings the mailman is going to say "yes" to me instead of
just shaking his head. One thing I have done during this past
week is catch up on writing letters. You see I wrote 2 or 3 every
evening, regardless of whether receiving any or not.*

*The picture of Ester's 3 boys is very nice. I have shown it
around and everyone comments on that. Getting them to pose
that way was something in itself. Paulie seems to be much
taller than when I last saw him, and Johnny and Jimmy are
no longer babies. I do hope they aren't too grown up by the
time I get back, as I'd like to enjoy them as infants for a while.
To paraphrase, Mom—there is no use being an uncle if I can't
get some pleasure out of it.*

Am enclosing 4 more snapshots.

Love,
Fred.

P.S. Just smelled some popcorn, so am tracking it down

Somewhere in the Palaus.
Fri. 2 March 1945.

Dear Folks:—

Well, the mail finally got in, and so this evening everyone is happy. I have plenty of reason to, myself, for I received 4 letters and 3 packages, all of them from you. One contained a fruit cake; the second contained the popcorn (I believe, from the sound, though I didn't open it) and oil and book and writing paper. The third contained the thumb tacks, paper clips, sardines and anchovies. Maybe I got them here listed a bit mixed up, but I tried to mention all the big things so you could recognize which packages they were. Thank you so very much for it all.

This morning I forgot all about there being a First Friday so I went to Confession and Mass this evening. There now are 2 priests on the island; one says daily mass at 7 A.M., the other at 6 P.M. With both of them here there now are 6 Sunday Masses. For a time only one priest was around and the 3 Sunday Masses he said were pretty crowded.

Berkowsky taking a photograph "at one of the prettiest spots here," January 1945, Angaur.

I haven't attended a Lenten service yet, though they are held
2 or 3 times during the week as well as on Sunday evening. I'll
have to try to do better along that line during the rest of Lent.
Gosh! it scarcely seems possible that Easter is only a matter of
weeks away. I don't like for time to pass by so quickly.

Am enclosing a few more snapshots; as I did in last nite's
letter. I hope they give you some idea of our setup here. Three
are hospital scenes, one is of myself and the last is one I took
of my tent mate, Herman Berkowsky, one Sunday afternoon
in January when he and I took a jeep and went sight-seeing
around the island. This picture was taken near a very pretty
spot of which there aren't too many around here.
Well, until tomorrow then,

Love,
Fred.

————— ⇥⇤ —————

[V-Mail]

SAT. 3 MARCH 1945
Somewhere in the Palaus

Dear Folks—

This afternoon Mal Parker (one of our Dental officers) and
I walked down and looked over the new area. Work on it is
progressing well, and the setup is going to be quite nice. I
hear we officers are to have 2 barracks instead of 1, which
is really as it should be. The wards are big and airy, and the
arrangement of them is nice, as will be the mess hall. I'll write
you more about these things later.

Had a busy time again today, and evening now finds me
tired and ready for bed. Usually stay up until around 11:00,
but am going to retire a bit earlier if I can.
Until tomorrow.

Love,
Fred.

[V-Mail]

SUN. 4 MARCH 1945
Somewhere in the Palaus.

Dear Folks—

Lights go out in a few minutes, so I have an excuse for making this short.

I always hated Sundays, and I hated this one. I worked a while this morning and a while after dinner, even though it was my afternoon off. Then Manny Feit and I went shell hunting. It was fun, especially since I used my diving mask. Didn't get many shells, however.

Had a nice mail call today—4 letters. Two were from Danbury, 1 from Erie and 1 from you. I wrote Louie and Joe both this evening.

Until tomorrow then.

Love,
Fred.

---- →← ----

Monday 5 March 1945.
Somewhere in the Palaus.

Dear Folks—

This has been a much nicer day than I expected it to be. One of the lab boys is now a patient in the hospital and that leaves us a bit short-handed, but the others fared quite well without him. Fortunately my work on the ward was light and I was able to spend most of the time here.

These past couple days have been unusually hot and humid, even for here. Weather like this makes me lazy (at least that is my story) and tire easily. Right now I could fall asleep here at this desk. I believe that residence in a climate like this begins to sap a person's energy after a time.

Our meals continue to be quite good. We have steak tonite and are due for fried eggs tomorrow morning, which will make the 3rd time within a week. We have been having fresh butter and fresh potatoes at least once daily for the past several days.

Your last letter mentions that the snow has melted somewhat, and that danger of flood downstate is lessening. A severe flood right now really would be rough on all concerned, and I trust there will be none of it.

According to one of the last "Eagles" I received, the local Rotary Club recently helped commemorate the 40th anniversary of the organization. Are you still a faithful member, Pop? I was very surprised to read in the "Newsletter" that Fr. Liebel had dropped out. Come to think of it, he mentioned to me once that he might do just that.

Every time I receive a package, I try to remember to mention it to you and as far as I know, I haven't missed any. Just a few days ago I got 3 all at once, one of which was a fruitcake. Another contained the sardines and anchovies; the third was the candy, popcorn and Mazola oil. Incidentally, I can get oil like that from our mess hall, so you need not send me any more of it.

I believe I read that Mrs. Aselin and Elizabeth returned to Princeton, N.J. after spending some time in Eldred. Are they (Mrs. Aselin and the 3 girls) all living together? That would be very nice if they were. I had been wondering just before I read that item where they were.

I believe, too, that I read something about Virginia and Betty Myron being in Eldred en route somewhere. Long time no see them.

Enclosed are a few more snapshots. I'll keep sending you a few until I get them home. I didn't realize I had so many. All of them are valuable to me and will become more so as time goes on.

Well, will close now.

Love,

F.

[V-Mail]

TUES. 6 MAR. 1945
Somewhere in the Palaus.

Dear Folks—

Tomorrow or the next day we begin to move down to the new area. It will be quite a job moving all the lab equipment, but I am sure we can manage it okay. I don't know when we will move our personal belongings, but it probably will be tomorrow. I will have plenty to move, but I am going to throw it all in a pile and get going.

This was another hot and busy day, but like most of them, it went by quickly. That is one nice thing—time moves right along for us here.

No mail again today. This seems to be one of those bad spells we go through occasionally. Still, it all eventually catches up to us.

Love,
Fred.

————— →← —————

Wed. 7 March 1945.
Somewhere in the Palaus.

Dear Folks—

I won't be writing you many more letters from this particular building, as tomorrow, Friday and Saturday we move into the new hospital area. Tomorrow will be for moving the enlisted and officer personnel. Friday the departments— like Lab, Pharmacy, Surgery, the Clinics, etc. and finally Saturday the patients! By doing it that way things should move smoothly and we will have a little time to get all set for the patients before moving them.

One nice thing about this move is that it isn't a long one— merely a 5 minute walk.

Things continue to go well here. These past couple weeks have been a bit busier for me than preceding ones but I manage okay. My ward is less than half full; consequently I am able to devote most of my time to the Laboratory. That is well, for one of the lab men being a patient left the others a bit *rushed. However, so far all has worked out very well. I am hard to please, huh?*

An evening newscast is now on, and they are telling about the fall of Cologne.[32] *Really, I fail to understand how Germany can hold out much longer. The American, Canadian, French and British armies in the West seem all-powerful right now and getting tougher all the time. The way they are eating up the miles, they should be in Berlin even before the Russians are.*

I believe I told you how I have been kidded by the other officers because Syria officially entered the war on the side of the Allies, and how they called me "Co-belligerent."[33] *Come to think of it—this coming conference of the Allies in San Francisco in April is pretty wonderful.*[34] *Don't you agree?*

No mail again but one of these days I should get a big handful of it. I hope so, anyway. As it is, I am a bit behind in answering the last batch I got.

Just heard on the radio that Ed. McKeever, current head football coach @ N.D., has been signed up by Cornell.[35] *That is a good break for him, but will be a bit tough on the school in replacing him. Well, N.D. has faced that situation before.*

This has been an unusually nice day—not as hot as most and with a bit of a breeze along (over) towards the later part of the afternoon. Right now the sky is clouding up but I doubt that it will rain.

As soon as I finish this I am going to the movie. It is good, I hope. Some we have seen lately have been pretty punk. Monday evening we saw a picture made in 1927—believe it or not!

Today lectured to the men on something I'll not mention here. I still have not gotten away from these lecture assignments.

Enclosed are 6 more snapshots. You will note that the workmanship on some of them is excellent. I had it done in Honolulu.

Until tomorrow, then,

Love,
Fred.

[V-Mail]

THUR. 8 MAR. 1945
Somewhere in the Palaus.

Dear Folks—

Am tired now, after spending the afternoon moving my personal belongings down to the new quarters. They are pretty nice and really are some improvement over what we had. Will tell you more about that setup after things get a bit settled.

This morning the enlisted men moved. This afternoon we officers did and tomorrow the lab and other departments will go. Moving tomorrow will be a much bigger job than today's but I am sure all will work out fine.

No mail again this morning. Otherwise—this has been a pretty nice day, though there was a heavy rain early this morning.

Until tomorrow.

Love,
Fred.

———— ➜ ❮ ————

[V-Mail]

TUES. 13 MARCH 1945

Dear Folks—

Missed writing to you last nite, and don't want to repeat tonite, so here is a half note.

Had a very good mail call this morning, 8 letters in all. Included was one from Louie.

All goes well here. I am very busy and it keeps me going until rather late each nite.

Will write you a long letter tomorrow.

Love,
Fred.

[on air mail stationery; similar to other letters]

Wed. 14 March 1945.
Somewhere in the Palau Islands

Dear Folks—

Just to kill 3 birds with 1 stone, I'll answer your last 3 letters (Feb. 20, March 2, March 6) with this one. As I told you, yesterday there were 2 letters from you and another today. The last letter got here in 8 days.

My addressing a letter to Eldred for Vic is nothing new, though usually I wake up before the thing is mailed. Invariably ELDRED is the place my hand prints, regardless of where I think I am thinking about. That probably is because my thoughts are home, don't you suppose?

It is nice that you are hearing from Louie more regularly now. He wrote me lately, too. You probably know as much about what he is doing as I do, so there is no need of my repeating here. I am glad the souvenirs he sent the children arrived okay. They'll be very proud of them. Incidentally, what ever became of the Jap canteen I sent home from Guadalcanal?

Uncle Mike had plenty of overseas duty but that won't prevent his getting more. The War Department is getting tough about some things, and that may be one of them. I hope, that should he be sent abroad, that it is to a warm climate. A cold place might be rough on him.

Okay—if I need anything to wear or to eat I'll not fail to let you know. The fruit cake comes through okay. However, gum and most candies do not arrive to me in usable condition. Even airmailed gum is all dried out—or is it merely the kind of gum being made nowadays?

Am returning the German stamp. Am glad to have it, but don't want it here, as it might become lost or spoiled. Come to think of it, I have a Jap stamp to send only if I can find it. I sent some to Ester's sons.

Someday soon I am going to begin sending home pictures, negatives that are spoiling here in this climate. Also some clothes for which I have no use at present. As far as I know, you *have mentioned receiving all the packages I have sent. Have they arrived in good shape, or all moldy and banged up?*

It is nice that you are planning to go visit Joe. I hope you do and make it a worthwhile one. Gabriels, though, favor the brief visit, don't we? Except me when I went to Charleston, remember? Remember when I came home you used to ask me how come I rushed right back?

Joe might want the sleeping bag, but I doubt if he (an enlisted man) would be allowed to carry it along with him. Officers, you know, have more leeway about things like that. If it isn't used—please oil the zipper to keep it from rusting and put some mothballs inside to keep it hole-proof. When I get home, I'll take the boys camping and we'll need it then.

I and my roommates—got a big kick out of your writing that I should let you know if I thought you were sending me too many packages. In the last letter before this one you said you had made up your mind to send one each week.

Today I am O.D. again, and while making rounds this evening one of the ward men handed me a newspaper clipping his folks in Rochester, N.Y. had sent him for me. It was a picture of Mrs. Leo Hofschneider and their 8-months old son, taken on a visit to his people. Remember Leo at N.D.? He met his wife in Australia where she was an Army nurse and they were married there. She lives in Indiana. She went home when she became pregnant. I believe that is one way a nurse can get out of the Service. I'll send the clipping on to Louie.

Enclosed are a few more pictures. Am taking some of this new area, which really is very nice. In my next letter I will start telling you about it beginning with our quarter.

Love,

Fred.

P.S. had a very nice letter from Lorraine the other day. In their letters of the same mail, both Vic and Louie mentioned how nice they thought she was. I guess we all agree on that point now. The "now" refers to me.

[V-Mail]

THURS. 15 MARCH 1945

Dear Folks—

   Am really tired tonite, having slept poorly last night and putting in a long, hard day. In addition, these last few days have been hotter than usual, which doesn't pep me up any. In spite of these few little things, however, all goes well here, and we are getting more fixed in this new setup.

   Am way behind in answering letters, so plan on catching up tomorrow (my afternoon off).

   Until tomorrow,

Love,
Fred.

———————— ➜ ← ————————

[V-Mail]

SAT. 17 MARCH 1945
Somewhere in the Palaus.

Dear Folks—

   Well, all goes as usual here. Today had a couple admirals here, inspecting us. I guess they liked our set-up. The weather continues to be hot and humid, with heavy rains late evening and this afternoon and I believe we are due for more.

   Saw a basketball game yesterday and played ping pong before supper. Plan to start going swimming once in a while, something we do little of down here. Too busy, I guess.

   Your weekly ads are very good and very patriotic. Several of the officers always read them. I told them Henry Morgenthau[36] was a personal friend of the family.

   Until tomorrow.

Love,
Fred.

[V-Mail]

SUN. 18 MARCH 1945
Somewhere in the Palaus.

Dear Folks—

Instead of going to a movie this evening, I took in a basketball game, watching the hospital team win another league game. The team is good, and I get a big kick out of watching them. They play on an outdoor, concrete court, which is nearby.

This afternoon I played a set of tennis with Manny Feit. He beat me but it was fun anyway, and neither of us were in nearly as good shape physically as we would like to be. Guess we will have to get out and play oftener, which is just what we plan to do.

The weather continues to be very hot and a couple good rains these past few days have done little more than lay the dust. From the way the wind was kicking-up this evening we are due for still more rain. Like you people, we here are approaching the spring season, and it must be the rainy season too.

Work was not too rushing this weekend, but then it usually is not. The fore part of the week commonly is the busiest. Had a letter from Uncle Mike today, from Camp Swift, Texas.[37] Until tomorrow.

Love,
Fred.

——————— ➜ ← ———————

[V-Mail]

MON. 19 MARCH 1945

TO DAD—
BIRTHDAY GREETINGS
19 MARCH 1945.
Fred.

Handmade V-mail birthday card, March 19, 1945, Angaur.

[V-Mail]

MON. 19 MARCH 1945
Somewhere in the Palaus

Dear Folks—

My roommates and I—Hyde, Burt and Parker—just finished playing cribbage. It is a game I learned on the boat en route here and one we played by the hour. That and bridge. Our new recreational hall will be finished in a day or 2. Then we expect to play cards plenty.

A good rain is falling now and unless I miss my guess badly—there will be a lot of wind along with it. Rains here usually last but a few minutes but this one sounds like it will hang on.

No mail came in today. I dislike mailless days but they do give me a chance to get caught up in my correspondence.

When Berkowsky was evacuated 3 weeks ago, he left behind a lot of canned food.[38] Now we hear he might be back, so we are eating this food fast so we won't have much of it left to give back. Good system, huh?

Until tomorrow.

Love,
Fred.

———————— ➔ ← ————————

[V-Mail]

TUES. 20 MARCH 1945
Somewhere in the Palaus.

Dear Folks—

Well, tomorrow is the first day of spring, and we will celebrate in style. A good rain is coming down and has been more or less all day long. The storm I predicted last night failed to materialize. I like to make mistakes like that.

Today's letter from Ester bore the good news that Mama had gone to Bayonne, to visit Joe. I am glad she did and hope she does not rush right back. Maybe she can go on up to Danbury

*while out that way. In every letter they mention how they
would like to have you people go up there.*

*My ward has a few vacant beds now, which means a little
less work. The whole hospital was quite busy for a while there,
and now things are beginning to let up a bit.*

Well, until tomorrow.

Love,
Fred.

———————— ➔← ————————

[V-Mail]

WED. 21 MARCH 1945
Somewhere in the Palaus.

Dear Folks—

*Being O.D. yesterday, I had this afternoon off. However it
didn't work out so well because I had to work a couple hours
this evening to catch up. Anyway—I got a couple hours sleep
out of the deal.*

*Our rainy weather continues off and on, and I doubt that
it is over with yet. In fact, today I heard that we can look
forward to several months more of it, as spring here is the
rain season. This wet weather raises Cain with the athletic
program of the island, necessitating cancellation of several
scheduled games.*

*I have been going to 6 o'clock Mass for the past week or so.
Tonite being Wednesday Novena service,*[39] *there was quite
a large group in attendance. Afterwards there was choir
practice getting ready for the Mass on Easter Sunday, which is
approaching very fast.*

Until tomorrow, then—

Love,
Fred.

[V-Mail]

FRI. 23 MARCH 1945
Palau Islands.

Dear Folks—

   I just finished my third shower of the day. One was my daily cleaning; the other 2 were needed because I got all sweating playing ping pong. I have been playing it a lot since the table was put up in our recreational hall. Which reminds me, this evening we had our first meal in the Officers' mess. Heretofore we had been using a corner of the patients' mess. Officer patients eat in the same mess we use. This new one is a Quonset hut, with one end devoted to use as a kitchen. In front are tables that accommodate 4 people. We are served by 2 enlisted men.

   Our rainy weather continues. In fact, we seem to be getting more of it right along.

   This has been a rather busy day for me but also one that passed very quickly. The way my schedule is arranged makes the days just seem to fly.

Love,
<u>*Fred.*</u>

P.S. Have many of my letters been censored since I arrived here?

———— ➔ ← ————

[V-Mail]

SAT. 24 MARCH 1945
Somewhere in the Palaus.

Dear Folks—

   No mail today, but sometime soon I hope I get one telling me all about Mom's trip to Bayonne. I hope she doesn't make it too short and that she goes up to Danbury, too.

   I haven't heard from Joe in over 2 weeks now. Of course I realize he must be much busier at this school than he was in Florida. I wish I knew more about what he is studying there, etc.

This afternoon I mailed you a wooden box that contains some woolen clothes, a couple books, and a few smaller items. You'll probably receive it around the 1st of June. Let me know when and in what condition.

Our rains continue—frequently, briefly and not for long at a time. It drove me away from the movie this evening, so I came back here and played ping pong.

Love,
Fred.

————— ➔ ← —————

[V-Mail]

SUN. 25 MARCH 1945

Dear Folks—

This is Palm Sunday, and for us here it was a palmless one. How was it home? Were palms distributed after Mass? I remember what a big occasion that seemed to me when I was younger. It is yet, for that matter, but in a different way.

We had a lot of rain again today. Mass was held in the Red Cross building, which has a tin roof. The rain on the roof made so much noise that we could not hear what the priest was saying.

I believe I mentioned before that our new officers mess now is in use. It has a much better environment than the other place, and we all enjoy our meals more now. Which reminds me, we had steak for supper tonite. For some reason we have not been doing so well on fresh foods of late.

Today received a letter from Vic. She mentioned that Mama had phoned her from Danbury. Also—she enclosed some cute snapshots of the children. They all look so well and seem to be growing quite fast.

We got beer 5 times this week. I am drinking some right now.

Love,
Fred.

[V-Mail]

> MON. 26 MARCH 1945
> *Somewhere in the Palaus.*

Dear Folks—

Am O.D., and as such, must sleep in the Dispensary. Am writing from there and fortunately all is quiet. I have seen only 2 patients all evening and trust that is all. One just left a few minutes ago.

Had a fair time at mail call. Nothing from you but did get last week's "Eagle." Have noted all the news therein. Apparently spring has arrived, if grass fires are on hand and people have to be warned about trash. Incidentally, those pictures of young children are sweet. I keep looking for one of the boys, but as they were photographed in a group, doubt very much if I will be seeing them in the paper.

Read in the "Personals" column that Mom had gone a-visiting, which makes it official now. It didn't say how long she stayed or what kind of a time she had, which is what I wanted to know now.

Still having some rain.

> Love,
> <u>Fred.</u>

———————— →← ————————

[V-Mail]

> TUES. 27 MARCH 1945

Dear Folks—

Haven't much to write, so this will be brief.

I didn't get so much sleep last night after all, as a few patients came in after I wrote you. However, I was off this afternoon and slept for an hour. After that, I played 2 sets of tennis. That was quite enough, especially in this heat.

Just finished to writing to Joe, a letter, I began last evening. I haven't heard from him in a couple weeks now. Hope I do soon.

More rain today, but still the thermometer and humidity stay way up.

Heard a refrigerator ship just came into the harbor today. If true, that means fresh eggs, fresh butter, and STEAK!!

Until tomorrow.

Love,
Fred.

———————— ➔ ← ————————

[V-Mail]
WED. 28 MARCH 1945

Dear Folks—

Just a few minutes ago I was rained away from a swell movie, which I suggest you all try to see—"A TREE GROWS IN BROOKLYN." [40] *These rains have been coming down real hard and often these past few days. Fortunately, this coral sand absorbs water very well; otherwise we might be flooded here.*

Received four letters today—from you, Ester, Lorraine, and Fr. Liebel's Easter Newsletter. Lorraine and Evelyn plan to go to Oklahoma right after Easter to visit Evelyn's husband, who is in camp there.

Am glad that Mama is making her visit worthwhile and not rushing right back. Hope Papa can get away for a while now. So you are Victory-gardening again already. It hardly seems possible that planting time is here once more! Come to think of it—we have been here longer than we were in the desert. [41]

The war news is closely listened-to over here. A person has to, to keep up.

Love,
Fred.

———————— ➔ ← ————————

[V-Mail]

THURS. 29 MARCH 1945.
Somewhere in the Palau Islands.

Dear Ester:—

This is evening of Holy Thursday, and I just returned from a 6:30 Mass. It was a High Mass with a surprisingly good choir, all male of course. Religious services are well attended here, with myself present practically every day for the past 2 weeks.

An official tour of this island is required of all here, and today I took a "looksee." Although I previously had been to most of the points of interest, I still enjoyed this afternoon's excursion. For a small place, there is considerable to be seen. I added one item to the commentary by pointing out a kind of tree that is a breeding place of a species of mosquito not yet identified completely. We all came back from this jaunt tired and dirty but a wonderful supper awaited us—fresh chicken, fresh potatoes and fresh butter! What a treat! And did we all go for it in a big way.

All goes well here in our new hospital area.

I read in the Easter "Newsletter" where the souvenirs Louie sent the boys have arrived.[42] I can imagine what a lot of fun they are having with them.

Love,
<u>Fred.</u>

———————— →← ————————

[V-Mail]

THURS. 29 MARCH 1945.

Dear Folks:—

Three big things happened this afternoon and evening: — 1) I attended a High Mass 2) We took an "official" tour of the island to visit all the spots of interest 3) for supper we had fresh chicken, butter and potatoes. Quite a day, don't you agree?

Luckily, there was no rain this afternoon while we were out looking over the island, but last night I got a good soaking while at the movie. Tonite so far it hasn't rained, either.

Things are a bit less busy now than they were for the past couple weeks. My ward is about only half-full now. But that's how it often seems to go—either a feast or a famine. Which reminds me that tomorrow is a day of fast.

Well, Easter is practically here. I won't have any new toggery to strut around in, but I'll have a good day. I know you will, too. Maybe next year we'll be together.

Love,
Fred.

———————— ➔ ⬅ ————————

[V-Mail]

FRI. 30 MARCH 1945.
Somewhere in the Palaus.

Dear Folks—

Another mail-less day, which makes 2 in a row. Maybe tomorrow will see a change. Tomorrow means another month gone by, a fourth of the year. Isn't it surprising? Here we have already been on this island over 5 months.

I just finished playing ping pong with Malcolm Parker, who is one of the 5 of us who lives in this section. I have been playing a lot of late. Also walking. By these means I am trying to keep my waistline down. It is showing a tendency to expand of late largely because of the beer I am drinking. We get 2 cans a day and I usually drink all mine.

I heard that officers' clothing can be purchased here on the island now, and first chance I get, I plan to go down. Some of this clothing I have been using since I entered the service is beginning to become a bit worn.

Hoping I hear from you tomorrow.

Love,
Fred.

[V-Mail - typed]

EASTER SUNDAY [APRIL 1] 1945.
SOMEWHERE IN THE PALAU ISLANDS.

DEAR FATHER LIEBEL:

*AM ON DUTY HERE IN THE DISPENSARY, THERE IS AN
UNUSED TYPEWRITER ON HAND, SO WHY NOT A V-MAIL? AND
BEFORE I FORGET IT, THANKS MUCH FOR THE FINE SNOW
SCENES. THEY EVOKE A WHOLE WAVE OF SIGHING AND
REMINISCING FROM ALL WHO SEE THEM.*

*EASTER HERE WAS NOT STATESIDE IN ALL ITS DETAILS (NO
EASTER PARADE) BUT WE CATHOLICS DID ALL RIGHT ON THE
OTHER ASPECT OF IT. THERE WERE THE USUAL SIX MASSES
ON THE ISLAND, WITH THAT HERE AT THE ISLAND THEATRE,
WHICH IS AN OUTDOOR JOB IN THE HOSPITAL AREA, BEING
A HIGH MASS. THERE ARE VERY MANY PAPISTS HERE, AND
FROM THE LOOKS OF THINGS EACH SUNDAY, MOST OF THEM
GET UP IN TIME. THE SINGING THIS MORNING, ALL MALE,
OF COURSE, WAS VERY GOOD, AND COMMUNION TOOK
ABOUT AS MUCH TIME AS THE REST OF THE SERVICE. THIS
IS ESSENTIALLY AN AIRBASE AND SURPRISING NUMBER OF
THESE BOYS ARE DAILY COMMUNICANTS. LENTEN SERVICES,
THOSE I SAW, SEEM QUITE WELL ATTENDED. A COLLECTION
WAS TAKEN UP AT ALL MASSES THIS MORNING TO RESTORE
THE CATHOLIC MISSION HERE.*[43]

*THREE WEEKS AGO WE MOVED INTO THIS NEW HOSPITAL
AREA, JUST DOWN THE ROAD FROM THE OTHER. WE HAVE A
NICE SETUP HERE, EVEN TWO NEW CONCRETE SIDEWALLS.
WARDS ARE LARGE AND AIRY, THE MEN'S BARRACKS
ARE ADEQUATE AND THE OFFICERS' QUARTERS ARE
COMFORTABLE, SO WE HAVE NO BIG COMPLAINING TO MAKE,
NOT FOR NOW ANYWAY. TIME RUNS OUT, SO WILL SIGN OFF
NOW.*

SINCERELY,
Fred.

[V-Mail]

Wed. 4 April 1945.
Somewhere in the Palaus.

Dear Folks—

   I hear that we get a landslide of mail tomorrow, which will come in handy after these lean past few days. Incidentally, I did not get around to writing you last nite, the first miss in several weeks. Yesterday I did get one letter—from Joe. He mentioned what a fine visit he had with Mom; also that he might be moving out soon. Should he do so, and come this way, I do hope we can get together.

   Another thing of interest—there was no rain today, though it was an unusually hot day. Everyone remarked about it. We also were served a good supper, as we have been for the past 3 days. We really eat well when fresh food comes to the island.

   Well, until tomorrow. I forgot all about Louie's birthday until the last minute.

Love,
Fred.

——————— ➤◄ ———————

[V-Mail]

Thurs. 5 April 1945.
Somewhere in the Palaus.

Dear Folks—

   This letter is being written Friday morning on the ward. Last nite after the show a few of us got together and had a little popcorn party, and by the time that was over it was "lights out."

   Yesterday was a beautiful day and this promises to be just as nice. And there has been no rain for 3 days now.

   The movies we have been seeing of late are easily the best we've had here.

   I heard that lots of mail came in but so far I have seen no sign of it. Maybe today.

Love,
Fred.

[V-Mail]

Fri. 6 April 1945.

Dear Folks—

Was going to write you a long letter tonight, but instead it will be this. We just finished a little "midnight snack" after the movie. The movie was punk but the food good.

We have been favored with another nice day, good in everything but one—no mail. A lot of it is supposed to be nearby and waiting for us. Maybe tomorrow will be our lucky strike.

Tomorrow evening we are having a party, a sort of farewell for Capt. Feit, who recently was transferred to another unit here on the island. Will write you about it.

Love,
Fred.

———— →← ————

[V-Mail]

Sunday 8 April 1945.
Somewhere in the Palaus.

Dear Folks—

The party last evening was very enjoyable. The food was excellent, we all were in a good mood, and there was only brief after-dinner speaking which pleased all present. Oh yes—there was also "dinner music" by a 3-piece orchestra. Some class, huh?

I was O.D. yesterday and as such, had to sleep in the Dispensary. Fortunately, I had no night calls and only 1 in the evening. We aren't nearly as busy as we were, as you can notice.

I went to 8 o'clock Mass this morning. Those later are too darn hot, and they break up the ward work too much. The priest announced that the collection taken up last Sunday to replace the destroyed Catholic Mission here amounted to one thousand dollars.

Manny Feit's farewell dinner, including the three-piece band, April 7, 1945, Angaur.

No mail again today. Maybe will do better tomorrow. Until then—

> Love,
> <u>Fred.</u>

———— ➔ ← ————

[V-Mail]

> Wed. 11 April 1945.
> Somewhere in the Palaus.

Dear Folks—

Just returned from a "live" USO Camp show. It had a cast of 5 girls and 3 fellows. Most everyone I talked to was disappointed in it. This is the 4th "live" show I have seen since being overseas and I have yet to see one that seemed to me to justify the time and expense to keep it on the road, and a surprisingly large number of people share that view.

Today was another real hot day. I am beginning to notice the heat more here than on the "Canal." A little rain would cool things off fine, and by the looks of the sky this evening, we may have rain. No mail from you today, but service is better now than it was last week.

Love,
Fred.

———— ➔ ◄ ————

[V-Mail]

THURS. 12 APR. 1945
Somewhere in the Palaus.

Dear Folks—

Received 2 letters from you today, both of which got here in swell time (8 and 10 days). Also had 1 from Vic from Buffalo. Glad you were able to do some good at the Merchandise show. More stock should be generally available by midsummer, the way the war in Europe is going. Today's news put the Americans 57 miles from Berlin.

I held Medical Clinic this afternoon and was it tiring!! I saw about 15 patients and was not through until after supper. We had steak tonite, by the way.

Certainly am glad that I am not around while the house is torn apart by spring cleaning. I want you to be careful about that flu. Be sure to call the doctor right away if you get sick. Be sure, now.

Love,
Fred.

———— ➔ ◄ ————

[V-Mail]

SAT. 14 APR 1945.
Somewhere in the Palaus.

Dear Folks—

Missed writing you last nite on account of a little party we had. Will write you about it tomorrow. Almost did not get around to writing tonight, but don't want to miss 2 nites in a row.

*Of course the big item of interest here is the sudden death of
President Roosevelt.*[44] *Most people, whether or not they liked
him, feel he was the best man to have on our side at the peace
conference.*

*Second and third class mail came in today. I did [receive] 3
old newspapers and a package from you (sandwich spreads,
figures [?], sardines). Thanks a lot.*

Love,
Fred.

———————— ➔ ← ————————

[V-Mail]

SUN. 15 APR. 1945.
Somewhere in the Palaus.

Dear Folks:

*We are having a very heavy rain right now, and a few
minutes ago it drove me away from a very fine movie:
"Wilson."*[45] *I just got back and switched into pajamas from my
ringing-wet clothes. There must have been about 3,000 fellows
at the movie, so you can figure out how many wet feet there are
around here now.*

*This was my afternoon off but I worked anyway. My ward
is filling up once more and I did not want to get behind. The
whole past week has been a very busy one, come to think of it.*

*At Mass this morning and at the Protestant services,
there were special prayers for Roosevelt, and at noon we all
observed a 5-minute silence.*

*I have some new pictures that I'll be sending along to you.
They are both of this new area and the old one. I have some of
natives, too, which I will send the children. Poor kids! I wish
I could send them some souvenirs or something, but none are
available. And I haven't time to write to them. Which reminds
me—both Pop and Ester mentioned their names (the boys)
being in the "Eagle." I received that of the 6th today and could
not find anything about them in it, nor in the one preceding it.
Am I overlooking something?*

*The rain is continuing hard and heavy, which is unusual.
Usually they are brief. This rain will help out the plants just
put in all over the hospital grounds.*

Love,
Fred.

———————— ✈✦ ————————

[V-Mail]

MON. 16 APR. 1945.
Somewhere in the Palaus.

Dear Folks—

Just finished writing to Lou and Joe, airmails and enclosed
a few snapshots of the area. Plan to do the same for you and
the girls tomorrow. Am having a bit of trouble keeping up in
my correspondence these days.

Received another package from you today, the one
containing the desk supplies (daily calendar and stapling
machine). Thanks for it. Forgot to mention that I got the wallet
in yesterday's package.

Went to watch the hospital team play basket-ball tonite but
the game was called off on account of rain. Guess we are due
for more of it, too.

Love,
Fred

———————— ✈✦ ————————

[V-Mail]

TUES. 17 APR. 1945.
Palau Island.

Dear Folks—

This has been a pretty routine day all the way around, and
without any effort at all I found enough to keep me busy. My
ward has several very interesting patients on it right now.
Although it is designated as the Communicable Disease ward, I
have other kinds of patients.

*Packages are still coming in for us and I have received 2,
as I write you—one with the desk equipment; the other with
the wallet and canned figs etc. Thank you very much for
everything.*

*Had a letter from Lorraine, from Oklahoma, where
she and Evelyn are visiting Evelyn's husband at an army
camp. She wanted to know what you people thought of our
corresponding. That will be easy to answer—huh. Until
tomorrow.*

Love,
<u>*Fred.*</u>

———————— ➔ ← ————————

[V-Mail]

SAT. 21 APR. 1945.
Palau Islands.

Dear Folks—

*Just returned from the movie and it was another swell
one—A SONG TO REMEMBER.*[46] *We have been seeing some
excellent movies lately, some of them soon after they are
released. Well, we can stand something outstanding over here,
just for contrast.*

*My room-mates are discussing a common question—will
we want to go to the movie 7 nites a week after we return to
civilian life or will we be fed up with them by then?*

*Hearing the word "boy scout" tonight reminded me that
when Louie and I were young we weren't allowed to join the
Scouts, because later on if there was a war, we would have
to join the army! Remember. And now look at us. I got a real
laugh thinking about it.*

Love,
<u>*Fred.*</u>

[V-Mail]

SUN. 22 APR. 1945.

Palau Islands.

Dear Folks—

This has been a quiet, hot Sunday. Now, in the evening, the sky has clouded over a lot and rain probably will follow. I have been pretty busy so far and have a little work yet to do.

Just came from supper—fried chicken, not too tough. Our meals have been pretty good of late, with chicken, steak and ice cream at least once weekly. Our beer ration is 2 cans per day. We now have a place to cool it and a cold beer in the middle of the afternoon really hits the spot. It also makes one put on weight around the belt line.

Your letter of the 13th arrived yesterday. Glad all is going well with you and am glad you seem so calm about Joe leaving his clothes at home. About the packages you sent me—yes I did receive the bedroom slippers. Also the ink and so forth. Sorry, thought I had mentioned receiving those 2 packages. I have received several from you, just how many I do not know. About a dozen, I estimated. Two arrived last week, the first in about two months. I will make it a point to let you know in my next letter every time I get a package from you. Okay?

I received only 1 letter today—from Brady. He is back at a rest camp after the Iwo Jima campaign.[47] *Jake expects to head for home about July. His wife lives in Olean, so he will drop in to see you when he gets up that way. These Navy men are lucky in that respect: they are returned to the States after 18-months foreign service.*

Cannot honestly say that I would like to be home to help out with the housecleaning. I hate that business and probably always will. Which reminds me that I just learned something— how to sew on a Singer. You ought to see me pump.

Love,

Fred.

[V-Mail]

MON. 23 APR. 1945.
Palau Islands.

Dear Folks—

Today received v-mail from you and Ester, both dated the 12th. Was surprised to learn that you had a spell of mailless days because I have been writing daily. But come to think of it—mail to us was slow about that time too, so apparently it was working both ways. Don't worry about not hearing from Lou very often. One of these days you will receive a whole handful of letters from him.

Packages and papers came in today. I got 3 "Lake Shore Visitors" and a package from you containing Zwieback,[48] pigs feet, tuna and ham. Thanks for it, but you might omit the Zwieback. This was the second box of it, and both had to be thrown away. Funny thing—the post office doesn't date those packages so I cannot let you know which ones I received.

Love,
Fred.

——————— →← ———————

[V-Mail]

TUES. 24 APR. 1945.
Palau Islands.

Dear Folks—

My roommates and I just returned from the movie, after which we had a little lunch with beer. At present we get 2 cans of it a day and have facilities for cooling it. A cold beer really is good in this climate.

No mail today, so apparently we have another of those weak spells on hand. Some pkgs. arrived yesterday and I received the one containing the pig's feet, tuna and devilled ham. Much obliged for it. We haven't been having as many late lunches here in our quarters as I thought we would, but occasionally we do get hungry at nite.

I haven't heard from Lou in some time so was glad to know you had an Easter greeting from him. Do you ever hear from Martha? I do not. Until tomorrow.

Love,
Fred.

──────── ➔ ← ────────

[V-Mail]

WED. 25 APR. 1945.
Palau Islands.

Dear Folks—

I just did something very unusual for me—walked out on a movie and Deanna Durbin at that.[49] *The name of it was "Can't Help Singing."*[50]

Well, today (our time) the San Francisco Conference begins. Do hope the members work out something very worthwhile. Come to think of it—just the idea of such a meeting is wonderful. We here rather expected that their first official act could to announce that the Allied and Russian armies had joined forces inside Germany.[51] *Germany is getting a real pasting now and Berlin can't be much to look at anymore. The Nazis will have to make some kind of a settlement soon.*

No mail from you again today, but only very little came in. Tomorrow will be my duty.

Until then.

Love,
Fred.

──────── ➔ ← ────────

[V-Mail]

THURS. 26 APR. 1945.
Palau Islands.

Dear Folks—

Golly—hasn't this month gone by very fast? 4 days more and May will be here. That is one nice thing I must say about life overseas—time does seem to really move along. Or is it

because I am getting older? I was blaming onto my age the
unusual bitterness towards my life in general that I have been
feeling these past 2 weeks. I really have been sour and sore
about something.

Contrary to my usual practice, I am writing this before
going to the movie. Right now I am in the lab and have just
completed making rounds of all the wards. Yes, I am O.D.
again. Every time we lose an officer our turn as O.D. comes
just that much oftener.

Love,
Fred.

———————— ➔ ← ————————

[V-Mail]

FRI. 27 APRIL 1945.
Palau Islands.

Dear Folks—

I have been pitching horse-shoes this evening and my right
arm and hand are pretty sore. However, that will not interfere
with my daily letter to you.

Your letter of the 18th is on hand. Isn't that grand service?
Glad you did get 5 letters from me in 1 day but you must not
have received any for about a week. By now you must know
that I am beginning to get your packages again.

Am glad that Pop is able to get out on these business trips,
and hope that he does stop at Sayre to see Martha and the
children. They must be growing fast, and they'll wonder who I
am when they first see me. For that matter, probably only Eddy
and Paulie will remember me, though the others may also.
They all are pretty bright and may just walk up to me and
say: Hi—Uncle. Where in hell have you been? Then I will show
them my pictures of Texas, Arizona, Guadalcanal, and here.

Love,
Fred.

[V-Mail]

SUN. 29 APR. 1945.
Palau Islands.

Dear Folks—

That was really some letter Pop wrote about the President's death—quite a nice eulogy. I had not realized that the people generally were so shaken by his sudden passing. It was saddening news to us, too, but aside from special church services and a period of silence, we continued on our daily tasks.

That and now the San Francisco conference have been the big items of news around here. Today a new one was added— the rumors of Germany surrendering. However, Truman's announcement that it was groundless seems to have settled that.[52]

Have been busy all day preparing for a school I am going to tomorrow. It is here on the island and will last one 12 hours. I will write you about it later.

Everybody here closely follows the newscasts; isn't the news really good from Europe.

Love,
Fred.

———————— → ← ————————

[V-Mail]

TUES. 1 MAY 1945.
Palau Islands.

Dear Folks—

Your letter of the 22nd carried the surprising news of Joe being in the hospital with [an] ulcer. Had one from him today, telling the same. Apparently it is not very serious, thank gosh.

Today finished giving a 2-day school in Insect Control. It went off quite well but I would be just as well satisfied if someone else had that job. Still, I know I can handle it.

One of my roommates, Parker—a dental officer, received his promotion to major today. We are all happy about it and are having a little party tonite to celebrate.

Had a letter from Lorraine today.

All is well here. Hope it is with you, too, and take care of your colds.

Love,
Fred.

[The envelope contains a Mother's Day card on V-mail. It is a sketch of a woman in a frame and says "To Mother [on top] With Love" [bottom], along with a short poem:

You've patched up my quarrels
So neatly it seems,
And mended the breaks
In my wishes and dreams.
So just picture me
And you're seeing the one
Who thinks you're the DEAREST MA
under the sun!!]

[V-Mail]

WED. 2 MAY 1945.
Palau Islands.

Dear Folks—

Have noticed that many of my negatives are getting moldy so will send them home to you. This morning sent 13 in an envelope and will do so again occasionally until you have them all.

Had only 1 drink at the party last nite but felt pretty rocky all morning anyway. Either I am getting older or I am way out of practice. Maybe we need to have parties like that oftener.

No mail from you today, but did get one from a Kane nurse (Bradford hospital) who is on Saipan, the same hospital as the Dorrion boy.[53]

Until tomorrow.

Love,
Fred.

[V-Mail]

THURS. 3 MAY 1945.
Palau Islands.

Dear Folks—

Earlier this evening I sent you 10 pictures and 10 negatives in an envelope. Will send you more occasionally.

Just finished writing Joe and plan to write to Lou and Duffy also. I like to get letters and knowing one way to do that is to write, I write. Our mail has been a bit slight this week, though some is coming through. No second class mail has come to us in over a week, so some of that should be along soon. A fresh-food vessel came in today, which is good news. However, our meals have been good—steak, chicken and ice-cream at least once weekly. We cannot kick about that, can we?

This has been a quite-cool day and we liked it that way. Of late the weather has been very hot. Has not rained in 5 days.

Love,
Fred.

———————— ➔ ← ————————

[V-Mail]

SAT. 5 MAY 1945.
Palau Islands.

Dear Folks—

Our 5-star inspecting visitor did not show up; at least we saw nothing of him. But that is how it commonly goes. Literally dozens of times we have gotten ready for visitors who did not show up, or if they did—just hurried through.

I didn't go to the movie because of rain but afterward did go over to the lab where a few of us popped some corn. It really was delicious—as Mom would say—and I ate more than my share, probably enough so that I won't sleep tonite.

This afternoon I ran all over the island collecting equipment and supplies for my Insect-Control detail. Had good luck however and even had a vehicle and trailer assigned to us. I have been kidding the boys—and vice versa—about my "town-car." All is well here, and I trust with you, too.

Until tomorrow,

Love,
Fred.

———————— ➔ ← ————————

Palau Islands.
Sunday 6 May 1945.

Dear Folks—

This has been the coolest day in a long time. Last night a heavy rain began and lasted all nite and this morning. This afternoon the sun came out and things cleared off nicely, so that there was a beautiful sunset this evening.

I spent a couple hours this afternoon painting my trunk. It needed it, too. The outside was badly scratched up and the metal parts were rusting. I painted it a regulation olive drab color, with jet black trim. It looks pretty good now. The job had to be finished this evening, after which I went to the movies. The movie was very funny—Rosalind Russell in "What a Woman."[54] Incidentally, we had fresh turkey for supper, plus fresh potatoes and butter.

Haven't had any letters from you in 2 or 3 days, but today received the April 27th "Eagle." Therein I read that Mama had gone to N.J. to visit Joe. I think it is a good idea that one of you went because while he is in the hospital he will have plenty of time to be with you. Hope he is coming along okay, and I am anxious for further word about his disposition.

There isn't much doing here. Tomorrow I will have to really get my Insect control detail in action. Just how much that will entail I will be better able to tell you tomorrow.

Included are a few more pictures.

Love,
Fred.

[V-Mail]

MON. 7 MAY 1945.
Palau Islands.

Dear Folks—

Well, by the time you get this Mama probably will be home again. That is why I am writing her c/o Joe. Hope she brings back with her the story that all is well with Joe and that his trouble is not serious enough to warrant discharge from the Army.

This was another rather quiet day though hotter than blazes. Maybe yesterday being relatively cool made it seem so hot. This afternoon the Island Surgeon and I drove around the island, locating work for my Insect Control detail. I think it will be a job that I can handle without much trouble.

Our basket-ball team has a game this evening at 9, but doubt that I will go. Instead I will write a couple letters and then read a while. No mail came in today, a thing that does happen once in a while. We still listen to all the news, hoping to hear that it is officially over in Europe.

Love,
Fred.

———— ➔ ← ————

[V-Mail]

TUES. 8 MAY 1945.
Palau Islands.

Dear Folks—

Among 4 letters received today was yours of the 29th, bearing the good news that you had just Rcd. a cablegram from Lou: Am glad to hear that, and know how worried you must have been. Well Thank God, all that is over now, for the radio today reported that all that is needed now is official announcing that Germany has surrendered unconditionally. It is now 10 P.M. and we mainly are trying to pick up the speech President Truman is scheduled to give at 9 A.M. your time so we will know it is the real McCoy.[55]

I didn't ask but I was wondering about the Rotary, too. Somehow I had the idea it broke up. Glad it hasn't; also am glad that the children aren't very sick with the whooping cough.

Until tomorrow,

Love,
Fred.

———————— ✈✈ ————————

Palau Islands
Wed. 9 May 1945.

Dear Folks—

This is about 6:30 in the evening and is my favorite period of the day. This evening is especially pleasant—cool, quiet and the sky very clear, possibly because the air was cleared by a brief but heavy rain about 5 o'clock. The whole day was a bit cooler than usual and the sun noticeably less hot. Have I ever told you about the sunsets here? Occasionally they are colored, and when they are—they are really beautiful. Somehow the sun appears to get behind the cloud bank in the west, giving the sky gorgeous blue and pink colors like I have never seen elsewhere. They seem to be "wet" pink and blue, not the ordinary ones.

For the last 2 days the radio has repeatedly told of the unconditional surrender of Germany to the Allies. Yet we have not been officially notified of it here, which makes us wonder just what is going on. Gosh! it is hard to believe just how much it means that the war in Europe is over. Regardless of how long it will be before any particular person gets home from over there, at least he needn't continually think of enemy attack and his people can stop worrying about him being killed.

Well, what do you hear from Joe? I imagine that by now Mom is back home, reporting a good time for herself and that all is well with Joe. I anxiously await word from him.

Had a letter from Charley Schaaf in Paris the other day. He has a nice assignment—CO of a hospital train working out of Paris. He has another medical officer, several nurses and several medical technicians working for him—not a bad setup, huh?

I haven't heard from Uncle Mike in quite a while now. I presume he still is in this country and that he will remain here.

Well, I'll close now.

Love,
Fred.

P.S. Enclosed are a few more pictures.

———————— →← ————————

[V-Mail]

THURS. 9 [10] MAY '45.
Palau Islands.

Dear Folks—

Just returned from the movie a few minutes ago. It rained during the early part of it but not enough to drive me away. But did it rain last nite! And what bright lightning! That is the second storm like that this week. One good thing they do anyway—they cool off the weather.

I had Medical Clinic again today. It was considerably lighter than usual but even at that it lasted 3 hours. My ward work is picking up again, and I have some interesting cases on hand. For instance, one is a 19-year-old sailor, whom we suspect having been born with only one kidney. Another fellow has a liver abscess, probably due to amoebic dysentery.

Tomorrow or the next day I am sending a package of pictures and negatives home. Some, of the family, I wanted to keep with me but they are getting moldy and I don't want to lose them. No mail from you today.

Love,
Fred.

[V-Mail]

FRI. 11 MAY 1945.
Palau Islands.

Dear Folks—

Got rained out of the movie tonite but it was not very good, anyway. The rain came at the end of a hot day. I didn't work so much this afternoon but did this morning. My ward was changed again, and that is a task that takes a little while.

A letter from Ester was the only one I received today. Still am awaiting word about Joe. Hope all goes well with him. It does with me.

Love,
Fred.

——————— →← ———————

[V-Mail]

SAT. 12 MAY 1945.
Palau Islands.

Dear Mom—

It is May 12th—your birthday. So with this letter to you goes my wishes for many happy returns of the day. I hope to be there with you next year.

Love,
Fred.

P.S. Today received 4 of your packages. Can't tell you just which ones they are, as they bear no dates. All contain canned goods, candy, etc. Thanks loads for them. Now I have on hand enough "snack-makings" for the next several weeks.

F.

[V-Mail]

MON. 14 MAY 1945.
Palau Islands.

Dear Folks—

Your letters of the first of the month telling of snow again, are on hand. The weather there must be changeable, all right, and I can see how a late frost is going to kill a lot of blooms.

Glad Mom enjoyed her second trip to New Jersey and that she found Joe not so sick. I am relieved to know his condition wasn't as serious as I was expecting. So little Tommy is quite a talker, huh? I don't suppose he asked about his Uncle Fred, did he? Ma, how many times a year does Mrs. Markey have a birthday? Or are the more than 1 Mrs. Markeys in your club? Sure doesn't seem like a year since her last party.

Today was a routine day, and rather quiet. I am O.D. and trust tonite is quiet, too. Generally they are, though I had one bloody case this evening—a fellow accidentally cut off 2 toes with an axe.

Until tomorrow.

Love,
Fred.

———— ➜ ← ————

[V-Mail]

TUES. 15 MAY 1945.
Palaus.

Dear Folks—

Someone just called me to listen to the radio. The program now on is "News from Home"[56] and this one is about Pennsylvania. Of course I was pleased to listen to it though the city discussed was New Kensington.[57] It is nice just to hear the word "Pennsylvania."

Your letter of the 5<u>th</u> arrived today. My letters arriving in bunches of 3 and 4 may be because most are V-mails. I guess too you have your mailless days, just like I do. Today was one. In general, however, mail service certainly is fine—both ways.

That 500-plane raid on Japan[58] must have really been

terrible, and must make some impression on the Nips. I don't
see how they can stand many like it. Hope they realize that
and give up soon. If they don't, there won't be much left to their
islands.

Love,
<u>Fred.</u>

————— ➔← —————

[V-Mail]

WED. [THURS.] 17 MAY 1945.
Palau Islands.

Dear Folks–

   Had about 4 letters from you today. Also, had a beer or 2 too
many this evening, so will make this short and snappy.

Love,
<u>Fred.</u>

————— ➔← —————

[V-Mail]

FRI. 18 MAR. [MAY] 1945.
Palaus.

Dear Folks—

   Dr. Bly came ashore again today and stopped in to see me.
We had a nice visit but I happened to be busy in the lab at the
time. He is much heavier and grayer than I remembered him,
but then I had met him only once, and that was several years
ago now. I am going out to his ship for dinner tomorrow.

   This was a pleasant day. Work in the lab and on the ward
has picked up some, but still I manage to not work too hard. A
real warm rain fell lazily this evening and afterwards the sky
was so clear and the air seemed so clean that it was fun to sit
outside and take deep breaths.

   No mail from you in 2 days; maybe one of those short
slumps is upon us.

   Until tomorrow,

Love,
<u>Fred.</u>

[V-Mail]

SAT. 19 MAY 1945
Palau Islands.

Dear Folks—

Just returned from having dinner with Dr. Bly aboard his ship. The dinner was good and I thoroughly enjoyed the 4 hours I spent with him. Needless to say—most of it was passed talking with a few minutes taken out to look over the vessel. Between us we have seen a lot of the world during the last 2 years, but we both agree that none of it looked nearly so nice as N.W. Pennsylvania.

Another pleasant day was had by me, all the way through. Last night was cool and swell for sleeping, so I slept in late this morning. There wasn't much to be done before noon. And after noon I took things easy until 3, when I began to clean up. At 4:30 I went down to the dock and met Bly.

Your letter of the 9<u>th</u> arrived today. Glad you finally had a letter from Lou; I should be getting one soon myself.

Love,
<u>Fred.</u>

———— ➜ ᚜ ————

[V-Mail]

MON. 21 MAY 1945.
Palau Islands.

Dear Folks—

Just returned from the movie. It wasn't so good but the sunset this evening was, and so is the sky now. Honestly, the colors here are beautiful and a person can see so many at one time.

This is now a couple hours later. I was called (I am O.D. tonite) to see a patient aboard a ship in the harbor. The navy doctor, who ordinarily sees such patients, was busy at the time, so we were asked to send someone out. On the ship I met a fellow who lived in the same deckhouse I did on the "Mormacport," the ship we came here on. Some fun we people have, huh, and now that there is a war on, a person is apt to meet people he knows most anywhere.

Pop should be in N.Y. now. That is provided he went when he planned. Hope he did, and that he has a good time and that he finds Joe all right.

Until tomorrow,

Love,

Fred.

——————— ➤ ← ———————

[V-Mail]

TUES. *22 MAY 1945.*

Palau Islands.

Dear Folks—

I don't know whether it is the heat or because I have done a lot of manual labor today, but I have already taken 2 showers since noon and believe I need another. If this keeps up I surely will wash myself away.

Nothing startling to report from here. We are due to lose 3 enlisted men soon, two because they are over 42 years of age and the last one demobilization. That last surprises me, getting underway so fast. I had expected it to work much slower.

There was no mail at all today. I do not like such days, but they do crop up once in a while. One thing, they give me a little chance to get caught up on letter writing. Wrote Lou last nite, haven't heard from him or Uncle Mike in quite some time. Tomorrow I will tell you what I want for my birthday.

Love,

Fred.

——————— ➤ ← ———————

[V-Mail]

WED. *23 MAY 1945.*

Palaus.

Dear Folks—

Tonite the boys in the lab and those in the dental clinic are being given a little party by their bosses—myself and my 2 roommates, Parker and Burt.

I mentioned yesterday what I wanted for my birthday, but

*I don't care if I get [them] then or a couple weeks afterwards.
What I want is a studio picture of you and Pop. Don't you think
that is a reasonable enough request? And in a durable frame,
too, not one of these flimsy pasteboard things.*

*This was another hot day, and a mailless one again, too.
Maybe tomorrow I well get a big handful of it.*

Love,
Fred.

———— ✈ ————

[V-Mail]

FRI. 25 MAY 1945
Palaus.

Dear Folks—

*After an unusually hot day we are having a nice cool
evening. And the moon tonite is so big and bright. It really
lights up things and makes the palm trees beautiful. I
sometimes think they are prettier at nite than in the daytime.
Like some people, huh?*

*I shot baskets for about an hour this morning before the sun
got hot, which it usually is by 10 o'clock and stays that way
until after 5 in the evening.*

*A news-cast is on the radio now. That 550-plane raid on
Tokyo[59] must have been a terrific blow to the Japs and I hope
they come oftener and bigger.*

Until tomorrow.

Love,
Fred.

———— ✈ ————

[V-Mail]

SAT. 26 MAY 1945.
Palaus.

Dear Folks—

*Was glad to learn that Mama received her posies in time for
Mothers' Day, and that she liked them. And it was nice that she
received more from Sayre.*

*A point system for officers has been announced. Figuring
as though I were an enlisted man I have 54 points (33 months
service; 16 month overseas; 5 points for 1 campaign star).
However, efficiency and other factors enter into it in case of
an officer. Besides, most medical officers are "essential."[60] If I
were married and had a couple children, my score would be
pretty close to the needed number. My roommate, Heyde, has 2
girls, whom he calls "my beautiful, curly-haired 24 points."!*

Well, Dar Feheley at least came out alive.[61]

Love,

<u>Fred.</u>

———————— ➔ ← ————————

[V-Mail]

SAT. 26 MAY, 1945

Palaus.

Dear Ester—

*Have your last 2 letters on hand. I think it is good for all
concerned that Pop takes the boys to the lease with him so
often. Where will they—or he—go when he sells the lease? That
may be a problem, huh? Or didn't he sell Windfall and Nigger
Hill.[62]*

*Had a letter from Duffy today, which I already have
answered. What is this about his throat? I do believe I forgot to
ask. And while I think of it—just what is the true story about
Joe? If he has only ulcers, I think it is a mistake to keep it from
Mom. There is no need for it as far as I can see. I shall be sorry
to see him out of the Service, especially that way. But as you
say, his being home will make things much easier on the folks.
They both must be working too hard. You probably are too, for
that matter. Well, love to all. Tell the boys I said "hello" and to
be good.*

<u>Fred.</u>

[V-Mail]

TUES. 29 MAY 1945
Palau Islands.

Dear Folks—

This evening we officers played the enlisted men in basket-
ball, and we lost 24–17. It was fun playing, though very hard
on the lungs and legs. It was rather foolhardy for us to play
such a strenuous game without some practice.

No mail has come in to us in the last 3 days, but I just heard
that there will be plenty of 2nd class things tomorrow. About
20 sacks came in for us, so I should get my share.

Tomorrow is Memorial Day and services will be held in the
morning at the local military cemetery; I plan to attend. This
evening I saw a burial at the native cemetery just behind us.
Prayers were said by a Marine priest chaplain. The native
cemetery has been beautified by the Army and really looks very
nice.

Love,
Fred.

———————— ➔ ← ————————

[V-Mail]

WED. 30 MAY 1945.
Palau Islands.

Dear Folks—

I attended Memorial Day services at the Military Cemetery
this morning. It was quite nice and attended by a large group,
including a contingent of natives. The native kids were just
like those home—wanting to know why they had to keep quiet
and wondering what it was all about. The Island Commander
gave a nice, brief talk; a Marine band furnished the music. The
weather was beautiful, though this evening we had rain again.

Plenty of 2nd class mail came in and I got 3 packages of food
from you. Only 1 package bore a date, a white card on which
Mom printed April 16. Fruit cake was in 2 of the packages; also

candy, pecans, popcorn, olives, canned fish, etc. Thank you
very much. I have plenty of food on hand now.

Love,

Fred.

──────── ➔ ← ────────

Thurs. 31 May 1945.

Dear Folks—

This is early afternoon, and we have had rain all night
and all morning. Today is ideal for staying in, therefore, and
catching-up on reading and writing.

Our USO show was postponed until tonite; hope it stops
raining by then. Whether or not it rains won't make much
difference really, for we will go anyway.

Got paid this morning and bought a 25-dollar bond at the
same time because I was building-up too much spare cash. I
don't like to have very much on hand. Am enclosing the bond
with this letter. Please put it with my others and don't forget
about it when my next income-tax is figured.

Two days ago I sent you a small package of pictures and
negatives; let me know when you receive them.

Today's was the first 1st class mail in 4 days. I got 2 letters
from you, one from Ester and last week's "Eagle." Am glad to
hear that your rainy spell has broken, and to know that Joe
isn't very sick. I will be glad to see what the Medical Board
decides about him. I trust you take good care of these pictures
I am sending home. You will notice that some of them have
started to spoil—to mold and to turn color. I'll have a nice
collection, won't I?

This fellow mentioned in the clipping Ester enclosed must
be with a unit down the road about a quarter-mile. I'll inquire
about him.

Well, until tomorrow.

Love,

Fred.

[V-Mail]

FRI. 1 JUNE 1945
Palaus.

Dear Folks—

The USO show last evening was quite well received and
certainly was much better than the last one we were subjected
to. The troupe was small, too, being only 4—2 men and 2
women.

I saw an unusually good movie this evening, "Music for
Millions."[63] There were 4 or 5 stars in it and all seemed to
have the leading role. There was very good music in it too.
One of my favorite stars, little Margaret O'Brien,[64] was in the
movie. I think she is very sweet, and how she can act!!

No mail at all came in today, but I did so well yesterday that
I cannot complain. Am glad to know that you are getting my
letters regularly and in such short time.

In yesterday's letter I enclosed a 25-dollar bond; please let
me know when you get it.

Love,
Fred.

———————— ➔ ⬅ ————————

[V-Mail]

Sun. 3 June 1945
Palaus.

Dear Folks—

The dedication of the native chapel this afternoon was
interesting; will write you all about it tomorrow. Planned to do
so this evening, but instead we got involved in a bull-session
and a short letter is all I have time for yet tonite.

No mail from you today. Yesterday had one from Timon. He
had been in a hospital for a minor illness and was due to go to
a rest camp for a few days' rest.

Today started out cool and rainy and stayed that way until
early afternoon, after which we had the usual hot and dry
stuff. No movie played at our theatre this evening, which left

*us with time on our hands and nothing to do. Such a state is
unusual for us.*

Love,
Fred.

──────── ➔ ← ────────

Palaus.
Mon. 4 June 1945.

Dear Folks—

*This is another day that is good for "staying in the sack," or
if a person does get up for staying indoors. It hasn't rained yet,
actually, though it has been threatening all day long.*

*The native chapel that was dedicated yesterday is built
along the design of the one it replaces and was patterned
from photographs and description. It is of poured concrete
throughout, and has a small arm to the left of the front of
the church proper. It bears a cross on top; the churchyard is
surrounded by a low stone wall.*

*Inside the church is the usual confessional; the pews are
made of plywood and I estimate they will seat 144 persons.
The altar railing is rather plain, as is the altar itself. The back
of the altar has places for 3 statues. The entire woodwork of
the inside of the church—pews, rafters and ceilings—has been
stained with flame, which gives a very nice appearance.*

*A 2-star general was on the island yesterday and dropped
around for the services, though he did not take part in them.
The Island Commander laid the cornerstone and spoke for a
few minutes. He said $500 had been raised by the servicemen
here for the chapel and that it was built somehow through the
Society for the Propagation of the Faith.*[65]

*After the dedication service there was a wedding of a native
couple. I don't believe either was over 19 years old, and they
dressed and acted pretty much like an American couple. The
wedding service was in English.*

*When I finish with this I will write to both Lou and Joe.
I haven't heard from either in quite some time now, which*

makes me wonder why. I trust all is well with them. According to a letter from Ester today, Joe has yet to go before the board, so the disposition of his case is problematical. Often they are returned to duty; often not, too, as getting special diet in the Army generally is not easy. I can't figure out why Lou doesn't write. Maybe he is traveling. Haven't heard from Uncle Mike either in several weeks. Uncle must be 40 and thereby eligible for discharge.

I received the "Eagle" of the 25th today. Everyone seems to be right behind this 7th Bond drive and intent on putting it over. Hope they do, but, gosh that seems like a very high quota. 185 thousand is big money. Well, I think these bonds and bond drives are good things, but hope that this can be the last one.

This issue of the paper seemed more newsy than most. At least so it seemed to me. Of course all the issues are welcome to me. Several of the others glance over it every week, too. The "Eagle" is pretty well known in this unit.

Have heard that our ex nurses have left England and are going to France or Germany as part of the occupation forces. They are with a large numbered hospital and were in England all the time. Parker married one of the nurses, you will recall, and through her we keep track of the goings-on of the girls. There were some darn nice ones among them, and I often wish they hadn't been taken from us.

Capt. Johnson, who left this unit a couple of weeks ago, got a nice new assignment. He was given the abdominal surgery ward of a general hospital in Saipan. I believe that to be a much better assignment than what he had with us.

Several of our officers have left us during the past few months, all of which makes a person wonder just what is up—if anything. It may be nothing, as Tables of Organization change frequently, and we may only be getting in line with a new table.

Well, this is a rather long letter for me, and I have exhausted my supply of news. I'll close now, until tomorrow.

Love,
Fred.

[V-Mail]

Tues. 5 June 1945
Palaus.

Dear Folks—

Our spring must be somewhat like yours—plenty damp. There was a heavy rain last night and just a few minutes ago (it is almost noon) did the drizzle stop. I don't believe that much food-growing is done here, so this wet weather does not interfere much with planting.

Your letter of the 24th arrived this morning. Am glad Mom received and liked that Mother's Day letter; she deserves it and many more.

Also glad to know you heard from Lou. I can imagine that they were busy and know that he will write oftener now if he has time. Units like theirs will be busy for a time even after the fighting is over.

We here get a laugh from how optimistic you folks home and in Europe are about an early defeat of Japan. Most of us in the Pacific think we know better. The only people here who think Japan will be easy to knock out is the Air Force and they traditionally regard themselves as supermen. I believe you will find that another 18 months will be required before the Japs see the light of day.

No—I need <u>nothing</u> in line of shaving stuff. Thanks anyways. Yes, you can renew my subscription to the Lake Shore Visitor. It generally is weeks old by the time I get it, but its contents still is news to me, so please have it continued.

Isn't time going fast? Unless I am mistaken about it, Joe will be 22 on the 24th, huh? And my birthday is soon afterwards.

Love,
<u>Fred</u>

[V-Mail]

[no date][66]*, Palaus.*

Dear Folks—

    For dinner today we had fried chicken, and was it ever good! I ate 3 large pieces and now wish I had taken more. Fried chicken is one thing I'll never tire of.

    Had a short letter from Fr. Liebel today. He mentioned about Joe waiting for travel orders. Also had one from you. You say Joe definitely will be discharged. One of these days I will hear from Joe himself and get the true story.

Native children playing on the beach, May 1945, Angaur.

A group of native children have been swimming all afternoon on the beach just across the road. They are from 2 to 16 years old, and splash and shout and run around just like Americans. The little boys go in naked; the girls wear pants. They seem to take quite naturally to the water, though many seem to prefer playing in the sand.

This is the first rain-less day in about a week; it is a welcome change. Am glad your weather is warmer and that Pop was able to do some farming.

Love,
<u>*Fred*</u>

4

Saipan Introduction

Letters: June 14–December 27, 1945

On June 12, 1945, the 39th Station Hospital landed on Saipan, the second largest island in the Marianas. United States forces had seized the island eleven months earlier and then constructed airfields there to launch B-29 raids against the Japanese mainland. As was the case on Guadalcanal, the 39th was not activated, and instead most of its personnel served with other medical units on detached duty. Gabriel was assigned to the 148th General Hospital and by July 10 headed its laboratory's clinical microscopy and parasitology area. The 148th had been on Saipan since August 1944 and treated patients from multiple campaigns, including the Palaus, the Philippines, Iwo Jima, and Okinawa. By the time Gabriel joined the unit, many of these patients had been released or evacuated, but a new group was beginning to appear, liberated allied prisoners of war.[1] Gabriel worked diligently at the 148th, continuing his previous practices, as is seen in his July 1, 1945, Efficiency Report. Lieutenant Colonel Jewell R. Wilson, the 39th's commander, rated him "excellent" and wrote, "A quiet unassuming officer, friendly and cheerful. Very loyal and dependable. Very thorough in carrying out his duties. Manifests much interest and enthusiasm in his work. Always optimistic."[2]

As in his previous letters, Gabriel *spent* much of his time discussing his day-to-day activities, movies, and Notre Dame and Jefferson alumnus. He also commented on Saipan itself, which compared very favorably to malarial Guadalcanal and battle-scarred Anĝaur. In fact, Gabriel noted that the island

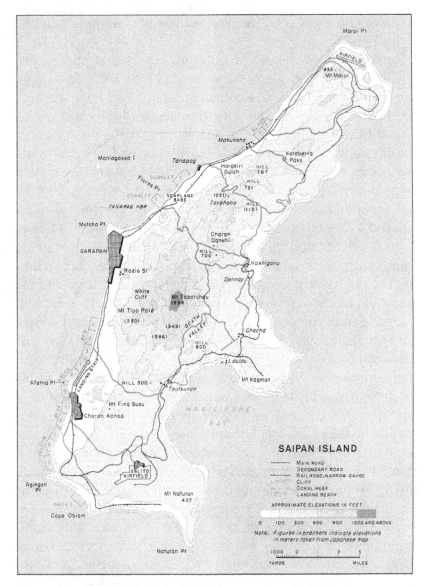

Saipan. Map II, from Philip A. Crowl, *Campaign in the Marianas*. Washington, DC>Office of the Chief of Military History, Department of the Army, 1960.

reminded him of the forested mountains of northern Pennsylvania, where he grew up. Gabriel's friend, Eddy Heyde also remembered Saipan favorably. One of his vivid memories of the war was, "Sunsets from high up on Saipan—our huts were about 800 feet above the sea. [Saipan] harbor was simply crammed with ships."[3]

Not surprisingly, many of Gabriel's letters and photos also deal with the final stages of the war. Upon learning of the atomic bomb, he wrote, "This new bomb is rugged, and I hope we don't live to regret its invention." Russia's declaration of war on Japan and the anticipation of official word that the war was over became important issues. With Japan's surrender, a new topic appears in many of his letters, when could he go home? On a form to tabulate the number of demobilization points that he had accumulated, Gabriel marked Category V, "I desire to be relieved from active duty at the earliest opportunity." In letters to his family, he dutifully reported the numerous changes to the point system. Gabriel also noted how quickly many of his fellow officers and friends, along with the enlisted men, returned to the States—sometimes with just a few hours' notice. For many men, including him, the pace of demobilization was not fast enough. With the end of mail censorship, Gabriel increasingly voiced his dissatisfaction with the process and with the military bureaucracy, more generally. On September 9, he complained to his parents, "Sometimes the apparent incompetence of the military service makes me wonder how we ever won the war. Guess our enemies' leaders do foolish things, too."[4]

One result of demobilization was that on October 1, Gabriel found himself the commander of the 39th Station Hospital, largely by default, as he explains. As commander, he oversaw the disposing of the unit's equipment, discharging of the enlisted men and awarding them their Good Conduct Medals, and writing monthly reports. For example, on November 2, he reported that the 39th had made "No direct contribution ... to the War Effort; however, personnel of the Unit have been on detached service with other active medical installations of this command." He further noted that 30 percent of the unit—now reduced to fifty men—purchased war bonds, showing that this remained important. Gabriel also compiled the 39th's last medical history and presided over its official deactivation on November 16, 1945.[5]

The last letter of this collection, dated December 27, 1945, finds Gabriel a patient in the 148th General Hospital. In May 1945, while still on Angaur, Gabriel experienced chest pain for six hours after climbing a ship ladder, and he had a similar attack in June. In August a chest X-ray for an upper respiratory infection revealed a large cyst or tumor that did not exist when he first entered the military. Monthly X-rays revealed no changes in the cyst, but on December 13, he was admitted to the hospital for "diagnostic studies." A week later, the cyst ruptured, which left him in intense pain for two days and the doctors prescribing him morphine.[6] Interestingly, none of Gabriel's letters to his parents in May, June, or August, make any mention of this serious medical condition.

Somewhere on Saipan.
Thurs. 14 June 1945.

Dear Folks:—

Well, now it can be told. I now am stationed "somewhere on Saipan" and we came here from Angaur, which is the southernmost of the Palau Island group.[7] Angaur was not very well known, as newspapers usually mentioned only the nearby island of Pelilieu. Pelilieu was invaded by Marines, Angaur by the Army.

I can't tell you much about our present status here. In fact, I don't know much about it. Right now both our officers and men are spread out over several of the hospitals here, mainly for board and quarters, though maybe later we'll work at these various hospitals. I believe this does not mean that our unit will be broken up. This merely is a temporary arrangement until a place can be found for us all or until we begin to function.

Seven of us officers are here at this hospital, which I cannot name (please notice that my address for now is 39th <u>Station</u> Hospital, A.P.O.# <u>244</u>, C/o P.M. San Francisco. We seven are in 2 compartments. Parker, Heyde, [Captain Richard E.] Bower and I being together. This hospital we are with has been here quite some time but just began to use these officers' quarters 2 days before we did, so you'll understand that they are new. They are prefabricated and resemble ours on Angaur but are arranged a bit nicer on the inside. Here, there is no breakdown of a compartment into 2 sleeping quarters and living-room in between. Instead there is only one nice large room. Our place on Angaur was kid stuff in size compared to this, which means that a person can do a lot of walking here in getting around this hospital. Incidentally, it is located on a hill and it is surprising how little waste of space because of hilliness there is.

This island is very pretty. All I have seen of it so far has been wooded hills that closely resembles northern Pennsylvania, as several have remarked to me. I have seen several well-kept small native farms and a few oxen and wild hogs.

The natives are Chamorros and many to me are dead ringers for Japs in appearance. And of course it is entirely possible that they do have Japanese blood. I believe the Japs

148th General Hospital barracks. Note the ships in the harbor, Summer 1945, Saipan.

controlled this island from the last war until last June. Wish I could tell you how much the Americans have built-up this base in those 12 months. I cannot, except to say that it is plenty.

While I think of it:—do not have the "Eagle," etc. change my address just yet, as we may get another soon and then another change would be needed. Of course, on my letters I will indicate on the envelop the correct return address.

Received 4 letters yesterday and 1 today. Some from you are included, as well as the "Eagle." The others read the paper and told me to tell someone that Palau is the correct spelling, not "Pallow." And I got the N.D. [Notre Dame] "Alumnus," too. Thanks.

Love,
Fred.

P.S. Better discontinue sending me packages for a few weeks.

There is another hospital here with a name very similar to mine;[8] that will mix-up our mail plenty for a time, I expect.

———————— ➜ ← ————————

PLEASE ADDRESS ME AS SHOWN BELOW UNTIL OTHERWISE ADVISED

CAPTAIN   FREDERICK   R   GABRIEL   0-485524
(Grade)   (First Name) (Initial) (Last name) (Army serial number)

39th Station Hospital
(Company, battery, etc.) (Regiment, groups or other organization)

A.P.O. No. 244, c/o Postmaster, San Francisco.
THE ABOVE COMPLETE ADDRESS SHOULD BE PLACED ON ALL MAIL SENT TO ME

MY CODE CABLE ADDRESS (SIX LETTER WORD) IS AMUFUN

DATE <u>15 JUNE 1945</u>
NORMAL SIGNATURE <u>Fred. R. Gabriel</u> [signed]
[INCOMPLETE]
[V-Mail]

Sat. 16 June 1945

Dear Folks—

There is nothing new to report about our possible disposition here. We heard stories that we were to take over another unit; then later that story was denied. And thus the rumors continue. None of the officers here with me have been put to work yet, though some of those at other hospitals have been. We might next week begin to work here.

Yesterday I hitched to the end of the island to visit the boys there, and also a nurse from Kane[9] I know. Was she surprised to see me! She trained at Bradford, and we hadn't seen each other since the summer at

———— ➔ ← ————

[V-Mail]

Saipan
Sunday 17 June 1945

Dear Pop—

With sincerest best wishes for a Happy Father's Day this year and for all the years to come. May they be numerous.

Your son,
<u>Fred.</u>

———— ➔ ← ————

[V-Mail]

Mon. 18 June 1945
Somewhere on Saipan.

Dear Folks—

I am pretty tired but want to write this before I go to bed. Why I am tired, I do not know for about all I did all day long was sit down in the lab and read. For Monday and in such a large lab, it seemed liked a light day's work.

Today wasn't very warm, and this evening is nice and cool, with a bright half-moon lighting up the place. The climate here is about the best we have hit since being overseas, and this island isn't bad, either. Many of our men do not like this place at all, because it is so big, I believe.

No mail from you today, but I did get 3 letters; all took over 2 weeks to get here.

Love,
Fred.

——————— ✦ ✦ ———————

[V-Mail]

Somewhere on Saipan.
Thurs. 21 June 1945.

Dear Folks—

Today is the first of spring [summer] and was a wet one for us. It rained several times including during the movie. However, a good show ("The Picture of Dorian Gray")[10] was playing, so we all sat through it. Afterwards, we sat around, discussing it and eating sardines.

I had another good mail call. One was from Joe and was 4 ½ weeks getting here. He sent it "free." Today I received, too, the air-mailed can opener, with the enclosed note about Pop and Joe going to W. Va. Am glad they were able to take the trip, and I know it will do them both good. Hope they don't hurry home.

Uncle Mike came through with a letter, too, that was written even earlier than Joe's. You probably have heard from him since then, but at that time all was well, and he thought he might get a discharge.

Until tomorrow.

Love,
Fred.

[V-Mail]

Saipan.
Sun. 24 June 1945.

Dear Folks—

I didn't write last night. After we came back from the movie, Parker, Hyde, Bower, and I started playing cards. We didn't stop until about eleven, which though early, is our bedtime. I am due at work at 7:30, which means that I get up about 6:15.

This has been a very pleasant day, all the way through, and entirely without rain. That is the first time we haven't had rain since we have been here. This afternoon was warm, something like Angaur weather. I worked all day, tho' actually there wasn't much for me to do. When things get slack I read, so time goes by pretty fast. Then, too, we have coffee at 9:30 to break up the morning routine

Today, I finally got a letter from Louis. It was written about 12 days ago, about the same time he wrote you. You know, for a time I thought he wasn't writing because he probably was sick, but I know better now. He just has been busy. He did start a letter to me 3 or 4 weeks previously but never finished it so enclosed it with the other letter.

Well, today is Joe's birthday. I wonder if he is celebrating it in Eldred or Charleston. It will be too bad if he and Pop rush right back as soon as they get there. Pop said he planned to be gone about a week.

Also had a letter from Charley Schaaf today. He no longer is with a hospital unit, but he is still located in France, wondering where he goes from there.

Love,
Fred.

[V-Mail]

Saipan.
Mon. 25 June 1945.

Dear Folks:—

   As I write this, Parker, Heyde, and Bower, armed with a shoe, slipper, and knife, respectively, are chasing a mouse about an inch long all around the room. I keep warning them not to injure each other, and so far no one has been hurt. I will let you know later how the mouse makes out.

   This has been a nice day, rather warm though now a slight rain is falling. Fortunately, it held off until after the movie, which was pretty good, for a change. Last week's movies all were on the weak side; some good ones are scheduled this week. Tonite's was Sonja Henie[11] and was in Technicolor—very pretty.

   No mail today. One of these days I'll have to write Fr. Liebel. Haven't done so in quite a while.

Love,
Fred.

——————— ➜ ← ———————

[V-Mail]

Saipan
Tues. 26 June 1945

Dear Folks—

   That mouse I wrote about last evening was finally stabbed to death. He never had a chance.

   This is early evening and we have just returned from a medical meeting. I did a little work on one of the cases presented at the meeting, so had to be there. We didn't go to the movie afterwards because while we were on Angaur we saw the show that is playing. Besides, the weather threatens rain.

Received the "Eagle" of June 8 and letters from Ester, Aileen and Jim Eastman today. Am glad to know that everyone is doing well. The same goes for me too.

Found out a classmate from Jeff is here nearby on the island. [12]

Love,

Fred.

————————— ➤ ❮ —————————

[V-Mail]

Saipan

Wed. 27 June 1945

Dear Folks—

This evening I dropped around to the Lab for what was supposed to be a few minutes work; actually I was there for 3 hours. And there it goes. But as long as that isn't repeated too often, I guess I can stand up under the strain.

Today received a letter from Vic and the "Eagle" of the 15th. Vic mentioned P.J. had his tonsils removed like an old timer. I knew he would act that way. She also mentioned the summer weather finally had put in an appearance back there. I am glad to hear though, as I was beginning to wonder if you would get warm days at all.

Regardless of all else, the "Eagle" regularly records births, deaths and marriages, doesn't it.

Love,

Fred.

[V-Mail]

Saipan.
Thurs. 28 June 1945.

Dear Folks—

Today had a letter from Lorraine, written the 17th in which she mentioned Pop and Joe's visit in Charleston, where they had arrived a week earlier. They planned to leave for home the next morning so by now are back home recuperating from the trip, I presume. I trust that I soon will be hearing from Joe, telling me all about Charleston and Lorraine.

Put in a full day in the lab again today and even went back a couple hours after supper. By that time it was too late for the movie, so here I am, writing you people my nitely letter. Wish I could write more each time but 1 page nicely is enough for all I usually have to say.

This is going to be another wet nite but our roof doesn't leak so we don't mind.

Love,
Fred.

———————— ➤ ← ————————

[V-Mail]

Saipan
Sat. 30 June 1945.

Dear Folks—

Today received your birthday card, with Mom's enclosed note—Am glad the weather is warming up enough for Pop to go ahead with the garden.

By the way—why wait until next year to have your picture taken? Why not do it now? It won't matter if I don't get a print of it exactly on my birthday. So how about it?

Also heard from Ester today. She too mentioned the hot weather and how well P.J. behaved in the hospital. You tell him I am very proud of him.

I put in another full day today and guess I will for a while. Two of the Lab officers left today, which means that the 3 of us who remain really will have our hands full.

Love,
Fred.

———————— ✥ ————————

[V-Mail]

Saipan
Sunday Morning 1 July 1945.

Dear Folks—

Didn't write last evening, and as things are slack here in the lab this morning, I decided to do so now. Last nite being Saturday, we stayed up late.

Burt, who is at another hospital working, came down to see us yesterday evening, and we all had supper together and later went to the movie. The movie, by the way, was very funny (Bob Hope and Virginia Mayo in "The Princess and the Pirate).[13] *Later, 7 of us crammed into a jeep and went along while the Chaplain drove Wesley (Burt) home. It was a pretty drive, but we couldn't see much as it was nite. Afterwards, we ate cookies and sardines and played cribbage until 11:15, when we hit the sack.*

Some evening this week the Chaplain is going to drive us around the island so we can see the sights. He is our own Chaplain (39th), by the way.

Love,
Fred.

[V-Mail]

Saipan
Sunday 1 July 1945.

Dear Folks—

Just returned from seeing the movie "God is My Co-Pilot,"[14] which was pretty good. I read the book, which I enjoyed very much.

I worked all morning and most of the afternoon. Rather, I put in my time. Next week I am going to ask for the afternoon off or maybe an afternoon during the week. This Jeff classmate of mine—John Brogan[15]—called me today and wants me to come out to dinner at his place.

Today had a letter from Joe (of the 20th), telling about the trip to Charleston. Too bad they didn't stay a little longer since they went that far, but I know they had to get back home. I'll write him in a couple days, telling what I know about those colleges he asked about.

Love,
Fred.

———— ➜ ❮ ————

[V-Mail]

Saipan
Tues. 3 July 1945.

Dear Folks—

Now I know you know my location, as a birthday card from Joe today used "244" and mentioned "Saipan."

Last nite's movie was Humphrey Bogart and Lauren Bacall, whom I believe to be grossly overrated.[16] There was a funny one tonite—Tallulah Bankhead in "Royal Scandal."[17] This week's movies are much better than last week. One thing, though—the seats here are absolutely the hardest I ever have sat on.

This evening the Chaplain drove Parker, Heyde, Bower, and I around the island for a couple hours. This really is a beautiful spot (in its ways) and our ride reminded me of the McCree Brook road to Ceres.

Today and yesterday were unusually hot; a lot like Angaur.

Love,

Fred.

———————— ➜ ← ————————

Saipan

Thurs. 5 July 1945.

Dear Folks—

Decided to address this letter to Joe, and thus answer 3 or 4 letters with one. Among 6 I received today were 2 from you and 1 from Vic.

I knew there were a couple fellows from home here, and rather suspected Anise was here, as Lorraine once wrote that he was in the Marianas. Now that I have his address I will try to contact him. I don't have too much time for that sort of thing and getting around at times is difficult, but meeting some of these people will be fun.

Joe, I don't know just how much I can advise you about a school. However, I think the first 2 things to settle are the course and the probable schools. Do you plan to continue with Commerce, and have you narrowed it down to either Bonas [St. Bonaventure University] or Hamilton? By the way, is Hamilton co-ed? I think that there are some advantages to a co-educational institution. Another thing to decide is if a school near home is desired; at the same time remember that if you are going away, 100 miles is the same as 500, as far as getting home often is concerned. For some reason or other, I don't take very well to the idea of driving to college every day and if you go to Bonas, it might be well to live there, coming home a couple times a week. By the way—I am enclosing a local newspaper supplement on a subject that should be interesting to you and Uncle Mike.

What is he planning to do, have you heard? I have an idea he will get into a business for himself. He should know the grocery business pretty well, and any concerned with food

seems to do okay if run at all well. Whatever he plans to do—I
hope he can get going easily.

A heavy rain is fall[ing] now—1800—and it seems like
the kind that will hang on all nite long. Rain here makes the
darnest, stickiest mud. Fortunately the hospital roads just
have been macadamized, so we shouldn't have to slush around
too much. July to October are the rainy months here and I
have been told that I can expect plenty of it.

Rumors concerning the 39th have started to circulate again.
Time will tell if they progress beyond the rumor stage. I'd hate
to see us broken up, and I rather like it here. Most of the 39th
are anxious to move forward and set up again, and I am too.

Are you doing anything with your painting these days?
Heyde, one of my compartment mates, is doing a scene in
pastels occasionally and doesn't do too badly. Last night he
did a shore-line one that is real nice. I wish I had some talent
along that line; I think it will be fun to do something creative
with my hands.

We have been playing cards a bit since being here, mostly
gin rummy and old-fashioned solitaire. To my regret, we
haven't been playing bridge since on the "Mormacport," en
route to Angaur. I was just getting sure of myself too, when we
stopped our daily sessions. The fellow who was teaching us
(another and myself) is at another hospital or otherwise we'd
resume our lessons. Bridge is a nice game, all right.

I had a long letter from Lou a couple weeks ago. He
surprised me when he said he had been taking, developing,
printing and enlarging his own pictures, which certainly is
nice. A lot of physicians go in for photography.

Am glad P.J. finally had his tonsillectomy. Undoubtedly he'll
stretch out this summer. It would be interesting to see how
much he grows in height and weight this summer.

Hope the shortages in merchandise let up soon. Darned,
however, if I can understand why you try to do too much about
getting substitutes. Looks to me like now would be a good time
to get rid of old stuff. Sell them that or nothing.

Have been seeing some fair movies lately, though those the first week were on the punk side. Guess I'll not go over tonite because of the weather. Also I am lab O.D. Instead, I think I will catch up on my letter-writing.

This is a pretty long enough one, so I'll close now with

Love,

Fred.

———————— ➔ ← ————————

[V-Mail]

Saipan

Tues. 10 July 1945.

Dear Folks—

Tonite for a while I thought I was back home. It began to rain and the sky darkened and the wind to blow. White coral dust on the shoulders of the road looked just like snow. Heyde and I were returning from a medical meeting, and we both at the same time thought how much it resembled the evening of a day in early winter. Incidentally, tonite has been very cool for over here.

We were going down to the Club for a couple beers, but the rain has lessened our thirst somewhat. Besides, Heyde is busy at another pastel drawing, and I just awakened from a nap. Parker is busy shining his brass.

Maj. Campbell, the Veterinary Officer on Angaur, came into lab today to see me.

Love,

Fred.

[V-Mail]

Saipan
Wed. 11 July 1945.

Dear Folks—

Know you'd prefer fewer V. mails, but darn if I can write longer letters unless I write less often. A v. mail a day is just about right for what I have to say.

Am listening to a newscast now, and am more optimistic about the end of the war. Still, it will be months yet. These bombing raids on Tokyo and elsewhere in Japan must be making the Nips pretty jittery and war-sick.

This evening was another wet one. It began while we were at an Orientation lecture, hearing about India. The rain continued so we stayed away from both the movie and the play "This is the Army,"[18] which is now here.

The radio program "Home Town News" ["News from Home"] is about Binghamton tonite, the home of the very excited major in the next room.

Love,
Fred.

———— ➔ ← ————

[V-Mail]

Saipan
Sun. 15 July 1945.

Dear Folks—

This is late Sunday evening. Being Sunday I thought I'd write you a long letter. Instead I slept a lot this afternoon and this evening went to the movie. Afterwards Heyde and I went down to the Club for a couple beers. I guess I had too much and right now bed is the place for me.

Until tomorrow, then.

Love,
Fred.

Saipan Island
Mon. 16 July 1945

Dear Folks—

This is the letter I should have written yesterday, but as I told you, when I returned from the Club last night had a little difficulty focusing my eyes.

Before I forget—here are 2 items of special interest.—1) in the July 10 issue of "Stars and Stripes"[19] the 14th Arm'd Division is listed as one of those scheduled to return home in September. 2) does Ma know that Schuschnigg,[20] the former premier of Austria, recently was liberated from a concentration camp by the Americans?

Had a good time at mail call again today, receiving letters from Ester, Vic, Lorraine and the July 6th "Eagle." Incidentally that was a most interesting letter Louie wrote Fr. Liebel.[21] Troops in Europe have it all over us as far as being in places of any size, etc., go. They can see places and things that have been known and famous for hundreds of years. Over here, on the other hand, are places most of us never heard of before war broke out, and which aside from military value, haven't much interest I suppose, just the same, that lots of the boys in the E.T.O. [European Theater of Operations] wish they had come this way and so it goes.

Vic mentioned the swimming party and lawn supper she had for Aunt Cecelia and Uncle Mike the Sunday before the 4th. No wonder she fed you on the lawn; I'll bet there wasn't room inside. It is nice you all were able to get together, and it is nice that she had Ester take the kids on picnics. Remember Mom used to take us on picnics in Dennis's Hill and up behind Lew Windsors'? I am not sure now where Windsors lived, but isn't it the Vaughn house at Haymaker? I recall going berrying over there once or twice.

What is Uncle Mike planning to do after he rests up a while, has he said? I know that at one time he talked pretty strongly of going to California to live. Of course that was a long while ago and much has happened since then.

Hearing all about the children makes me anxious to see them. Boy! I'll bet they will be big when I next see them. Not too big, I hope. Say—should Martha come visit you, or even if she doesn't, I wish you put the whole bunch of them together and take their picture.

The "Eagle" was newsy for a change and not so punctuated with mistakes as it often is. There were none at all that I noticed in the 2 columns devoted to Lou's letter. I wonder who set up the type for it. I note that a Wasson from Duke[22] is going to N.D. [Notre Dame] and that Richard Frisbee is now a father. I couldn't make out the reason for that notice by the Township School Board about not transporting Boro students in their busses. Are the Boro and Township feuding?

Well, I'll close now.

Love,
Fred

———— ➜← ————

[V-Mail]

Saipan
Thurs. 19 July 1945.

Dear Folks—

My only mail today was a "newsletter" from Fr. Liebel and a copy of that issue of the "Eagle" with Lou's letter, also one from Fr. Liebel. The newsletter was rather brief this time, though it was quite newsy. I hope Fr. Liebel doesn't discontinue it—I have enjoyed them very much and I am sure most of the others have, too.

Today was another rather easy one in the lab. We were through about 3 o'clock, though I stayed around until the usual 4:30 quitting time. I met the new officer this morning. He is quite young for a lt.-colonel and seems very nice.

I guess lab isn't the only department that is taking things easy now-a-days. My roommates say they aren't as busy as

*they were, either. The same probably is true throughout the
hospital, as the census is down right now.*

Well, until tomorrow,

Love,
Fred.

———————— ➜ ❖ ————————

[V-Mail]

Saipan
Friday, 20 July 1945.

Dear Folks—

*Believe it or not, this is the 3rd anniversary of our unit.
It surely doesn't seem like a year since our 2nd anniversary
party on the "Canal." We wanted to have one this year, but
decided it was a bit difficult now since we are spread out so
much here. Instead we'll celebrate when we are re-assembled
again as a unit.*

*Heyde and I were invited by our C.O. (39th) to have dinner
with him this evening at his place. He is at another hospital.
We had a good dinner, plus chocolate ice-cream for dessert.
We get ice-cream once a week but usually it is vanilla. We just
returned from there. The Colonel drove us back himself. It is a
nice 35-minute ride and is the traffic heavy on that road. Just
like a city.*

Until tomorrow.

Love,
Fred.

———————— ➜ ❖ ————————

[V-Mail]

Saipan
Saturday 21 July 1945.

Dear Folks—

*Just returned from the movie: "Son of Lassie";[23] it was
pretty good, and the technicolor scenery was beautiful.*

*Today had letters from you, Ester and Art Hand. Art wanted
me to look him up should I ever get down his way, which I*

*believe is Guam. I will, too. By the way, I believe Anise Cassab
has moved to Okinawa.*

*Four yards of that material is enough. Don't go out of your
way for the extra yard.*

*I am glad Aileen was able to visit you. By the way, who was
with her—Esther or Edna? Your letters mentioned both. Was
Uncle Louie still there, or had he gone back to Danbury before
the girls left for Olean?*

*Today was quite hot, though there was a little rain this
evening. Golly—tomorrow is Sunday again. Weeks seem to go
awfully fast here. Glad you liked the pocketbook.*

Love,
Fred.

———————— ➤ ← ————————

[V-Mail]

Saipan
Sunday 22 July 1945.

Dear Folks—

*Am listening to the Army radio program "COMMAND
PERFORMANCE"* [24] *right now. This week's hour is being
dedicated, they said, to a forgotten part of the Army—the
mules, horses, dogs and pigeons. They haven't been getting
much publicity have they?*

*Today received my birthday present from Lorraine—a
picture of herself. It is very good, and believe she posed for it
while Pop and Joe were down there. It is a face-view, about 6
by 4 inches and is covered with a plastic case so I won't have
to worry about it being spoiled by mold or finger prints.*

*This has been an easy day again, and a wet one, too, for
it has started and stopped raining a half dozen times this
afternoon. And more seems coming. Well, if it does rain I'll stay
in and read; if not I'll go to the movie. I don't know what is
playing but it might be a good picture.*

*A bus service within the hospital area was started
yesterday, using a big, enclosed truck for the vehicle. It
operates from 6:30 in the morning to 7:30 at evening.*

Personally I won't ride it much, but I do think it is a handy thing to have around with these sudden rains.

The 39th enlisted men who are here played a soft-ball game yesterday, and as usual a couple of them got banged up. One broke his arm in the same place (and in the same way) as on Angaur. Our fellows must play hard or something, because after practically every game one or more used to be hurt.

Haven't been hearing any rumors about us lately, but no news is said to be good news, so I am not worrying.

All is well with me, and you too, I hope.

Love,
Fred.

———————— →← ————————

[V-Mail]

Saipan
Mon. 23 July 1945.

Dear Folks—

The chaplain was over for a few minutes this evening, and while here he read the "Eagle," as he often does. Some of the things in it always amuse him; but mostly he reads it in earnest. I'll bet there isn't a man in our outfit who doesn't know I am from Eldred, though perhaps half of them don't know the state.

I laid down after supper and fell asleep. Thus missed going to the movie. It didn't seem to be very good anyway—an all British pictured named, "By Candlelight in Algiers" [Candlelight in Algeria].[25] For some reason or other I have been doing a lot of sleeping this past week. Maybe it is a good idea to get plenty of it while I can; besides 6:15 in the morning comes around awfully fast.

Until tomorrow.

Love,
Fred.

[V-Mail]

> Saipan
> Tues. 24 July 1945.

Dear Folks—

After the movie this evening, a few of us 39'ers had a little get-together at the Club. The liquid was only beer, however, and the food pretzels and peanuts. No food is served there though the Club will supply cheese for sandwiches if the person brings his own bread.

There is a clumsy comical dog around here whom everybody pets. Tonite someone had him drinking beer off the floor, after which this darn pooch tried to get into the Men's Room. It really was funny to watch him.

No mail from you today but I did have a letter from a nurse in Philly. She writes the most ambiguous letters at times, and today was one of them. Sometimes I just can't figure her out no how.

> Love,
> <u>Fred.</u>

———————— ➔ ← ————————

> Saipan,
> Thurs. 26 July '45

Dear Folks—

Our generator broke down yesterday. Hence we went to bed early and without writing any letters. I have had 3 from you in the past couple days, today receiving a V-mail from Joe.
Am glad Joe is progressing so with the painting, and I am sure the store now looks much better.

This visitor from Eldred I am expecting hasn't shown up yet, but I believe it is the Dorrion boy.[26] I checked-up on my informant and find this fellow is at the Dorrion boy's hospital, so probably it is he. I may get over that way tomorrow, and if so, will look him up.

Sunday, we local Jeff men are going to have a picnic. We find there are at least 8 of us here—mostly Navy. The picnic is scheduled down at one of the beaches and my friend Brogan is *supplying the food. Navy usually can get things like that easier than Army men. We will have a good time provided it doesn't storm.*

Before I forget any longer—yes I did get that wallet. I received it along in April sometime, several weeks before we left Angaur. I thought I had mentioned it, but probably didn't. I am sorry my request for cloth caused so much trouble. I forgot that cotton goods were so scarce. All I wanted was 4 or 5 yards of remnant, nothing fancy. In fact, if I had thought you would have to go out of town for it, I would not have asked for it. I might just as well still try to surprise you, now that you have done all the hard work in getting me material. However, you won't be much disappointed in why I wanted it—I hope.

Typewritten letters from both Pop and Joe (the 14th and 15th) arrived yesterday. The typed ones generally are longer, but any kind is welcome.

There was a heavy rain for about a half-hour this morning, after which the sun has been hot and bright. In fact, these past 3 days have been unusually hot and close. By the end of the afternoon I am bathed in sweat, and not necessarily from hard work, either. Work continues to be on the light side of the ledger. These people deserve a respite, too, as they certainly worked hard during the Iwo and Okinawa campaigns.[27] This is a large unit, and their patients are mainly chest and extremity cases, practically all of whom are evacuated to them. In other words, they do not service local garrison troops. Other hospitals here do that.

The Chief told me today that I could take time off occasionally, which I shall do. The rub is, however, that I may have no place or no way to go anywhere.

I am considerably behind in my correspondence, and think I shall make a determined effort to catch up.

The movie last evening was quite a disappointment—"No one Lives Forever."[28] A supposedly good one is showing tonite: "The Valley of Decision."[29] I read the book and enjoyed it very much. It centers on Pittsburgh.

Am enclosing a copy of the local "daily." [30]

Until tomorrow,

Love,

Fred

P.S. Jake Brady may drop in on you one of these days.

The *Daily Target*, July 26, 1945, Saipan.

[V-Mail]

Saipan
Fri. 27 July 1945

Dear Folks—

Heyde and I just returned from the Club, where we had a little "night-cap." There is a dance there tonite, but there isn't much doing.

Today received some snapshots from Lorraine. They were the ones taken while Pop and Joe were there. She sent 4; all are nice, especially the one of her alone, which is swell. She is very nice-looking, to say the least. I believe Lorraine sent Joe copies of these pictures, so you must know what I am talking about.

This was another hot, humid day, and an easy one again as far as work goes. I was going down to another hospital to visit one of [our] men who is sick but I couldn't get away. Maybe I can make it tomorrow. Sunday I am going on this Jeff picnic at one of the local beaches.

It is getting late so I must close now.

Love,
Fred.

———————— ➔ ← ————————

[V-Mail]

Saipan
Sat. 28 July 1945.

Dear Ester—

Looks like I'll be rained away from the movie this evening so can put in a few hours at letter-writing, of which I have several to take care of. I haven't been doing so well along that line this past couple weeks.

The local Jefferson alumni are going to have a beach picnic tomorrow. About 8 of us—all we could locate—are coming along. A naval officer is furnishing the luncheon and transportation. Only 1 besides myself is Army; he is Maj. White, who was on Angaur while we were there. I met him last nite at the officers' club.

*Still is no news about us (the 39th). The 20th we were
3 years old and we now are working on our 20th month
overseas. 4 days ago I finished my 3rd year in the Army. Time
is moving along, huh?*

*Did you see the pictures Lorraine sent Joe? She sent me
a set, too; also a portrait of herself for my birthday. How are
the 3 tykes doing? I must write them or send them something
soon.*

Love,
Fred.

────────── ⇥⇤ ──────────

[V-Mail]

Saipan
Sunday 29 July 1945.

Dear Folks—

*"Last minute cancellations" postponed our picnic for this
afternoon. Just the same, Maj. White, Brogan, and I met here
and then went out to Brogan's place for a few hours. Out there
we had sandwiches and beer and just sat around talking.
Although we did nothing exciting, we did have fun. Brogan
brought us back a few minutes ago, and I believe, just in time,
too.*

*It looks like are due for a big rain storm. The sky has
darkened and the wind has started to blow. Any time now the
rain will come.*

*Several score new nurses arrived at this hospital this week,
fresh from the States. In general, they are a young, nice-looking
group. The older girls were very pleased to see them arrive, for
now possibly some of them can go home. Whether or not they
do, however, remains to be seen.*

Love,
Fred.

[V-Mail]

Saipan
Mon. 30 July 1945.

Dear Joe—

I'll address this one to you.

You probably know our picnic had to be postponed yesterday, and we'll try again some afternoon this week. The effort wasn't totally lost yesterday, as the 3 of us who did show up stowed-away (internally) a part of the prepared luncheon.

The weather suddenly turned cool last night, which is probably why I now have a little head-cold, the first in a long time. It isn't very bad but I did stay away from the lab all day. The rest was fine, and I feel much better this evening and plan to go back to work tomorrow.

Some evening when things get slack I wish you would see how our microscope and otoscope[31] are doing; be sure there are no batteries in the latter. Someday I hope to use those instruments and want them to be in good working order. Has Pop read "Syrian Yankee"?

Love,
Fred

————— ➔ ← —————

[V-Mail]

Saipan
Monday [Tuesday] 31 July 1945.

Dear Folks—

My cold is about all gone, and I expect to be back to work tomorrow. I did drop over to the lab for a few minutes today. All is well there without me.

Our weather continues wet and surprisingly cool, so much so that we keep our door closed in the evenings.

Pop's letter of the 22nd is in. Am glad all goes fine home and that Joe is having no trouble. He should do okay provided he watches his diet. Why don't you make up your minds definitely whether or not you'd prefer Joe to begin school this fall, and

*if so, if he should go to Bonas? I have an idea he will go there
because you want him to. I don't believe he can go to school
and run the store both [at] the same time.*

Maybe Louie is writing me, but I am not receiving them.

Love,
Fred.

———— ➜ ← ————

[V-Mail]

Saipan
Wed. 1 Aug. 1945.

Dear Folks—

*Today has been the nicest day in the last 4; in fact, it was
hot. Maybe the sun did it, but my cold is all gone now, and I
worked all day.*

*No mail today, but I did receive the package containing the
cloth. Thanks for it. That stuff put you to more trouble and
expense than I realized it would. I didn't think it would weigh
so much.*

*Tonight I am attending a movie that is required of us all; it
is the sequel to the one we saw just after V-E day. Hope this one
reveals some good news, but doubt it.[32] Got paid today.*

*New critical scores for officers have been announced (100
for males; 50 for females). Against a goal like that, my 54
points are a bit weak, huh?*

Until tomorrow.

Love,
Fred.

———— ➜ ← ————

[V-Mail]

Saipan
Thurs. 2 Aug. 1945.

Dear Folks—

*I have just returned from dinner at Brogan's place. It
was a good meal too—fried chicken. Our meals here have*

not been so good for the last 2 weeks, which also is the case with most units on the island. Apparently not much fresh food is coming in.

Did hear some news today: the 39th <u>probably</u> will set up somewhere in the Marianas, though maybe not for a few months. Meanwhile we stay here,—I guess. That is the first definite news about us in weeks.

Your letter of the 24th came in today. Glad to know all is well with you; hope the Buffalo shopping trip was successful.

Love,
<u>Fred.</u>

———— →← ————

Saipan
Saturday 4 Aug. 1945.

Dear Folks—

Well, the local "Jeff Club" finally got together. This afternoon at 3 o'clock, 11 of us met at the Navy Officers Club for a session of beer and "bull." Both flowed freely. We were there 3 hours, going strong all the time. 6 of us were Army; the others Navy. One was from the class of '37; one from '39; two from '40; 2 from '41; 4 from '43 and 1 from '44. Some of these younger fellows remembered me, though I didn't recall them. I guess they knew me during my resident year there.[33]

It didn't take us long to get acquainted. The drinking helped out a bit, as did the fact that we had our professors, etc. to talk about. It is fun to get together like that and next Sunday we plan to do so again, this time at a beach somewhere on the island.

Mail has been a bit lean this week, though today I did get a V-mail from Ester (26 July). I thought Vincent Wood was Earn Wood's grandson, thou' of course I wasn't sure; and I believe that Bob Ring left Angaur last December, not recently. They went to Pelilieu from Angaur.

There seems to be an awful lot of little insects flying around the room tonite. They do not bite or sting, thank goodness, but

they are pesky and seem to get a big kick out of crawling along
my back.

I think I will write to Lou after I finish this. I haven't written
to him in almost a month now, nor have I heard from him
during that time. I suppose he is busy now and doesn't have
the time or inclination to do much writing. I do hope his unit
comes home next month.

Yesterday I received another package from you—the second
in 2 days. The first one contained the cloth; this last one
contained anchovies, sardines, powder and shaving lotion,
etc. Thanks for it. I can always use things like that. We haven't
been having any midnite lunches lately. For one reason, we
can't get things out of the mess hall like we did in our own
unit. Another reason is that we can get sandwiches down to
the Club during the evening.

I am completely over my cold now. Aside from it, I have
felt swell during the last several months. Am not sure of my
present weight but think it hasn't changed much since we left
Angaur. I believe I weighed a bit less on the 'Canal, but that is
because we played ball so much there. I was in better physical
condition then than I am now. We haven't had the time or
facilities for athletics since like we had there. Swimming
classes are being held here—required, more or less, I believe.
If I can I am going to try to attend them, for I still am very
anxious to learn how to swim fairly well.

A good rain is falling now. This wet weather probably is
the big reason why the bugs are so numerous. Fortunately
the mosquito population hasn't increased much. Actually this
island is a very healthy place, though such always was not the
case. Flies and mosquitoes were pretty rough here before aerial
spraying with D.D.T. was started. D.D.T. is great stuff.

I'll close now.

Love,
Fred.

[V-Mail]

Saipan
Sunday, 5 Aug. 1945

Dear Folks—

No letters from you came in today, but I did receive 2 packages of food. One was from you and the other from Vic. The packages were mailed the 10th and 19th of May respectively. In them (both) were a bath-towel, wash-cloth, candy, popcorn, anchovies, mayonnaise, sandwich cheese and luncheon meat. Thanks for it. I guess we'll have to have a few little parties to eat up all the food I now have on hand.

This afternoon Neil Dorrion came up to see me. We had a nice visit, and he was here a couple of hours. He looks a little like his father. He told me that a Netzel boy and James Morrison of Bullis Mills[34] are around here somewhere with the Navy. I believe Netzel came here to visit him some time ago.

A couple of visiting 39'ers just dropped in, and we are having a good 39 discussion. No one seems to have any new rumors or stories concerning us, so I can't pass anything on to you.

Love.
Fred.

——————— ➜ ← ———————

Saipan
Monday 6 Aug. 1945.

Dear Folks—

Today had 2 letters from Ester, one from Vic, one from you and the "Eagle" of July 27th. In addition there was some airmail stationery. Don't recall now if I asked for it or if it is merely a hint, but I'll try to write fewer V-mails in the future. However, as long as I write daily I am not going to be able to get off very newsy or interesting letters.

In yesterday's letter I mentioned that Neil Dorrion had spent a couple hours visiting me yesterday afternoon. We had a good talk, and he brought me up to date on the Bullis Mills– Haymaker[35] items.

*My roommate, Heyde, is doing a lot of work on pastels
these days. He is on the other side of the table now, drawing.
Heyde does good work and is going to give me a couple of his
productions. I wish I could do work like that. It doesn't seem
too difficult, so maybe I can. Never having tried, I do not know.*

*We often thought we would like to have a radio here in the
room, but the way the fellows next door play theirs, it amounts
to about the same thing. Their radio seems to be always tuned
to the local station. Some of its programs are good; others not.
One good thing is that it has no commercials to annoy us. We
are spared that.*

*Someone else from around Eldred is here but I do not know
whom. One of my friends had this fellow as a clinic patient.
While taking the history, this fellow said he lived in N.W.
Pennsylvania. When asked if he knew where Eldred was, he
said that he ought to, as he lived 4 miles from there. Have any
idea who it is? Next time I see my friend I'll see if he recalls the
name and unit of that patient.*

*In her letter Ester said that Jimmy had not been feeling
well. I hope it is nothing serious and that it is over with now.
I haven't had any very recent pictures from her but the boys
must be growing fast. I'll be especially interested in P.J.'s case,
especially since his tonsillectomy. P.J. will be going back to
school before very long, too, come to realize it. Hope he is
having a good summer.*

*How is Joe progressing on the painting job? It is a good-
sized undertaking for one person. I hope these shopping tours
are producing some stock to put on the shelves, now that he
has them all brightened up.*

Well, I'll close now.

Love,
<u>Fred</u>.

[V-Mail]

Saipan
Tues. 7 August 1945.

Dear Folks—

The movie this evening ("Murder She Says") [Murder, He Says][36] *was pretty punk, so Parker and I walked out on it and went down to the Club for a beer and sandwich. The movie tomorrow is supposed to be very good—"Those Endearing Young Charms."*[37]

This place just buzzed all day long with speculation about the new atomic bomb we have just announced possession of.[38] *From what little I have heard, it must be terrible. Rather makes me wish it never had been invented for in a few years other nations will be making ones just like it. One good thing— I'll bet if we drop a few more on Japan they'll reverse their decision to fight to the bitter end. They won't want to be totally destroyed, as they surely will be if they fight on.*

No mail from you today; in fact very little came in to the hospital. However, I did receive a nice letter from Lorraine.

Love,
Fred.

——————— →← ———————

Saipan
Thurs. 9 Aug. 1945.

Dear Folks—

Last night a practice blackout, a stage show and a couple movie shorts kept me from writing you. By the time we got back here it was eleven—our bedtime. I had nothing much to write about anyway, so really it didn't matter.

We just got back from the movie a few minutes ago. It wasn't too good but was enjoyable, a story of bobbysoxers.[39] *In general it probably presented an exaggerated view [of] things but the main idea is true. Bobbysoxers apparently are a distinct way-of-life back home from what I read.*

I thought that news of the atomic bomb had caused a lot of

*optimism here but how it has jumped with the announcement
of Russia warring on Japan!*[40] *Some people, from the way they
are talking, must have started to pack already. Estimates as to
how long Japan will hold out range from 6 days to 6 months.*

*The B-29s alone had the Air Corps fellows saying "3 months."
My own opinion is about 5 weeks. The negotiations alone will
take almost that long. This new bomb is rugged, and I hope we
don't live to regret its invention.*

*This hospital is having a party tomorrow nite to celebrate
1 year here. Don't know whether I'll go—I have been invited—
because it'll more-or-less be a family affair, I believe. We didn't
have our 3rd anniversary party on July 20th because we
39'ers were spread out too much.*

*We have lost several men and a few officers during the past
few weeks by illness, discharge, etc. One officer was a medical
evacuation and 2 more are up for it, besides which we lost a
couple some time before we left Angaur.*[41] *My roommate Heyde
may leave this hospital (not our unit) within a few days. There
isn't much of his work here right now, and a nearby hospital
does need a man. I'll hate to see him go as he is a fine fellow,
and he and I get along swell. Still—that is how things often go,
huh?*

Until tomorrow.

Love,
<u>*Fred.*</u>

———————— ➔ ← ————————

[V-Mail]

Saipan
Fri. 10 Aug. 1945.

Dear Folks—

*I watched a soft-ball game this evening. The 39th team
played, and lost 8 to nothing. If they keep losing, I guess I'll
have to reform my old "Eagles" to help them out.*

*Quite a lot of mail came in today. I received 2 letters—one
from Ester and the "newsletter." It is news to me that Johnny
Gabriel is married again and to a nurse.*[42] *The last I knew his*

wife was a nite-club entertainer from Tennessee. Is his present wife an Army nurse? I mean—was she?

This has been the hottest afternoon in a couple weeks. Mornings here are usually the warmer but not today. Today both were hot. Right now, though, it seems like a rain is blowing up.

Parker just told us that in a recent letter his father mentioned that back there in N. Jersey there was rain every day for 2 weeks as a result of which vegetable crops were largely spoiled.

> Love,
> *Fred.*

———— ⟶⟵ ————

[V-Mail]

> Saipan
> Sunday 12 Aug. 1945.

Dear Folks—

Have a couple other letters to write tonite before going to bed, so this will be V-mail instead of longer.

This place was pretty much excited today. Early this morning (very early) the story got around that the war officially was over. And of course there was considerable celebrating. The same thing happened this afternoon, the story possibly coming via the Navy. The reason I say that is that all at once several ships in the harbor suddenly began blowing their whistles and shooting flares. Apparently that story was a bit premature for I have heard several newscasts since then, and nothing official has happened.

My personal opinion is that the thing is in the bag but that a day or 2 yet is needed to complete the paper work.

This afternoon Heyde left to begin work at another hospital here on the island. Parker and I are left in this compartment now.

> Love,
> *Fred.*

Saipan
Monday, 13 Aug. 1945.

Dear Folks—

All the newscasts today keep telling us that yesterday's peace celebrations were a bit premature. Apparently a lot of people were fooled, especially that Canadian radio station.[43] *Well, come to think of it, the negotiations alone will require a few days to be cleared through all those national capitals.*

Today received the package containing the stationery and swim trunks. Thanks for them. I'll try to see that you get most of that paper back—written upon. I can use the other things included, though hope I am not over here long enough to need to do much sewing.

Today, too, received a V-mail written by Joe on the 4th. Am glad that Martha and the boys came over to visit you for a while. Sure would like to be there now. Joe writes that the children—all 8—are growing right along. I'll probably have to get re-acquainted with them all except Eddy and P.J. I doubt that the others will remember me—except by name.

It is nice that Joe has taken definite steps to go back to school this fall. Is he going back under the G-I Bill of Rights? In a way, I am none too keen on his driving back and forth, though he knows more about that than I do. Getting him a car will be a problem, all right.

I was quite surprised to learn that we still own property on Park Avenue. Somehow or other—perhaps only wishful thinking—I had the idea that all those houses had been sold. It will be swell if good buyers can be found for the others. I realize they probably are a good investment but they probably require considerable looking-after, too. Some time I wish Pop or Joe would bring me up to date on the actual ownership of those houses, as well as the status of that loan we got from the Bradford Building and Loan in July of 1942. After all, it was in my name (I am not sure, actually, or I never really knew what the transaction was about), and I'd like to know. Such information may save me time and opportunity someday.

Incidentally, how about that picture of Mom and Pop I was supposed to get for my birthday? I have heard nothing concerning it. Certainly that request is reasonable enough. I know Mom doesn't actually like to pose for pictures but surely she will for this one. All she has to do is smile sweetly 3 or 4 times. Have the photographer keep taking proofs until he gets one she likes. Really it is simple.

Considerable 2<u>nd</u> class mail came in this afternoon. I received several papers and magazines, including the "Eagle" of the 2nd. There is a lot wedding-bell ringing going on now. I suppose I can expect to hear about Joe anytime, can't I? Still, I wouldn't be too surprised for I have been expecting something like that. I can just hear Mom say "how about you?" Well, maybe one of these months.

Until tomorrow.

Love,
<u>*Fred.*</u>

———————— → ← ————————

Saipan
Tues. 14 Aug. 1945.

Dear Folks—

Well, we over here are still awaiting "word." How about you people? Know anything we don't? I rather imagine our news is about the same, as we get hourly newscasts.

This afternoon was the first it has rained in several days, and it put off a ballgame between this hospital and the 39th. There was considerable interest (and money bet) on this game, and for it the old 39th team of Guadalcanal and Angaur days was reassembled. Our boys were all primed to win, too. I hope the game is rescheduled.

I was wondering today—did you ever have my winter Army dress blouse shortened? Joe knows which one. I wanted it done some time ago but don't recall now how you answered me. The coat is about 3 inches too long, now. Maybe I'll never use it again but I'll be surprised if I don't. So if you have

Gabriel (*right*) and Eddy Heyde (*left*), V-J Day 1945, Saipan
(courtesy of Muriel Youmans).

Gabriel and 148th General Hospital laboratory personnel celebrate V-J Day,
August 15, 1945.

not already done so, please have it fixed for me. How is my
summer worsted uniform I bought in Chicago? That was tailor
made and fit okay.

Wes Burt, my old roommate, came around to see us tonight.
Saturday nite we had a little "going-away" party at his place
for Heyde. About 6 of us were present, and we had a good
time. Before the party we went to a movie, which wasn't too
good, and then went over to his place for a few drinks and
sandwiches.

Lots of B-29's went out today, so maybe Japan is being urged
a bit to make up its mind. The radio says that today's raid may
be the biggest of the war and is the first by B-29's on railroad
yards, etc.[44]

The Russians seem to be doing okay by themselves in
Manchuria.[45] *Apparently the Japs aren't used to fast land*
fighting with armor. The Russians can capitalize now on the
lessons they learned fighting the Germans. Actually, I don't
believe the war will go on over a few days more, if that long. I
believe it is all over now but the shouting. Hope I am right and
that soon I'll be headed for the States.

Love,
Fred.

---------- →← ----------

[V-Mail]

Saipan
Fri. 17 Aug. 1945.

Dear Folks—

Well, rumors continue to fly thick and fast about the fate of
the hospital here, but still they are only rumors. Concerning us,
the story is the same. I now believe we will not go forward, but
that is only a hunch.

Apparently the Japs are a bit mixed up about this surrender
business, but they should get the idea soon. Still, it will be
difficult to get some of those fanatics to see the light. According

to today's news, a little trouble takes place occasionally
between their planes and our ships.[46]

Capt. Hughes moved in with us today, taking the portion
of the room occupied by Heyde before he left. Hughes is our
adjutant and was in a neighboring barracks.

Love,
Fred.

——————— →← ———————

[V-Mail]

Saipan
Sunday, 19 Aug. 1945

Dear Folks—

Am real tired tonite and anxious for bed, so this will be
another brief one. However, I believe I have been sending
rather long letters, so this one will be a change.

I wish you would start building up my checking account—
i.e.—put all my allotment in it until I have 7 or 800 dollars. I
expect to draw rather heavily on it within a few months and
don't want to have to fool around with an interest one.

Also—you can stop putting blank stationery in your letters.
With this air-mail variety you just sent me, I now have enough
on hand to last a few months. When that begins to run low I
will let you know.

A heavy rain now is falling. It should cool off this hot
weather we have been having.

Love,
Fred.

[V-Mail]

Saipan
Mon. 20 Aug. 1945

Dear Folks—

Just returned from seeing "Thirty Seconds over Tokyo,"[47]
*one of the best war pictures I have seen. What pleased me most
was that there was very little flag-waving, something I dislike.*

*Friday, Saturday, and Sunday were very hot. Today was
much cooler because of a heavy rain. In fact, it was one of the
longest rains so far. Generally they last but a few minutes.*

*"When" we get back to the States is the big item of
conversation around here. All kinds of stories float around but
very little official news has been given out. Most of this hospital
[148th General Hospital] are ready and willing to leave, as
they have been overseas over 38 months, which is long enough
for anybody.*

Until tomorrow.

Love,
Fred.

———— →← ————

Saipan
Tues. 21 Aug. 1945.

Dear Folks—

*Just returned from seeing one of the best movies of the
year—Danny Kaye in the "Wonder Man."*[48] *It very funny, so see
it if you have the chance. I think you will enjoy it.*

*"What will happen to this hospital" and "when do we go
back" continue to be the talk around here. So far nothing
definite has been said and stories are a dime a dozen. I
have an idea that as soon as V-J Day is proclaimed, things
will begin to really happen, including redeployment and
reconversion. I believe that units with over 18-months
overseas time will be coming home much sooner than they
expected, and I do hope we are amongst them.*

Mail service to us has been a bit slow this past week. I heard the planes that ordinarily carry the mail were diverted to some other use for a few days. Today, however, a little airmail did get through, so I believe we can expect more tomorrow.

We here follow with interest MacArthur's progress with the Japanese.[49] *They seem to me to be acting funny. I don't know if there is treachery afoot or if it is only the Oriental way of doing things. Or should I say "Jap" way of doing things? Anyway, I believe that for a time at least occupation duty in Japan is going to be rough duty.*

The regular 39th softball team played this hospital today and lost 3–2. I saw only the end of the game, and that was exciting. I believe that if the 2 teams meet again the 39th will win.

Incidentally, the 39th officers are planning a party this Saturday nite. It will be the first time many of us have been together since we arrived here some 9 weeks ago. We are to meet at our C.O's place, which is at another hospital where he is temporarily. I'll let you know what kind of time we have.

Until tomorrow.

Love,
<u>Fred</u>.

P.S. Am enclosing 2 snapshots.

[V-Mail]

Saipan
Wed. 22 Aug. 1945

Dear Folks—

Just received 2 letters from you and before I forget, I want to answer a few questions: —

I'll try to get in touch with Bill Llewelyn.[50]

Did you ever receive a $25.00 bond I mailed you about the first of May?

Yes, I received the swim trunk; they fit fine.

The "Notre Dame Alumnus" does come to me directly. I received 1 only last week.

The "Eagle" of the 10th came today, too. It was rather newsy. I was surprised that the Frison-Dennis wedding took place in Church. How long has she been a Catholic, and what is being done with her young children? Did she have a boy named Bernard?

Tomorrow I am going to attend a Mass said by Archbishop Spellman.[51]

Love,
Fred.

———— →← ————

[V-Mail]

Saipan
Thurs. 23 Aug. 1945

Dear Folks—

This morning I attended a Mass said by Archbishop Spellman. About 15,000 people were there, and afterwards a good share of them—including me—shook hands with him. The Archbishop is a kindly-looking man, just like his pictures. He gave a nice sermon after Mass, which was said in a movie [theater] on the other side of the island. About 20 of us officers and nurses drove out in a hospital bus; I don't know how many enlisted men went out.

This evening Parker and I had dinner with Herbie Weisberg—another of our officers—at the place where he is

*working. We had lamb chops, fried right, and I enjoyed myself
on 4. Afterwards we played cribbage for a couple of hours.*

Until tomorrow.

Love,

Fred.

———————— ⇥⇤ ————————

Saipan Island

Mon. 27 Aug. 1945.

Dear Folks—

*I went visiting last nite out to Brogan's, and by the time I got
back here it was too late to write you. Golly! They had a swell
meal out there last evening—delicious steak (done as desired),
fried potatoes, toast, cheese-and-pineapple salad, apple pie
and ice-cream. There are tablecloths, 2 spoons, 2 knives and 2
forks and negro serving-boys. They seem to do things like that
much nicer than we do it in the Army, which reminds me—the
food here has been unusually poor for the last 3 weeks.*

*After dinner we went over to their Club for a few drinks,
after which we saw a pretty good movie. It was Charles
Laughton and Ella Raines in "The Suspect,"[52] a type of picture
in which he really stands out.*

*Yesterday afternoon I went out and saw Bill Llewelyn.
I tried to get transportation to go out, and since there was
none available immediately, I hitched out. At that I made
good time, since it is only about 2 miles from the hospital. Bill
surely was glad to see me. He looks good, and has a dandy
tan. He said I was the first person from home he has met
since being out here. Bill arrived here the first of the month;
he has been in the Army 38 months but has been overseas
only 2 of them. He is in a Replacement Depot and probably is
awaiting reassignment.*

*One of the heaviest rains we have had is falling now. It has
been raining off-and-on since midnight, and mud is pretty
common right now. Mud is one of the biggest reasons why
I will be glad to get back to where there are sidewalks and
hard roads everywhere. But to get back to the rain: I knew*

nothing about last night's storm until I awoke this morning, so apparently I sleep much sounder than I thought I did.

Today received a letter from Ester, dated the 16th. In it she told about the celebrating home when news got around that Japan had surrendered. Apparently you received that premature report, too, just as we did. We heard the "official thing" at 9:07 AM on Wednesday, which would be about 7:07 PM back home. Is that about the time you heard of Truman's announcement?[53] *Wish I could have seen the 3 tykes in the parade.*

The "Eagle" of the 17th arrived today, too. It wasn't a particularly newsy issue, I don't think. I'll send it over to Bill tomorrow.

Incidentally, are Ann NcNulty and Len Hensel engaged? I am not sure if that is what she was writing or not, and there was no mention of it in the paper.

Just heard a swell rumor, in which the 39th was included, about local hospitals going back to the States. Should it be true and materialize, I might *see a football game this season, albeit a bowl game on New Year's Day. Remember—it is only a rumor so far.*

> *Love,*
> *Fred.*

──────── ➔ ← ────────

[V-Mail]
Saipan

Wed. 29 Aug. 1945.

Dear Folks—

Parker and I just got in from spending a very enjoyable evening with the Chaplain at the place where he is working temporarily. He called for us at 5 o'clock and drove us to the area. We had a drink (coke) before we sat down, in a nice dining room, to a dinner of lamb and mashed potatoes, followed by apple pie and ice cream, and preceded by soup. I described the meal and setting a bit because they are in so much contrast to what we have been getting here.

View of Saipan from the mountains. Gabriel is on the left, summer 1945.

After dinner we drove and climbed to the top of the highest mountain around. From there we could see for miles and miles, and what a beautiful sight it was! The views were just like pictures.

We capped our evening by seeing the movie "The Seventh Cross," starring Spencer Tracy.[54] *It was a Nazi war picture but quite good.*

All in all, we had a nice evening, huh?

Love,
Fred.

Saipan
Fri. 31 Aug. 1945.

Dear Folks—

I saw an interesting soft-ball game this evening (shades of Guadalcanal, huh?), the 39th winning 1–0 in an overtime game. It was one of the best games I have seen here. I don't go to many of the games but do usually try to go when our team plays.

George Hughes (our new roommate), Parker and I are having a lot of laughs this evening at George's expense. He had his eyes dilated this morning for a refraction and can't see very well yet. He goes around try[ing] to read per usual, and of course he can't do it. He looks and acts so funny reading with one eye and then the other, holding the letters close and then far away, etc. To make matters more humorous, he isn't feeling well anyway, and he says now he really is a sad sack.

We are following the occupation of Japan closely, and are pleased that it is progressing so smoothly. The easier and faster it goes, the fewer troops will be required there, and the sooner lots of people will get back to the States. We probably will be included therein. Rumors concerning all medical units out this way are still a dime-a-dozen. Some are about us and some sound pretty good. At this stage of the game, though, I have wised up and do not believe anything until it actually happens.

In a package you sent me quite a while ago was a blotter advertising a typewriter repair shop in Tampa, Florida. The fellows want to know how I came to have it, and aren't satisfied with a simple, "it was sent to me from home." Incidentally, on the blotter is the name of a city spelled YBOR.[55] *We are having quite a discussion on the correct pronunciation of it. I say it is E-bo, for such I was told a long time ago. I recall that in the 7th grade Florence Parmeter once raised her hand and said she knew a word none of us could pronounce and then she sprung it. I believe her people had been down that way, so she knew. Isn't it odd how I always remembered that incident?*

Today I received a letter from Timon, in the Philippines. He has been reclassified and now is in a non-combat engineering outfit. The letter was a short one and did not say much other than that. He apparently is now recovered from his sickness that he had a few weeks ago.

Today received also your letter of the 21st. That V.J. celebration Eldred put on must have been worth seeing.

Was it actually put on the air, or just mentioned on the radio newscast?

Thanks for offering to send me some food but please do <u>not</u> do so unless I request it. We have plenty on hand yet and are using it up only slowly. I am trying to reduce (I weighed 148# 2 weeks ago) and the others do not often eat before going to bed. Our meals haven't been very good lately but there has been some improvement yesterday and today.

Tonight Captain Johnson and I are going to pop some corn, as we have been planning to do for the last 2 months. He and I used to do that often back on Angaur before he was transferred out. It so happened he was sent to this hospital here.

It was nice that Louie met Williams[56] and Leffler in Bavaria or whatever the name of the place is. I haven't heard from him in about 2 months now, so do not know just where they are located. I can understand why he probably isn't writing so often—he just has had a letdown. I often feel that way myself, and I suppose it is the same with Joe.

Love,
<u>*Fred.*</u>

———————— ➔ ← ————————

[V-Mail]

Saipan
Monday 3 Sept. 1945

Dear Folks—

Today, Labor Day, was supposed to be a holiday here. However, it didn't turn out that way for me, and I worked until about 4 o'clock. I can't complain, though, as I really have things pretty easy.

Today had a letter from Lou, in which was enclosed a picture of himself. He looks good, tho' maybe a bit heavier. He wrote very interestingly of the trips he has taken, the things he had seen, etc. Lou will have plenty of stories to tell, all right, when he gets home. Incidentally, he wrote as though their unit will leave for the States within a few weeks. Hope it does.

Kind of thought Bill Llewelyn would be around today but he didn't. Maybe they had to train today, I don't know. I sent him a couple "Eagles" the other day.

Love,
Fred.

——————— ➔← ———————

[V-Mail]

Saipan
Wed. 5 Sept. 1945

Dear Folks—

Although there is nothing definite, I feel quite optimistic about being back in the States within a few months. This plan of not sending overseas men with 45 points, suggests to me that the big boys have decided that not-too-many of us really are needed over here. [57]

I didn't do very much today. Took off for a couple hours this morning and spent the greater part of the afternoon making a pop-corn popper. One of these evening I will see how it works.

There has been plenty of rain this evening; hard, too. It was just the kind of evening for staying in. Weisberg (one of our men who just moved in with us), Parker and I just finished a couple hours of cribbage. Until tomorrow.

Love,
Fred.

[V-Mail]

Saipan
Sunday 9 Sept. 1945

Dear Folks—

I missed writing the last 2 evenings. On Friday it was because the generator was on the blink, and we had no lights; last evening it was because we tried out my new popcorn popper, and we sat around and talked (and ate) until way past our bedtime.

Am in the lab now. Things are quiet this morning, fortunately, so I think I will take off early and go down to the quarters to clean up the mess I made last evening.

I don't qualify according to the new point system for officers announced a couple of days ago, but just the same am in high hopes of being back in the States in a few months.[58]

Love,
<u>*Fred*</u>

———— →← ————

Saipan
9 Sept. 1945.

Dear Folks—

I had planned to see "A Tree Grows in Brooklyn" this evening (which would make the 3rd time) but it is raining quite hard so I stayed in. Parker and Weisberg are here, too, writing letters. We just finished our daily session of cribbage with myself winning 2 out of 4 games. Our other roommate, George Hughes, is still in the hospital. We dropped in to see him this P.M. He is feeling fine and thinks he will be discharged within a few days.

This afternoon I went swimming for the first time since being here on Saipan. The beach wasn't very good but the sun was hot and the sand soft, so we did lie around a while, trying to reinforce our rapidly fading tans. Five of us went along. Parker, Weisberg, and I drove over to the other side of the island where we picked up C.O. Lt. Col. Wilson, and Ed Heyde.

Afterwards Heyde came down here with us to see Hughes. Incidentally, now that censorship is over[59] I believe I can safely reveal that I am at the 148th General Hospital. When we arrived here their bed capacity was 2,600. Now, however, it has been made a 1,000 bed unit again.

Work has been rather slack this week although the week previously I was quite busy. I doubt that we'll be rushed again—thanks goodness—though we may have an occasional busy day. For instance—I hear that tomorrow we are to receive a few dozen of Americans liberated from Japanese prison camps. If so, my part of the lab may get considerable work. You see, I do the parasitology here, and these men may need plenty of work. In my part of the lab we examine specimens— mainly urine and stools—for evidence of human tropical diseases, especially intestinal infections. The most feared one, of which we find a few all the time, is amebic dysentery. There seems to be considerable amebiasis of a non-serious nature. The commonest thing, I believe, is hookworm. Fortunately, there is no malaria here. There was considerable dengue a few months ago, but it has been controlled very effectively by aerial spraying of D.D.T.

The new point system for officers is causing a lot of talk here.[60] It sounds pretty good on paper, but the famed red tape and snafu will horse it up. Already I have heard that medical officers are not included in it. I realize medics are essential theoretically but there are so many over here doing nothing that it is a shame. Sometimes the apparent incompetence of the military service makes me wonder how we ever won the war. Guess our enemies' leaders do foolish things, too. Seeing how the Army is run only makes me more determined to have as little to do as possible with any system of state or socialized medicine unless it is run by the doctors, and not by the others. One thing that seems very unfair to me is granting 12 points for a dependent child. I believe dependency is being made too much of. Just think—some poor devil could storm 2 enemy beaches and he'd only have 10 points for it, whereas the fact that a man has a young child will give 12. Maybe dependency should carry some weight, but certainly not that much.

Am glad Joe's study at Batavia [61] *showed all is well. The news that he can have a more liberal diet must have been welcome to him, as I know how he must have felt on a restricted one. He'll be going to school soon, won't he? I hope he takes things easy and doesn't try to do too much work in the store and study too.*

Pop's letter about the real estate came several days ago. Am glad to know that most of the houses have been sold; I assume everybody is prompt in their payments. Can't recall just now which are the Mechanic, Edson, and King Street properties. Are they the Hensel, Standard and Howell houses, respectively? That restaurant building on Main Street is sort of a white elephant. Why not make a nice offer to the electric company and try to sell it to them? About the Annex property—I didn't know anything about my helping Ester. How am I doing it—financially or just how? I knew it had been deeded to her.

Well, it is getting late, so will close now.

Love,

<u>Fred.</u>

P.S. The other day sent home by P.P. [parcel post] 2 Japanese dolls. One is for Mom; I wish you would send the other to Lorraine. The dolls are almost identical.

[V-Mail]

Saipan
Friday 11 Sept. 1945

Dear Folks—

   Nothing new of importance to write about. The rain is still plentiful and sudden and a person had best confine his walking to the roads or sidewalks or run the risk of being mired.

   Mail has been a bit lean lately but I heard that plenty came in today, much of it papers and packages.

   Had a letter from Uncle Mike and Aunt Cecelia 2 days ago. He said he was working in a chemistry laboratory but didn't say where. I suppose one of the local refineries. Anyway—he said he liked the work.

Love,
Fred.

———— ➛ ➛ ————

[V-Mail]

Saipan
Thurs. 13 Sept. 1945

Dear Folks—

   Just returned from our meeting of the Saipan Medical Society, which was held at the Navy Military Government Hospital. It was an interesting meeting, especially since cases of filariasis, leprosy and yaws (native) were shown. There was quite a nice turnout, and afterwards we were taken over to the Club for refreshments.

   The mailman brought me 4 letters including those from Vic and Fr. Liebel. Mail has been poor all this week, so should begin to pick up any day now. There have been lots of packages and papers coming in these last 2 days, however, but not letters.

   Our weather continues to be wet and windy, any [and] every loose window and door is almost constantly rattling and

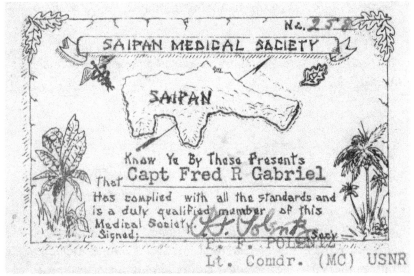

Gabriel's Saipan Medical Society membership card, summer 1945.

slamming. *I have eliminated some of it today, so hope I won't*
be kept awake again tonite.

> *Love,*
> *Fred.*

———— ➔← ————

[V-Mail]

> Saipan
> Fri. 14 Sept. 1945

Dear Folks—

This was quite a busy day for my part of the lab. 60
American prisoners of war from Japanese concentration
camps came in Thursday, and we got work on practically all
of them. My headache ached this evening from looking thru' the
microscope so steadily. Most of the fellows, by the way, were in
much better condition physically than I expected.

Our mail was on the blink again today, and none at all
came in for us. I heard that most of the planes were grounded

*because of the heavy storms raging in this part of the Pacific.
That well may be true.*

*We just got back from the Club, where we had a beer
and sandwich after seeing a second-rate movie "Out of this
World."* [62]

Love,
Fred.

Saipan
Sunday 16 Sept. 1945.

Dear Folks—

*Before I forget—I have notified "Readers Digest" to send
the magazine to my home address instead of out here. One
of the others here gets it, and I can read that. Also perhaps it
would be best if you didn't send me any Christmas packages
this year. Maybe I am wrong, but I have an idea that I might
be back in the States around the first of the year. The way the
point score is being lowered I should be eligible pretty soon
now. Every month I add 2 points and already have 62.*

*Today received the "Eagle" of the 7th, and read therein that
Louie expects to be home soon. Hope he is. Also read about my
meeting Bill Llewelyn.* [63] *I don't know if he is still here or not.
He hasn't come around, and I haven't had time to go up there
again, though I have sent him the "Eagle" a couple times.*

*Parker and Weisberg really felt sick today. They slept most of
the afternoon, and Parker is in bed now.*

*I went to the movie this evening but didn't stay as it was one
I had seen on Angaur. Before I go to bed early, I'll try to write a
few back letters. Generally I try to answer them promptly but
during the past few weeks haven't had much "stomach" for
corresponding. Incidentally, all the mail I expected today failed
to show up, and all that came for me was the newspaper.*

*Today worked until 4 but not hard. Not much work came in,
probably because this is Sunday, but we'll catch it in the neck
tomorrow. Fifty more prisoners came in last nite, and we'll
receive work on all of them, plus the routine stuff.*

I have a batch of pictures to send you and will do so soon.
Also, I plan to send a box of things I no longer need. I am
going to get rid of everything I am not using, so that when
I do move I can travel light, and if orders come suddenly, I
won't be caught unprepared. Some of the officers have left here
suddenly, one on 2 hours' notice. That isn't long to pack and
get other things ready, is it?
    Until tomorrow.

Love,
Fred.

---------- ➔ ← ----------

[V-Mail]

Saipan
Wed. 19 Sept. 1945.

Dear Folks—
    Our fourth roommate, Hughes, is out of the hospital now,
and is this place crowded. 4 beds, 2 clothes closets, a table and
our gear don't leave much extra space in a room, which must
be about 16 x 16. We jokingly tell each other that it isn't bad,
since we still don't have to come outside to turn out [around].
    This noon and this evening I cleaned out my footlocker,
and got a few things together to send home. I am going to cut
my clothing, etc. down to a bare minimum, so "when" comes
along, I can travel light. More officers and enlisted men left
here today, and more are due to leave anytime now.
    No mail came in today, but I still have plenty on hand to
answer.

Love,
Fred.

Did you take my Army blouse to the tailor?

Saipan.
Friday 21 Sept. 1945

Dear Folks—

　Two years ago I either was home or was not far away, as on the 20th we left Sheppard Field on leave. My leave was up on Oct. 4, so we left back about the 2nd. If I recall correctly, my captaincy became effective the 5th, though I didn't know about it until several days later. Speaking of promotions—I doubt that I'll ever make major but that doesn't bother me a bit for I am quite content with things as they are.

　Today received the V-mail Joe wrote on the 11th, just after returning from Utica. I am glad he had such a nice time. He didn't say when he's trying marriage, did he? Incidentally, just what kind of a radio program are young Eade and his bride appearing on—one for newly married couples?

　A friend of the Chief (in the lab) stopped in to visit—en route to Japan—and I spent several hours entertaining him. He is a young second lieutenant in the Sanitary Corps by the name of Friedman, a very nice fellow. His home is in Albany, N.Y., and he did premed at Johns Hopkins. However, he did not enter Medical School before he went into the Service, though he plans to do so later, I believe.

　Enclosed are a few more snapshots. In case you can't recognize anyone shown just look on the back. I usually write on them so strangers can read it and also so I will know who the subjects are years from now.

　This letter is a bit mixed up because I am trying to listen to the radio and write too. The news just finished mentioned what General Marshall told Congress about the new lowering of points for discharge. It doesn't apply to male officers but I feel it is a very healthy sign anyway.[64]

　Earlier this evening Parker and I swapped our beds (not such good ones) for 2 swell ones from the next compartment. The former occupants left for home [the] day before yesterday, and we decided to make the exchange before anyone else grabbed them. I have a bit of trouble getting up in the morning as it is, so it probably will be worse with my new bed.

The "newsletter" of September 12 arrived this morning, which reminds me that I haven't written to Fr. Liebel in quite some time. I'll try to do so this weekend. I really do enjoy receiving the "newsletter," and wish now that I had saved them all. It would be a very nice souvenir to have later on. I think that when all the local service men and women get home we ought to have some kind of a big dinner for Fr. Liebel to thank him for all the time and effort he has gone to with that project.

Well, until tomorrow.

Love,
Fred.

———— ➜ ⬅ ————

[V-Mail]

Saipan
Tues. 25 Sept. 1945.

Dear Folks—

About the only newsy news I have is that the 39th now is turning in its equipment and supplies, so apparently someone feels we'll not serve as a unit again. Some of our lab supplies are being brought to this lab, so as long as I am here I'll have old "friends" around me. Funny thought, huh?

Played volley-ball again this evening with a group of officers. Had a lot of fun, a lot of good exercise, and I hope I lost a little weight. My waistline can stand to be a little less. I believe I weigh about 148#, which is about 8# too much (at least 8).

Work was noticeably less today, and I hope it doesn't go booming again. At least not for a while. Chances are it won't, but I heard some of the other hospitals may close, sending us their patients. In that case we can expect to be busier all right. Have heard so many rumors about hospitals closing that I am skeptical of it all until I see it happen.

Love,
Fred.

Saipan
Thurs. 27 Sept. 1945.

Dear Folks—

Was pleased to learn today from your letter of the 20th that Lou had arrived in Boston. I can imagine how happy you are about the matter, and how anxious you must be to see him. Wish I could be there. Among other things, the thought of those Syrian dishes is enough by itself to make one hurry home, let along being back. I wonder how Tommy and Donny will act when they see him. Tommy probably does remember him.

This is a bit of news. Although I haven't yet received the orders, apparently I am to be the new C.O. of the 39th Sta. Hospital. Just how much this entails, I don't know but I imagine that the deactivation of our unit will not be easy. Getting rid of our supplies in a satisfactory manner may be quite a headache. I came to be C.O.-nominee by a process of elimination. There are others around in the Unit with more rank but they are either Dental Corps or Medical Administrative and therefore are ineligible. I hope this new deal won't delay my going home when that event comes due. I don't believe it will.

Today was an unusually warm day, but rather light as regards work. I hope lab does have a let-up for I probably will be relieved of duty there for a while. Afterwards I probably will be assigned to the 148th permanently.

Other hospitals in the islands are being closed down and some of their officers sent here. 2 or 3 old 39'ers came here, and all of us being together is like old times.

Incidentally, our roommate, Lt. Herb. Weisberg left for home today. Heyde is due to go soon, as is our regular C.O. Col. Wilson. His going is why I am the next C.O.

I am awfully sleepy, so will close now.

Love,
Fred

P.S. Enclosed are 2 pictures. Give one to each of the girls for their offspring. The scene is a schoolroom full of Chamorro children on Angaur.

Saipan.
Sunday 30 Sept. 1945.

Dear Folks—

I guess it is definite that tomorrow I assume command
of the 39th Station Hospital. This falls to me because I am
about the only one in the unit who can hold it. Others are
ineligible because they are not M.C., or else have recently
been transferred out of the 39th. Our hospital is being deactivated, the big problem of which is turning in our supplies.
Fortunately, I have a good adjutant and a good supply man to
do all the actual work. Just what I, as C.O., will have to do I
do not know. Time alone will tell. However, I am not worrying.

Heyde and Weisburg have already received their orders to
go back to the States for discharge. They were around this
afternoon for a little farewell and left only a couple hours ago.
They'll probably leave the island in a day or 2. We all hate to
see them go, as they were swell fellows. I got along especially
well with Heyde, who came probably the closest to being a
"chum" to me of anyone I ever have known. He lives in Ohio,
is married and has 2 young daughters. He is a couple years
older than myself and is an idealistic type of fellow. He has the
best general all-around intelligence of any layman I know, and
obtained it largely through reading. He's that type of person.
In case you are wondering what he looks like, he is in many of
my pictures—the one with the brush haircut, mustache, and
glasses. [65]

Today has been an unusually wet day, and did it come
down hard today! Seemed like it was in pailsful instead of
drops. The rainy season, however, is about over—according to
the calendar—so we should begin to have less and less of this
weather.

"When do we go home" continues to be the best subject of
conversation around here. Rumors still cloud the air, but one
or 2 things seem to be fact—there soon will be only 1 or 2 Army
hospitals here, and within a couple or 4 months this place is to
be largely cleared of Army personnel. I don't understand how
we can but be sent back soon.

*Plenty over here are bitter about the whole matter of
getting back to the States. There seems to be so much politics
and incompetence involved that at times it is disgusting.
And the fact that there are frequent changes of plans and
contradictions in them doesn't make us feel any better about
the matter. At times I can't help but think that they are doing
plenty to keep us over here, while those back in the States
are getting all the breaks. I wonder at some of these figures
published about discharge, etc.—how many are overseas
personnel and how many are those back in the States to begin
with.*

*The "Eagle" of the 21st arrived yesterday. According to it Joe
is going to Bonas and Louie is back in the States. In your next
letter I expect to read that he is home. I assume he soon will
get his discharge from the Army.*

*Over our glasses this afternoon, we 39'ers agreed to keep
in touch with each other after we get home, and to hold a
reunion every few years. All this is very agreeable to me, as
they are a swell group, and I'd hate to lose contact with them.
We are going to have a "letter" like my intern group has. Did
you know my fellow interns and I still keep in touch with each
other? Incidentally, has Brady ever tried to get in touch with
you? He should be back by now.*

*Boy! Is Parker irked! Today an order came out that T.D.R.R.
(leave home for Temporary Duty for Rest and Recuperation)
has been dropped from a 24-month overseas requirement to
18-months but those who can get it are only those who: (1) are
Regular Army or (2) are those who signed that they desired to
stay in the Service for the duration plus 6 months. (We recently
were given a chance to express a preference—Yes or No—on
this latter matter.) The whole thing seems quite unfair to me,
seeming like we who signed "no" are being penalized for so
signing, or else we are being "squeeze-played" into changing
over to "yes." Or if T.D.R.R. is being denied us because a plan
is imminent whereby we soon will be discharged, I think we
should be told so so we'll know what is going on; they should*

not let us feel we are being discriminated against.

Well, I have written enough, so I had better close now.

Love,

<u>Fred</u>.

Saipan

Wed. 3 October 1945.

Dear Ester—

The work of folding up the 39th is progressing okay. At least to date we have hit no bottle-necks and have received no kick-backs. We hope to complete the job per schedule. My duties are not exacting. About all I have done so far is sign a lot of papers and make a few decisions.

We have had the rainiest weather the past few days, some of it with strong wind. Fortunately, today was a clear one [and] things have had a chance to dry. This included a wash I hung out about 3 days back. Most things [I] send to the regular Quartermaster laundry but socks I do myself. Socks are the items most often lost or mixed up.

Joe wrote me that he liked school okay, and only Accounting was giving him any trouble. Apparently he has been away from it for too long. I don't know what subjects he is carrying. Nor did I know, incidentally, that girls attended classes at Bonas during the regular winter session. Louie must have been home by now. [From] that last letter, he wired the folks [to expect] him in a few days, meanwhile preparing [for] a determined onslaught on the Syrian foods in their kitchen. He'll do it, too. I believe he missed Syrian food more than I did, though right now I could put away plenty of it sans difficulty.

How are the 3 tykes doing these days? I'd really enjoy seeing them now. They'll probably all be much bigger than when I saw them, just 2 years ago. I am glad P.J. is doing so well in school. He draws like I do.

Your letter arrived yesterday. That "Cold" part confused me for a moment. Mama won't receive the dolls for a couple

*weeks yet, I expect. I think you are a bit wrong about Bill L.
[Llewelyn] being too stuck-up to visit us. Some enlisted men
are a bit reticent about looking-up officers, though no-one can
accuse me of high-hatting them. I don't think Bill is where
he was. I haven't gone back, but I believe [he] would have
dropped around were he here. Maybe I am wrong, though.*

*During the past few weeks we have lost several men and
officers on age, points, etc. Today our chaplain went home on
emergency leave due to the illness of his wife. Tomorrow our
regular C.O. leaves, on points. They wouldn't give him travel
orders until a C.O. had been named for the 39th, which was me.*

Well, it is bedtime, so I'll close now.

Love,
Fred.

*P.S. I still think I will be home by Christmas, so don't bother to
send me any packages. Tell the boys that when I get home I'll
help them make a snowman.*

F.

Saipan
Thurs. [Friday] 5 Oct. 1945.

Dear Folks—

*Being that our adjutant, Capt. George Hughes, is going back
to the States tomorrow my work is a bit tougher from here on
in. He is an excellent man to have around, and I was planning
on him doing all the heavy work. However, we are very glad
to see him go back. For a long time he has wanted to go to a
Staff school (he plans to stay in the Army), and now he has his
wish.*

*Hughes' leaving will reduce the 39th officers to 3—Burt,
[Wendell L.] Putt and myself. A few others are around but
they have recently been transferred to other units. They really
consider themselves 39'ers, though.*

*Work is progressing nicely in turning in our supplies. Most
of the lab stuff has been taken care of, and if the rest is doing*

as well, we certainly [are] doing all we expected. We were having a little trouble getting rid of 7 Quonset huts, (nobody wants to be burdened with them now) but finally someone has agreed to take them off our hands.

We haven't had as much rain yesterday and today as we had, and it has been a relief. I thought the rainy season was just about over, but today heard that this was it, which isn't hard to believe at all. Right now the wind is howling like a prelude to a gale.

In a letter that I received from Joe a few days ago, he asked about sending me packages for Christmas. I believe it best not to send me anything as I expect to be home by then. Maybe I am too optimistic but at least that is the way I feel about the matter.

I'll close now.

Love,
Fred.

———— ➔ ← ————

[V-Mail]

Saipan
Fri. 12 Oct. 1945

Dear Folks—

Just received another nice letter from Loraine; we have been corresponding quite regularly of late, as I have told you. I have been trying to persuade her to pay you all a visit. Maybe she will. I hope so. She says it has been 5 years; also—she says she hasn't heard from any of you in some time.

Last nite, while at the Club with a couple of Parker's friends, we saw some old friends of ours from the 41st Sta. Hospital. They were activated when we were and we have [been] plenty pretty near each other since. These we saw last nite are going home.

Today is awfully hot again; or maybe I am working too hard. Anyway, my shirt is wet with sweat.

Love,
Fred.

[Typed]

Saipan

Tuesday 16 Oct 1945

Dear Folks—

I have been pretty busy these past few days again, part of it due to a bit of sight-seeing around the island. Captain Feit, who formerly was with us and who left us on Angaur, is on this island awaiting to go home. He came around to see us, and being one of the "charter members" of the Unit, naturally we all were happy to see each other.

He came over Saturday evening, early. He had dinner here, and then we spent the rest of the time reminiscing about the early days of the 39th. He stayed overnite, as Parker and I have an extra bed in our room, and all day yesterday we were on the road. I have been driving lately, and did it all yesterday. We must have covered 75 miles, seeing everything of interest on the island. Feit really got a bang out of it as he is very interested in things like that.

The turning-in of our supplies is going okay by itself, though it is some job. Most of the smaller things have been turned over, and now we are working on the bigger things, like generators, refrigerators, etc. These latter were somewhat of a worry as we had no heavy equipment to move it, and had to shop around for it. The way things look now, those items should all be off our hands in two days more.

Mail service has been off for the past few days, though during that time I have had letters from you, Father Liebel and Ester. Am glad to know that all continues to go well [at] home, and that Louie was home. I can imagine how happy you all were. No news definitely changes points for me, but rumor has it that a change will be in effect some time in November. Don't know what it will be, but it must lower points. I still am holding out to be home around the first of the year.

While I think of it—did you shorten my blouse, as I requested? So far you have made no mention of it.

I am typing this in the office while awaiting chow call. V-mail will no longer be photographed, as of yesterday, so

*chances are you will receive no more of it from me. If it will be
sent on unphotographed, a person might just as well write an
air-mail in the first place, had not they?*

*You probably have heard how Okinawa was banged-up by
a typhoon a week and a half ago, ruining most of the Army
installations up there.* [66] *We had a couple days of it here, thou
not so severely. It reminded me of the storm we had while on
Angaur on Nov. 7, 8, and 9, 1944.* [67] *That really was something.*

*In his last letter Joe mentioned that he was considering
joining the American Legion. In most places that organization
is not too well thought of. I suggest he inquire around a bit
before he join with them. The VFW [Veterans of Foreign Wars]
generally is a better group.* [68]

Time to go put on the feedbag, so I will close now.

Love,
Fred.

*P.S. Am enclosing a few photographs that I got from Don
Johnson.*

————— ➔ ⬅ —————

Saipan
Thurs. 18 Oct. 1945.

Dear Folks—

*Duties up in Headquarters have kept me unusually busy for
the past few days. We are losing men all the time, are turning
in our suppliers and have to assemble material for a medical
history of the unit, all of which require considerable time and
effort. Just the same, things are going along fine.*

*I just returned from a visit to the 5th Convalescent Hospital
with Lt. Putt, my adjutant. We saw Joan Davis in "George
White's Scandals" out there.* [69] *It was not good but was better
than I expected.*

*Yesterday evening I drove out and got Col. Wilson and Capt.
Feit, both of whom are awaiting transportation home, to come
in for a visit. Feit stayed all night here, and while he and I
were coming back from returning the Colonel to the Transient*

Camp at Kobler Field,[70] *we had quite an experience. A heavy rain was falling and on the hillside just below the hospital the road was almost a washout. Great big stones were strewn all across it and a young river flowed down its middle.*

Mail service continues to be very poor. I did get a letter yesterday, so have no reason to complain, I guess.

I am sleepy, so I'll close now.

Love,
Fred.

P.S. Am including a few negatives.

Saipan
Sat. 20 October 1945

Dear Folks—

The mail finally broke through to us, and I received 3 letters and the "Eagle" of the 12th. And before I forget, please have the "Eagle" correct the statement that I am C.O. of the 39th General *Hospital. It should be, instead, 39th* Station *Hospital. General hospitals usually have full colonels or generals as commanders. My affiliation is to the 39th Station, and has been for over 3 years. I want no truck [?] with that 39th General outfit.*

Yesterday and today have been the nicest, sunniest days, a bit on the hot side, if anything. I sunbathed for about 30 minutes this noon, and that was enough to make my skin smart a bit. I think that I shall start acquiring a tan like I had on the Canal. Since then I haven't had too much exposure to the sun and gradually have lost my "native" look.

Work is coming along fine. Thank goodness it is, because this week we lost by points all the key supply men, the ones who actually were doing the heavy work of turning in equipment. We begin to lose the 60-point men, of whom we have about 70, the first of the month. When they go, our unit will shrink down to less than half. I am trying to have a final Detachment party for the men sometime this week, and believe I will be able to do so. Also, when the men leave the organization I am giving them their Good Conduct medals. They should have received them months ago, but they were obtainable only after we got here. Col. Wilson never gave them out because he kept hoping to be able to do so at an appropriate ceremony. I feel we can never get the men together again for anything like that, so I am giving them their medals individually as they leave, and believe they'd rather receive them from their own unit rather than from strangers. After all, they did earn them with us.

This is Saturday nite, traditional time for stepping out. I just returned from supper and now am writing a few letters before I get cleaned up for going down to the Club.

This afternoon I drove out to the Casual Depot to see if Capt. Feit wanted to come back and spend the evening here with us. I was unable to locate him, however, so will probably go after him again tomorrow.

In her letter, Ester enclosed some of P.J.'s schoolwork. His drawings really amuse me. I think I'll save some of it for my scrap-book. He'll never believe it is his work when I show it to him about 1965. Apparently he is doing okay by himself in school, however.

How are you folks feeling these days? I hope you are well and are taking care of yourselves. Winter is a bad season of the year as far as health goes. The very thought of snow is pleasant but cold never-the-less. Chances are I'll get home at the height of a storm, and me with no woolens. I have an idea. I can get some before I leave, though, and will investigate the matter Monday.

Well, I'll close now.

Love,
Fred.

P.S. Enclosed are a few more negatives.

Saipan
Mon. 29 Oct. 1945.

Dear Folks—

Our party Saturday evening was quite a success. At least all comments I have heard about it were favorable. There were 105 present, about 20 less than we figured on. Several men on their way home didn't attend as they heard that their ship might leave that night, and no one wants to miss a trip home on account of a party. I am glad we were able to have the party for the men and am glad also that it is over. Now we can concentrate our efforts on the supplies.

That part of our deactivation is just about complete, needing only a day or so more to pick up the loose ends (and the trash). Then we'll have only the records to dispose of, and already we have received instructions on where to forward them, and how.

We aren't the only hospital around here that is being deactivated but I believe we'll be finished first. Being first will be of some advantage because the people receiving our supplies are becoming hard to deal with.

I received the Christmas cards the other day. Thanks for them. You needn't send me anymore, though, as I don't care particularly if I send any this year or not.

Until tomorrow.

Love,
Fred.

———————— →← ————————

Saipan
Wed. 31 Oct. 1945.

Dear Folks—

Well, today we were informed that our deactivation date would be the 16th. That is the first definite date we have had and it gives us 2 weeks to "get ready." About a couple days will clean up the supplies: I am not sure how long it will take to dispose of the records and close headquarters.

*This morning 53 of our men left on the first leg of the trip
home. I ran around like mad last night and early this morning
getting them ready, especially one fellow, who was in the
hospital. He is an Indian, and strangers don't understand him
so I wanted him to go with the rest and not alone a day later.*

*My classmate, Brogan, is back on the island from Marcus
Island, where he went with the Marines and CB's who accepted
the Jap surrender.[71] He was around for a few minutes this
afternoon and will be here again tomorrow. He'll probably have
some stories to tell me, if he is around long enough. He expects
to be ordered back to the States any day now.*

*Tonite an officer from the Surgeon General's Office in
Washington will be here to give us a chance to air our
"grievances" about getting home, etc. From what I have
heard from several local officers, this man will have plenty to
explain. The officers here are plenty tired of the bungly way
medics are being discharged. It seems like someone is doing
everything they can to keep us over here. It is a shame how
many doctors and nurses here have no business being here,
since there is nothing for them to do. I believe the public would
be pretty disgusted if they knew the true facts.[72]*

*While returning from the Medical Supply Depot this
afternoon I looked up Johnny Abdo and had a nice visit with
him. He told me where I could find Tommy Tucker. We 3 are
going to get together soon.*

> *Love,*
> *Fred.*

———— ➜ ← ————

> *Saipan*
> *Friday 2 Nov. 1945.*

Dear Folks: —

*Today we finally received our deactivation orders. The date
is 16 November, and it is to occur here (we'll not go back as a
unit to the States). That gives us just 2 weeks to get everything
ready, and we should be finished easily in good time.*

This afternoon I looked up Tommy Tucker. It took me a couple of hours and a lot of driving but I finally located him. I found him fast asleep in his sack. I don't think he would have known me if he were fully awake and he surely didn't when he was suddenly awakened, like it happened. I wouldn't have known him, either. He is a pretty big boy and doesn't resemble the Syrians too much. Still he has that Tucker look.

Mail is a bit slow again but I did receive the "Eagle" of 26 October. I read it over pretty carefully, noting that Eldred is to have another clothing store. The death of that Mullen infant was pretty tragic.

I can't figure out who Mrs. Mullen is unless it is Alice. Is it? It said she was a sister of Mrs. J. H. MacNulty.

Recently I have met 2 other Syrians here at the 148th. One is a 2<u>nd</u> Lt. Medical Administrative Officer from Des Moines, Iowa, by the name of Simon. The other is an enlisted man from Brooklyn, whose name I have forgotten. Both are pretty nice fellows.

Well, until the next time.

Love,
[unsigned]

———————— ➔ ← ————————

Saipan
Mon. 5 Nov. 1945.

Dear Folks—

I just returned from having dinner out at Brogan's place. We had steak, one that could be cut, which made it quite different from the kind we get here. In general, though, our meals haven't been too bad these past few weeks.

Parker, my roommate, has been declared surplus here. In a couple days he is leaving for Oahu, and if they have no assignment for him there, he will go on back to the States for one. In a way I hate to see him go. He is one of the oldest men in the unit and always has been one of my best friends. The old 39th really is being whittled down, all right.

*Our unit is just now getting belated recognition for its work
on Angaur. Two of the officers—Major Vermilya and Captain
[Kersey C.] Riter—neither of whom are with us anymore, are
getting the Bronze Star.[73] Several others probably deserve them
just as much but no one is envious. It probably would have
been better, however, if we had a Unit Citation, in which all
could have shared equally. Did I ever tell you that practically
every unit on Angaur but the hospital did get some kind of an
award or commendation? The island commander, or someone
there, had very little use for us and that was one way of
showing it.*

*Today received a letter from Charley Schaaf. He is a
patient in an Army hospital in Germany, suffering with Acute
Hepatitis. He isn't very ill and is coming along okay. I haven't
heard from any of the others in a couple weeks. Most of them
should be back in the States any time now. We plan to hold a
reunion in Erie if and when we all can get together. If all these
planned reunions materialize, I am doing a lot of traveling in
the next few years.*

Until tomorrow.

Love,
Fred.

————— ➔ ← —————

Saipan
Tues. 13 Nov. 1945.

Dear Folks—

*While I think of them I'll answer a couple questions you
have asked in recent letters.*

*Yes, we caught some of that storm last month. Fortunately
we got only the tail of it but for a few hours it was plenty rough.
Reminded me of a similar storm about a year ago on Angaur.
Remember me mentioning it on Nov. 7–8 and 9? I remember so
well because it was Election Day and I was O.D.[74]*

*By all means please shorten my green woolen army blouse.
I thought it had been done by this time. You can measure my*

*summer Army blouse to get the correct length. You'll find there
is about 3 inches difference. Please have this matter taken care
of now.*

*Just three more days until the 16th, when we sing our swan
song. We'll be ready but it meant we worked most of Sunday
and Monday, which was a sort of holiday since the 11th came
on Sunday.*

*Last evening we went up to Burt's place, where we ate
popcorn and played bridge, and had a good time doing both.
There is a new dental officer up there, who finished at N.D.
[Notre Dame] in 1938. He is from Ohio and is a very nice
fellow by name of Haggerty.*

*Yesterday morning I took off for a while and took some
pictures. There is a road sign here about a girl named Lorraine
and the real one wanted to see what her namesake looked
like. There are several clever road signs about the island.
Most of them show girls who advise us to drive carefully.[75]
That drive carefully is a good idea, too, as in the last 2 months
a surprisingly large number of people were killed here in
accidents.*

*What kind of weather are you having back home? Ours has
been unusually hot this last week. Hope you have a short, easy
winter. Has Joe found anyone to drive with him? I hope so, as
I know that drive daily can become monotonous. I hope, too,
that Joe isn't studying and/or working too hard. It isn't worth
it, either of them. What I'd advise him to do is to do only a
reasonable amount of studying, a reasonable amount of work
and being sure meanwhile to have considerable amount of
social life. That is important no less than the work. I am glad
he went to the Fresh Hop; was it Joan Cawley he took?*

*There are a lot of Cawley's teaching around home, aren't
there? Rosamond, Margaret, Joan, Bobby, Genevieve, and
June's husband.*

I'll close now.

*Love,
Fred.*

Saipan
Monday 17 Dec. 1945.

Dear Folks—

I believe fall actually has come our way. Midday is as warm as ever but evenings and mornings are definitely cooler. So much so, in fact, that I began <u>thinking</u> of using a blanket for a bedcover instead of the usual sheet.

You know, I believe, that Tony Kaminsky of Erie is assigned here now. He was on the staff at St. V. Hospital there while I was interning. It is nice talking over with him all about the Hospital and the staff, etc. Tony is only 4 or 5 years older than myself. Yesterday he gave me a copy of the little magazine put out by the Erie County Medical Society. I enjoyed seeing it. One interesting item in it was that St. V. is going to have— beginning next July—2 surgical residences, open only to former interns or staff men returning from Service. They will be worth investigating, but I doubt if they would be too good, especially when just instituted. Of course they would be a better residency after they had been in effect a few years.

Saturday received your letter of the 29th. Am sorry you were so disappointed about my change of address. I was, too, but knew that I would not get home just because the 39th was inactivated. And actually my being assigned to the 148th was merely a transfer on paper for I have been living here at the 148th ever since we hit Saipan last June. Gosh—we have been here over 6 months already. Scarcely seems true but time does go by fast these days. Just about a week until Christmas. Thanks, but don't bother sending me any Christmas packages. There is nothing I need.

So there was an explosion at the Powder plant,[76] and a couple were found asphyxiated? Too bad. I'll get the details in the "Eagle" about both accidents. The number of people killed each year in home accidents is terrific, from what I have read, and yet it continues over and over. Which reminds me—how is Mrs. Splain doing with her fractured hip?

Christmas cards are beginning to come in, and yesterday I got one from Paris, no less. It was an American-style card,

*from a Red Cross girl who was a Jeff technician. She hasn't
been there long. At first she thought she was coming this way
but at the last minute the orders were changed.*

*Just finished reading an interesting book, "The Brother"
by Dorothy Clarke Wilson.*[77] *It is about the family life of
Jesus, and centers about his brother James. In many ways it
reminded me of "The Robe."*[78]

*Saw a good movie the other nite—"Our Vines Have Tender
Grapes," with Margaret O'Brien, Edward G. Robinson, and
Jackie Jenkins.*[79] *I had seen it before but enjoyed it very much
anyway. It may have come to Eldred by now; if not see it. I
think you'll like it.*

*Our meals are better now than they were a couple months
back. Now we are getting better fresh meat oftener, as well as
more fresh fruit. Speaking of food reminds me that another
book I just read kept making me think of home by mentioning
big family dinners.*

On that I will close.

Love,
Fred.

--------------- →← ---------------

Saipan
Thurs. 27 Dec. 1945.

Dear Folks—

*Things are the same here. I am still in the hospital and
feeling just fine, good enough to be out, I think. However, the
ward officer keeps telling me to take things easy for a few more
days, so that I'll probably do.*

*Am writing this on my lap, in bed, which accounts for the
lines running uphill.*

*Have been reading and hearing a lot lately of the influenza
epidemic back in the States. It is news to me. Do hope it
isn't serious and that it doesn't last long. Hope, too, it is light
around home. How about it? Have any of you had it? This flu*

can be tricky business so please all of you be careful of your health.

This has been a nice day though a bit on the cool side and with heavy rain for a while early in the morning. I wish the sun would come out real strong as I'd like to bolster my suntan.

The news is on the radio now. The part about how many people were killed in accidents over Christmas is bad, but how well the meeting of Byrnes, Bevin and Molotoff went off is gratifying.[80] Hope they really did accomplish something.

Mail is a bit slow again but yesterday I received a letter from Lorraine, and today got one from Wes Burt in Oahu. Also got two "Lake-Shore-Registers [*Lake Shore Visitors*]."

Love,
<u>Fred</u>.

→←

Afterword

Gabriel was evacuated from Saipan on January 2, 1946, and arrived at Hamilton Field, California, just north of San Francisco, four days later. On January 10, he was transferred to Kennedy General Hospital, in Memphis, Tennessee, where doctors surgically removed the cyst on March 6. Gabriel was released from the hospital on June 10 and received his official discharge from the army on September 23, at Fort George G. Meade, Maryland.[1]

Following his release from military service, Gabriel did a residency at Wayne State Hospital in Eloise, Michigan, and then returned to Erie, Pennsylvania, in the early 1950s. There he married Elizabeth Brown, a nurse from Saint Vincent Hospital

"Freddy recently home," with nephews Johnny and Jimmy Farris, April 1946, Eldred.

in May 1952, opened his own practice, and eventually specialized in radiology, doing clinical work at the University of Pennsylvania. In 1966, after moves to Auburn, New York, and Dalton, Massachusetts, Gabriel, Betty, and their seven children settled in Bradford, Pennsylvania, about sixteen miles from his home town of Eldred. There he headed the Radiology Department at the Bradford Hospital. Gabriel always remained a devoted Notre Dame fan, returned to the university for class reunions multiple times, and took his children there. Gabriel also fondly remembered Jefferson and his fellow interns from Saint Vincent, and he occasionally mentioned his service during the war, but never in great detail. He retired in 1981 and died on August 17, 1985. He is buried in Saint Raphael Cemetery in Eldred near his brother Lou.

Appendix

A typed copy of this poem was found with Gabriel's letters. He likely met its author, Major E. Murray Burns of the 46th General Hospital, in Autumn 1942, when they both took an eight-week tropical medicine course at the Army Medical School in Washington, DC.[1]

TROPICAL PARADISE

"Life in the tropics is a simple thing!"
With this "truth" our ears did ring.
When first we sat in the A.M.S.*
We believed it, too (more or less).
Here are the rules, it's up to you
Follow them closely, or you'll get what's due
Stay in all night, or you'll get malaria;
Stay in all day or you'll get filaria.
Anopheles at night does prey;
Simulian prefers the day.
You take a bath and the schistosome
Will cirrhose your liver and lay you prone.
Hematobium cause hematuria
And with mansoni it's hard to cure ya.
But <u>don't</u> you bathe and then, oh, fie!
Your skin will rot with bad fungi
Eat your food, you'll pass some blood
Histolytica's inside you, Bud!
Don't you eat; avoid your food,
Then lack of vitamin disturbs your mood

Deficiency states will surely accrue
Until you come down with a good case of sprue [?]
Quaff some water; oh, boy, the flux!
Cholera and dysentery go through like lux.**
If you don't drink, you'll only get
Dehydration because of your sweat
Touch the natives to get the yaws
A Treponema is the cause.
Ticks and lice, they are a curse
I can think of nothing worse
Unless it's that beast that takes the cake
A wriggling coiling, hissing snake.
And if you ache it may be dengue,
Because Aedes must have stung you,
And plague is only a bit bubonic
Septicemic or pneumonic
Flies will give you ghastly myiasis,
Creeping eruption or trypanosomiasis—
Not to mention pappatici
Or Salmonella paratyphi
Cyticerious and saginata
Hydatid cysts and fasciola—
These and others just to make you
Wish the tropics would forsake you.
Nothing serious—just prostration
Caused by lack of sanitation.
You can't do this, you can't do that
You can't be thin, you can't be fat.
Wear a net and a high top boot
The humidity's up. Who gives a hoot!

E. Murray Burns
Major, Medical Corps

* Army Medical School
** For readers in the year AD 3000—Lux was a proprietary
soap product used in AD 1942.

Leo Hofschneider Letter,
"The Things I Dream of Now"

Initially appearing in the April 12, 1944, edition of the *Buffalo News*, Gabriel sent a clipping of this letter to the *Notre Dame Alumnus*, which reprinted it in its June 1944 edition (vol. 22, page 29). See April 28, 1944, Letter to Parents.

"I've gotten so used to this business in the past couple of years that I sometimes wonder if there is any other way to live.

"I've done enough and seen enough to last me for two lives. I've eaten yams and coconuts with natives, and traded razor blades for bunches of bananas; I've picked and eaten pineapples hot from the sun, with juice so sweet I've needed water afterwards. But I've changed a bit—and now I eat my meat and beans from cans—without a fork; it smears my face, but I can wipe that off. My sleeves are dirty anyway.

"I've watched our planes go out in numbers, and when they came back, I've counted them and breathed a silent prayer for those whose place in the line was vacant. I've seen planes fight, in spiraling arcs over the sea, and jumped and shouted for joy when a red Rising Sun turned black and fell in flames, with streamers reaching out behind. I've watched our Air Corps bomb and blast the little buzzards to their Shinto heaven, and I've been below while Japs bombed us and tried to send me onto mine! I've groveled on the ground at night when bombs fell near, and prayed for dawn, yet feared its coming because it meant attack!

"I've counseled men who feared what's coming next, and I've sought advice from grizzled veterans of 23 to learn how to protect myself—they taught me, too. I've seen these same men dash to certain death; I've seen others crack—and cry and curse, and still go back for more. I've held them in my arms to die, and laughed and joked with them to keep their spirits up.

"I've seen big ships, and crouched in a small boat beneath the scream of their shells passing overhead, while smoke and

flame obscured the guns, and noise like thunder shook our small assault craft.

"I'm with the infantry. I've seen that queen of battles charge from boats upon a hostile beach and plunge into the stinking jungle where you couldn't see a foot ahead. I've gone with them—so scared I shook and sweated—yet couldn't give my feelings any vent because my men were near, and I'm supposed to be a man to lead. I've slept in water to my waist, and used my poncho to cover my supplies instead of me. I've lugged a pack so heavy that I couldn't straighten up – because men with bullets in their bellies need plasma right away, and chafes across my back don't hurt as much.

"I've stood out on the beach and watched a hundred dawns, and looked towards home across the sea and wondered how the traffic was on Main St. It can't go on forever, and some day I hope I can get home to do the things I dream of now. To sit and smoke and listen to a band; to take a rum and coke; to eat fresh mayonnaise and lettuce; to go to church and see the gang around the corner afterward. Simple things, themselves, but their importance grows.

"Now I have a wife, and a family will be mine pretty soon, and there's nothing I want more than to come home and watch it grow, but if coming home means that I have to turn my back just once and shirk my duty, then, I won't be back. I rather like this life, thought at times I get discouraged, but I realize that I'm useful here, and I enjoy the respect and confidence of the men it's my job to patch up.

"Occasionally, these Japs drop bombs on us—they're either bombs or something else. They scream when they come down. They may be just old peanut roasters. I don't think so though, because I've looked into the holes they make, and never found a whistle, or any peanuts, either."

Notes

Introduction

1. Clarence McKittrick Smith, *The Medical Department: Hospitalization and Evacuation, Zone of Interior* (Washington, DC: Center of Military History, United States Army, 1989); Charles M. Wiltse, *The Medical Department: Medical Service in the Mediterranean and Minor Theaters* (Washington, DC: Center of Military History, United States Army, 1987); Graham A. Cosmas and Albert E. Cowdrey, *The Medical Department: Medical Service in the European Theater of Operations* (Washington, DC: Center of Military History, United States Army, 1992); Mary Ellen Condon-Rall and Albert E. Cowdrey, *The Medical Department: Medical Service in the War against Japan* (Washington, DC: Center of Military History, United States Army, 1998); Albert E. Cowdrey, *Fighting for Life: American Military Medicine in World War II* (New York: Free Press, 1994).

2. Brendan Phibbs, *The Other Side of Time: A Combat Surgeon in World War II* (Boston: Little, Brown, 1987); Allen N. Towne, *Doctor Danger Forward: A World War II Memoir of a Combat Medical Aidman, First Infantry Division* (Jefferson, NC: McFarland, 2000); Paul A. Kennedy and Christopher B. Kennedy, eds, *Battlefield Surgeon: Life and Death on the Front Lines of World War II* (Lexington: University Press of Kentucky, 2016); Lawrence D. Collins, *The 56th Evacuation Hospital: Letters of a World War II Army Doctor* (Denton: University of North Texas Press, 1995); James S. Vedder, *Combat Surgeon: Up Front with the 27th Marines* (Novato, CA: Presidio Press, 1998); Michael J. Lepore, *Life of the Clinician* (Rochester, NY: University of Rochester Press, 2002).

3. Anne Bosanko Green, *One Woman's War: Letters Home from the Women's Army Corps, 1944–1946* (Saint Paul: Minnesota Historical Society Press, 1989); Peter A. Witt, *Edith's War: Writings of a Red*

Cross Worker and Lifelong Champion of Social Justice (College Station: Texas A&M University Press, 2018).

4. With each letter reduced to approximately five by four inches, V-mail was an innovative microfilming process that the military used during World War II to save shipping space. For a good account of the technology behind V-mail and its advantages, see "V-Mail: Letters Home," *History Magazine* 16 (June/July 2015): 17–22.

5. For the history of the 39th Station Hospital, see three somewhat duplicative files found at the United States National Archives and Records Administration, College Park, MD: 39th Station Hospital 1942, RG 112, Entry 54A, Box 156; 39th Station Hospital POA 1942–1944, RG 112, Entry 54A, Box 489; Unit Histories 39th Station Hospital, RG 112, Entry 1012 HUMEDS, Box 110.

6. John J. McGrath, *The Other End of the Spear: The Tooth-to-Tail Ratio (T3R) in Modern Military Operations*, The Long War Series Occasional Paper No. 23. (Fort Leavenworth, KS: Combat Studies Institute Press, 2007), 16–24.

7. James H. Cawley, ed., *Fr. Liebel's Letters: To the Men and Women Serving Our Country, 1943–1945* (n.p.: 2002).

Chapter 1

1. Information concerning Gabriel's military service comes from documents located in his personnel file or on his Travel Log, unless otherwise noted. "Classification Questionnaire of Medical Department Officers," March 15, 1945, pages 37–38, Frederick R. Gabriel Personnel File, National Personnel Records Center, Saint Louis, MO [hereafter Gabriel Personnel File]; Gabriel Travel Log.

2. "Application for Appointment and Statement of Preference for Reserve Officers," January 12, 1940; "Appointment in the Officers' Reserve Corps," February 13, 1940, pages 178–79, 181, Gabriel Personnel File.

3. WW2 US Medical Research Centre, "WW2 Military Hospitals: General Introduction," accessed October 28, 2016, https://www.med-dept.com/articles/ww2-military-hospitals-general-introduction/.

4. "Medical History of the 39th Station Hospital Prepared by Lt. Col. Isaac F. Hudson," January 26, 1943, pages 1–4, 39th Station Hospital 1942, RG 112, Entry 54A, Box 156.

5. "History of the 39th Station Hospital," May 27, 1943, pages 1–4, Unit Histories 39th Station Hospital, RG 112, Entry 1012 HUMEDS, Box 110; Gabriel to Parents, September 19, 1943.

6. "Medical History of the 39th Station Hospital Prepared by Lt. Col. Isaac F. Hudson" [January 26, 1943], pages 3–11, 39th Station Hospital 1942, RG 112, Entry 54A, Box 156.

7. Gabriel Travel Log.

8. "History of the 39th Station Hospital," May 27, 1943, page 3, Unit Histories 39th Station Hospital, RG 112, Entry 1012 HUMEDS, Box 110.

9. "History of the 39th Station Hospital," May 27, 1943, page 3, Unit Histories 39th Station Hospital, RG 112, Entry 1012 HUMEDS, Box 110; "Medical History of the 39th Station Hospital prepared by Major Jewell R. Wilson," April 6, 1944, pages 2–3, 9, 39th Station Hospital POA 1942–1944, RG 112, Entry 54A, Box 489. Pages 6–7 of the document "Medical History of the 39th Station Hospital prepared by Major Jewell R. Wilson" list the nurses' names.

10. "History of the 39th Station Hospital (Addendum)," July 5, 1943, page 1, Unit Histories 39th Station Hospital, RG 112, Entry 1012 HUMEDS, Box 110; "The Heroine on the Cover," *Collier's*, April 15, 1944, 65.

11. Gabriel Travel Log.

12. "Headquarters 39th Station Hospital, Special Order No. 57," June 29, 1943; "Headquarters 39th Station Hospital, Special Order No. 64," June 29, 1943; "Officer's and Warrant Officer's Qualification Card," [1945]; "Headquarters 39th Station Hospital," September 1, 1943, pages 100, 103, 184, 146–47 (quote 147), Gabriel Personnel File.

13. "Medical History of the 39th Station Hospital prepared by Major Jewell R. Wilson," April 6, 1944, pages 2–3, 39th Station Hospital POA 1942–1944, RG 112, Entry 54A, Box 489; Gabriel Travel Log.

14. A Thomas Jefferson Medical University [Philadelphia, PA] annual all-college dance sponsored by the Kappa Beta Phi fraternity. Thomas Jefferson University, "Black and Blue Marks: History of the School Colors," accessed May 18, 2015, http://jeffline.jefferson.edu/SML/Archives/Highlights/School_Colors/.

15. Dr. John "Jake" Brady was a classmate of Gabriel at both Notre Dame and Jefferson Medical College, and they then interned at Saint Vincent Hospital in Erie, Pennsylvania. Brady also served in the Pacific during the war. *Jefferson Medical College Yearbooks, 1940*, 102, accessed September 24, 2015, http://jdc.jefferson.edu/jmc_yearbooks/50.

16. Located in Arlington, Virginia, Fort Myer served as a processing center for soldiers during World War II. Joint Base Myer-Henderson Hall, "Fort Myer History," accessed May 18, 2015, http://www.jbmhh.

army.mil/WEB/JBMHH/AboutJBMHH/FortMyerHistory.html.

17. Fort Oglethorpe, Georgia, was located near the Chickamauga National Battlefield, south of Chattanooga, Tennessee. South Carolina History Net, "History: Fort Oglethorpe, Georgia, US Army Installation," accessed May 18, 2015, http://www.schistory.net/fortoglethorpe/History.htm.

18. Dr. Alfred M. Tocker also did an internship at Saint Vincent Hospital in Erie, Pennsylvania. Serving in the 29th Infantry Division, Tocker landed on Omaha Beach on June 6, 1944, and later witnessed German concentration camps. For his service, see Joe Rodriguez, "Deaths Seared in Battle Physician's Memory," *Twenty-Niner* 45 (March 2001): 49.

19. Timon J. Phelan (1917–1992) of Eldred, Pennsylvania, was a high school classmate of Gabriel's. Unless otherwise cited, all birth and death dates for Eldred area residents are from Joel Frampton Gilfert, "Military History of McKean County, Pennsylvania, World War II: Community Honor Rolls—Eldred and Vicinity," accessed December 12, 2014, http://jfgvictoryverlag.com/WWIIhonorrolls/Eldred%20N-Z.html.

20. Camp Barkeley housed the Medical Administrative Officer Candidate School. Established in May 1942, the school trained 12,500 physicians and nurses to be army officers. Camp Barkeley Tactical Training Center, "A Proud History," accessed May 19, 2015, http://www.campbarkeleytactical.com/camp-barkeley-history.html.

21. Fort Benning is located near Columbus, Georgia. Fort Benning, "Welcome to Fort Benning," accessed September 15, 2015, http://www.military.com/base-guide/fort-benning.

22. A reference to the rationing of gasoline, rubber tires, and other consumer goods needed for the war effort.

23. Torrential rain, totaling as much as 30.8 inches in 4.75 hours, fell over much of north central Pennsylvania and adjoining counties of New York on July 18, 1942, causing widespread flooding. John Harrison, "Extreme Events: Graphs, Photos, Videos," 3–7, accessed May 19, 2015, http://www.schnabel-eng.com/wp-content/uploads/2013/12/Extreme-Events.pdf. For photographs of the devastation in Eldred, see Painted Hills Genealogy Society, "Miscellaneous Photos Of Eldred, Pa. During the July 1942 Flood," accessed May, 19, 2015, http://www.paintedhills.org/MCKEAN/EldredFlood/.

24. Probably a reference to the people from Olean referred to earlier in the letter. The town had a large Middle Eastern population, thus the humorous reference to "camel-riders."

25. The US Navy began a Naval Reserve Officers Training Corps at the University of Notre Dame in September 1941. Following the United States' entry into the war, the navy expanded its presence on campus. It took over four dormitories and constructed both a drill hall and a combination headquarters/classroom building to train officers. Approximately 12,000 naval officers received training at the university between 1942 and 1946. Lou Somogyi, "God, Country, Notre Dame: The United States Military has been Part of Notre Dame's Fabric," accessed May 18, 2015, http://www.und.com/genrel/111011aaa.html; V. R. Cardozier, *Colleges and Universities in World War II* (Westport, CT: Greenwood, 1993), 12, 52, 115. The Knute Rockne Memorial Gymnasium, named after the legendary football coach, opened in 1937.

26. William DeGan, Brother Maurilius, served as the rector of Carroll and Brownson Halls for over three decades. Find a Grave, "Br. Maurilius DeGan," accessed March 23, 2015, http://www.findagrave.com/cgi-bin/fg.cgi?page=gr&GRid=46594296.

27. Once the largest hotel in the world, Chicago's Stevens Hotel opened in 1927. The army purchased it in 1942 as a barracks and classroom building for 10,000 air force cadets. Historic Hotels of America, "Hilton Chicago," accessed May 18, 2015, http://www.historichotels.org/hotels-resorts/hilton-chicago/history.php.

28. Gabriel's paternal uncle. He served in Panama during the war.

29. First Lieutenant George B. Hughes Jr., served as the 39th Station Hospital's adjutant.

30. For a photograph of civilians assessing the damage from this mock air attack, see Chicago Tribune, "World War II: Life in Chicago," accessed January 6, 2016, http://galleries.apps.chicagotribune.com/chi-130320-arsenal-democracy-world-war-ii-pictures/.

31. James Campbell Todd and Arthur Hawley Sanford's *Clinical Diagnosis by Laboratory Methods* (Philadelphia: W. B. Saunders) was originally published in 1908 and was in its twentieth edition by 2001, although the title varied slightly over time. Worldcat, accessed October 19, 2015, http://www.worldcat.org/title/todd-sanfords-clinical-diagnosis-by-laboratory-methods/oclc/465670173/editions?referer=di&editionsView=true.

32. Established in early 1941, Sheppard Field mainly trained personnel for the Army Air Corps. Sheppard Air Force Base, *A Brief History of the 82d Training Wing and Sheppard AFB* (n.c.: n.p: n.d), 25–27, accessed May 19, 2015, http://www.sheppard.af.mil/shared/media/document/AFD-120424-046.pdf.

33. Gabriel apparently had some financial stake in his father's real estate investments.

34. Mae Russell served as the longtime editor of the *Eldred Eagle*.

35. Edmond Lambillotte (1920–1970), an Eldred resident, served in the Army Air Corps. His brother, Lawrence, was killed at Anzio on February 12, 1944. See letter of March 30, 1944. *Service Record Book of Men and Women of Eldred & Vicinity* (Eldred, PA: PVT Myron Burn's Post No. 2092, VFW, n.d.), 8, 25.

36. General George C. Marshall (1880–1959) served as the chief of staff of the United States military during World War II.

37. Major General James A. Ulio (1882–1958) served as the army's adjutant general from 1942 to 1946. Arlington National Cemetery, "James Alexander Ulio," accessed May 19, 2015, http://www.arlington cemetery.net/jaulio.htm.

38. Herman Berkowsky was an officer in the 39th Station Hospital.

39. Joe was serving with the Army Air Force Training Command at Hamilton College in Clinton, New York.

40. Louis Dan, also known as Louis Abdo, the brother of Gabriel's mother, resided in Danbury, Connecticut, with his five daughters, one of whom was Ailene, and two sons. Louis's wife, Fumia, was Gabriel's father's sister.

41. The O'Dells, close family friends of the Gabriels, moved to San Francisco.

42. A small suitcase built over a rigid frame.

43. Established in Pittsburg, California, in early 1942, Camp Stoneman was a major staging area for troops deploying to the Pacific from San Francisco. California Military History Foundation, "Camp Stoneman," accessed May 19, 2015, http://californiamilitaryhistory .org/CpStoneman.html.

44. Pinks is slang for an officer's winter uniform trousers. WWII Impressions, Inc., "US Army Regulation, Winter Officer's Service Uniform," accessed June 1, 2015, http://www.wwiiimpressions.com/newu sarmyofficerwinteruniform.html.

Chapter 2

1. Stanley Tryzbiak, *Official Log of Cruises and Narrative War History of the U.S.S. West Point AP 23, World War II, 1941–1946* (n.c.: USS *West Point* Reunion Association, 2008), 4, accessed October 22, 2013, http://www.usswestpoint.com/newsletters/The%20shipslog.pdf.

2. Eddy Heyde to author, October 27, 1987; Atabrine was a medicine

use to treat the symptoms of malaria but was extremely unpopular among soldiers, who erroneously believed that it would cause impotence or permanently stain their skin. John Miller, Jr., *United States Army in World War II: The War in the Pacific, Guadalcanal; The First Offensive* (Washington, DC: Historical Division, Department of the Army, 1949), 227.

3. For a good overview of this traditional ceremony involving King Neptune and the uninitiated "pollywogs," see David Moore, "Pollywog or Shellback: The Navy's Line Crossing Ceremony Revealed," *Veterans United Network*, accessed August 7, 2016, https://www.veteransunited.com/network/the-navys-line-crossing-ceremony-revealed/.

4. "Unit History, 39th Station Hospital, Second Half 1944," January 3, 1945, Unit Histories 39th Station Hospital, RG 112, Entry 1012 HU MEDS, Box 110.

5. Historians have documented the struggle for Guadalcanal many times. Two of the best works on this decisive action are Jack Coggins, *The Campaign for Guadalcanal: A Battle That Made History* (Garden City, NY: Doubleday, 1972) and Richard B. Frank, *Guadalcanal* (New York: Random House, 1990).

6. "Medical History of the 39th Station Hospital prepared by Major Jewell R. Wilson," April 6, 1944, pages 1, 5, 39th Station Hospital POA 1942–1944, RG 112, Entry 54A, Box 489.

7. Originally launched in 1940 as the SS *America*, the navy acquired this large passenger liner in June 1941 and converted into a troop ship, the USS *West Point* (AP 23). The ship made a total of fifty-six voyages in both the Pacific and European Theaters and often sailed unescorted because of its great speed. During the course of the war it carried tens of thousands of soldiers, including over 4,000 German prisoners of war, and sailed 436,144 miles. Tryzbiak, *Official Log of U.S.S. West Point*, 2–7, 9, accessed October 22, 2013, http://www.usswestpoint.com/newsletters/The%20shipslog.pdf.

8. The second letter is omitted from this collection because it is identical to the first.

9. The *West Point* arrived at Noumea, the capital of the French colony of New Caledonia, on January 24 and left two days later. According to his Travel Log, Gabriel went ashore on Thursday, January 25. Tryzbiak, *Official Log of Cruises*, 4, accessed October 22, 2013, http://www.usswestpoint.com/newsletters/The%20shipslog.pdf.

The United States Navy constructed a major naval base at Noumea in 1942 because of its extensive harbor. Department of the Navy, Bureau of Yards and Docks, "Building the Navy's Bases in World War II: History of the Bureau of Yards and Docks and the Civil Engineer Corps, 1940–1946," 194, accessed June 1, 2015, 194, http://www.ibiblio.org/hyperwar/USN/Building_Bases/bases-24.html; John Miller Jr., *United States Army in World War II: The War in the Pacific, Guadalcanal; The First Offensive* (Washington, DC: Historical Division, Department of the Army, 1949), 7.

10. Army Air Forces Technical Training Command.

11. A formal written message that was transmitted by the radio.

12. He actually wrote to his parents four times while on the *West Point*, but two were identical letters on January 19.

13. Possibly Arthur F. Hoffman, who graduated from Jefferson Medical College in 1941, and who earned his undergraduate degree at the University of Notre Dame. *Jefferson Medical College Yearbooks, 1941*, accessed November 3, 2015, http://jdc.jefferson.edu/jmc_yearbooks/53/.

14. A key naval base in Vallejo, California, on San Francisco Bay, Mare Island also contained a large hospital, which specialized in producing prosthetic limbs, for wounded military personnel in the Pacific. Calexplornia, "A Historical Look at the Mare Island Naval Hospital," accessed September 18, 2015, http://www.calexplornia.com/a-historical-look-at-the-mare-island-naval-hospital/.

15. The US military employed a variety of rations, designated by letters. Soldiers serving in rear areas in the Pacific usually received B field rations, which consisted of canned and dehydrated foods. Locally produced food sometimes supplemented these, as did care packages from home. Alvin P. Stauffer, *The Quartermaster Corps: Operations in the War against Japan* (1956; Reprint, Washington, DC: Office of the Chief of Military History, Department of the Army, 1971), 55, 309–10; the Pacific War Online Encyclopedia, "Rations," accessed November 25, 2016, http://www.pwencycl.kgbudge.com/R/a/Rations.htm.

16. For an interesting study on the importance of the PX in maintaining soldiers' morale, see James J. Cooke, *Chewing Gum, Candy Bars, and Beer: The Army PX in World War II* (Columbia: University of Missouri Press, 2009).

17. The Solomon Islands average nearly thirteen inches of rain in February. The World Bank Group, "Climate Change Knowledge Portal: Solomon Islands," accessed August 31, 2016, http://sdwebx.worldbank.org/climateportal/index.cfm?page=country_historical_climate&ThisCCode=SLB.

18. Dr. Leonard. See May 18, 1944, letter to parents.

19. Bradford, Pennsylvania, is located about sixteen miles west of El-dred. In all likelihood, the doctor was Joseph A. Kervin (1896–1965), a longtime Bradford resident and Naval Reserve officer, who served with Naval Mobile Hospital 8 on Guadalcanal. Dr. Kervin was probably detached to Naval Base Hospital 7 on Tulagi. "Dr. J. Kervin Dies of Heart Attack at 69," *Bradford Era* [PA], May 12, 1965, 1, 16; Joseph L. Schwartz, "Chapter I: Facilities of the Medical Department of the Navy," *History of the Medical Department of the United States Navy in World War II*, 21–22, accessed September 3, 2015, https://www.ibiblio.org/hyperwar/USN/USN-Medical/I/USN-Medical-1.html. Also see May 8, 1944, letter to parents.

20. A small religious artifact usually associated with a saint.

21. Arctics were a type of rubber boot.

22. For a discussion of Japanese radio propaganda in the Pacific war, see Namikawa Ry , "Japanese Overseas Broadcasting: A Personal View," in *Film and Radio Propaganda in World War II*, ed. K. R. M. Short (Knoxville: University of Tennessee Press, 1983), 319–33.

23. Suntans referred to the lightweight tan slacks of a summer uni-form. WWII Impressions, Inc., "US Army Regulation, Winter Officer's Service Uniform," accessed June 1, 2015, http://www.wwiiimpressions.com/newusarmyofficerwinteruniform.html.

24. Possibly Roosevelt transferring a destroyer escort to the Free French. The American Presidency Project, "Franklin D. Roosevelt: 11—Remarks on Transferring a Destroyer Escort to the French," February 12, 1944, accessed December 4, 2015, http://www.presidency.ucsb.edu/ws/?pid=16464.

25. Jeanette M. Long worked in Gabriel's parents' store.

26. Troops serving overseas were routinely issued a ration of weak, 3.2% alcohol, beer. The Pacific War Online Encyclopedia, "Alcohol," accessed November 25, 2016, http://www.pwencycl.kgbudge.com/A/1 / Alcohol.htm.

27. The Kniesers were Gabriel's cousins who owned a clothing store in Olean, New York.

28. O.D. refers to olive drab uniforms. WWII Impressions, Inc., "United States Army Regulation Uniforms," accessed June 1, 2015, http://www.wwiiimpressions.com/newusarmyuniforms.html.

29. Ronson manufactured some of the first commercial lighters starting in 1913. W. R. Case and Sons Cutlery Company, "Our Com-panies," accessed June 1, 2015, http://www.zippo.com/about/article.aspx?id=1577.

30. Hendrik Willem Van Loon's *Story of Mankind* described the rise of Western civilization to the early twentieth century. Published in 1921, it received the first Newberry Award for children's literature the following year. The Baldwin Project, "The Story of Mankind," accessed June 12, 2015, http://www.mainlesson.com/display.php?author=van loon&book=mankind&story=_contents.

31. George Gabriel, the brother of Gabriel's father, ran a grocery store in Olean, New York. Gabriel's uncle Louis Abdo Dan resided in Danbury, Connecticut; see December 20, 1943, letter to parents. Gabriel's father's cousins lived in Bayonne, New Jersey.

32. For a thorough discussion of the importance of the Special Service Division, a branch of the military designed to maintain morale through the use of the USO, movies, and other recreational efforts, see James J. Cooke, *American Girls, Beer, and Glenn Miller: G.I. Morale in World War II* (Columbia: University of Missouri Press, 2012).

Welsh-born Ray Milland (1907–1986) was barred from service in the Army Air Corps during World War II because of a hand injury, so he made repeated USO tours to support the troops. He is best remembered for his roles in such movies as *Beau Geste* (1939), *The Lost Weekend* (1945), and *Dial M for Murder* (1954). John A. Garraty and Mark C. Carnes, *American National Biography* (New York: Oxford University Press, 1999), 15:459–60 (hereafter, Garraty, *ANB*); Mary Elliott (1917–2000) worked as a singer, actress, and model. IMDb.com, "Mary Elliott," accessed September 19, 2015, http://www.imdb.com/name/nm0254551/; Frances Faye (1912–1991) appeared in a number of movies. IMDb.com, "Frances Faye," accessed September 19, 2015, http://www.imdb.com/name/nm0269662/?ref_=fn_al_nm_1; Rosita Moreno (1907–1993) was a Spanish-born actress who made movies in several countries including the United States. IMDb.com, "Rosita Moreno," accessed September 19, 2015, http://www.imdb.com/name/nm0604174/?ref_=fn_al_nm_2.

33. See February 6, 1944, letter to parents.

34. Ikuko Toguri [Iva Toguri d'Aquino] (1916–2006), better known as "Tokyo Rose" to US troops in the Pacific, played "Orphan Ann" on the Japanese radio program *Zero Hour*. Beginning in 1943, *Zero Hour* featured music, news, and letters from Allied prisoners of war designed to lower morale among American military personnel. Toguri, a US citizen, was visiting Japan in 1941 to care for an ill family friend when she was stranded by the outbreak of the war. Toguri then began working for Nippon Hoso Kyokai, the Japanese Broadcasting Corporation. She was convicted of treason in 1949 and sentenced to prison for ten years,

but only served six. Gerald Ford pardoned her in January 1977. Ry, "Japanese Overseas Broadcasting," 324–27; Frederick P. Close, *Tokyo Rose, An American Patriot: A Dual Biography* (Lanham, MD: Scarecrow Press, 2010); Ann Elizabeth Pfau, *Miss Yourlovin: GIs, Gender, and Domesticity during World War II* (New York: Columbia University Press, 2008; Project Gutenberg, 2008), chapter 5, "The Legend of *Tokyo Rose*," http://www.gutenberg-e.org/pfau/index.html.

35. The Eldred area experienced a series of floods in the 1940s, with an especially damaging one in July 1942. St. Bonaventure University Archives, "The Floods of 1942 and 1972," accessed June 12, 2015, http://web.sbu.edu/friedsam/archives/buildings/Floods.htm.

36. Jamestown is a city located in Chautauqua County in western New York.

37. James W. Eastman (1917–1982), an Eldred resident who served in the Army Signal Corps, ran a radio-teletype on Guadalcanal. *Service Record, Eldred*, 14.

38. Curiously, Gabriel mentioned the *Eagle* in the previous letter.

39. Probably a reference to Loop Hollow, the site of the National Munitions Company plant that operated in Eldred during World War II. Eldred World War II Museum, "About Us," accessed June 13, 2015, http://eldredwwiimuseum.net/about-us/.

40. Axis radio broadcasts reported the sinking of the *West Point* seven different times during the war, in both theaters. Tryzbiak, *Official Log of Cruises*, 7–8, accessed October 24, 2013, http://www.usswestpoint.com/newsletters/The%20shipslog.pdf.

41. Sister Margaret Carmencita Tuohy, a Sister of Saint Francis nun, died in Allegany, New York, on May 27, 1943. Franciscan Sisters of Allegany, "Necrology of the Franciscan Sisters of Allegany, New York," accessed September 20, 2015, http://www.alleganyfranciscans.org/necrology_chron.html; "June 1943 Newsletter," in Cawley, *Fr. Liebel's Letters*, 25.

42. Edna Dan was another of Gabriel's Danbury cousins.

43. Military medical personnel often formed local societies to promote camaraderie among the various hospitals and to disseminate current findings. Similar societies existed on Saipan, Tinian, and Espiritu Santo in the New Hebrides. Lepore, *Life of the Clinician*, 236; Joseph L. Schwartz, "Chapter II: Experiences in Battle of the Medical Department of the Navy," *History of the Medical Department of the United States Navy in World War II*, accessed July 13, 2015, http://www.ibiblio.org/hyperwar/USN/USN-Medical/I/USN-Medical-2.html.

44. Frances Selzer Talbot (1914–2010) served as a lieutenant in the Army Air Corps. Waller Funeral Home, "In Memoriam of Frances Selzer Talbot," accessed December 21, 2014, www.wallerfuneralhome.com/memsol.cgi?user_id=264693.

45. Van Loon's *Story of Mankind*. See letter of February 19, 1944.

46. *Ten Gentlemen from West Point* (1942) was an action film set in the early 1800s about the first West Point cadets battling Native Americans in the West. Leslie Halliwell, *Halliwell's Film Guide*, 2nd. ed. (London: Granada Publishing, 1979), 858.

47. Julia, Gabriel's cousin, was the Knieser brothers' sister. See February 16, 1944, letter to parents.

48. Johnnie Mansour lived in Olean, New York. Abdo Dan was the son of Gabriel's Uncle Louie, and he resided in Danbury, Connecticut.

49. Captain Bergen W. Birdsall served as the 39th Station Hospital's chaplain.

50. *A Journey for Margaret* (1942) featured Robert Young as an American war correspondent who adopts an orphan during the Blitz. Halliwell, *Film Guide*, 460.

51. Lorraine Sadd [Moses], a distant cousin, lived in Charleston, West Virginia.

52. Evelyn Thabet, Lorraine Sadd's sister.

53. Dr. Andrew G. Lasichak graduated from Thomas Jefferson Medical College in 1940. *Jefferson Medical College Yearbooks, 1940*, accessed September 24, 2015, http://jdc.jefferson.edu/jmc_yearbooks/50.

54. James W. Eastman. See February 28, 1944, letter to parents. Barden Brook is a small stream located on the north edge of Eldred.

55. Dr. Charles Schaaf, an intern with Gabriel at St. Vincent Hospital in Erie, Pennsylvania, later served in Europe during the war. See April 14, 1944, letter to parents.

56. Lawrence "Nunny" Lambillotte, an Eldred resident, was killed at Anzio, Italy, on February 12, 1944. *Service Record, Eldred*, 8. His brother Edmond was stationed at Sheppard Field, Texas, with Gabriel. See September 15, 1943, letter to parents.

57. The *Alumnus* was the University of Notre Dame's bimonthly alumni publication.

58. See February 13, 1944, letter to Father Liebel.

59. *Eyes in the Night* (1942) featured Edward Arnold as a blind detective who discovers a Nazi plot to steal military secrets. Halliwell, *Film Guide*, 269. Arnold (1890–1956) appeared in over 150 films, including *Diamond Jim* (1935). IMDb.com, "Edward Arnold," accessed

July 17, 2015, http://www.imdb.com/name/nm0036427/bio?ref_=nm_ov_bio_sm.

60. *Air Force* (1943) was a film about a B-17 crew that sees combat in the South Pacific following Pearl Harbor. *Mrs. Miniver* (1942), starring Greer Garson and Walter Pidgeon, told the story of an English housewife during World War II. Halliwell, *Film Guide*, 14–15, 591.

61. Lewis Frank. See April 9, 1944, letter to parents.

62. The island chaplain designed this building, and native workers built it.

63. Lewis P. Frank earned his bachelor of science degree at Lebanon Valley College, and then did a residency at St. Louis University Hospital after graduating from Jefferson. *Jefferson Medical College Yearbooks, 1940*, 113, accessed September 24, 2015, http://jdc.jefferson.edu/jmc_yearbooks/50.

64. Founded in 1882, the Knights of Columbus is a Catholic fraternal and charitable society initially designed to provide insurance for working-class families. Douglas Brinkley and Julie M. Fenster, *Parish Priest: Father Michael McGivney and American Catholicism* (New York: William Morrow, 2006), 109–207.

65. Herbert J. Geuder was an airman in a four-day battle between March 15 and 19, near Wewak, New Guinea, that resulted in the sinking of five Japanese ships. During the course of the war Geuder earned eight Air Medals, three Oak Leaf Clusters, and four Battle Stars. "SGT. Herbert Geuder of Eldred Helps Sink Five Jap Ships," *Eldred Eagle*, March 24, 1944, 1; *Service Record, Eldred*, 20 (this book misidentifies him as Herbert J. Gender, but his parents are listed as Geuder).

66. Sampson Naval Training Base was located on the east shore of Seneca Lake in Seneca County, New York. New York State Military Museum and Veterans Research Center, "Sampson Naval Training Base," accessed July 9, 2015, https://dmna.ny.gov/forts/fortsQ_S/sampsonNavalTrainingBase.htm.

67. Liz Farris was Gabriel's sister Ester's sister-in-law. Liz helped Ester when her husband Duffy served in the navy.

68. Ingrid Bergman starred in *Intermezzo: A Love Story* (1939), a film about a famous violinist who falls in love with his protégé. Nominated for twelve Academy Awards, *The Song of Bernadette* (1943) was the story Saint Bernadette, a French peasant girl who saw visions of the Virgin Mary in the 1850s. Halliwell, *Film Guide*, 434; Turner Classic Movies, accessed July 16, 2015, http://www.tcm.com/tcmdb/title/90836/The-Song-of-Bernadette/.

69. John Hersey's *Into the Valley: A Skirmish of the Marines* (New York: Alfred A. Knopf, 1943) contained personal accounts of the Solomon Island campaign. Worldcat, accessed October 21, 2015, http://www.worldcat.org/title/into-the-valley-a-skirmish-of-the-marines/oclc/396087&referer=brief_results.

70. Possibly Allied landings at Aitape and Hollandia on the northern coast of New Guinea. Wesley Frank Craven and James Lea Cate, eds., *The Army Air Forces in World War II*, vol. 4, *The Pacific: Guadalcanal to Saipan, August 1942 to July 1944* (Washington, DC: Office of Air Force History, 1983), 603–7; "Naval Operations in the Pacific from March 1944 to October 1945: Capture and Occupation of Hollandia," accessed February 19, 2015, http://www.shsu.edu/~his_ncp/Compac45.html.

71. George Rubenstein was from Dunkirk, a town located in Chautauqua County, New York, on Lake Erie. See letter of May 22, 1944.

72. Red Cross women arrived in the Solomon Islands in spring 1944, where they distributed coffee and doughnuts to military personnel. United States Online Historical Newspapers, "Red Cross Girls Reach Guadalcanal," *Eugene Register-Guard* [Eugene, Oregon], April 26, 1944, 8, accessed July 13, 2015, https://sites.google.com/site/online-newspapersite/Home/usa. For the Red Cross's role in the South Pacific, see Foster Rhea Dulles, *The American Red Cross: A History* (New York: Harper and Brothers, 1950), 465–88.

73. Sergeant Richardson.

74. Leo Hofschneider graduated from the University of Notre Dame in 1936, attended medical school, and served in the Medical Corps in the South Pacific. His letter was reprinted in the Notre Dame alumni magazine. "The Things I Dream of Now," *Notre Dame Alumnus 22* (June 1944): 29. See appendix.

75. The description on the back of several photographs from this trip and Eddy Heyde's letter to the author indicate that they went to Savo Island.

76. Located in Allegany County in central New York near the Pennsylvania border.

77. Savo Island is now being investigated as a possible site for a geothermal power station. See Geodynamics Limited, "Savo Island Geothermal Power Project," accessed April 3, 2015, http://www.geodynamics.com.au/Our-Projects/Pacific-Islands/Savo-Island.aspx, and Welkam Solomons, "Sunset Lodge, Savo Island," accessed April 3, 2015, http://welkamsolomons.com/places/central/savo/index.html.

78. The newspaper of the Catholic Diocese of Erie, Pennsylvania.

79. Dr. Joseph A. Kervin. See February 6, 1944, letter to parents.

80. *Spotlight Scandals* (1943) is the story of a vaudevillian and a barber who become a comic duo. Turner Classic Movies, accessed July 21, 2015, http://www.tcm.com/tcmdb/title/91137/Spotlight-Scandals/. Bonnie Baker (1917–1990)an American actress and singer. IMDb.com, "Bonnie Baker," accessed July 12, 2015, http://www.imdb.com/name/nm0048284/.

81. US Online Historical Newspapers, "Red Cross Girls Reach Guadalcanal," *Eugene Register-Guard* [Eugene, Oregon], (April 26, 1944), 8, accessed July 13, 2015, https://sites.google.com/site/onlinenewspapersite/Home/usa.

82. Lewis Frank. See April 9, 1944, letter to parents.

83. Eastman Kodak, *How to Make Good Pictures* (Rochester, NY: Eastman Kodak, 1943). The book was reprinted and updated multiple times.

84. In *Tarzan's New York Adventure* (1942) Tarzan (Johnny Weissmuller) and Jane (Maureen O'Sullivan) attempt to rescue a boy kidnapped by a circus. Turner Classic Movies, accessed July 17, 2015, http://www.tcm.com/tcmdb/title/3594/Tarzan-s-New-York-Adventure/.

85. Army Post Office 708 was Espiritu Santo, New Hebrides Islands, about 630 miles southeast of Guadalcanal. United States, Adjutant-General's Office, *Numerical Listing of APO's January 1942–November 1947* (Washington, DC: Adjutant-General's Office, 1949; Internet Archive), 158, accessed, July 19, 2015, https://archive.org/details/NumericalListingOfApos.

86. Gino L. Baldoni (1915–1983), an Eldred native, served in the navy. *Service Record, Eldred*, 34.

87. The friend is Dave Chase. See July 18, 1944, letter to parents.

88. Wynette O'Dell was a close friend and high school classmate of Gabriel's sister Ester. Also see December 20, 1943, letter to parents.

89. *Ladies' Day* (1943) features Eddie Albert as a professional baseball pitcher who loses his edge after meeting a lively Mexican actress. Turner Classic Movies, accessed July 17, 2015, http://www.tcm.com/tcmdb/title/15165/Ladies-Day/.

90. Gabriel is referring to an atmospheric phenomenon called crepuscular rays. This occurs when the sun, low on the horizon, sets behind irregular clouds, mountains, or other obstructions, and casts long converging rays and shadows. *Encyclopedia Britannica*, "Crepuscular Rays," https://www.britannica.com/science/crepuscular-ray; NASA

Earth Observatory, "Crepuscular Rays: India," https://earthobservato ry.nasa.gov/images/76261/crepuscular-rays-india, both accessed February 17, 2019.

91. Lieutenant Edith Greenwood was the first woman to receive the Soldier's Medal for helping evacuate patients from a burning hospital near Yuma, Arizona, on September 16, 1942. "The Heroine on the Cover," *Collier's*, April 15, 1944, 65.

92. *Cowboy in Manhattan* (1943) is the story of a Broadway producer trying to finance a musical about Texas. Turner Classic Movies, accessed July 18, 2015, http://www.tcm.com/tcmdb/title/71677/Cowboy-in-Manhattan/.

93. See incomplete letter of May 24 to parents.

94. The editor's family still has this ashtray, but it is actually from a 75 mm shell.

95. A copy of this Travel Log is found following the Introduction of this work.

96. *Going My Way* (1944). Bing Crosby starred as a young priest assigned to assist an elderly pastor at a struggling church. The movie won seven Academy Awards, including Best Actor (Crosby), Best Supporting Actor (Barry Fitzgerald), and Best Picture. Thomas Hischak, *The Oxford Companion to the American Musical: Theatre, Films, and Television* (New York: Oxford University Press, 2008), 291, 844.

Bing Crosby (1903–1977), a gifted singer and actor, starred in such movies as *Holiday Inn* (1942), *The Bells of St. Mary's* (1945), and *White Christmas* (1954), along with a series of *Road* movies with Bob Hope. Hischak, *American Musical*, 175–76.

97. Orientation officers gave lectures to the enlisted men about current events, health issues, and war objectives to help maintain morale. For an overview of the goals of orientation, see Samuel A. Stouffer, *The American Soldier* (Princeton, NJ: Princeton University Press, 1949), 1: 458–85.

98. *This Land Is Mine* (1943). Charles Laughton and Maureen O'Hara star in this film about a schoolteacher who fights the Nazis in occupied Europe. Halliwell, *Film Guide*, 876.

99. *The Great Impersonation* (1942). During World War I, a German spy murders a British aristocrat, who is his double, and takes his place. Halliwell, *Film Guide*, 351.

100. Captain Edward C. Heyde. See June 6, 1944, letter to parents.

101. *The Spoilers* (1942) is a film about two prospectors who battle over land claims and a singer in the Yukon goldfields. Halliwell, *Film Guide*, 818.

Marlene Dietrich (1901–1992) enjoyed a long career as a singer and actress, appearing both on film and the stage. A fervent anti-Nazi, Dietrich participated in bond drives and did five hundred USO performances, earning the Medal of Freedom; Randolph Scott (1898–1987) is best remembered for his roles in westerns such as *Ride the High Country* (1962); John Wayne (1907–1979) was a legendary actor who starred in a wide array of films including *The Fighting Seabees* (1944), *The Quiet Man* (1952), and *True Grit* (1969). Garraty, *ANB*, 6: 590–92; 19: 504–5; 22: 829–31.

102. Gabriel's uncle in Danbury, Connecticut, and his son. See December 20, 1943 letter to parents.

103. Allied forces entered Rome on June 4, 1944, the first Axis capital to fall.

104. *Always in My Heart* (1942). A convict returns home to find his family shattered and his wife preparing to remarry. Halliwell, *Film Guide*, 24.

105. *Princess O'Rourke* (1943) is the story of a princess living in New York who falls in love with an ordinary American. Turner Classic Movies, accessed September 24, 2015. http://www.tcm.com/tcmdb/title/87158/Princess-O-Rourke/.

Olivia de Havilland (b. 1916) won two Academy Awards and appeared in many major films including *The Adventures of Robin Hood* (1938) and *Gone With the Wind* (1939). *Encyclopedia Britannica*, "Olivia De Havilland," accessed February 10, 2019, https://www.britannica.com/biography/Olivia-de-Havilland; Robert Cummings (1918–1990) enjoyed a long career in both movies and on television, frequently appearing in comedies. Hischak, *American Musical*, 178.

106. Allied forces landed in Normandy, France, on June 6, 1944.

107. Esther Dan was another of Gabriel's cousins from Danbury, Connecticut.

108. The Schaffners were family friends of Gabriel's sister, Victoria Fagouri, who also lived in Bolivar, New York.

Father Gabriel Naughton was the first friar from St. Bonaventure University to become a navy chaplain in World War II. St. Bonaventure University, "World War II Chaplains from St. Bonaventure," accessed July 14, 2015, http://students.sbu.edu/astrong/chaplains.htm.

109. *The Devil with Hitler* (1942). To save his own position, Satan masquerades as Hitler's valet and astrologer to show that even the führer has good qualities. Turner Classic Movies, accessed September 24, 2015, http://www.tcm.com/tcmdb/title/493723/The-Devil-with-Hitler/.

110. *Rhythm of the Islands* (1943). A group of cannibals complicate

two New Yorkers' scheme to sell a South Pacific island to wealthy tourists. Turner Classic Movies, accessed September 24, 2015, http://www.tcm.com/tcmdb/title/88164/Rhythm-of-the-Islands/.

111. This is the package that he refers to in his May 31 letter to his brother Joe.

112. *Meanest Man in the World* (1943). Jack Benny plays the role of a good-natured lawyer who attempts to blacken his reputation to expand his business. Turner Classic Movies, accessed September 24, 2015, http://www.tcm.com/tcmdb/title/83172/The-Meanest-Man-in-the-World/.

Jack Benny (1894–1974) was a comedian and actor who achieved great success in vaudeville and on the radio, television, and in the movies. Garraty, *ANB*, 2: 600–602.

113. Coudersport and Gaines are small towns located in Potter and Tioga Counties, Pennsylvania, respectively.

114. *Girl Trouble* (1942). Don Ameche plays a Venezuelan playboy who rents an apartment from a New York City socialite whom he mistakes for a maid. Turner Classic Movies, accessed September 21, 2015, http://www.tcm.com/tcmdb/title/76396/Girl-Trouble/.

Don Ameche (1908–1993) was a popular actor and radio master of ceremonies in the 1930s and 1940s. He revived his career in the 1980s with roles in such movies as *Trading Places* and *Cocoon*. Garraty, *ANB*, 1: 403–4.

115. Joe served at MacDill Air Force Base located near Tampa.

116. Sartwell and Duke Center are villages neighboring Eldred in McKean County.

117. The United States Naval Training Center, Bainbridge, was located in Port Deposit, Maryland. "USNTC Bainbridge Association," accessed July 14, 2015, http://www.usntcb.org/.

118. On June 15/16, seventy-five B-29s, flying from Burma, bombed the steelworks at Yawata in northern Kyushu, the first attacks on the Japanese mainland since General Jimmy Doolittle's Tokyo raid on April 18, 1942. Norman Polmar and Thomas B. Allen, *World War II: The Encyclopedia of the War Years, 1941–1945* (Mineola, NY: Dover, 2012), 37, 79, 772.

119. Walter Lippmann's *US Foreign Policy: Shield of the Republic* (1943). See letter to his sister Ester, June 30, 1944.

120. Frank Buck (1888–1950) was a writer and actor best known for his works on wild animals and jungles. IMDb.com, "Frank Buck," accessed July 14, 2015, http://www.imdb.com/name/nm0118353/bio.

121. Harold B. Morris, an Eldred resident who served in the Pacific. *Service Record, Eldred*, 28; "June 1, 1944 Newsletter," in Cawley, *Fr. Liebel's Letters*, 76.

122. The officer Class A uniform included a jacket, white collar shirt, tie, and dress pants. Byron Connell, "WWII US Army Officers' Uniforms," accessed November 6, 2015, http://www.siwcostumers.org/newsletter-archive/VirtCostV9-I2–2011/VirtCostV9-I2–2011_37-army.pdf.

123. The movie could have been either *Tarzan Triumphs* or *Tarzan's Desert Mystery*, both of which appeared in 1943. Turner Classic Movies, accessed September 24, 2015, http://www.tcm.com/search/?text=tarzan&type=allSite.

124. Dr. Joseph A. Wintermantle practiced in Olean, New York.

125. *Sing a Jingle* (1944). A radio singer, working incognito at a factory, helps a sorority girl organize a benefit dance to sell war bonds. Turner Classic Movies, accessed September 21, 2015, http://www.tcm.com/tcmdb/title/90230/Sing-a-Jingle/.

126. United States troops captured Cherbourg, a key port on the Cotentin Peninsula, in heavy fighting between June 22 and June 27. Max Hastings, *Overlord: D-Day and the Battle for Normandy* (New York: Simon and Schuster, 1984), 163–66.

US forces seized Saipan in the Mariana Islands between June 15 and July 9, 1944, and then used it to launch B-29 raids against Japan. Harold J. Goldberg, *D-Day in the Pacific: The Battle of Saipan* (Bloomington: Indiana University Press, 2007).

Soviet offensives in the second half of 1943 through the summer of 1944 inflicted heavy losses on the Germans and drove them steadily westward. Keith Cumins, *Cataclysm: The War on the Eastern Front, 1941–45* (Solihull, England: Helion, 2011), 197–223.

127. *Coastal Command* (1943). A documentary featuring Royal Air Force personnel guarding convoys and attacking Nazi U-boats and aircraft. IMDb.com, *Coastal Command*, accessed September 22, 2015, http://www.imdb.com/title/tt0034603/?ref_=fn_al_tt_1.

128. On June 9, 1944, the Soviet Army launched a major offensive against Finland, which had reluctantly allied itself to Germany during the 1940 Winter War. Although they eventually contained the Soviet offensive, the Finns, exhausted by five years of war, signed an armistice with the Russians in September. Cumins, *Cataclysm*, 220–22.

129. The fourth team was the Oklahoma Oakies. See July 3, 1944, letter to parents.

130. *Strange Death of Adolph Hitler* (1943). A minor Austrian offi-

cial is forced to act as Hitler's double, only to be killed by his wife, who mistakes him for the real führer. Turner Classic Movies, accessed September 22, 2015, http://www.tcm.com/tcmdb/title/91585/The-Strange -Death-of-Adolf-Hitler/.

131. Thomas E. Dewey and John W. Bricker ran as the Republican candidates for president and vice president in the 1944 presidential election.

132. Scopa is a traditional Italian card game that is often played in teams, similar to bridge. BoardGameGeek.com, "Scopa," accessed November 6, 2015, https://boardgamegeek.com/boardgame/15889/scopa.

133. Duke Center is a small town near Eldred, Pennsylvania.

134. *Salute to the Marines* (1943). A tough marine sergeant trains Filipinos to resist the Japanese during the early stages of the war, while trying to save his family. Halliwell, *Film Guide*, 754.

Wallace Beery (1885–1949) won an Academy Award for Best Actor for his role in *The Champ* (1931), and he later appeared in such films as *Treasure Island* (1934) and *Viva Villa!* (1934). Garraty, *ANB*, 2: 477–78.

135. A technique to apply vivid colors to movies. James Layton and David Pierce, *The Dawn of Technicolor, 1915–1935* (Rochester, NY: George Eastman House, 2015).

136. Robert Lee Scott Jr.'s autobiographical account of his service as a fighter pilot in Burma and China (New York: Charles Scribner's Sons, 1943). Worldcat, accessed November 23, 2015, http://www.worldcat. org/title/god-is-my-co-pilot/oclc/1216391&referer=brief_results.

137. Walter Lippmann's *US Foreign Policy: Shield of the Republic* (Boston: Little, Brown, 1943) offered an assessment of where American global commitments should lie in the postwar era. Patrick Garrity, "US Foreign Policy: Shield of the Republic (1943)," *Classics of Strategy and Diplomacy*, accessed September 18, 2016, www.classicsofstrategy. com/2008/09/us-foreign-policy.html.

138. *Lost Angel* (1944). Margaret O'Brien stars in this film about a child adopted by a reporter. Halliwell, *Film Guide*, 526.

139. *The Sullivans* (1944). The inspirational story of five brothers who were killed aboard the USS *Juneau*. Halliwell, *Film Guide*, 839.

140. Eldred resident Thomas V. Slavin (1923–2008), who served in the navy. Gilfert, "Military History of McKean County, Pennsylvania, World War II: Community Honor Rolls—Eldred and Vicinity," accessed July 15, 2015, http://jfgvictoryverlag.com/WWIIhonorrolls/Eldred%20 N-Z.html.

141. St. Francis Hospital, once one of the largest in Pittsburgh, ceased operating in 2002 after 137 years. Pittsburgh Catholic Publishing Associates, "St. Francis Medical Center's long history comes to a close," accessed July 15, 2015, http://www.pittsburghcatholic.org/ News/st-francis-medical-centers-long-history-comes-to-a-close.

142. Berenice Thorpe's *Reunion on Strawberry Hill* (New York: Alfred A. Knopf, 1944) is a novel about six adult children returning home to celebrate their parents' forty-eighth anniversary. Worldcat, accessed September 22, 2015, http://www.worldcat.org/title/reunion- on-strawberry-hill-a-novel/oclc/1655751&referer=brief_results.

143. *Gangway for Tomorrow* (1943). Five defense workers riding in a car reflect on their earlier lives. Turner Classic Movies, access September 22, 2015, http://www.tcm.com/tcmdb/title/75985/Gangway- for-Tomorrow/.

144. The Quartermaster Corps began experimental farming on Guadalcanal in 1943 to ease logistical demands. By 1944 both soldiers and local natives worked a large farm that eventually encompassed over two thousand acres near the Malimbo River. Smaller, yet similar farms also operated on Bougainville, Espiritu Santo, Efate, New Caledonia, and other islands. Stauffer, *Quartermaster Corps*, 129–33; Judith A. Bennett, *Natives and Exotics: World War II and the Environment in the Southern Pacific* (Honolulu: University of Hawai'i Press, 2009), 78–85.

145. The War Department began Badge Pay on June 30, 1944, to improve morale of infantry soldiers and recognize the risks that they faced. Those who possessed the Combat Infantry Badge or the Expert Infantryman's Badge earned an extra $10 or $5 per month. Brandon R. Gould and Stanley A. Horowitz, *History of Combat Pay* (Alexandria, VA: Institute for Defense Analyses, August 2011), iii, 5–11.

146. Soviet offensives in spring and summer 1944 pushed Axis forces steadily westward toward the prewar border, but at horrific cost to both sides. Cumins, *Cataclysm*, 203–57.

147. *Sahara* (1943). Humphrey Bogart plays a hard-bitten American tank commander who leads a collection of Allied soldiers in a desperate battle against the Nazis in the North African desert. Turner Classic Movies, accessed September 24, 2015, http://www.tcm.com/ tcmdb/title/88884/Sahara/.

148. Gabriel's nephews, Paul and John Farris. A Lebanese custom was for uncles to address their nephews as "uncle."

149. Corporal Carmelo Mangion.

150. *Boston Blackie Goes to Hollywood* (1942). A reformed criminal and his sidekick try to recover a stolen diamond. Turner Classic Movies, accessed September 24, 2015, http://www.tcm.com/tcmdb/title/69459/Boston-Blackie-Goes-Hollywood/.

151. Chase sent him camera equipment. See May 22, 1944, letter to parents.

152. Eldred resident Dermond J. Tuohy served in the military in World War II. Gilfert, "Military History of McKean County, Pennsylvania, World War II: Community Honor Rolls—Eldred and Vicinity," accessed November 8, 2015, http://jfgvictoryverlag.com/WWIIhonorrolls/Eldred%20N-Z.html.

153. See June 22, 1944, letter to parents.

154. Camp Bowie is located near Brownwood, Texas. "Camp Bowie," accessed July 15, 2015, http://army.com/info/posts/camp-bowie.

155. The Royal New Zealand Air Force Band was formed in 1935 and performed throughout World War II. Air Force, "Royal New Zealand Air Force Band," accessed November 8, 2015, http://www.airforce.mil.nz/about-us/who-we-are/band/default.htm.

156. Shigetaro Shimada (1883–1976), the Japanese Navy minister, and Hideki Tojo (1884–1948), the Chief of the Imperial Japanese Army General Staff, were forced out of office on July 17 and 18, respectively, after American forces seized Saipan. John Toland, *The Rising Sun: The Decline and Fall of the Japanese Empire, 1936–1945* (New York: Random House, 1970), 2: 656–58.

157. Japanese Emperor Hirohito (1901–1989).

158. On July 6, 1944, the tent of the Ringling Brothers and Barnum & Bailey Circus caught fire during a performance in Hartford, Connecticut, killing 168 and injuring hundreds of others. Eleven days later two explosions ripped through a naval ammunition depot at Port Chicago, just north of San Francisco. The blast killed 320 and wounded 390, most of whom were African Americans. When 258 African American enlisted men refused to resume loading ammunition several weeks later, fearing another explosion, they were charged with various crimes, including mutiny, and convicted. McKinley Albert, "Saving Face and Losing the Circus: The Hartford Circus Fire and Its Disgraceful Aftermath," *Connecticut History* 48 (Spring 2009): 62–77; Robert L. Allen, "From Disaster to Desegregation," *Naval History* 29 (February 2015): 16–24.

159. *No Time for Love* (1943). A construction worker accepts employment from the photographer who inadvertently caused him to lose

his job. Turner Classic Movies, accessed October 29, 2015, http://www
.tcm.com/tcmdb/title/85164/No-Time-for-Love/.

Claudette Colbert (1903–1996) was born in France and arrived in the
United States at age three. She went on to have a career that spanned
over three decades and included three Academy Award nominations.
IMDb.com, "Claudette Colbert," accessed November 13, 2015, http://
www.imdb.com/name/nm0001055/bio?ref_=nm_ov_bio_sm.

Fred MacMurray (1908–1991) was a versatile actor who appeared in
a wide range of movies, including *Double Indemnity* (1944), *The Caine
Mutiny* (1954), and *The Absent-Minded Professor* (1961), along with
starring in the television series *My Three Sons* (1960–72). Garraty,
ANB, 14: 277–78.

160. Following the seizure of Saipan, United States forces landed
on nearby Guam and Tinian on July 21 and 24, respectively. Philip
A. Crowl, *Campaign in the Marianas* (Washington, DC: Office of the
Chief of Military History, Department of the Army), 1960.

161. The Royal New Zealand Air Force Band. See July 20, 1944,
letter to parents.

162. The quota for the Fifth Loan bond drive for McKean County,
Pennsylvania, was $5,200,000. Eldred held a bond rally on July 8,
1944, and residents and local businesses purchased approximately
$115,000. "July 1, 1944 Newsletter" and "July 29, 1944 Newsletter," in
Cawley, *Fr. Liebel's Letters*, 78, 80.

163. In early 1944, Donald Nelson, the director of the War Production Board, the agency charged with overseeing the economy, suggest-
ed reconverting some factories back to the manufacturing of civilian
goods. The process did not get underway, however, until early 1945.
Christopher J. Tassava, "The American Economy during World War
II," *EH-net*, accessed September 23, 2016, https://eh.net/encyclopedia/
the-american-economy-during-world-war-ii/.

164. Each unit appointed a Soldier Voting Officer to insure that the
troops had the necessary information and ballots to participate in
the fall 1944 election. *Manual for Soldier Voting Outside the United
States in the November 1944 General Election* (War Department Pamphlet No. 21–11, 5 June 1944), 12. Fold3.com.

165. Villa Maria College was located in Erie, Pennsylvania, and
merged with Gannon University in 1989. Gannon University, "Villa
Maria College," accessed July 17, 2015, http://www.gannonalumni.
org/s/740/index.aspx?pgid=1199.

166. *Doughboys in Ireland* (1943). An American band leader serv-

ing in the military falls in love with a beautiful Irish lass. Turner Classic Movies, accessed October 29, 2015, http://www.tcm.com/tcmdb/title/73523/Doughboys-in-Ireland/.

167. Colonel Francis S. Gabreski (1919–2002), born in Oil City, Pennsylvania, shot down twenty-eight German planes between 1943 and 1945 and destroyed three others on the ground. He went on to become an ace in the Korean War. Polish American Cultural Center, "Colonel Francis S. Grabreski, WWII Air Ace," accessed February 16, 2015, http://www.polishamericancenter.org/Gabreski.html.

Gabreski's brother, Thaddeus, graduated from Notre Dame in 1934 and became a physician. "Col. Gabreski Missing," *Notre Dame Scholastic* 82 (August 4, 1944): 13.

168. Camp Van Dorn, located near Centreville, in Amite and Wilkinson Counties, Mississippi, began functioning in November 1942, and was primarily used to train troops for the European theater. "Camp Van Dorn World War II Museum," accessed July 18, 2015, http://www.vandornmuseum.org/.

169. *Moontide* (1942). A dock worker, who may have killed a man while in a drunken fit, falls in love with a troubled woman, who discovers the actual murderer. Turner Classic Movies, accessed October 29, 2015, http://www.tcm.com/tcmdb/title/83967/Moontide/.

170. Bob Hope (1903–2003), the legendary actor and comic, visited countless military installations throughout World War II and continued this into the 1990s during the Persian Gulf War. William Robert Faith, *Bob Hope: A Life in Comedy* (New York: Da Capo, 2003).

171. *Roxie Hart* (1942). A young showgirl confesses to a murder she did not commit to reinvigorate her career. Halliwell, *Film Guide*, 745.

Ginger Rogers (1911–1995), a dancer and actress, is best remembered for her movies with Fred Astaire, including *The Gay Divorcee* (1934) and *Follow the Fleet* (1936). Garraty, *ANB*, 18: 756–57.

172. On August 1, 1944, white Philadelphia Transit Company (PTC) workers went on strike when eight African American employees were promoted to trolley car drivers. This hurt military production because 300,000 defense workers could not get to their jobs. The strike ended on August 7 after President Franklin Roosevelt ordered troops to take control of the PTC, and workers were threatened with losing their draft deferments. Temple University, "Philadelphia Transit Strike of 1944," accessed July 19, 2015, http://northerncity.library.temple.edu/node/30260; Allan M. Winkler, "The Philadelphia Transit Strike of 1944," *Journal of American History* 59 (June 1972): 73–89.

173. Frances Langford (1913–2005) was a singer and actress who frequently appeared with Bob Hope on the radio; Jerry Colonna (1904–1986) was a comedian and composer who was a member of Hope's radio program. Hischak, *American Musical*, 417, 161. Pennsylvania native Patty Thomas (1922–2014) was an actress who was best known for her roles in such films as *Smooth Sailing* (1947) and *The Ladies Man* (1961). IMDb.com, "Patty Thomas," http://www.imdb.com/name/nm0859331/. Born in Italy, musician Tony Romano (1915–2005) was one of the four original members of Hope's USO show that performed before thousands of troops during World War II. Colonna, Langford, and Hope were the other original members. IMDb.com, "Tony Romano," http://www.imdb.com/name/nm0738966/. Barney Dean was one of Hope's writers. Faith, *Bob Hope: A Life in Comedy*, 163. The Library of Congress's "Veterans History Project" website contains a photo of these performers, http://lcweb2.10c.gov/diglib/vhp-stories/loc.natlib.afc2001001.08272/enlarge?ID=ph0002001&page=1. Footage of the troupe performing for Americans soldiers on Bougainville on August 2, 1944, is available on YouTube at "Bob Hope and Frances Langford in U.S.O. tour, entertain US troops Bougainville," https://www.youtube.com/watch?v=eX2V5ySCqnU. All the sites listed in this citation were accessed on July 19, 2015.

174. The stationery contains a SHEPPARD FIELD, Wichita Falls, Texas, letterhead, with a Latin motto "Sustineo Alas."

175. Lewis P. Frank. See April 9, 1944, letter to parents.

176. On August 1, 1944, elements of General George Patton's Third Army swept out of the Normandy beachhead and drove west into the Brittany Peninsula to seize Brest, Saint-Malo, and other ports. Some historians have argued this was a strategic error because it diverted crucial American strength from advancing east toward Germany. Hastings, *Overlord*, 280–83; Rick Atkinson, *The Guns at Last Light: The War in Western Europe, 1944–1945* (New York: Henry Holt, 2013), 149–53.

177. *Holy Matrimony* (1943). A reclusive painter takes the identity of his deceased valet. Halliwell, *Film Guide*, 395.

Gracie Fields (1898–1979) was a British-born singer, actress, and comedienne. IMDb.com, "Gracie Fields," accessed November 13, 2015, http://www.imdb.com/name/nm0276247/bio?ref_=nm_ov_bio_sm.

Monty Woolley (1888–1963), an actor and director, was a one-time English instructor and drama coach at Yale, who taught such students as Stephen Vincent Benet. Woolley was twice nominated for Academy

Awards and is best known for his role in *The Man Who Came to Dinner* (1942). Garraty, *ANB*, 23: 852–53.

178. "T-SGT. Geuder With_'Ken's Men,'" *Eldred Eagle*, July 28, 1944, 1.

179. Lieutenant John Long who accompanied them to Tulagi. See May 8, 1944, letter to parents.

180. The 39th was preparing to leave Guadalcanal for service in the Palaus Islands.

Chapter 3

1. Eddy Heyde to author, October 27, 1987; Gabriel Travel Log.

2. For the best account of the attack of Angaur, see Bobby C. Blair, *Victory at Peleliu: The 81st Infantry Division's Pacific Campaign* (Norman: University of Oklahoma Press, 2011), 1–118, especially 117–18 for casualties and comparison to Iwo Jima; Army, 81st Infantry Div., HDQTRS, "Report of Operations in the Capture of Angaur Island, Palau Island, 9/15/44–10/22/44," World War II War Diaries, Fold3.com; Office of the Surgeon, United States Army Forces, *The Palau Operation (15 September to 27 November 1944)* (N.p.: 1946?), 4–5, 51–52, US Army Heritage and Education Center, Carlisle, PA; "Final Historical Report of Medical Department Activities at APO 264," June 1, 1945, pages 1–3, Unit Histories 39th Station Hospital, RG 112, Entry 1012 HUMEDS, Box 110; The Stamford Historical Society, Inc., "The Battle of Angaur," accessed October 23, 2016, http://www.stamfordhistory.org/ww2_angaur.htm. For a good overview of the controversy if the invasion of the Palaus was necessary, see Stephen C. Murray, *The Battle over Peleliu: Islander, Japanese, and American Memories of War* (Tuscaloosa: University of Alabama Press, 2016), 84–85; Hiroshi Funasaka, *Falling Blossoms*, trans. Hiroshi Funasaka and Jeffrey D. Rubin (Singapore: Times Books International, 1986) provides a view of the fighting on Angaur from a Japanese soldier who was wounded and captured there.

3. For the location of Yellow Beach, see "Report of Unloading Operations on Peleliu & Angaur Is, Peleliu Is, November 20, 1944," page 3, World War II War Diaries, Fold3.com. Eddy Heyde to author, October 27, 1987.

4. Eddy Heyde to author, October 27, 1987; "Medical History of the 39th Station Hospital prepared by Lt. Col. Jewell R. Wilson, MC," January 12, 1945, pages 2–3, 7–12, 39th Station Hospital POA 1942–1944, RG 112, Entry 54A, Box 489; "Final Historical Report of Medical Department Activities at APO 264," June 1, 1945, pages 3–13, 16–19,

Unit Histories 39th Station Hospital, RG 112, Entry 1012 HUMEDS, Box 110; Murray, *Battle over Peleliu*, 99–100.

5. "Final Historical Report of Medical Department Activities at APO 264," June 1, 1945, pages 3–4, 21; "Medical History of the 39th Station Hospital Prepared by Captain Frederick R. Gabriel," November 16, 1945, pages 1–2, 10–13; "Headquarters Western Pacific Base Command, APO 244, General Orders 111," October 24, 1945; all documents are found in Unit Histories 39th Station Hospital, RG 112, Entry 1012 HUMEDS, Box 110. Also see November 5, 1945, letter to parents.

6. USS *Sabik*, War Diaries, 6/1–24/1945, World War II War Diaries, Fold3.com.

7. The reference to the other ship, not ships, coupled with the comment "tired of doing nothing," suggests that this voyage was to the Palaus, not the original deployment to the Pacific or to Saipan in June 1945.

8. The letter's reference to Gabriel large amounts of time to read and his nephew's first day of school suggests he wrote it in fall 1944 during the thirty-eight days aboard the *Mormacport*.

9. Possibly slang for watching the ocean.

10. Bess Streeter Aldrich's 1928 novel about a young family's struggle to survive on the Nebraska prairie in the 1800s. Worldcat, accessed May 21, 2015, http://www.worldcat.org/title/lantern-in-her-hand/oclc/279805&referer=brief_results.

11. The 39th Station Hospital landed on Angaur on October 13, and it began to function as a unit eight days later when it received 373 patients from the 17th Field Hospital.

12. The night force consisted of the nurses, orderlies, and other hospital personnel who were on duty after dark. M. H. Foster, *Manual of Hospital Management for US Marine Hospitals*, Miscellaneous Publication No. 29 (Washington, DC: United States Government Printing Office, 1930; Google Books), 155, https://books.google.com/books?id=f6VIAQAAIAAJ.

13. United States forces led by General Douglas MacArthur landed on Leyte in the central Philippines on October 20, 1944, fulfilling his promise, "I shall return." M. Hamlin Cannon, *Leyte: The Return to the Philippines* (Washington, DC: Office of the Chief of Military History, Department of the Army, 1954).

14. The Florida-Cuba Hurricane, which occurred in mid-October 1944, killed more than three hundred people and caused $100,000,000 damage. H. C. Sumner, "The North Atlantic Hurricane of October 13–

21," *Monthly Weather Review* 72 (November 1944): 221–23, http://www.aoml.noaa.gov/hrd/hurdat/mwr_pdf/1944.pdf.

15. Rock City, a popular tourist area near Olean, New York, features a hiking trail and scenic overlooks through massive formations of quartz conglomerate. Enchanted Mountains, "Rock City Park," accessed October 25, 2016, http://enchantedmountains.com/place/rock-city-park.

16. *Syrian Yankee* (Garden City, NJ: Doubleday, Doran, 1943). The autobiography of Salom Rizk, a Syrian orphan who came to the United States. Worldcat, accessed October 21, 2015, http://www.worldcat.org/title/syrian-yankee/oclc/170534&referer=brief_results.

17. Louie served in France with the 14th Armored Division.

18. Donald H. Frisbee (1917–1985) lived in Eldred and served in the Army Air Corps in the South Pacific. *Service Record, Eldred*, 17.

19. *Casanova Brown* (1944). Cas Brown (Cooper) is on the verge of marrying another woman when he learns that his annulled wife is putting their newborn daughter up for adoption. Turner Classic Movies, accessed October 29, 2015, http://www.tcm.com/tcmdb/title/17062/Casanova-Brown/.

Teresa Wright (1918–2005) was the only performer ever nominated for Academy Awards for her first three films. She appeared in such movies as *Mrs. Miniver* (1942) and *Pride of the Yankees* (1942). IMDb.com, "Teresa Wright," accessed October 29, 2015, http://www.imdb.com/name/nm0942863/?ref_=fn_al_nm_1.

Gary Cooper (1901–1961) often played all-American heroes. A popular Academy Award–winning actor, Cooper appeared in over one hundred films including, *Beau Geste* (1939), *Sergeant York* (1941), and *High Noon* (1952). Garraty, *ANB*, 5: 436–39.

20. *The Doughgirls* (1944). Three newlywed couples struggle to start their lives and find housing in wartime Washington, DC. Turner Classic Movies, accessed November 16, 2015, http://www.tcm.com/tcmdb/title/118/The-Doughgirls/.

21. Staff Sergeant Joseph M. Kunkel of Eldred was killed on December 21, 1944, during the Battle of the Bulge. Gilfert, "Military History of McKean County, Pennsylvania, World War II: Gold Stars," accessed September 29, 2016, http://www.jfgvictoryverlag.com/mckean.goldstars/WWII%20H-L.html; Eldred resident David D. Feheley's B-24 was shot down over Vienna on October 7, 1944, and he was reported missing in action. On January 9, 1945, Feheley was declared a prisoner of war. Gilfert, "Military History of McKean County, Pennsylvania, World War II: Prisoners of War," accessed September 20, 2016, http://www.jfgvicto

ryverlag.com/POW/001temp.html. Also see "February 1, 1945 Newsletter," in Cawley, *Fr. Liebel's Letters*, 94; May 26, 1945, letter to parents.

22. *Strike Up the Band* (1940). A high school band raises money to compete in a Chicago music contest. Hischak, *American Musical*, 717.

Judy Garland (1922–1969), a talented singer and actress, is best remembered for her portrayal of Dorothy in *The Wizard of Oz* (1939), one of the most popular films ever made, and *Easter Parade* (1948). Garraty, *ANB*, 18: 727–30.

Mickey Rooney (1920–2014) first appeared on a vaudeville stage at age fifteen months and went on to a film career that spanned from 1926 until the early 2000s. Hischak, *American Musical*, 640–42.

23. Soviet offensives in late 1944 and early 1945 pushed the German army into Hungary, Poland, and East Prussia. Cumins, *Cataclysm*, 264–73.

24. Possibly *Knute Rockne, All American* (1940), but it seems that Gabriel would have liked this film, considering his devotion to Notre Dame.

25. The 39th Station Hospital's officer roster does not indicate that any officers left the unit in February 1945, but the March 19 letter to parents suggests that one of them was Lieutenant Herman Berkowsky. "Medical History, 39th Station Hospital," November 13, 1945, pages 3–4, in Unit Histories 39th Station Hospital, RG 112, Entry 1012 HUMEDS, Box 110.

26. Smethport is the county seat of McKean County, Pennsylvania. The patient was possibly William J. Gustafson, who was wounded in the Philippines. Gilfert, "Military History of McKean County, Pennsylvania, World War II: Community Honor Rolls—Smethport," accessed November 16, 2015, http://www.jfgvictoryverlag.com/WWIIhonorrolls/Smethport.html.

27. The editor's family still owns this pair of carved elephants.

28. Father N. A. Chemaly was the pastor of St. Joseph's Church in Olean, New York.

29. Neil K. Dorrion, an Eldred resident, served as a technician in the Medical Corps in the South Pacific. *Service Record, Eldred*, 14.

30. Rew is a small village near Eldred.

31. *Keys of the Kingdom* (1945). Gregory Peck starred in this film about a Catholic priest in nineteenth-century China. Halliwell, *Film Guide*, 470.

32. Elements of the United States VII Corps captured Germany's

fourth largest city, Cologne, after two days of heavy fighting on March 7, 1945. Previously, the city had been largely destroyed by repeated Allied air attacks. Charles B. MacDonald, *Victory in Europe, 1945: The Last Offensive of World War II* (Mineola, NY: Dover, 2007), 189–91.

33. Taking advantage of the disruption caused by World War II, Syria declared its independence from France, and both the United States and the Soviet Union recognized this in 1944. On February 26, 1945, Syria declared war on Germany and Japan, making it eligible to participate in the San Francisco Conference, which resulted in the formation of the United Nations. Tabitha Petran, *Syria* (London: Ernest Benn, 1972), 77–79; Alan Axelrod, *Encyclopedia of World War II* (New York: Facts on File, 2007), 1: 269.

34. A meeting of forty-six nations to discuss the postwar world. The United Nations was created at this conference. The United Nations, "History of the United Nations," accessed November 17, 2015, http://www.un.org/en/aboutun/history/sanfrancisco_conference.shtml.

35. Edward McKeever (1910–1974), who briefly attended Notre Dame in the early 1930s, returned to the school as an assistant coach to Frank Leahy. After Leahy enlisted in the navy in 1944, McKeever became head coach and subsequently accepted a position at Cornell University. University of Notre Dame Athletics, "Ed McKeever," accessed November 17, 2015, http://www.und.com/sports/m-footbl/mtt/mckeever_ed00.html.

36. Henry Morgenthau Jr. (1891–1967) served as Secretary of the Treasury under both Franklin Roosevelt and Harry Truman from January 1934 to July 1945.

37. Located twenty-eight miles east of Austin in Bastrop County, Camp Swift opened in 1942 and became the army's largest training center in the state. Nearly 3,900 German prisoners of war were also housed there. Texas State Historical Association, "Camp Swift," accessed November 18, 2015, https://tshaonline.org/handbook/online/articles/qbc27.

38. Probably one of the two officers evacuated because of stomach ulcers. See February 8 and 28 letters to parents.

39. Novenas are a series of prayers for a special intention said on nine consecutive days.

40. *A Tree Grows in Brooklyn* (1945) tells the story of a young girl growing up in a poor Irish neighborhood. Turner Classic Movies, accessed November 18, 2015, http://www.tcm.com/tcmdb/title/93886/A-Tree-Grows-in-Brooklyn/.

41. The 39th Station Hospital was stationed at the Army Desert Training Center near Yuma, Arizona, from March to September 1943.

42. The boys' souvenirs included two German helmets and a Nazi battle flag for their grandfather. "March 17, 1945 Newsletter," in Cawley, *Fr. Liebel's Letters*, 97; also see letter to parents, March 14, 1945.

43. Catholic missionaries worked in the Palaus, and they constructed a new church on Angaur in 1939 to replace two small chapels. The Japanese restricted the work of these priests once the war broke out, and they detained and ultimately executed six Jesuits who ministered in the islands. The Catholic Church in Micronesia, "The Catholic Church in Palau," accessed November 18, 2015, http://www.micsem.org/pubs/books/catholic/palau/index.htm.

44. Franklin D. Roosevelt died at Warm Springs, Georgia, on April 12, 1945, after suffering a cerebral hemorrhage.

45. *Wilson* (1945). This biography of the twenty-eighth president won half of the ten Academy Awards for which it was nominated. Turner Classic Movies, accessed September 24, 2015, http://www.tcm.com/tcmdb/title/95931/Wilson/.

46. *A Song to Remember* (1945). The story of the famous Polish composer Frédéric Chopin and his struggles to aid his homeland. Turner Classic Movies, accessed November 19, 2015, http://www.tcm.com/tcmdb/title/4840/A-Song-to-Remember/.

47. Numerous works have examined the United States Marines' seizure of Iwo Jima, a small volcanic island less than seven hundred miles south of Japan, between February 19 and March 26, 1945, in vicious fighting. For a good overview, see Max Hastings, *Retribution: The Battle for Japan, 1944–45* (New York: Alfred A. Knopf, 2008), 247–65.

48. Zwieback is a type of crisp sweet bread.

49. Deanna Durbin (1921–2013), a highly successful singer and actress, began appearing in films as a teenager, and by the mid-1940s was a box office superstar. She disliked the notoriety, however, and, at age twenty-seven, retired and never performed again. Hischak, *American Musical*, 218.

50. *Can't Help Singing* (1945). The story of the misadventures of a senator's daughter who heads for California on a wagon train during the gold rush. Hischak, *American Musical*, 124.

51. United States and Soviet troops met at Torgau, Germany, on the Elbe River on April 26, 1945. MacDonald, *Victory in Europe*, 453–456.

52. On April 28, a rumor circulated at the San Francisco Conference that Heinrich Himmler, the head of the Nazi SS, intended to surrender

Germany to the British and Americans. That evening President Harry Truman gave a brief statement saying that the rumor was untrue. "Nazis' End Near: But President on Word from Eisenhower Corrects Rumor," *New York Times*, April 29, 1945, 1.

53. Neil K. Dorrion. See February 24, 1945, letter to parents.

54. *What a Woman!* (1943). A female literary agent tries to transform a staid college professor into a romantic actor. Turner Classic Movies, accessed November 20, 2015, http://www.tcm.com/tcmdb/title /95414/What-a-Woman/.

Rosalind Russell (1908–1976), a versatile actress of both comedy and drama, was nominated for four Academy Awards. Garraty, *ANB*, 19: 113–14.

55. For a transcript of Truman's address, see Harry S. Truman Library and Museum, "Broadcast to the American People Announcing the Surrender of Germany. May 8, 1945," accessed November 20, 2015, http:// www.trumanlibrary.org/ww2/veday.htm.

56. *News from Home* was an NBC Radio program hosted by Mel Allen. Stephen Borelli, *How About That!: The Life of Mel Allen* (Champaign, IL: Sports Publishing, 2005), 63.

57. New Kensington is located in Westmoreland County.

58. On May 14, 542 B-29s dropped incendiary bombs on Nagoya, destroying large parts of the city. Three days later a similar-sized force devastated the city again. Richard B. Frank, *Downfall: The End of the Imperial Japanese Empire* (New York: Random House, 1999), 73–74.

59. On the nights of May 23/24 and May 25/26, incendiary-carrying B-29s ravaged large portions of the Japanese capital. Frank, *Downfall*, 74

60. On May 10, the War Department announced a "point system" to determine which soldiers would be discharged first. A soldier earned one point per month in service since September 1940; one point for each month overseas; five points for each decoration; and twelve points for each child under the age of eighteen, up to three children. Soldiers who had accumulated eighty-five points or more would be the first eligible for discharge. There were some variations of this scale based on a soldier's particular rank, age, and specialty. The discharge number was periodically lowered as the war wound down. Still, many military personnel and their families believed that the demobilization rate was too slow, and the system produced widespread discontent. "Army Plan Telling Just How a Soldier will be Demobilized," *New York Times*, May 11, 1945, 11; "Priorities in Army," *New York Times*, Sep-

tember 11, 1945, 1, 11; Stouffer, *American Soldier*, 2: 529–31, 546–48; Kent Roberts Greenfield, Robert R. Palmer, and Bell I. Wiley, *The Organization of Ground Combat Troops* (Washington, DC: Center of Military History, United States Army, 1987), 442–43, 490.

61. Eldred resident David "Dar" Feheley lost both legs when his B-24 was shot down over Vienna, Austria, in 1944. Captured by the Germans, American forces freed him on April 1, 1945. *Service Record, Eldred*, 34; "SGT. D. D. Feheley Home on Furlough," *Eldred Eagle*, May 18, 1945, 1.

62. Windfall is located about three miles outside of Eldred, while Nigger Hill is near Bolivar, New York.

63. *Music for Millions* (1945). A pregnant musician raises her young sister while worrying about her missing soldier husband. TCM.com, accessed November 22, 2015, http://www.tcm.com/tcmdb/title/2704/Music-for-Millions/.

64. Margaret O'Brien (b. 1937), a gifted child actress, appeared in her first movie at age four. She is best remembered for playing Judy Garland's little sister in *Meet Me in St. Louis (1944)*, Hischak, *American Musical*, 537–38.

65. Established in 1822 in Lyon, France, partly through the efforts of Pauline Jaricot, the Society for the Propagation of the Faith offers prayers and donations to assist Catholic missionaries. New Advent, "The Society for the Propagation of the Faith," accessed March 11, 2018, http://www.newadvent.org/cathen/12461a.htm.

66. The letter's reference to Joe being discharged indicates that it was probably written in June 1945.

Chapter 4

1. 148th General Hospital—Annual Report, October 1945, RG 112, HUMEDS, Box 38; History—148th General Hospital January 1945–20 February 1946, pages 2, 8–9, RG 407, Entry 427, Box 17296, United States National Archives and Records Administration, College Park, MD; "Medical History of the 39th Station Hospital Prepared by Captain Frederick R. Gabriel," November 16, 1945, page 3, Unit Histories 39th Station Hospital, RG 112, Entry 1012 HUMEDS, Box 110.

2. "Efficiency Report," July, 1, 1945, page 280, Gabriel Personnel File.

3. Eddy Heyde to author, October 27, 1987.

4. For indicating his desire to be discharged as soon as possible, see Gabriel Personnel File, pages 86–87.

5. "Headquarters 39th Station Hospital, General Order Number 2," October 1, 1945, page 33, Gabriel Personnel File; "Headquarters 39th Station Hospital, November 2, 1945," Island Command Saipan: War Diary, October 1945, page 56, World War II War Diaries, Fold3.com; "Medical History of the 39th Station Hospital Prepared by Captain Frederick R. Gabriel," November 16, 1945, page 13, Unit Histories 39th Station Hospital, RG 112, Entry 1012 HUMEDS, Box 110.

6. "Brief Clinical Abstract, Captain Frederick R. Gabriel," no date, pages 270–71, Gabriel Personnel File.

7. The 39th Station Hospital departed Angaur aboard the USS *Sabik* (AK-121) on June 7 and landed five days later on Saipan, the second largest island in the Marianas. See Frederick R. Gabriel Travel Log; also see USS *Sabik*, War Diary, 6/1–24/1945, World War II War Diaries, Fold3.com.

8. The 39th General Hospital was also stationed on Saipan in 1945. John B. Flick, "Chapter XII: Pacific Ocean Areas," *Medical Department, United States Army: Surgery in World War II, Activities of Surgical Consultants*, Volume II, 633, 638, 641, accessed November 22, 2015, http://history.amedd.army.mil/booksdocs/wwii/actvssurgconv012/chapter11.htm.

9. Kane is a town in McKean County, Pennsylvania, about forty miles southwest of Eldred.

10. *The Picture of Dorian Gray* (1945). A Victorian gentleman never ages, but his portrait shows the effects of time and debauchery. Halliwell, *Film Guide*, 685.

11. Sonja Henie (1912–1969) was born in Norway and won medals in skating at three consecutive Olympics. She then parlayed these skills into a successful acting career. Hischak, *American Musical*, 337.

12. John Brogan. See July 1, 1945, letter to parents.

13. *Princess and the Pirate* (1944). A ham actor and a princess are captured by an infamous pirate who is searching for a stolen treasure map. Turner Classic Movies, accessed September 24, 2015, http://www.tcm.com/tcmdb/title/87150/The-Princess-and-the-Pirate/.

Virginia Mayo (1920–2005) appeared in a wide range of dramas and musicals, often with Danny Kaye. Hischak, *American Musical*, 478.

14. *God Is My Co-Pilot* (1945). A fighter pilot, deemed too old for combat, battles the Japanese in China. The movie was adapted from Robert Lee Scott Jr.'s 1943 book about his experiences serving with the Flying Tigers. Turner Classic Movies, accessed September 22, 2015, http://www.tcm.com/tcmdb/title/2343/God-Is-My-Co-Pilot/.

15. Dr. John J. Brogan graduated from Jefferson Medical College in 1940 and then did a residency at St. Vincent's Hospital in New York City. *Jefferson Medical College Yearbooks, 1940*, 103, accessed September 24, 2015, http://jdc.jefferson.edu/jmc_yearbooks/50.

16. The movie must have been *To Have and Have Not* (1944), the first movie Bogart and Bacall appeared in together. Humphrey Bogart (1899–1957) was a legendary film and stage actor best remembered for his roles in such movies as *The Maltese Falcon* (1941), *Casablanca* (1942), and *The African Queen* (1951), for which he won an Academy Award. Garraty, *ANB*, 3: 107–8.

Lauren Bacall (1924–2014) started her career as an aspiring Broadway actress and model, before going to Hollywood. She married Bogart in 1945, after starring with him in *To Have and Have Not* (1944). Hischak, *American Musical*, 44.

17. *A Royal Scandal* (1945). Catherine the Great's court is filled with intrigue as the czarina is infatuated by a young officer involved in a plot to overthrow her. Turner Classic Movies, accessed November 19, 2015, http://www.tcm.com/tcmdb/title/88721/A-Royal-Scandal/.

Tallulah Bankhead (1902–1968). The daughter of one of the Speakers of the House of Representatives, Bankhead had a long career on the stage, with occasional roles in motion pictures. Garraty, *ANB*, 2: 109–11.

18. *This is the Army* (1942). An Irving Berlin musical that initially appeared on Broadway and then toured for the next three years. Allmusic.com, *This is the Army* [Original Broadway Cast], accessed November 24, 2015, http://www.allmusic.com/album/this-is-the-army-original-broadway-cast-mw0000599946.

19. *Stars and Stripes* is the newspaper of the United States military. Stars and Stripes, "About Stars and Stripes," accessed November 25, 2015, http://www.stripes.com/customer-service/about-us.

20. Kurt von Schuschnigg (1897–1977) was the Austrian chancellor who initially cooperated with Nazi Germany but then sought to maintain his country's independence. The Nazis arrested him shortly after they annexed Austria in March 1938. Encyclopedia Britannica, accessed November 25, 2015, http://www.britannica.com/biography/Kurt-von-Schuschnigg.

21. The *Eldred Eagle* published a June 17, 1945, letter that Gabriel's brother Lou wrote to Father Liebel describing the end of the war and the first weeks of the American occupation of Bavaria. Lou mentioned the reaction of German civilians as US troops entered their towns,

encountering hundreds of liberated POWs from many different countries, and the discovery of a mass grave containing 2,500 bodies, most of whom were Jewish. "Louis Gabriel Writes of Present Conditions in Germany," *Eldred Eagle*, July 6, 1945, 1.

22. Duke is a reference to Duke Center, Pennsylvania, a small town approximately eight miles west of Eldred.

23. *Son of Lassie* (1945). Laddie, the son of the famous collie, helps a British pilot escape German-occupied Norway. Turner Classic Movies, accessed November 25, 2015, http://www.tcm.com/tcmdb/title/3066/Son-of-Lassie/.

24. *Command Performance* was a radio variety program produced by the War Department from 1942 to 1949 for troops serving overseas. Modesto Radio Museum, "Command Performance," accessed November 25, 2015, http://www.modestoradiomuseum.org/command%20performance.html.

25. *Candlelight in Algeria* (1944). An American woman gets involved with a German spy who is trying to gain information about a meeting of Allied leaders in North Africa. IMDb.com, *Candlelight in Algeria*, accessed November 26, 2015, http://www.imdb.com/title/tt0036693/plotsummary?ref_=tt_ov_pl.

26. Neil K. Dorrion. See February 24, 1945, letter to parents.

27. United States forces captured Okinawa, the largest of the Ryukyus Islands, between April 1 and June 22, at a cost of over 57,000 killed and wounded, with another 36,000 nonbattle casualties. Hastings, *Retribution*, 369–403.

28. This title is apparently wrong. The closest one is *Nobody Lives Forever*, the story of a con man who falls in love with a wealthy widow, whom he had swindled, but the film was not released until 1946. Halliwell, *Film Guide*, 632.

29. *Valley of Decision* (1945). Greer Garson plays an Irish housemaid who falls in love with the son of the owner of a large steel mill in Pittsburgh. Turner Classic Movies, accessed October 1, 2015, http://www.tcm.com/tcmdb/title/1188/The-Valley-of-Decision/. The film is based on Marcia Davenport's 1942 book of the same name.

30. The letter contains the Thursday, July 26, 1945, issue of the island newspaper, the *Daily Target: Saipan*.

31. An otoscope is a medical device to designed to look into the ears.

32. The two required films were possibly *Two Down and One to Go* and *On to Tokyo*, shorts made by Frank Capra for the United States Army. Both films were in production for several years, but were re-

leased on May 10 and 31, 1945, respectively. *Two Down* explained the necessity of completing the war, even though Hitler and Benito Mussolini were no longer threats. *On to Tokyo* featured General Marshall telling troops in Europe why they would be redeployed to the Pacific. Mark Harris, *Five Came Back: A Story of Hollywood and the Second World War* (New York: Penguin Press, 2014), 380; John C. Sparrow, *History of Personnel Demobilization in the United States Army* (Washington, DC: Department of the Army, July 1952), 117–25, accessed December 18, 2015, http://www.history.army.mil/html/books/104/104-8/CMH_Pub_104–8.pdf; IMDb.com, *Two Down and One to Go*, http://www.IMDb.com/title/tt0185734/?ref_=fn_al_tt_1; *On to Tokyo*, http://www.IMDb.com/title/tt0187370/?ref_=fn_al_tt_5, both accessed December 19, 2015.

33. Gabriel did a residency at Thomas Jefferson Medical College in 1942. See the first letter in this collection.

34. Bullis Mills is a small village located about three miles northeast of Eldred, just south of the Pennsylvania–New York border.

35. Haymaker is a small settlement located near Eldred, Pennsylvania.

36. *Murder, He Says* (1945). Fred MacMurray starred in this film about an insurance salesman who encounters a family of murderous hillbillies. Halliwell, *Film Guide*, 603.

A three-minute cartoon short, *It's Murder She Says*, about malaria control was released in 1945, but it seems unlikely this was the movie to which Gabriel referred. IMDb.com, *It's Murder She Says*, accessed November 25, 2012, http://www.imdb.com/title/tt0154659/?ref_=fn_al_tt_4.

37. *Those Endearing Young Charms* (1945) tells the story of a perfume sales clerk who is romantically pursued by a hometown boy and a smooth-talking air force pilot. Turner Classic Movies, accessed September 28, 2016, http://www.tcm.com/tcmdb/title/2622/Those-Endearing-Young-Charms/.

38. On August 6, 1945, President Harry Truman announced that an American aircraft had dropped an atomic bomb on Hiroshima, Japan, destroying most of the city. Public Broadcasting Service, "American Experience, Primary Resources: Announcing the Bombing of Hiroshima," accessed November 27, 2015, http://www.pbs.org/wgbh/americanexperience/features/primary-resources/truman-hiroshima/.

39. Named for the socks they wore with their saddle shoes, bobbysoxers were usually exuberant teenage female fans of singers, such as Frank Sinatra. Some critics saw them as a sign of declining moral

values. Robert Sickels, *The 1940s* (Westport, CT: Greenwood, 2004), 35–36.

40. The Soviet Union declared war on Japan on August 8, 1945, as Joseph Stalin agreed it would at the July 1945 Potsdam Conference. Hastings, *Retribution*, 480–81; Toland, *Rising Sun*, 2: 984–86.

41. 39th Station Hospital records reveal that Major Glen E. Snyder, Captain Richard E. Bower, and Lieutenant Albert S. Elliot left the unit in July and August 1945. "Medical History, 39th Station Hospital," November 13, 1945, pages 3–4, in Unit Histories 39th Station Hospital, RG 112, Entry 1012 HUMEDS, Box 110.

42. Johnny Gabriel was the eldest son of Gabriel's Uncle George, who resided in Olean, New York.

43. On August 12, an erroneous news report circulated at 9:34 p.m. that Japan had surrendered. Although this report was retracted two minutes later, it set off uproarious celebrations in the United States, Canada, Britain, and elsewhere. The Canadian Broadcasting Company interrupted its normal programing and aired a pre-recorded message from Prime Minister W. L Mackenzie King hailing the surrender and announcing a national day of Thanksgiving the following Sunday. "Erroneous 'Flash' of Surrender Starts Many Wild Celebrations," *New York Times*, August 13, 1945, 1, 3.

44. Nearly six hundred American bombers, escorted by almost two hundred fighter planes, struck Japanese arsenals and railroads, among other targets. Frank, *Downfall*, 313.

45. On August 9, following their declaration of war on Japan, Soviet forces invaded Manchuria. Hastings, *Retribution*, 482–503.

46. For examples of Japanese forces unwilling to surrender, see Toland, *Rising Sun*, 1056–58, 1060–61, 1068–69; Hastings, *Retribution*, 519–20.

47. *Thirty Seconds Over Tokyo* (1944). Van Johnson and Spencer Tracy starred in this movie about General Jimmy Doolittle's 1942 air raid on Japan. Turner Classic Movies, accessed November 27, 2015, http://www.tcm.com/tcmdb/title/451/Thirty-Seconds-Over-Tokyo/.

48. *Wonder Man* (1945). The spirit of a murdered nightclub singer inhabits his twin brother's body and gets him to testify against a gangster. Turner Classic Movies, accessed October 1, 2015, http://www.tcm.com/tcmdb/title/96239/Wonder-Man/.

Danny Kaye (1911–1987) was a singer and actor who tried to serve in the military during the Second World War but was rejected because of a bad back. He starred in such films as *The Secret Life of Walter*

Mitty (1947) and *White Christmas* (1954). Garraty, *ANB*, 12: 411–12.

49. Douglas MacArthur (1880–1964) served as commander in chief of United States Army Forces Pacific and was subsequently named supreme commander for the Allied Powers for the occupation of Japan. For his arrival in Japan and initial actions, see Toland, *Rising Sun*, 1068–78.

50. William J. Llewelyn (1913–1963), a resident of Eldred, served in the army. Gilfert, "McKean County During World War II: Community Honor Rolls—Eldred and Vicinity," accessed December 12, 2014, http://www.jfgvictoryverlag.com/WWIIhonorrolls/Index.html.

51. Francis Joseph Spellman (1889–1967), the Archbishop of New York, "embodied the image of the American Catholic as patriot." He strongly supported the war effort and visited US troops throughout the world. Garraty, *ANB*, 20: 435–38, quote 437.

52. *The Suspect* (1945). A tobacco shop owner is driven to double murder when he befriends and then falls in love with a young woman. Turner Classic Movies, accessed October 1, 2015, http://www.tcm.com/tcmdb/title/92020/The-Suspect/.

A World War I veteran who had been wounded, Charles Laughton (1899–1962) enjoyed a long career in Hollywood, appearing in such movies as *Mutiny on the Bounty* (1935), *The Hunchback of Notre Dame* (1939), and *Witness for the Prosecution* (1957). Garraty, *ANB*, 13: 253–54.

Ella Raines (1920–1988) was a singer and actress who appeared in numerous movies and a 1950s television series, *Janet Dean: Registered Nurse*. IMDb.com, "Ella Raines," accessed October 1, 2015, http://www.imdb.com/name/nm0707048/bio?ref_=nmmi_bio_sm.

53. Harry S. Truman Library and Museum, "100. The President's News Conference, August 14, 1945," accessed November 28, 2015, https://www.trumanlibrary.org/publicpapers/index.php?pid=107.

54. *The Seventh Cross* (1944). Seven Germans escape from a Nazi concentration camp and are ruthlessly pursued by the Gestapo. Halliwell, *Film Guide*, 778.

Spencer Tracy (1900–1967). One of the most honored American actors, Tracy won two Academy Awards and was nominated for seven more for his roles in such films as *Old Man and the Sea* (1958) and *Judgement at Nuremberg* (1961). Garraty, *ANB*, 21: 796–98.

55. Ybor City is now a neighborhood in Tampa, Florida.

56. Richard M. Williams Jr. of Eldred served in the 9th Infantry Division in the European theater. *Service Record, Eldred*, 34.

57. On September 4, the War Department announced new regulations on the deployment of troops. No soldier would be sent outside of the continental United States if they were between age thirty-four and thirty-six with more than one year of service, were age thirty-seven or older, or had earned forty-five or more points by May 12. William S. White, "Army Gives Plan to Keep 665,000 From Going Abroad," *New York Times*, September 5, 1945, 1.

58. On September 6 the War Department released a point system to discharge officers, under which captains would be eligible for release from the army if they had accumulated eighty-five points. "Point Plan Set Up For Army Officers," *New York Times*, September 7, 1945, 4.

59. The military stop censoring mail shortly after Japan surrendered in August 1945. For a good discussion of mail censoring, see Smithsonian National Postal Museum, Ann Pfau, "Postal Censorship and Military Intelligence in World War II," http://postalmuseum.si.edu/ symposium2008/pfau-postal_censorship.pdf, and Louis Fiset, "Return to Sender: US Censorship of Enemy Alien Mail in World War II," *Prologue Magazine* 33 (Spring 2001), https://www.archives.gov/publica tions/prologue/2001/spring/mail-censorship-in-world-war-two-1.html, both accessed December 4, 2015.

60. On September 14 Major General Norman T. Kirk, the surgeon general, announced plans to release 13,000 army doctors, along with 3,500 dentists and 25,000 nurses, by January 1, 1946. Under this plan, doctors would be eligible for discharge if they met one of three criteria: had entered active service before the attack on Pearl Harbor, were age forty-eight or older, and had eighty points or more. Kirk also noted that these qualifications would be lowered as demobilization proceeded. "Army To Release 13,000 Doctors," *New York Times*, September 15, 1945, 1.

61. Batavia, New York, is located between Buffalo and Rochester and is the site of a Veteran's Administration hospital.

62. *Out of this World* (1945). A female band leader oversells stock in a shy singer, who makes his audience swoon. Turner Classic Movies, accessed November 11, 2015, http://www.tcm.com/tcmdb/title/85972/ Out-of-This-World/.

63. Both of these articles appeared in "Men and Women in Service," *Eldred Eagle*, September 7, 1945, 5.

64. Marshall addressed Congress on September 20 and announced that effective October 1, enlisted men with seventy or more points would be eligible for discharge, and the number would drop to sixty on

November 1. The discharge scores for enlisted women would be lowered from forty-one to thirty-six on October 1 and to thirty-four on November 1. "Marshall Speaks," *New York Times*, September 21,1945, 1, 2; "New Army Discharge Plan," *New York Times*, September 21, 2.

65. In 1958 Heyde identified a syndrome related to gastrointestinal bleeding that now bears his name. Joseph Loscalzo, "From Clinical Observation to Mechanism—Heyde's Syndrome," *New England Journal of Medicine* 367, no. 20 (November 15, 2012): 1954–56.

66. On October 9, 1945, Typhoon Louise unexpectedly struck Okinawa with over 100 mile-per-hour winds and 30–35 foot waves. The storm sank twelve ships and landing crafts and grounded 222 others, in addition to destroying over 80 percent of the buildings on the island. This resulted in the loss of most of the supplies and provisions on Okinawa, and the storm left thirty-six dead, one hundred seriously injured, and forty-seven missing. Naval History and Heritage Command, "Typhoons and Hurricanes: Pacific Typhoon at Okinawa, October 1945," accessed December 12, 2015, http://www.history.navy.mil/research/library/online-reading-room/title-list-alphabetically/p/pacific-typhoon-october-1945.html.

67. A typhoon struck the Palaus in early November 1944, slowing American military operations on Pelelieu. Robert Ross Smith, *The Approach to the Philippines* (Washington, DC: Center of Military History, United States Army, 1996), 571.

68. Gabriel's comments on the American Legion and the Veterans of Foreign Wars are difficult to understand. Both organizations had millions of members and advocated for veterans' rights and benefits. They both opposed "un-American" ideas and radicalism in the 1920s and 1930s, emphasizing the actions of labor unions and immigrants, in some cases. Critics tended to focus such criticism on the Legion, however, partly because of its larger membership. Any veteran could join the American Legion, while the VFW was restricted to those who had served overseas. William Pencak, *Encyclopedia of the Veteran in America*, 2 vols. (Santa Barbara, CA: ABC-Clio, 2009), 1: 57–69; 2: 410–17.

69. *George White's Scandal* (1945). The third Hollywood movie with this title, the film features a couple falling in love while producing a musical. Hischak, *American Musical*, 280–81.

Joan Davis (1907–1961) was a comedienne and actress who appeared in two dozen musicals and starred in the 1950s television series *I Married Joan*. Hischak, *American Musical*, 190.

70. Kobler Field was built from August to October 1944 near the southern end of Saipan to base the B-29s from the 20th Air Force that were bombing Japan. It served as Saipan's main airport until the mid-1970s and is now a housing development. Abandoned and Little-Known Airfields: Western Pacific Islands, "Kobler Field, Saipan, Mariana Islands," accessed December 14, 2015, http://www.airfields-freeman. com/HI/Airfields_W_Pacific.htm#kobler.

71. American forces launched repeated airstrikes on Marcus Island, located about 1,200 miles southeast of Tokyo, but bypassed the atoll rather than landing troops on it during the war. Its garrison of 2,455 sick and emaciated Japanese naval personnel surrendered to Admiral F. E. M. Whiting aboard the USS *Bagley* on August 31, 1945. "Marcus Garrison of Foe Gives Up," *New York Times*, September 1, 1945, 2; for a photograph of the ceremony, see "The Japanese Surrender on Marcus Island," *New York Times*, September 4, 1945, 4. For a firsthand account of the surrender, see National Naval Aviation Museum, "Surrender at Marcus Island," accessed December 14, 2015, http://www.navalaviation museum.org/history-up-close/surrender-at-marcus-island/.

72. For a good overview on the general discontent with the slow pace of demobilization by both civilians and military personnel, see R. Alton Lee, "The Army 'Mutiny' of 1946," *Journal of American History* 53 (December 1966): 555–71.

73. Vermilya received his Bronze Star for overseeing the 39th Station Hospital's surgical services between October 13 and December 15, 1944, "under emergency conditions and inclement weather, while caring for heavy casualties." Kersey's award recognized his role in establishing the unit's Ear, Nose and Throat Clinic under the same conditions, which resulted in the "swift recovery and return to duty of all patients not requiring prolonged treatment." Copies of each officer's citation are found in "Medical History, 39th Station Hospital," November 13, 1945, pages 13, 15–17, in Unit Histories 39th Station Hospital, RG 112, Entry 1012 HUMEDS, Box 110.

74. For more on the typhoon, see October 16, 1945, letter to parents.

75. For photographs of five of these road signs, see Southern Methodist University, "Frank K. Davis World War II Photographs—road signs," accessed October 19, 2016, http://digitalcollections.smu.edu/ all/cul/fjd/.

76. An early morning explosion destroyed a building at the National Powder Company plant in Eldred on November 28, 1945, but fortunately caused no injuries. "Explosion Occurs at Powder Plant; No One

Injured," *Bradford Era*, November 25, 1945, 1.

The plant had a history of such explosions dating back to 1885, but especially in the mid-twentieth century. Five men were killed in a blast on October 18, 1939, and eight more on September 12, 1950. Coincidentally, Gabriel was visiting his family in Eldred at the time of this second explosion, and he rushed to the scene to administer first aid to the survivors. An explosion killed one worker the following year, and another blast shook the plant in 1968 but resulted in no fatalities. Joel Frampton Gilfert, "Historical Eldred & Vicinity: National Powder Company," accessed September 30, 2016, http://www.jfgvictoryverlag. com/eldred/nationalpowder.html.

77. This novel, originally published by Westminster Press in 1944, was reprinted through the 1980s.

78. *The Robe* (1942). Lloyd C. Davis's fictional account of what happened to the Roman soldier who won Jesus's robe by casting lots at the Crucifixion. The book was made into a five-time Academy Award nominated movie in 1953. 20th-Century American Bestsellers, "The Robe," accessed December 15, 2015, http://unsworth.unet.brandeis .edu/courses/bestsellers/search.cgi?title=The+Robe; Turner Classic Movies, accessed December 15, 2015, http://www.tcm.com/tcmdb/title/ 88469/The-Robe/.

79. *Our Vines Have Tender Grapes* (1945). The story of Norwegian immigrants living in a small Wisconsin farming village. Turner Classic Movies, accessed November 11, 2015, http://www.tcm.com/tcmdb/ title/360/Our-Vines-Have-Tender-Grapes/.

Romanian-born Edward G. Robinson (1893–1973) had a long career in movies, frequently portraying gangsters. In 1973 he was awarded a posthumous Academy Award for lifetime achievement. Garraty, *ANB*, 18: 649–51.

Jackie Jenkins (1937–2001) was a popular child star who left the film industry after a short career. IMDb.com, "Jackie Jenkins," accessed November 11, 2015, http://www.imdb.com/name/nm0420862/ bio?ref_=nm_ov_bio_sm#mini_bio.

80. From December 16 to 26, 1945, American secretary of state James F. Byrnes, British foreign minister Ernest Bevin, and Russian minister of foreign affairs Vyacheslav Molotoff met in Moscow to discuss the postwar world. Some of the topics included establishing peace treaties with Axis countries, the governance of occupied Japan, and the creation of the United Nations Commission for the Control of Atomic Energy. The Avalon Project, "Interim Meeting of Foreign Ministers of

the United States, the United Kingdom, and the Union of Soviet Socialist Republics, Moscow, December 16–26, 1945," accessed December
15, 2015, http://avalon.law.yale.edu/20th_century/decade19.asp.

Afterward

1. "Officer's and Warrant Officer's Qualification Card, no date, pages
196–97; "Brief Clinical Abstract, Captain Frederick R. Gabriel," no date,
pages 270–71; "Separation Qualification Record," page 193, Gabriel Personnel File.

Appendix

1. Edgar Murray Burns (interviewee) and Linda A. Weimer (interviewer), "Interview with E. Murray Burns" (1998), Oral History
Collection, Paper 30, page 4, accessed October 1, 2016, http://digital-
commons.ohsu.edu/hca-oralhist/30.

Bibliography

Manuscript Sources

Fold3.com

Army, 81st Infantry Div., HDQTRS, Report of Operations in the Capture of Angaur Island, Palau Island, 9/15/44–10/22/44.

"Headquarters 39th Station Hospital, November 2, 1945." Island Command Saipan: War Diary, October 1945.

Report of Unloading Operations on Peleliu and Angaur Island, Peleliu Island, November 20, 1944.

USS *Sabik*, War Diary, 6/1–24/1945.

World War II War Diaries, 1941–1945.

Heyde, Edward. Letter to author, October 27, 1987.

National Personnel Records Center, Saint Louis, MO.

Frederick R. Gabriel Personnel File.

United States National Archives and Records Administration, College Park, MD.

39th Station Hospital POA 1942–1944, RG 112, Entry 54A, Box 489.

39th Station Hospital 1942, RG 112, Entry 54A, Box 156.

148th General Hospital—Annual Report, October 1945, RG 112, HUMEDS, Box 38.

History—148th General Hospital January 1945–20 February 1946, RG 407, Entry 427, Box 17296.

Unit Histories 39th Station Hospital, RG 112, Entry 1012 HUMEDS, Box 110.

US Army Heritage and Education Center, Carlisle, PA.

Office of the Surgeon, United States Army Forces, *The Palau Operation (15 September to 27 November 1944)* (N.p., 1946?).

Published Primary Sources

Cawley, James H., ed. *Fr. Liebel's Letters: To the Men and Women Serving Our Country, 1943–1945*. N.p., 2002.

Collins, Lawrence D. *The 56th Evacuation Hospital: Letters of a World War II Army Doctor*. Denton: University of North Texas Press, 1995.

Funasaka, Hiroshi. *Falling Blossoms*. Translated by Hiroshi Funasaka and Jeffrey D. Rubin. Singapore: Times Books International, 1986.

Green, Anne Bosanko. *One Woman's War: Letters Home from the Women's Army Corps, 1944–1946*. Saint Paul: Minnesota Historical Society Press, 1989.

Hofschneider, Leo. "The Things I Dream of Now." *Notre Dame Alumnus* 22 (June 1944): 29.

Kennedy, Paul A., and Christopher B. Kennedy, eds. *Battlefield Surgeon: Life and Death on the Front Lines of World War II*. Lexington: University Press of Kentucky, 2016.

Lepore, Michael J. *Life of the Clinician*. Rochester, NY: University of Rochester Press, 2002.

Manual for Soldier Voting Outside the United States in the November 1944 General Election. War Department Pamphlet No. 21–11, June 5, 1944. Fold3.com.

Phibbs, Brendan. *The Other Side of Time: A Combat Surgeon in World War II*. Boston: Little, Brown, 1987.

Towne, Allen N. *Doctor Danger Forward: A World War II Memoir of a Combat Medical Aidman, First Infantry Division*. Jefferson, NC: McFarland, 2000.

Vedder, James S. *Combat Surgeon: Up Front with the 27th Marines*. Novato, CA: Presidio Press, 1998.

Secondary Sources

Albert, McKinley. "Saving Face and Losing the Circus: The Hartford Circus Fire and Its Disgraceful Aftermath." *Connecticut History* 48 (Spring 2009): 62–77.

Allen, Robert L. "From Disaster to Desegregation." *Naval History* 29 (February 2015): 16–24.

Atkinson, Rick. *The Guns at Last Light: The War in Western Europe, 1944–1945*. New York: Henry Holt, 2013.

Axelrod, Alan. *Encyclopedia of World War II*. 2 vols. New York: Facts on File, 2007.

Bennett, Judith A. *Natives and Exotics: World War II and the Environment in the Southern Pacific*. Honolulu: University of Hawai'i Press, 2009.

Blair, Bobby Charles, and John Peter DeCioccio. *Victory at Peleliu: The 81st Infantry Division's Pacific Campaign*. Norman: University of Oklahoma Press, 2011.

Borelli, Stephen. *How About That!: The Life of Mel Allen*. Champaign, IL: Sports Publishing, 2005.

Brinkley, Douglas, and Julie M. Fenster. *Parish Priest: Father Michael McGivney and American Catholicism*. New York: William Morrow, 2006.

Cannon, M. Hamlin. *Leyte: The Return to the Philippines*. Washington, DC: Office of the Chief of Military History, Department of the Army, 1954.

Cardozier, V. R. *Colleges and Universities in World War II*. Westport, CT: Greenwood, 1993.

Close, Frederick P. *Tokyo Rose, An American Patriot: A Dual Biography*. Lanham, MD: Scarecrow Press, 2010.

Coggins, Jack. *The Campaign for Guadalcanal: A Battle That Made History*. Garden City, NY: Doubleday, 1972.

"Col. Gabreski Missing." *Notre Dame Scholastic* 82 (August 4, 1944): 13.

Condon-Rall, Mary Ellen, and Albert E. Cowdrey. *The Medical Department: Medical Service in the War against Japan*. Washington, DC: Center of Military History, United States Army, 1998.

Cooke, James J. *American Girls, Beer, and Glenn Miller: G.I. Morale in World War II*. Columbia: University of Missouri Press, 2012.

———. *Chewing Gum, Candy Bars, and Beer: The Army PX in World War II*. Columbia: University of Missouri Press, 2009.

Cosmas, Graham A., and Albert E. Cowdrey. *The Medical Department: Medical Service in the European Theater of Operations*. Washington, DC: Center of Military History, United States Army, 1992.

Cowdrey, Albert E. *Fighting for Life: American Military Medicine in World War II*. New York: Free Press, 1994.

Craven, Wesley Frank, and James Lea Cate, eds. *The Army Air Forces in World War II*. Vol. 4, *The Pacific: Guadalcanal to Saipan, August 1942 to July 1944*. Washington, DC: Office of Air Force History, 1983.

Crowl, Philip A. *Campaign in the Marianas*. Washington, DC: Office of the Chief of Military History, Department of the Army, 1960.

Cumins, Keith. *Cataclysm: The War on the Eastern Front, 1941–45*. Solihull, England: Helion, 2011.

Dulles, Foster Rhea. *The American Red Cross: A History*. New York: Harper and Brothers, 1950.

Eastman Kodak. *How to Make Good Pictures*. Rochester, NY: Eastman Kodak, 1943.

Faith, William Robert. *Bob Hope: A Life in Comedy*. New York: Da Capo, 2003.

Foster, M. H. *Manual of Hospital Management for US Marine Hospitals*. Miscellaneous Publication No. 29. Washington, DC: United States Government Printing Office, 1930; Google Books. https://books.google.com/books?id=f6VIAQAAIAAJ.

Frank, Richard B. *Downfall: The End of the Imperial Japanese Empire*. New York: Random House, 1999.

———. *Guadalcanal*. New York: Random House, 1990.

Garraty, John A., and Mark C. Carnes. *American National Biography*. 24 vols. New York: Oxford University Press, 1999.

Goldberg, Harold J. *D-Day in the Pacific: The Battle of Saipan*. Bloomington: Indiana University Press, 2007.

Gould, Brandon R., and Stanley A. Horowitz. *History of Combat Pay*. Alexandria, VA: Institute for Defense Analyses, August 2011.

Greenfield, Kent Roberts, Robert R. Palmer, and Bell I. Wiley, *The Organization of Ground Combat Troops*. Washington, DC: Center of Military History United States Army, 1987.

Halliwell, Leslie. *Halliwell's Film Guide*. 2nd ed. London: Granada Publishing, 1979.

Harris, Mark. *Five Came Back: A Story of Hollywood and the Second World War*. New York: Penguin Press, 2014.

Hastings, Max. *Overlord: D-Day and the Battle for Normandy*. New York: Simon and Schuster, 1984.

———. *Retribution: The Battle for Japan, 1944–45*. New York: Alfred A. Knopf, 2008.

"The Heroine on the Cover." *Collier's*, April 15, 1944, 65.

Hischak, Thomas. *The Oxford Companion to the American Musical: Theatre, Films, and Television*. New York: Oxford University Press, 2008.

Layton, James, and David Pierce. *The Dawn of Technicolor, 1915–1935*. Rochester, NY: George Eastman House, 2015.

Lee, R. Alton. "The Army 'Mutiny' of 1946." *Journal of American History* 53 (December 1966): 555–71.

Loscalzo, Josesph. "From Clinical Observation to Mechanism—Heyde's Syndrome." *New England Journal of Medicine* 367, no. 20 (November 15, 2012): 1954–56.

MacDonald, Charles B. *Victory in Europe, 1945: The Last Offensive of World War II*. Mineola, NY: Dover, 2007.

McGrath, John J. *The Other End of the Spear: The Tooth-to-Tail Ratio (T3R) in Modern Military Operations*. The Long War Series Occasional Paper No. 23. Fort Leavenworth, KS: Combat Studies Institute Press, 2007.

Miller, John, Jr. *United States Army in World War II: The War in the Pacific, Guadalcanal; The First Offensive*. Washington, DC: Historical Division, Department of the Army, 1949.

Murray, Stephen C. *The Battle over Peleliu: Islander, Japanese, and American Memories of War*. Tuscaloosa: University of Alabama Press, 2016.

Pencak, William, ed. *Encyclopedia of the Veteran in America*. 2 vols. Santa Barbara, CA: ABC-Clio, 2009.

Petran, Tabitha. *Syria*. London: Ernest Benn, 1972.

Pfau, Ann Elizabeth. *Miss Yourlovin: GIs, Gender, and Domesticity during World War II*. New York: Columbia University Press, 2008; Project Gutenberg, 2008. http://www.gutenberg-e.org/pfau/index.html.

Polmar, Norman, and Thomas B. Allen. *World War II: The Encyclopedia of the War Years, 1941–1945*. Mineola, NY: Dover, 2012.

Rodriguez, Joe. "Deaths Seared in Battle Physician's Memory." *Twenty-Niner* 45 (March 2001): 49.

Ry, Namikawa. "Japanese Overseas Broadcasting: A Personal View." In *Film and Radio Propaganda in World War II*, edited by K. R. M. Short, 319–33. Knoxville: University of Tennessee Press, 1983.

Service Record Book of Men and Women of Eldred and Vicinity. Eldred, PA: PVT Myron Burn's Post No. 2092, VFW, n.d.

Sickels, Robert. *The 1940s*. Westport, Connecticut: Greenwood Press, 2004.

Smith, Clarence McKittrick. *The Medical Department: Hospitalization and Evacuation, Zone of Interior*. Washington, DC: Center of Military History, United States Army, 1989.

Smith, Robert Ross. *The Approach to the Philippines*. Washington, DC: Center of Military History, United States Army, 1996,

Stauffer, Alvin P. *The Quartermaster Corps: Operations in the War against Japan*. 1956. Reprint; Washington, DC: Office of the Chief of Military History, Department of the Army, 1971.

Stouffer, Samuel A. *The American Soldier*. 2 vols. Princeton, NJ: Princeton University Press, 1949.

Toland, John. *The Rising Sun: The Decline and Fall of the Japanese Empire, 1936–1945*. 2 vols. New York: Random House, 1970.

"V-Mail: Letters Home." *History Magazine* 16 (June/July 2015): 17–22.

Wiltse, Charles M. *The Medical Department: Medical Service in the*

Mediterranean and Minor Theaters. Washington, DC: Center of Military History, United States Army, 1987.

Winkler, Allan M. "The Philadelphia Transit Strike of 1944." *Journal of American History* 59 (June 1972): 73–89.

Witt, Peter A. *Edith's War: Writings of a Red Cross Worker and Lifelong Champion of Social Justice.* College Station: Texas A&M University Press, 2018.

Newspapers

Bradford Era
"Dr. J. Kervin Dies of Heart Attack at 69." May 12, 1965, 1, 16.
"Explosion Occurs at Powder Plant; No One Injured." November 25, 1945, 1.

Eldred Eagle
"Louis Gabriel Writes of Present Conditions in Germany." July 6, 1945, 1.
"Men and Women in Service." September 7, 1945, 5.
"SGT. D. D. Feheley Home on Furlough." May 18, 1945, 1.
"SGT. Herbert Geuder of Eldred Helps Sink Five Jap Ships." March 24, 1944, 1.
"T-SGT. Geuder With 'Ken's Men.'" July 28, 1944, 1.

New York Times
"Army Plan Telling Just How a Soldier Will Be Demobilized." May 11, 1945, 11.
"Army to Release 13,000 Doctors." September 15, 1945, 1.
"Erroneous 'Flash' of Surrender Starts Many Wild Celebrations." August 13, 1945, 1, 3.
"The Japanese Surrender on Marcus Island." September 4, 1945, 4.
"Marcus Garrison of Foe Gives Up." September 1, 1945, 2.
"Marshall Speaks." September 21, 1945, 1, 2.
"Nazis' End Near: But President on Word from Eisenhower Corrects Rumor." April 29, 1945, 1.
"New Army Discharge Plan." September 21, 2.
"Point Plan Set Up for Army Officers." September 7, 1945, 4.
"Priorities in Army." September 11, 1945, 1, 11.
White, William S. "Army Gives Plan to Keep 665,000 from Going Abroad." September 5, 1945, 1.

United States Online Historical Newspapers
https://sites.google.com/site/onlinenewspapersite/Home/usa.
"Red Cross Girls Reach Guadalcanal." *Eugene Register-Guard* [Eugene, Oregon], April 26, 1944, 8. Accessed July 13, 2015.

Websites

Abandoned and Little-Known Airfields: Western Pacific Islands. "Kobler Field, Saipan, Mariana Islands." Accessed December 14, 2015. http://www.airfields-freeman.com/HI/Airfields_W_Pacific.htm#kobler.

Air Force. "Royal New Zealand Air Force Band." Accessed November 8, 2015. http://www.airforce.mil.nz/about-us/who-we-are/band/default.htm.

Allmusic.com. *This Is the Army* [Original Broadway Cast]. Accessed November 24, 2015. http://www.allmusic.com/album/this-is-the-army-original-broadway-cast-mw0000599946.

American Presidency Project. "Franklin D. Roosevelt: 11—Remarks on Transferring a Destroyer Escort to the French." February 12, 1944. Accessed December 4, 2015. http://www.presidency.ucsb.edu/ws/?pid=16464.

Arlington National Cemetery. "James Alexander Ulio." Accessed May 19, 2015. http://www.arlingtoncemetery.net/jaulio.htm.

Avalon Project. "Interim Meeting of Foreign Ministers of the United States, the United Kingdom, and the Union of Soviet Socialist Republics, Moscow, December 16–26, 1945." Accessed December 15, 2015. http://avalon.law.yale.edu/20th_century/decade19.asp.

Baldwin Project. "The Story of Mankind." Accessed June 12, 2015. http://www.mainlesson.com/display.php?author=vanloon&book=mankind&story=_contents.

BoardGameGeek.com. "Scopa." Accessed November 6, 2015. https://boardgamegeek.com/boardgame/15889/scopa.

Burns (interviewee), Edgar Murray, and , Linda A. Weimer (interviewer). "Interview with E. Murray Burns" (1998). *Oral History Collection.* Paper 30. Accessed October 1, 2016. http://digitalcommons.ohsu.edu/hca-oralhist/30.

Calexplornia. "A Historical Look at the Mare Island Naval Hospital." Accessed September 18, 2015. http://www.calexplornia.com/a-historical-look-at-the-mare-island-naval-hospital/.

California Military History Foundation. "Camp Stoneman." Accessed May 19, 2015. http://californiamilitaryhistory.org/CpStoneman.html.

Camp Barkeley Tactical Training Center. "A Proud History." Accessed

May 19, 2015. http://www.campbarkeleytactical.com/camp-barkeley-history.html.

"Camp Bowie." Accessed July 15, 2015. http://army.com/info/posts/camp-bowie.

"Camp Van Dorn World War II Museum." Accessed July 18, 2015. http://www.vandornmuseum.org/.

Catholic Church in Micronesia. "The Catholic Church in Palau." Accessed November 18, 2015. http://www.micsem.org/pubs/books/catholic/palau/index.htm.

Chicago Tribune. "World War II: Life in Chicago." Accessed January 6, 2016. http://galleries.apps.chicagotribune.com/chi-130320-arsenal-democracy-world-war-ii-pictures/.

Connell, Byron. "WWII US Army Officers' Uniforms." Accessed November 6, 2015. http://www.siwcostumers.org/newsletterarchive/VirtCost V9-I2-2011/VirtCostV9-I2-2011_37-army.pdf.

Department of the Navy, Bureau of Yards and Docks. "Building the Navy's Bases in World War II: History of the Bureau of Yards and Docks and the Civil Engineer Corps, 1940–1946." Accessed June 1, 2015. http://www.ibiblio.org/hyperwar/USN/Building_Bases/bases-24.html.

Eldred World War II Museum. "About Us." Accessed June 13, 2015. http://eldredwwiimuseum.net/about-us/.

Enchanted Mountains. "Rock City Park." Accessed October 25, 2016. http://enchantedmountains.com/place/rock-city-park.

Encyclopedia Britannica. http://www.britannica.com/.

Crepuscular Rays. Accessed February 17, 2019.

De Havilland, Olivia. Accessed February 10, 2019.

Von Schuschnigg, Kurt. Accessed November 25, 2015.

Find a Grave. "Br. Maurilius DeGan." Accessed March 23, 2015. http://www.findagrave.com/cgi-bin/fg.cgi?page=gr&GRid=46594296.

Fiset, Louis. "Return to Sender: US Censorship of Enemy Alien Mail in World War II." *Prologue Magazine* 33 (Spring 2001). Accessed December 4, 2015. https://www.archives.gov/publications/prologue/2001/spring/mail-censorship-in-world-war-two-1.html.

Flick, John B. "Chapter XII: Pacific Ocean Areas." Medical Department, United States Army: Surgery in World War II, Activities of Surgical Consultants, Volume II. Accessed November 22, 2015. http://history.amedd.army.mil/booksdocs/wwii/actvssurgconvol2/chapter11.htm.

Fort Benning. "Welcome to Fort Benning." Accessed September 15, 2015. http://www.military.com/base-guide/fort-benning.

Franciscan Sisters of Allegany. "Necrology of the Franciscan Sisters of Allegany, New York." Accessed September 20, 2015. http://www.alleganyfranciscans.org/necrology_chron.html.

Gannon University. "Villa Maria College." Accessed July 17, 2015. http://www.gannonalumni.org/s/740/index.aspx?pgid=1199.

Garrity, Patrick. "US Foreign Policy: Shield of the Republic (1943)." *Classics of Strategy and Diplomacy.* Accessed September 18, 2016. www.classicsofstrategy.com/2008/09/us-foreign-policy.html.

Geodynamics Limited. "Savo Island Geothermal Power Project." Accessed April 3, 2015. http://www.geodynamics.com.au/Our-Projects/Pacific-Islands/Savo-Island.aspx.

Gilfert, Joel Frampton. "Historical Eldred & Vicinity: National Powder Company." Accessed September 30, 2016. http://www.jfgvictoryverlag.com/eldred/nationalpowder.html.

———. "Military History of McKean County, Pennsylvania, World War II." http://www.jfgvictoryverlag.com/.

Community Honor Rolls—Eldred and Vicinity. Accessed December 12, 2014.

Community Honor Rolls—Smethport. Accessed November 16, 2015.

Gold Stars. Accessed September 29, 2016.

Prisoners of War. Accessed September 29, 2016.

Harrison, John. "Extreme Events: Graphs, Photos, Videos." Accessed May 19, 2015. http://www.schnabel-eng.com/wp-content/uploads/2013/12/Extreme-Events.pdf.

Harry S. Truman Library and Museum. http://www.trumanlibrary.org.

"Broadcast to the American People Announcing the Surrender of Germany. May 8, 1945." Accessed November 20, 2015.

"100. The President's News Conference, August 14, 1945." Accessed November 28, 2015.

Historic Hotels of America. "Hilton Chicago." Accessed May 18, 2015. http://www.historichotels.org/hotels-resorts/hilton-chicago/history php.

IMDb. http://www.imdb.com/.

Arnold, Edward. Accessed July 17, 2015.

Baker, Bonnie. Accessed July 12, 2015.

Buck, Frank. Accessed July 14, 2015.

Candlelight in Algeria. Accessed November 25, 2015.

Coastal Command. Accessed September 22, 2015.

Colbert, Claudette. Accessed November 13, 2015.

Elliott, Mary. Accessed September 19, 2015.

Faye, Frances. Accessed September 19, 2015.

Fields, Gracie. Accessed November 13, 2015.

It's Murder She Says. Accessed November 25, 2015.

Jenkins, Jackie. Accessed November 11, 2015.

Moreno, Rosita. Accessed September 19, 2015.

On to Tokyo. Accessed December 19, 2015.

Raines, Ella. Accessed October 1, 2015.

Romano, Tony. Accessed July 19, 2015.

Thomas, Patty. Accessed July 19, 2015.

Two Down and One to Go. Accessed December 19, 2015.

Wright, Teresa. Accessed October 29, 2015.

Jefferson Medical College Yearbooks, 1940. Accessed September 24, 2015. http://jdc.jefferson.edu/jmc_yearbooks/50.

Jefferson Medical College Yearbooks, 1941. Accessed November 3, 2015. http://jdc.jefferson.edu/jmc_yearbooks/53/.

Joint Base Myer-Henderson Hall. "Fort Myer History." Accessed May 18, 2015. http://www.jbmhh.army.mil/WEB/JBMHH/AboutJBMHH/FortMyerHistory.html.

Modesto Radio Museum. "Command Performance." Accessed November 25, 2015. http://www.modestoradiomuseum.org/command%20performance.html.

Moore, David. "Pollywog or Shellback: The Navy's Line Crossing Ceremony Revealed." *Veterans United Network*. Accessed August 7, 2016. https://www.veteransunited.com/network/the-navys-line-crossing-ceremony-revealed/.

NASA Earth Observatory. "Crepuscular Rays: India." Accessed February 17, 2019. https://earthobservatory.nasa.gov/images/76261/crepuscular-rays-india.

National Naval Aviation Museum. "Surrender at Marcus Island." Accessed December 14, 2015. http://www.navalaviationmuseum.org/history-up-close/surrender-at-marcus-island/.

Naval History and Heritage Command. "Typhoons and Hurricanes: Pacific Typhoon at Okinawa, October 1945." Accessed December 12, 2015. http://www.history.navy.mil/research/library/online-reading-room/title-list-alphabetically/p/pacific-typhoon-october-1945.html.

"Naval Operations in the Pacific from March 1944 to October 1945: Capture and Occupation of Hollandia." Accessed February 19, 2015. http://www.shsu.edu/~his_ncp/Compac45.html.

New Advent. "The Society for the Propagation of the Faith." Accessed March 11, 2018. http://www.newadvent.org/cathen/12461a.htm.

New York State Military Museum and Veterans Research Center. "Sampson Naval Training Base." Accessed July 9, 2015. https://dmna.ny.gov/forts/fortsQ_S/sampsonNavalTrainingBase.htm.

The Pacific War Online Encyclopedia. http://pwencycl.kgbudge.com/.

Alcohol. Accessed November 25, 2016.

Rations. Accessed November 25, 2016.

Painted Hills Genealogy Society. "Miscellaneous Photos of Eldred, Pa. During the July 1942 Flood." Accessed May, 19, 2015. http://www.paintedhills.org/MCKEAN/EldredFlood/.

Pittsburgh Catholic Publishing Associates. "St. Francis Medical Center's long history comes to a close." Accessed July 15, 2015. http://www.pittsburghcatholic.org/News/st-francis-medical-centers-long-history-comes-to-a-close.

Polish American Cultural Center. "Colonel Francis S. Grabreski, WWII Air Ace." Accessed February 16, 2015. http://www.polishamerican center.org/Gabreski.html.

Public Broadcasting Service. "American Experience, Primary Resources: Announcing the Bombing of Hiroshima." Accessed November 27, 2015. http://www.pbs.org/wgbh/americanexperience/features/primary -resources/truman-hiroshima/.

Saint Bonaventure University Archives. "The Floods of 1942 and 1972." Accessed June 12, 2015. http://web.sbu.edu/friedsam/archives/build ings/Floods.htm.

Schwartz, Joseph L. "Chapter I: Facilities of the Medical Department of the Navy." *History of the Medical Department of the United States Navy in World War II*, 21-22. Accessed September 3, 2015. https://www.ibiblio.org/hyperwar/USN/USN-Medical/I/USN-Medical-1.html.

———. "Chapter II: Experiences in Battle of the Medical Department of the Navy." *History of the Medical Department of the United States Navy in World War II*. Accessed July 13, 2015. http://www .ibiblio.org/hyperwar/USN/USN-Medical/I/USN-Medical-2.html.

Sheppard Air Force Base. *A Brief History of the 82d Training Wing and Sheppard AFB* (n.c.: n.p: n.d), 25–27. Accessed May 19, 2015. http://www.sheppard.af.mil/shared/media/document/AFD-120424-046.pdf.

Smithsonian National Postal Museum. Pfau, Ann. "Postal Censorship and Military Intelligence in World War II." Accessed December 4,

2015. http://postalmuseum.si.edu/symposium2008/pfau-postal_censorship.pdf.

Somogyi, Lou. "God, Country, Notre Dame: The United States Military has been Part of Notre Dame's Fabric." Accessed May 18, 2015. http://www.und.com/genrel/111011aaa.html.

South Carolina History Net. "History: Fort Oglethorpe, Georgia, US Army Installation." Accessed May 18, 2015. http://www.schistory.net /fortoglethorpe/History.htm.

Southern Methodist University. "Frank K. Davis World War II Photographs—Road Signs." Accessed October 19, 2016. http://digitalcol lections.smu.edu/all/cul/fjd/.

Sparrow, John C. *History of Personnel Demobilization in the United States Army*. Washington, DC: Department of the Army, July 1952. Accessed December 18, 2015. http://www.history.army.mil/html/ books/104/104-8/CMH_Pub_104-8.pdf; St. Bonaventure University. "World War II Chaplains from St. Bonaventure." Accessed July 14, 2015. http://students.sbu.edu/astrong/chaplains.htm.

Stamford Historical Society, Inc. "The Battle of Angaur." Accessed October 23, 2016. http://www.stamfordhistory.org/ww2_angaur.htm.

Stars and Stripes. "About Stars and Stripes." Accessed November 25, 2015. http://www.stripes.com/customer-service/about-us.

Sumner, H. C. "The North Atlantic Hurricane of October 13–21." *Monthly Weather Review* 72 (November 1944): 221–23. http://www .aoml.noaa.gov/hrd/hurdat/mwr_pdf/1944.pdf.

Tassava, Christopher J. "The American Economy during World War II." *EH-net*. Accessed September 23, 2016. https://eh.net/encyclopedia/the-american-economy-during-world-war-ii/.

Temple University. "Philadelphia Transit Strike of 1944." Accessed July 19, 2015. http://northerncity.library.temple.edu/node/30260.

Texas State Historical Association. "Camp Swift." Accessed November 18, 2015. https://tshaonline.org/handbook/online/articles/qbc27.

Thomas Jefferson University. "Black and Blue Marks: History of the School Colors." Accessed May 18, 2015. http://jeffline.jefferson.edu/ SML/Archives/Highlights/School_Colors/.

Tryzbiak, Stanley. *Official Log of Cruises and Narrative War History of the U.S.S. West Point AP 23, World War II, 1941–1946*. N.c.: U.S.S. *West Point* Reunion Association, 2008. Accessed October 22, 2013. http://www.usswestpoint.com/newsletters/The%20shipslog.pdf.

Turner Classic Movies. http://www.tcm.com.
    Boston Blackie Goes to Hollywood. Accessed September 24, 2015.

Casanova Brown. Accessed October 29, 2015.

Cowboy in Manhattan. Accessed July 18, 2015.

The Devil with Hitler. **Accessed September 24, 2015.**

Doughboys in Ireland. Accessed October 29, 2015.

The Doughgirls. Accessed November 16, 2015.

Gangway for Tomorrow. **Accessed September 22, 2015.**

Girl Trouble. **Accessed September 21, 2015.**

God Is My Co-Pilot. Accessed September 22, 2015.

Ladies' Day. Accessed July 17, 2015.

Meanest Man in the World. **September 24, 2015.**

Moontide. Accessed October 29, 2015.

Music for Millions. Accessed November 22, 2015.

No Time for Love. Accessed October 29, 2015.

Our Vines Have Tender Grapes. **Accessed November 11, 2015.**

Out of This World. **Accessed November 11, 2015.**

Princess and the Pirate. Accessed September 24, 2015.

Princess O'Rourke. Accessed September 24, 2015.

Rhythm of the Islands. Accessed September 24, 2015.

The Robe. Accessed December 15, 2015.

A Royal Scandal **(1945). Accessed November 19, 2015.**

Sahara. Accessed September 24, 2015.

Sing a Jingle. **Accessed September 21, 2015.**

Son of Lassie. Accessed November 25, 2015.

Song of Bernadette. Accessed July 16, 2015.

A Song to Remember. Accessed November 19, 2015.

Spotlight Scandals. Accessed July 21, 2015.

Strange Death of Adolph Hitler. **Accessed September 22, 2015.**

The Suspect. Accessed October 1, 2015.

Tarzan's Desert Mystery. **Accessed September 24, 2015.**

Tarzan's New York Adventure. Accessed July 17, 2015.

Tarzan Triumphs. **Accessed September 24, 2015.**

Thirty Seconds over Tokyo. Accessed November 27, 2015.

Those Endearing Young Charms. Accessed September 28, 2016.

A Tree Grows in Brooklyn. Accessed November 18, 2015.

Valley of Decision. Accessed October 1, 2015.

What a Woman! Accessed November 20, 2015.

Wilson. Accessed September 24, 2015.

Wonder Man. Accessed October 1, 2015.

20th-Century American Bestsellers. "The Robe." Accessed December 15, 2015. http://unsworth.unet.brandeis.edu/courses/bestsellers/search.cgi?title=The+Robe.

The United Nations. "History of the United Nations." Accessed November 17, 2015. http://www.un.org/en/aboutun/history/sanfrancisco_conference.shtml.

United States, Adjutant-General's Office. *Numerical Listing of APO's January 1942–November 1947*. Washington, DC: Adjutant-General's Office, 1949; Internet Archive. Accessed July 19, 2015. https://archive.org/details/NumericalListingOfApos.

University of Notre Dame Athletics. "Ed McKeever." Accessed November 17, 2015. http://www.und.com/sports/m-footbl/mtt/mckeever_ed00.html.

USNTC Bainbridge Association. Accessed July 14, 2015. http://www.usntcb.org/.

Waller Funeral Home. "In Memoriam of Frances Selzer Talbot." Accessed December 21, 2014. www.wallerfuneralhome.com/memsol.cgi?user_id=264693.

Welkam Solomons. "Sunset Lodge, Savo Island." Accessed April 3, 2015. welkamsolomons.com/places/central/savo/index.html.

World Bank Group, "Climate Change Knowledge Portal: Solomon Islands." Accessed August 31, 2016. http://sdwebx.worldbank.org/climateportal/index.cfm?page=country_historical_climate&ThisCCode=SLB.

Worldcat, www.worldcat.org.

    Aldrich, Bess Streeter. *A Lantern in Her Hand*. Accessed May 21, 2015.

    Hersey, John. *Into the Valley: A Skirmish of the Marines*. Accessed October 21, 2015.

    Rizk, Salom. *Syrian Yankee*. Accessed October 21, 2015.

    Scott, Robert Lee, Jr. *God Is My Co-Pilot*. Accessed November 23, 2015.

    Thorpe, Berenice. *Reunion on Strawberry Hill*. Accessed September 22, 2015.

    Todd, James Campbell, and Arthur Hawley Sanford. *Clinical Diagnosis by Laboratory Methods*. Accessed October 19, 2015.

W. R. Case and Sons Cutlery Company. "Our Companies." Accessed June 1, 2015. http://www.zippo.com/about/article.aspx?id=1577.

WW2 US Medical Research Centre. "WW2 Military Hospitals: General Introduction." Accessed October 28, 2106. https://www.med-dept.com/articles/ww2-military-hospitals-general-introduction/.

WWII Impressions, Inc. "US Army Regulation, Winter Officer's Service Uniform." Accessed June 1, 2015. http://www.wwiiimpressions.com/newusarmyofficerwinteruniform.html.

WWII Impressions, Inc. "United States Army Regulation Uniforms." Accessed June 1, 2015. http://www.wwiiimpressions.com/newusarmyuniforms.html.

Index Terms

Printed in the USA
CPSIA information can be obtained
at www.ICGtesting.com
LVHW021439300823
756644LV00006B/464